The Politics of Military Families

This book examines the politics of military families in relation to the tensions between the state, military organization, and private life.

It elaborates on the tensions between the advent of challenging worldwide deployment for the military and the prominence of the home front. The volume aims to understand the dynamics of conflict and change within triad figurations at the macro (society), meso (organizational), and micro (family) level and is guided by the following overarching research questions:

- What are the key issues in the three-party dynamics?
- What tensions exist in these dynamics?
- How do actors seek to arrive at a balance? What initiatives for change are made?

With contributions from international scholars, who examine the workings of politics in military families at all three levels, the book argues that members within military families deal with shifting power balances and these are impacted by demands from organizations and the state.

This book will be of much interest to students of military studies, sociology, organizational studies and politics.

René Moelker is an Associate Professor of Sociology at the Netherlands Defence Academy.

Manon Andres is an Assistant Professor at the Netherlands Defence Academy.

Nina Rones is a Senior Researcher at the Norwegian Defence Research Establishment.

Cass Military Studies

Israel, Strategic Culture and the Conflict with Hamas
Adaptation and military effectiveness
Niccolò Petrelli

War and Strategy in the Modern World
From Blitzkrieg to unconventional terrorism
Azar Gat

Military Strategy of Small States
Responding to external shocks of the 21st century
Edström Håkan, Dennis Gyllensporre and Jacob Westberg (eds)

Western Military Interventions after the Cold War
Evaluating the wars of the West
Marek Madej (ed.)

Countering Insurgencies and Violent Extremism in Asia
Shanthie Mariet D'Souza (ed.)

Commercial Insurgencies in the Networked Era
The Revolutionary Armed Forces of Colombia
Oscar Palma

The Politics of Military Families
State, Work Organizations, and the Rise of the Negotiation Household
René Moelker, Manon Andres, and Nina Rones (eds)

Organisational Learning and the Modern Army
A new model for lessons-learned processes
Tom Dyson

For more information about this series, please visit: www.routledge.com/Cass-Military-Studies/book-series/CMS

The Politics of Military Families

State, Work Organizations, and the Rise of the Negotiation Household

Edited by René Moelker, Manon Andres, and Nina Rones

LONDON AND NEW YORK

First published 2019
by Routledge
2 Park Square, Milton Park, Abingdon, Oxon OX14 4RN

and by Routledge
52 Vanderbilt Avenue, New York, NY 10017

Routledge is an imprint of the Taylor & Francis Group, an informa business

British Library Cataloguing-in-Publication Data
A catalogue record for this book is available from the British Library

Library of Congress Cataloging-in-Publication Data
Names: Moelker, R. (René), 1960-editor. | Andres, Manon, editor. | Rones, Nina, editor.
Title: The politics of military families : state, work organizations, and the rise of the negotiation household / edited by René Moelker, Manon Andres, and Nina Rones.
Description: First edition. | Abingdon, Oxon ; New York, NY : Routledge, [2019] | Series: Cass military studies | Includes bibliographical references and index.
Identifiers: LCCN 2019008081 (print) | LCCN 2019010408 (ebook) | ISBN 9780429651724 (Web PDF) | ISBN 9780429649080 (ePub) | ISBN 9780429646447 (Mobi) | ISBN 9780367134426 (hardback) | ISBN 9780429026492 (e-book)
Subjects: LCSH: Families of military personnel. | Soldiers—Family relationships. | Sociology, Military.
Classification: LCC U21.5 (ebook) | LCC U21.5 .P65 2019 (print) | DDC 355.1—dc23
LC record available at https://lccn.loc.gov/2019008081

ISBN: 978-0-367-13442-6 (hbk)
ISBN: 978-0-429-02649-2 (ebk)

Typeset in Times New Roman
by Swales & Willis Ltd, Exeter, Devon, UK

Contents

Figures

Tables

Contributors

Joanna E. Anderson received her PhD in social psychology from the University of Waterloo in 2012, and completed a postdoctoral fellowship at Cornell University in 2014. Since then, she has worked at Director General Military Personnel Research and Analysis (DGMPRA) as a personnel researcher on the Recruitment and Retention team. Much of her research focuses on the Reserve Force.

Manon Andres is an Assistant Professor at the Faculty of Military Sciences of the Netherlands Defense Academy. She holds a doctorate from Tilburg University. Her main research focus is on understanding military families.

Dotan Aviram is a Senior Research Officer at the Israeli Defence Forces Behavioral Science Center. His research focuses on public opinion, gender relations in the military, and organizational studies.

Gary L. Bowen is Dean and Kenan Distinguished Professor in the School of Social Work at the University of North Carolina at Chapel Hill (UNC-CH). He serves as Chief Scientist in the Jordan Institute for Military Members, Veterans, and Their Families. He also co-directs the School Success Profile (SSP) project with Dr. Natasha Bowen and Dr. Jack Richman. Dr. Bowen received his MSW in 1976 from UNC-CH and his PhD in Family Studies in 1981 from the University of North Carolina at Greensboro. Dr. Bowen is Past President of the National Council on Family Relations.

Amanda Bullock has a PhD in Experimental Psychology from Carleton University. Since 2015, she has been employed as a Defence Scientist with the Director General Military Personnel Research and Analysis (DGMPRA) in Ottawa. Her research expertise includes military families' stress and well-being and evaluation of military family programs and services. She is also an Adjunct Research Professor in Psychology at Carleton University, where she teaches undergraduate statistics and investigates the well-being of socially anxious emerging adults.

Sanela Dursun is Research Psychologist and Director of the Personnel and Family Support Research section at the Department of National Defence. She is responsible for managing and delivering research, analysis, and expert advice on strategies to improve the well-being of serving members, veterans, and their families. Dr. Dursun has published and disseminated research findings in these domains both within the Department of National Defence and in a variety of international fora. She holds a doctorate in health psychology.

Meytal Eran-Jona is Associate Researcher at Haifa University and Academic Consultant at Weizmann Institute of Science. As a sociologist and gender expert, she studies various aspects of gender in work organizations. Her research focuses on gender, work, and family aspects in the military and in the academy, enhancing gender equality in the workplace, civil–military relations in Israel, and on public opinions in Israel.

Nicola Fear is Professor of Epidemiology at King's College London. She specializes in the mental health and well-being of service personnel, veterans, and military families. She is currently the lead epidemiologist on a large cohort study examining the health (mental and physical), lifestyle, and career consequences of military deployments to Iraq and Afghanistan on UK personnel. Nicola also is involved in a number of family-focused projects aiming to understand further the impact of service life on families.

Sabina Frederic is Professor at the National University of Quilmes, Argentina, and Independent Researcher at the Argentine National Council of Scientific and Technical Research. She holds a PhD in Social Anthropology from the University of Utrecht, the Netherlands. Among her main books are *Traps of the Past: The Armed Forces and Their Integration to the Democratic State in Argentina* and as a co-editor with Helena Carreiras and Celso Castro, *Researching the Military* (Routledge, 2016). She was formerly Coordinator of the Gender Policy Council and Undersecretary of Education with the Argentine Ministry of Defense.

Irina Goldenberg is Section Head of Recruitment and Retention Research in Defence Research and Development Canada, managing the research program related to recruitment and retention of Canadian Armed Forces personnel. In addition, she specializes in military–civilian personnel collaboration in defense organizations. She is an internationally known and respected researcher and plays an active role within many international organizations, including the European Research Group on Military and Society (ERGOMAS), where she serves as Secretary General.

Laura Goodwin is Senior Lecturer and Lead for the Addiction Research Group at the University of Liverpool. Laura has a background in health psychology and psychiatric epidemiology. Interests include military health, links between mental health and addiction, and life course epidemiology, with expertise in cohort studies, electronic healthcare records, and development of electronic interventions.

Rachael Gribble is Lecturer in War and Psychiatry at King's College London. Based at the King's Centre for Military Health Research, her research focuses on the health and well-being of military families.

Anitta Hannola is Researcher at the Finnish Defence Research Agency, Human Performance Division, Finland. She holds a master's degree in Sociology and Work and Organizational Psychology. She has been working for the Finnish Defence Forces for a decade and her research interests include military personnel's well-being, especially work–family relationships and preventing work–family conflict.

Todd M. Jensen is Research Associate in the Jordan Institute for Families and Research Assistant Professor in the School of Social Work at the University of North Carolina at Chapel Hill. Dr. Jensen is committed to strengthening families and promoting youth well-being. He has studied extensively the experiences of families who face shifts in structure, particularly when parental figures exit or enter a household. During his doctoral studies at the University of North Carolina at Chapel Hill, this work was supported by two awards—a Chancellor's Fellowship from the Royster Society of Fellows and a pre-doctoral fellowship from the Eunice Kennedy Shriver National Institute for Child Health and Human Development. Dr. Jensen also currently serves as Co-Principal Investigator on a federally funded, nationwide project aimed at supporting the US Air Force Family Advocacy Program and its efforts to strengthen families and prevent family maltreatment among active-duty members.

George Karpetis an associate researcher at the University of Adelaide, Medical School (Robinson Research Institute, Critical and Ethical Mental Health Research Group), Australia, and a clinical practitioner. He has been trained in child psychoanalytic psychotherapy and worked for 20 years in mental health services. George is a practitioner-researcher and his research evaluates the effectiveness of clinical practice, the dynamics of aggression in organizations, and the formation of professional identity.

Kairi Kasearu is Associate Professor of General Sociology and Head of the research group Centre of Strategic Sustainability at the University of Tartu, Estonia. Her research interests have been related to family studies, intergenerational relations, and social exclusion. Since 2014 she has focused on military sociology, especially military families, conscription, and reservist-based armies. At the moment she is leading the Development of Resource Management in the Defence Sector project in cooperation with the Estonian Defence Forces (2018–2022).

Emma Long is a PhD researcher in the Sociology department at Lancaster University. Her primary research interests revolve around the army family and how members manage and negotiate their military lives. Her PhD explores how partners to serving personnel in the army experience reintegration after combat-related deployment, focusing on coping strategies and possible engagement with formal support services.

Elena Lysak is a PhD student in Sociology at the School for Advanced Studies in the Social Sciences, France. She is specialized in military and international studies, as well as in gender stratification of women in the family and at work. Her PhD will explore the role of the military spouses in the construction and development of the military profession in the contemporary world. She is doing a research in France and Russia and currently working in both those countries.

James A. Martin is a retired Army Officer and Professor of Social Work and Social Research at Bryn Mawr College.

Laura Masson is Professor at the National University of San Martín, Argentina, and a member of the Gender Policy Council of the Argentine Ministry of Defense (since 2007). She holds a PhD (2007) and master's degree (1999) in Social Anthropology from the Federal University of Rio de Janeiro (FURJ), Brazil. She is the author of *Politic in Female: Gender and Power in the Province of Buenos Aires* (Ed. Antropofagia) and *Feminists Everywhere: An Ethnography of Spaces and Feminist Narratives in Argentina* (Ed. Prometeo). She is Advisor to the National Direction of Human Rights and International Humanitarian Law, Ministry of Defense, Argentina.

René Moelker is an Associate Professor of Sociology at the Royal Military Academy, the Netherlands. He holds a doctorate from the Erasmus University, Rotterdam. His work in military sociology concentrates on the sociology of military families, military technology, the military profession, the military sociology of Norbert Elias, military education, conflict in Chechnya, and the media. His latest project focuses on veterans and veteran care.

Catherine Mogil is an Assistant Clinical Professor at the Semel Institute for Neuroscience and Human Behavior at the University of California, Los Angeles. Dr. Mogil's research focuses on family-centered and trauma-informed interventions for at-risk infants and toddlers and their families. She is a co-developer of the FOCUS (Families OverComing Under Stress) Program, which has been implemented at US Military installations around the world.

Eleonora Natale holds a PhD from Keele University, the United Kingdom and specializes in Politics and International Relations. In 2018 she held a Research Fellowship at Universidad Nacional de San Martín, Argentina. Her research interests lie primarily in the areas of military studies, violence, and ethnography.

Ann-Margreth E. Olsson holds a Professional Doctorate (Systemic Practice) from the University of Bedfordshire and is a trained social worker (BSc) and supervisor (MSc). She is currently employed as Senior Lecturer in Social Work at Kristianstad University. She is a Swedish representative in the NATO/OTAN team on the impact of military life on children from military families. Her professional interests include social services, coaching pedagogics and counselling, military families; and soldiers, veterans, and their extended families. Children's participation, "Barnahus" (Children Advocacy Centers), and parenting support programs constitute her major fields of research and publication. Her professional trajectory includes top managing positions in social services in Sweden and she was the CEO of AMOVE AB, a private consulting firm focusing on coaching, supervision, and organizational development.

Sven-Erik Olsson is a Researcher at AMOVE AB, Lund Sweden. He is a trained social worker (BSc) and worked at Kristianstad University, Sweden for 16 years as Senior Lecturer in Social Work. His work has focused on labor, social insurance, and evaluation of collaboration between healthcare, social care, and social work agencies. His latest project focused on prevention work against violence in close relations.

Sian Oram is a Lecturer in Women's Mental Health at the Institute of Psychiatry, Psychology & Neuroscience at King's College London and she jointly leads the Violence Abuse and Mental Health Network. Her research aims to reduce the risk and impact of violence through qualitative, epidemiological, and intervention research.

Blair Paley is a Clinical Professor in the Department of Psychiatry and Biobehavioral Sciences at the David Geffen School of Medicine at UCLA, and the Director of the Strategies for Enhancing Early Developmental Success (SEEDS) program. Dr. Paley's research and clinical work focus on prevention and intervention with high-risk children and their families.

Helen Pluut is Assistant Professor at the Department of Business Studies at Leiden University, the Netherlands. Before moving to Leiden University in 2016, she was a Visiting Fellow at the National University of Singapore. She defended her dissertation at Tilburg University, where she also obtained her bachelor's and master's degrees. Dr. Pluut's research examines numerous areas related to organizational behavior and psychology, such as job attitudes, moods and emotions, (eu)stress, social support, work–family interface, and group dynamics.

Lesleigh E. Pullman has a doctorate in Experimental Psychology from the University of Ottawa. She is a Defence Scientist under Director General Military Personnel Research and Analysis at the Department of National Defence. She investigates a variety of topics related to military personnel and their families, including financial stability, spousal employment and income, military family well-being, and sexual misconduct.

Kadri Raid is a PhD student in Sociology and Junior Researcher of Sociological Studies at the Institute of Social Studies at the University of Tartu, Estonia. She has specialized in the fields of family studies (e.g., family relations, family structures, children, family formation, cohabitation, and marriage). Her PhD thesis theme is "The Changing Family in Contemporary Society through the Lens of Ambivalence." She has also belonged to several research groups studying family relations and formation.

Gottfried Reiter is an Officer in the Austrian Armed Forces. He holds a master's degree in Military Leadership from the Theresian Military Academy and a doctorate in Sociology from the University of Vienna. His research interests include to the work–life balance of soldiers as well as their family life in connection with the stresses and strains of the military service.

Nina Rones is a Senior Researcher at the Norwegian Defence Research Establishment. She earned her doctorate at the Norwegian School of Sport Sciences with a thesis entitled: "The Struggle over Military Identity: a multi-sited ethnography on gender, fitness and 'the right attitudes' in the military profession/field." In addition to gender identity and the military profession, her research interests include military socialization, power relations, and the sociology of Norbert Elias.

Philip Siebler is a Mental Health Manager in the Department of Defense, Australia. He has worked in a range of child and family social work positions. He earned his doctorate in social work at Monash University, with a thesis entitled: "'Military People Won't Ask for Help': Experiences of deployment of Australian Defense Force personnel, their families, and implications for social work." His research and practice interest is in what constitutes best practice with the military family. He created an ecological model of the military family for social work.

Alla Skomorovsky has a PhD in Experimental Social Psychology from Carleton University, Ottawa, Canada. Since 2005, she has been working as a Research Psychologist at Director General Military Personnel Research and Analysis (DGMPRA) in Ottawa. Currently, she is a Team Leader of the Military Families Research Team. She conducts quantitative and qualitative research in the areas of resilience, stress, coping, personality, and well-being of military families. In addition, Dr. Skomorovsky teaches psychology at Royal Military College and Carleton University.

Kevin Spruce earned his BA (Hons), MSc, and MRes (converted to PhD) at Edinburgh Napier University. Kevin's academic background is in Keele University's Psychology and Counselling Psychology departments. He is Director and Senior Practicing Therapist at Veterans' Counselling Services and Cheshire Therapy Services. He feels privileged to have been asked to contribute to Lord Ashcroft's Veteran Transition Review, as an academic advisor, and to hold the position of being a War Veteran (Falkland Islands).

Tiia-Triin Truusa is a PhD student in Sociology; however, her background is social work. She works as an analysist at the Institute of Social Studies at the University of Tartu, Estonia. She is also Project Manager for the Centre of Strategic Sustainability research group. Her research focus has been on human resources in the defence sector. She is a part of the NATO research group HFM 263 RTG, The Transition of Military Veterans from Active Service to Civilian Life.

Cynthia Wan is a doctoral candidate completing her last year in the Experimental Psychology program at the University of Ottawa, Canada. Her dissertation focuses on social neuroscience, particularly the influences of culture and various psychosocial factors on physiological (i.e., biomarkers) and psychological patterns of stress. Other research interests include quantitative and qualitative investigations of health, quality of life, and well-being of individuals suffering from chronic conditions. Ms. Wan has been working as a Research Assistant at the Director General Military Personnel Research and Analysis (DGMPRA) in Ottawa since 2017. During her research assistantship at DGMPRA, she has been involved in various qualitative and quantitative studies on the health, well-being, and psychological outcomes of military personnel and their families.

Zhigang Wang leads the Methodology team at Director General Military Personnel Research and Analysis (DGMPRA) at the Department of National Defence, Ottawa. He received his PhD in Social Psychology from Carleton University. He conducts research on a variety of military personnel issues, including personnel and family support, diversity and employment equity, and harassment and sexual misconduct.

Part I

The state, the Armed Forces, and the rise of the negotiation household

1 Introduction

The politics of military families and the rise of the negotiation household—tensions between state, work, and families

René Moelker, Nina Rones, and Manon Andres

> Introducing Family Claus Pedersen: Danish Major Pedersen is deployed in Helmand, Afghanistan. He leads his company on patrols and tries to contribute to reconstruction in the best way he can. He helps the local population whenever possible, and motivates the men in his company that suffer the loss of a buddy by IEDs. His wife Maria meanwhile manages the family back home. The children Figne, Julius, and Elliot miss daddy very much and have a hard time adjusting to the separation. Besides work, Maria has to deal with problems at school, sibling rivalry, and of course her own emotional rollercoaster. On top of that the family is confronted with a premature repatriation and judicial hassles because Pederson ordered an air strike on a compound without proper friend-or-foe identification that resulted in collateral damage. Moral dilemmas weigh heavy on both spouses' consciences.
>
> (Abstracted from Krigen, 2015)[1]

Introducing power, politics, and families

"The love of power is the love of ourselves," William Hazlitt remarked,[2] but the power of love is somewhere in the balance of give and take. Sensible people know that giving a little bit more without counter-obligation brings profit because it builds up a relationship and that is what families are about. Besides being foremost a survival unit, the family harbors affection. Where the state is a power and security container (Moelker, 2009: 16), the family does provide survival within the context of being a container for emotions (Kövecses, 1990). How can we understand politics in our ideal typical military family, the Pedersens?

> Julius doesn't respond to his mother when she calls him to go home and he keeps playing soccer by himself at the schoolyard. In general, he defies her authority, never listens. . . he is annoying his older sister Figne, saying "Figne, your butt is fat. . ." Maria tells Figne to be patient. After dinner, dad is supposed to phone but he phones late, after the children have gone to bed. Claus tells Maria that one of his men, First Gunner Anders Holm, stepped on an IED and passed away. Worriedly, Maria asks "Are you OK?" whilst lighting a cigarette [tension relief]. She says "We are fine. . . they. . . sure, they behave from time to time, you know. . . they are annoying at times, it's funny for you, you can look forward to coming home to these little brats."

The power relations in this family scene are about to be contested. Claus is on deployment, but he is the head of the family. The Pedersens are a very democratic and equalitarian modern family, but with Claus being separated from home the middle son Julius feels a disbalance in the relationships and he applies disruptive tactics to destabilize Maria's authority. By behaving in an obnoxious way, he hopes to get attention and hopes for a return to the situation before the deployment, with father being back home. Maria quiets and reassures both Figne and Elliot, but cannot share her worries with Claus because Claus already has a large mental load to digest with a casualty among his men. She interprets Claus' story to be stressful to him and therefore does not communicate about the home front. This barrier for support weakens Maria's position further, because now she has to solve the problems on her own.

The micro politics at family level are already complicated by the separation of one of the parents, but they are also affected by the events in Afghanistan and by the intricate intersection of school and family. In this family scene the state level is out of sight, but it is at state level that the structure for the behavioral patterns is defined. We will discuss this in later sections, after first defining families and elaborating theory. In this book, we focus on three levels: the state level (macro), the organization level (meso), and the family level (micro), which impact each other. The politics of military families regard these tensions between the state, work organizations, and the family.

The (military) family as figuration: exploring the micro level process from command to negotiation household

> The Pedersens are a typical modern family. The composition is traditional, since they form a family consisting of a father, mother, and three children. Maria is a working mom, educated and emancipated. Claus is the main provider but Maria is an equal partner. The children are parented by coaching, and by explaining the things they do wrong. Moreover, reward and stimulation are prone in the interactions, whilst punishment or negative reinforcement is avoided at all times. The children have a voice in the management of the family. They are not the decision makers, but they have influence and their parents consider their needs, wishes and opinions. The Pedersens are a negotiation household.

"We speak of families as though we all knew what families are" (Laing, 2001: 3), and therefore the concept is susceptible for reification, but in reality definitions of the family as well as the dynamics and structures that determine families vary over time and cultures. Scholars using a reified concept of "the family" often refer to "an ideological stereotype of a heterosexual two-parent nuclear family with breadwinning husband and father, home-making wife and mother, and their biological children" (Edwards, Ribbens, McCarthy, and Gillies, 2012: 732), which does not correspond to the diversity of family forms. Modern families are not solely based on biological, marital, child-rearing structures, but on the performance of family roles. They include, for instance, single-parent families, childless couples, same-sex couples, transgender families, and newly remarried families (stepfamilies or blended families). The various family forms create different family dynamics and include various subgroups and relationships. Members of the family may be "close or apart, together or separate, near or distant, loving, fighting, etc." (Laing, 2001: 4). What constitutes a family is not only conceptually relevant. Professionals and practitioners also need a framework of how to approach "the family" for providing their services (Edwards et al., 2012).

The family is a figuration that mostly takes the form of a triad consisting of a father, mother, and one or more children. If the family composition diverts from this triadic form, for example, in the case of single-parent families or childless couples, the basic form is dyadic. The dynamic in a dyad is very different from a triad. Nonetheless, even with dyadic basic forms there is always a third relevant party nearby; for instance, in single-parent families there may be the co-parent, or perhaps grandparents or friends who play an important role. However, the typical military family is a triadic figuration.

The three parties in the figuration are interdependent. Norbert Elias defines the figuration as

> the changing pattern created by the players as a whole – not by their intellects but by their whole selves, the totality of their dealings in their relationships with each other. It can be seen that this figuration forms a *flexible latticework of tensions* [emphasis by the author]. The interdependence of the players, which is a prerequisite of their forming a figuration, may be an interdependence of allies or of opponents.
>
> (Elias, 1978: 130)

Elias' theoretical perspective came thus to be known as "figurational sociology," although Elias later came to prefer the term "process sociology" (Baur and Ernst, 2011: 123) in order to avoid static thinking on figurations. Following Elias, the family and the Armed Forces are shifting networks of living, constantly growing/aging, and socialized people who constantly do and reconstruct the family and the military in an ongoing process. And such formations/network/relationship (figurations) of interdependent people are, according to Elias, always characterized by interweaving processes of shifting power balances.

The dynamic in these figurations stems from the basic political mechanism of divide and rule. Lasswell (1936) defined politics as the answer to the question "who gets what, when and how?" and thus points to the fact that politics concern matters of distribution. This takes place at all levels of daily life, including the way a household is managed. Families, with their relationships, hierarchies, roles, and interactions, may form people's first experience with "politics to every day living" (Edwards et al., 2012: 737). Family members influence each other continuously and in a reciprocal manner. Lasswell's definition and the definition of figuration is in line with basic conflict theory since "tensions and conflicts arise when resources, power etcetera are unevenly distributed between groups in society and that these conflicts become the engine for social change."[3] The new element here is the concept of social change! In "trialectics" (Bröcklin, 2010) the change comes from the actors, who seek to arrive at a balance within a triadic system. Heider's Balance Theory (1958) also presumes the idea of triads in describing significant entities in one's environment and assumes that disharmony creates tensions, which enforce change. Elias (1939) refers to this system as the "royal mechanism," in which the king balances out the nobles against the commons, sometimes favoring the one side, sometimes favoring the other side. The principle is also referred to as the "rejoicing third" or the "tertius gaudens," since the power holder will profit from the rivalry of those beneath him and he will be in power because of the game of balancing out the ascendant and the descendent in the power triangle. Change will occur when the power holder is not able to balance the parties and one of the rivaling parties ascends to power. Mathematically, the options are manifold, as is illustrated in Figure 1.1.

The family is a figuration like many others. Since the Pedersen family is a modern family, the "king's position," which falls to Claus, is merely a *primus inter pares* position and the axis of cooperation with Maria is unbreakable when the family is united. But in times of deployment-induced separation this axis is feeble; Claus is far away and cannot always communicate, and Maria is forced into the "king's position" whilst not being able to manage well the axis of tensions between the children. Julius rebels both against his sibling sister and contests Maria's authority, and even though Maria knows how to get the other two on her side she is on the brink of an emotional breakdown. It only takes a small incident to collapse the powerhouse—and it does. The youngest, Elliot, swallows a large amount of pills, possibly paracetamol, and Maria has to take him to the hospital to have his stomach pumped. The other children go along because there is no one to take care of them. Maria is at the end of her wits and endurance. She recuperates a little bit by sharing her worries with a friend but her resources for resilience have definitely dried up. This scene ends with the Pedersens' home front in a power vacuum, and yet another crisis is impending.

Elias (1978) suggests regarding power as ever-shifting balances in power ratios, power chances, or power distribution, which form an aspect of all human relationships. Because the balances are ever-shifting, the relationships are always dynamic. Even the tiny child has power over its parents. Elias explains:

> It must also be born in mind that power balances, like human relationships in general, are bi-polar at least, and usually multi-polar . . . From the day of his birth a baby has power over its parents, not just the parents over the baby. At least, the baby has power over them as long as they attach any kind of value to it. If not, it loses its power. The parents may abandon the baby . . . if it has no function for them.
>
> (p. 74)

The child has power over his parents in proportion to his parents' dependence of him. "Even the tiny child has its trump-cards in weeping and laughter"

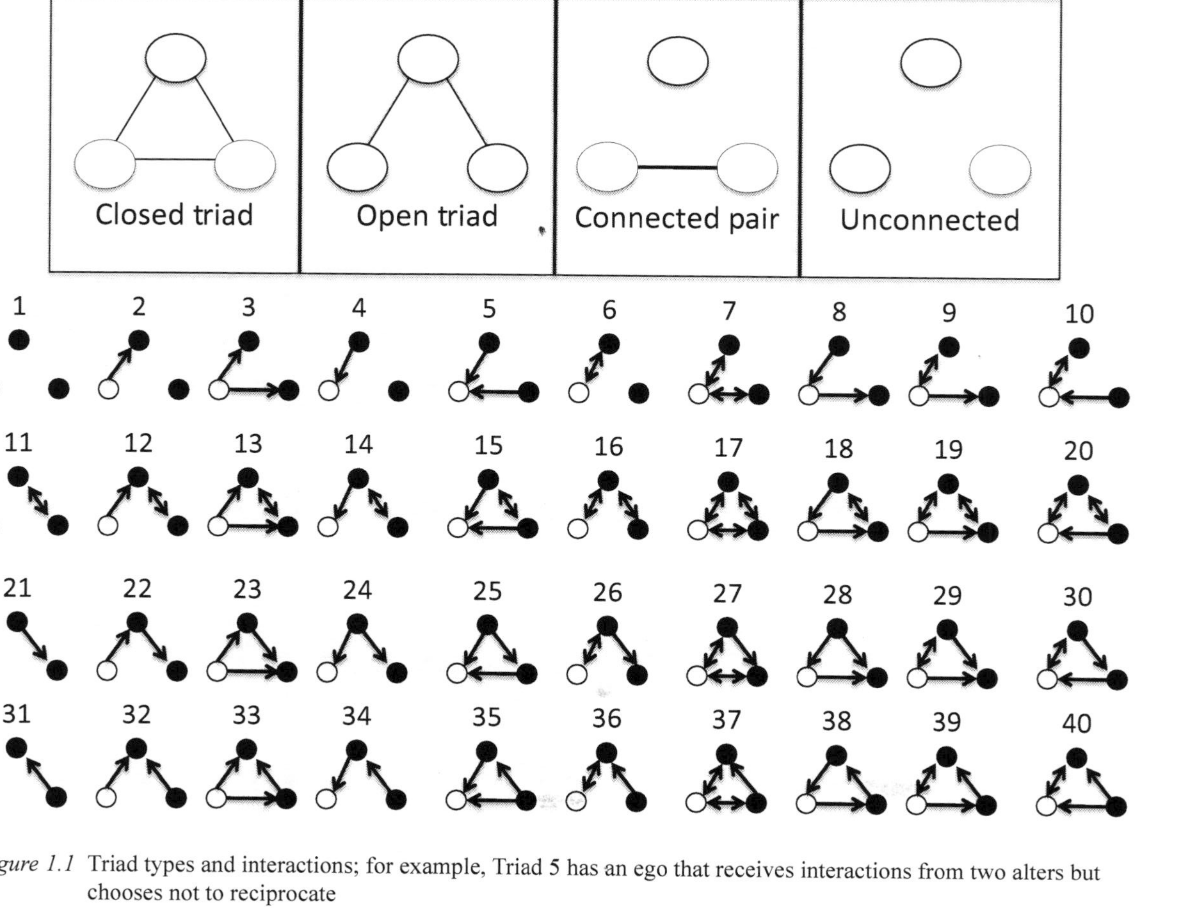

Figure 1.1 Triad types and interactions; for example, Triad 5 has an ego that receives interactions from two alters but chooses not to reciprocate

(p. 121). In relationships between parents and infants, power chances are distributed very unevenly. But whether the power differentials are large or small, balances of power are always present where there are functional interdependences between people. As a result of such ever-shifting power balances, social figurations are in a constant state of flux.

> At the core of changing figurations . . . is a fluctuation, tensile equilibrium, a balance of power moving to and fro, inclining first to one side and then to the other. This kind of fluctuating balance of power is a structural characteristic of the flow of every figuration.
>
> (Elias, 1978: 131)

By analyzing the axis of tensions in the figuration in a historical sequence one can reconstruct the process of change, and this analysis resembles Marx's dialectic approach.[4] But instead of two parties, Elias prefers to analyze three or more stakeholders, hence the abovementioned "trialectics" and the "tertius gaudens" that is implied in the "royal mechanism." Gilliam and Gulløv (2014) argue, among other things, that shifting power balances have altered cultural perceptions of ideals of child-rearing and that the development of institutional child-rearing is an interesting case for the discussion of civilizing processes. Others, such as Ariès (1960), have thus analyzed the genesis of childhood. Ariès (1960), in his book *Centuries of Childhood: A Social History of Family Life*, vividly claims that childhood was not discovered until well after the middle ages. Children used to be treated as adults, which implicates that the basic form of interaction often was dyadic. The triad "father, mother, child" is politically a more interesting game because the dynamic in this triad leads to a shift from a command household to a negotiation household (Swaan, 1982: 81–115).

The command household is the traditional form where the man is in control of all interactions; at the least, he has the last say regarding decisions. This ideal type does not really exist because even when legally and culturally the power lays with the head of the family, behind the curtain often the women manages many affairs and exerts much influence. But the discretionary powers of the man are disproportional in these households, more in front- than in back-office situations. Although the father is bestowed with authority he is normally not a dictator and the family can be just as caring and warm as any other type of family. Claus Pedersen meets a family like that in Afghanistan.

> On patrol the company finds an indigenous father whose daughter is ill and needs medical attention. She suffers from burns and the man is desperately asking for help. When they enter the *quala*, there are only women and children, and the little girl lies in bandages. The burns are hurting and need tending. The medic cleans the wound. The local is told that he can bring the little girl to the camp if things get worse.

In contrast to command households, negotiation households involve tensions and ever-shifting power balances that are discussed and negotiated: "Balancing out the power between man and woman [and other possible intimate relations] and parents and child requires verbal skills, far-sightedness, aptitude for reflection and tolerance, and the acceptance of limits despite all openness and freedom of choice" (Bois-Reymond, 1999: 82). Not all negotiation households are balanced and well managed, but when they are the spouses are collaborating based on equality and on the ways in which they supplement each other. The politics are more egalitarian and presuppose much communication. The same with children! Sociologists like Brinkgreve (2008) have noticed that childhood patterns have prolonged over the course of the family life span. Often children are physically and economically independent and mature, but emotionally still dependent on their parents for advice and coaching. Sometimes these adult "children" never leave home. The negotiation household relates to the triad "father," "mother," "child"—and "children" are often equal political agents in the family diplomatic system. Coercion is hardly an accepted praxis and/or discourse in family life. In many countries it is legally forbidden to physically correct one's children. The line between corrective punishment and maltreatment is thinner. Deployments, exercises, and military work obligations challenge the family diplomatic system in a different way from patriarchal times, when "father's will was law."

Wouters (2007) remarks that "informalizing" defines the interactions between people in general and this also applies to parent–child relations, meaning that everything (even intimate topics) can be discussed as without status or age being barriers to the communication. These two elements, the taboo of physical force inside family relations and the informal code between family members, call for an advanced emotion management that Wouters (2007) and Elias elaborated on by coining the concept of "controlled decontrolling of emotions." The controlled decontrolling of emotions in an informalized context implies that the political game in organizations and families is played in a more sophisticated manner. One can approach a colonel quite informally, whilst still knowing where the power balance lies. One can talk with children and "act" foolish for a fun moment like one is a child him/herself, and yet return to the adult position within the blink of an eye without losing control of the situation. One can "let go," whilst also being in control. Interactions within families are emotion work, and so is work at the office or work as an officer.

> Lasse (second gunner) is crying and laments, "I want to go home." He feels guilty because first gunner Anders took his place and died from an IED. It should have been him being hit by the IED. "I can't go through that gate again. I am useless." Claus responds: "I can't send you home, but I can give you camp duty for the next two weeks." After two weeks they will have another talk. He offers a cigarette and leaves the phone so that Lasse can call to his 16-year-old sister. Lasse is pleased to hear his sister and smiles.

The Danish soldiers interact with lowest power distance possible in almost informal fashion. But Claus is the commander and even though emotional himself, he can help his second gunner by listening and providing him with means of communication with the home front. Claus engages in emotion management and emotion work and he subtly knows to control the decontrolling of emotions. The stiff upper lip or "carry on" fashion would have aggregated Lasse's emotional hurt and led to a disfunctioning co-worker. The decontrolling of emotions can apply to "ego" and "alter," and requires psychological skills and above all empathy.

The state, the Armed Forces, and family (a macro elaboration of the shift from command to negotiation household)

> If the army had wanted you to have a family, it would have issued you one.
> (Anonymous)

In analyzing the politics of military families one can shift between the micro, the meso, and the macro level because these levels are intertwined and shifting will illuminate the interdependencies. It is the state that deploys soldiers, and it is the home front that is amongst the main operational success or fail factors. "War made the state, and the state made war," so Tilly claimed (1975: 42) but states could not win wars without support from the home front.

The method in this book reflects the intertwined character of the topic matter at hand. Elias asserts to reveal macrostructures by researching microstructures: "Makrostrukturen durch die Untersuchung von Mikrostructuren sichtbar zu machen" (Moelker, 2003: 378). This method implies that one can see the structure of the whole system reflected in a subsystem. Studying military families likewise reveals how the military organization and the state change. The triad "state," "Armed Forces," and "family" is interdependent on each other in reproducing a gender-based system of reproduction that is resistant to change because it is deeply rooted in cultural values and norms and transmitted by socialization. Historically, the tensions in this system are advantageous to the men in the family, but also to the state that thrives from the division of labor freeing men for conscription, and thus the monopoly of violence (Elias, 1939) coincides with hegemonic masculinity (Connell, 2009) and with the exclusion of women from war and soldiering. By limiting the role of women to the family realm the state was able to develop into a nation-state, the Armed Forces could become stationary instead of seasonal, and the family itself became a command household chaired by the *pater familias*.

The constructivist Connell (2009) defines gender as: "the structure of social relations that centers on the reproductive arena, and the set of practices that bring reproductive distinctions between bodies into social processes" (Connell, 2009: 11). Thus the objective of the figuration "state," "Armed Forces," and "family" is about physical reproduction (children), cultural reproduction, and power, and the practices that bring reproduction about such as socialization in families, conscripted service in the Armed Forces, and (combining the two) hegemonic masculinity. In studying masculinity we need to focus on processes and relationships through which men and women conduct gendered lives. "Masculinities are configurations of practice that are accomplished in social action and, therefore, can differ according to the gender relations in a particular social setting" (Connell and Messerschmidt, 2005: 836).

Hegemonial masculinity, a term that was inspired by the work of Gramsci, is "the form of masculinity in a given historical and society-wide setting that structures and legitimates hierarchical gender relations between men and women, between masculinity and femininity, and among masculinities" (Messerschmidt, 2016: 10). Hooper (1999) discusses how military combat has shaped the state and the soldier. As a result, men can only exist as men if they are willing to charge into war, thereby expressing their "enduring natural aggression." As a consequence, this leads to the "exclusion of women from combat," while furthering the myth "that military service is the fullest expression of masculinity." Hooper also points at the socialization of militarized masculinity in boys. More specifically, she sees military service as a "rite of passage" into manhood. As such, "war and the military represent one of the major sites where hegemonic masculinities are formed" (Hooper, 1999: 475–480).

This form of hegemony is similar to Bourdieu's symbolic violence, because the figuration does not depend on coercion but on cultural and ideological persuasion that results in (often unconscious or taken-for-granted) consent from those that are actually the most exploited or subdued actors in the figuration. Symbolic violence denotes "the violence which is exercised upon a social agent with his or her complicity" (Bourdieu and Wacquant, 2002: 167). In a command household, the mother may be revered in many ways, but the man is without dispute the lord, the hunter, the provider, the protector; the wife is his accomplice. This is the metaphoric symbolic capital and the hegemonial system in Western societies, and it is also the dominant culture of the Armed Forces (Enloe, 2000, 2007; Woodward and Winter, 2007).

The model of the command household as a specific form of hegemonial masculinity fits the military sociology of both Moskos (1977) and Segal (1986). In the Armed Forces as an institution, the spouse (and the family) are integral parts of the military community, whereas they are removed from the military community in situations where the military progressed toward an occupation. The position of the spouse was, in the institution era, supportive to the position of the soldier much in line to the saying "behind every great man there's a great woman." Segal elaborated on this theory and added on the Coser (1974)-inspired concept of greediness. The greediness concept works both ways; the military family is greedy and claims the devotion of both spouses to the job of parenting, and the military organization is greedy since it also claims devotion of the soldier. The concept is put to the test in this book since with the advent of the negotiation family, the work–family conflict is sharper today where relations between partners are more equal (Andres, De Angelis, and McCone, 2015) and the women have more resources to power to underline their claims to an equal workload in the family realm.

Figurations have changed from command household to negotiation household. Hegemonic masculinity or symbolic violence has transformed by a change to soft power that actually is an iron fist in a velvet glove. We can illustrate this by looking at the microcosmos of the kindergarten that reflects the macro cosmos at the state level. The kindergarten as a system exerts power paralleled to the Foucauldian panopticum. It is an example par excellence of state power controlling our lives and the lives of our model family Pedersen.

> The school staff member Brigitte approaches Maria with the most serious face you can imagine, and says: "I have to tell you that Julius has been in a fight with another boy today. . . he bit the other boy in the shoulder." Later, Maria will have to go back to school to talk about the incident. She knows that Julius is in big trouble because this behavior is not tolerated and she, the mother, is held responsible. So she discusses the incident with the other children, with her husband Claus (but he is occupied with a combat situation and is not really receiving the message), and with a friend.

Schools have lost the competence to understand the "biting kid" as a kid in need of communication and have outlawed all forms of violence without questioning what the meaning of this violence is. Gilliam and Gulløv (2014) argue that child-rearing institutions, kindergartens and schools, have been central to the civilizing process of the last century. In specific, they argue that child-rearing institutions have a role in forming and disseminating ideas about what it means to be a civilized person in the Danish welfare state (and many other countries). The Danish welfare state seems to be "unwilling to leave the practice of child-rearing to random parents, but must ensure and control the proper civilizing of the up-coming generation." Through the daily formative work with children, norms of social interactions are internalized. They are imposed and standardized as the proper way to behave (Gilliam and Gulløv, 2014).

As power balances shifted through the nineteenth and twentieth centuries, so did norms and values regarding child-rearing. The way in which child-rearing institutions are organized changed accordingly, allotting much more power to the state and state officials (staff of kindergartens) while regulating and surveilling parenting practices. Within negotiation households, equality is the norm, but—paradoxically—state coercion has more grip on modern families whilst parents do not.

Work organization, family, soldier

The lengthening of the "chain of interdependencies" (Elias, 1978) connects people all the way from Afghanistan to Denmark but also makes it more difficult to foresee, understand, or control the direction of the war game, the society, the institution, or the family they form together. To illustrate the chain of interdependencies one needs only to consider a mission abroad going astray and how this affects the home front in both its emotional and legal aspects. The global is connected with the local, and the state is connected with the family. Often the military is caught in between. This happened to Claus Pedersen when he was under enemy fire and requested air support.

> The local farmer (with an injured daughter) visits the camp with his family and complains that the Taliban come at night and want him to join the insurgents. Major Claus Pedersen promises that the Danes will "drive the Taliban out tomorrow." Next morning, they seek out the indigenous family. When they arrive at the *quala*, the platoon finds out that the whole family has been killed. Then there is an ambush. They are fired upon and first gunner Lasse is hit in the neck and needs assistance. They've asked for medevac but are still under fire. The enemy is westward but there is no clear enemy report; "Where the fuck are they?" one of the men exclaims. "Visual: negative." Lasse is getting critical and they want air support badly. Communications officer Butcher reports "no air support unless we have positive identification." The Tactical Operation Commander wants verification. Butcher: "7-5 wants to know who's in there." Claus Pedersen: "I don't care who's in there. Tell that to 7-5." Butcher: "We have positive identification on compound 6." Air support is delivered and enables the helicopter to land and Lasse is transported to safety. He survives. Back at the compound Pedersen is called to meet the commander and two judge advocates: "We want to interrogate you in connection with some civilian deaths." The commander concludes the meeting: "I have to inform you that you're charged with bombing a civilian target, resulting in the death of 11 civilians." Claus: "What does that mean?" The commander responds: "It means that you're going home, Claus."

The global meets the local because the political judicial situation abroad affects the home front on an existential level. The judiciary represents the state level and the prosecution gives the defense a hard time. The family triad (Claus, Maria, kids) is reinstated, the family is reunited, but the relational quality suffers because the legal verdict is approaching and the prospects look gloomy. If Claus tells the truth, meaning that he had no real identification on compound 6, he might face four years' imprisonment. His wife Maria confronts him with the dilemma that results from the question of whether the target was a military or a civilian target with innocent civilian victims, amongst whom were eight children.

> Claus: "I didn't know who was in that house Maria. . . I'll just have to suffer the consequences." Maria: "What about the children? What about me? You've been gone for a very long time. Julius is struggling with it." Claus: "What should I have done?" Maria replies: "The issue is not what you should have done, but what you do now. Will four years in prison help you? Will that make you feel better? Will the children feel better? We need you at home. The children need you." Claus is troubled by his conscience: "I dropped that bomb. It was my decision. I can't blame the men." Maria is really getting angry: "No, say you had the fucking identification. Say you don't remember who gave it to you. You may have killed eight children, but you have three living ones at home."

We will not reveal the ending of this story—no more spoilers—but to mirror the ethical dilemma to the reader: what would you do if you were in this position?

Tell the truth and face prison time, or lie and remain reunited with the family that you love dearly and that needs you desperately? What would you do if you were in the shoes of Major Pedersen?

At the meso level, the macro and micro processes often collide and conflict. The work–family conflict is played out at this level. Tensions pertain to competing work and family demands, incompatible expectations or behavior, and psychological, emotional, or moral conflicts (Greenhaus and Beutell, 1985; MacDermid, Wadsworth, and Southwell, 2011) such as in the dilemma described above. Common features of the military, such as frequent separations, relocations, the command structure, expected behavior, and discipline, could collide with expectations in the family domain. But family responsibilities can also interfere with work, particularly considering the shift toward negotiation households and the "sandwich generation" comprised of those who care for aging parents while also raising children. As stated earlier, in light of changes in military and family dynamics, work–family conflict is becoming even more prominent (De Angelis and Segal, 2015).

Politics is about forming coalitions. The triadic modeling is an abstraction from reality, but we understand the seemingly chaotic reality better if we contrast it with our constructed models. Models like these can successfully be applied to realistic situations such as the situation that Maria, Claus, and the children are in.

Overview of the book

The point of departure in this book lies in a triadic approach to reality (Figure 1.2). Three is company. Society starts with three. Political processes can best be studied by looking at the interdependencies in three-party figurations on three different analytical levels. Therefore, the book is divided into three parts: the society level, the organization level, and the family level, which regards individual families, parenting, and micro interactions. In these parts, the authors are guided by the following overarching research questions.

- What are the key issues in three-party dynamics?
- What tensions exist in these dynamics?
- How do actors seek to arrive at a balance? What initiatives for change are made?

Part I: the state, the Armed Forces, and the rise of the negotiation household

In Chapter 2, Kevin Spruce elaborates on the triadic approach and shows that the family itself is an (often) unconscious executioner of its own suppression; third-party symbolic violence invisibilizes the invisible, changing spouses of military personnel from being the victim, to being the perpetrator of their own symbolic violence. The role of the state is most interesting in Natale's chapter (3) on the embarrassing mutual pain in the tensions between family members of the former oppressive Argentine regime (perpetrator families), the attitudes of the present

Figure 1.2 Triadic figurations approach of understanding modern military families

population, and the Argentine state's ambivalent position, which aspires to be the rejoicing third in an act of electoral-motivated brinkmanship. Masson (Chapter 4) expands on this analysis by bringing in gender and gender regimes and applying this perspective to female officers in the Brazilian Air Force. Lysak (Chapter 5) examines the reason for the persistence of these figurations and finds the cause in the exploitation of spouses whose free labor is supporting both the soldier and the Armed Forces organization. She adequately coins this labor "the military–family industry" because families compose part of the machine. However, all this is challenged by the advent of new families like same-sex and transgender couples. Eran-Jona and Aviram (Chapter 6) argue that the Israeli Armed Forces are in need of a culture change in order to promote acceptance.

Part II: Organization, soldier, and military family: negotiating the tensions

Raid, Kasearu, and Truusa (Chapter 7) examine how drafted conscripts balance the power triad made up of the institutions of family, changing society, and military, and find that individual agency and the support of family (parents) play a significant role in successfully integrating conscription into one's lifecourse. Dursun, Wang, and Pullman (Chapter 8) examine the extent to which military lifestyle stressors and support influence military spouses' well-being. Pluut and Andres (Chapter 9) study the tensions in the military–employee–family triad and analyze how the work–family conflict influences employees' and partners' attitudes toward the organization. Satisfaction with support organized by the navy is positively associated with all attitudes towards the navy. Gribble (Chapter 10) describes a perceived lack of agency amongst her respondents. Yet, the military institution was also seen to provide a sense of connectedness for spouses. Anderson and Goldenberg (Chapter 11) look into the Canadian reserve forces, who often also hold civilian employment. Thus, members of the reserves are in the unique position of balancing a trio of responsibilities: family life, civilian work obligations, and military service.

In Finland, Hannola (Chapter 12) remarks that military greediness results in obligatory transfers and relocations, and thus may cause severe harm to one's family life. Even though relocated personnel and their families usually live in separation, familism is shown to be strengthened. The interesting finding from the UK study by Long (Chapter 13) regards a general decline in community spirit. The primary reason for the decline in community spirit is that families are less likely to regard the functioning of the military as part of their responsibility and they are no longer satisfied with the implicit expectation that they should put the soldiers' career and welfare above their own. Frederic (Chapter 14) studies the characteristics of the support the families render to soldiers in a study of Argentine peacekeeping operations in Haiti and defines the support as emotion work. Bowen, Jensen, and Martin (Chapter 15) focus on both organizational and family demands and develop a measure of USAF civilian spouse fitness.

Part III: Inside the negotiation household: tensions between the soldier-parent, the partner, and children

Siebler and Karpetis (Chapter 16) examine the phenomenon of intimate partner violence in Australian military families. Olsson and Olsson have conducted dialogical interviews in Sweden (Chapter 17). Although relatives are very supportive of their soldier, the Swedish families reject the concept of the "military family." Andres and Moelker (Chapter 18) study communication strategies of deployed military personnel and partners at home and focus on the question of whether it is better to actively communicate problems or to protect one's loved one from disrupting information. Skomorovsky, Bullock, and Wan (Chapter 19) study the stresses on Canadian single military parents. Reiter (Chapter 20) addresses family planning and fatherhood of male officers in the Austrian Army. This chapter offers a unique study into parenting as it departs from the father's perspective. A father who is also an officer! Mogil and Paley (Chapter 21) discuss the topic of parenting in military families.

In the concluding chapter (22), Moelker and Andres discuss dating from a distance and they challenge the "greedy institutions" concept. Instead of this dyadic concept, they propose a triadic approach to military families and by doing so they advance beyond the "greedy institution."

Notes

1 *A War* (Danish: Krigen) is a 2015 Danish war drama film written and directed by Tobias Lindholm, and starring Pilou Asbæk and Søren Malling. We apologize for the fact that this chapter contains so many spoilers.
2 As quoted by Galbraith (1983: 10).
3 http://sociology.about.com/od/Sociological-Theory/a/Conflict-Theory.htm.
4 Elias (2007) proposes a sociology of tensions resembling Marx's dialectical method. In particular, the concept of an "axis of tensions" is an example of this dialectical approach. But in a Paris lecture, Elias criticized Marx's two-party dialectics and presented the royal mechanism as at least a three-party kind of dynamic (Moelker, 2003).

References

Andres, M., De Angelis, K., and McCone, D. (2015). Reintegration, reconciliation, and relationship quality. In R. Moelker, M. Andres, G. Bowen, and P. Manigart (eds), *Military Families and War in the 21st Century: Comparative Perspectives* (pp. 145–160). London: Routledge.

Ariès, P. (1960). *Centuries of Childhood: A Social History of Family Life*, translated by Robert Baldick. New York: Alfred A. Knopf.

Baur, N. and Ernst, S. (2011). Towards a process-oriented methodology: modern social science research methods and Norbert Elias's figurational sociology. In N. Gabriel and S. Mennell (eds), *Norbert Elias and Figurational Research: Processual Thinking in Sociology* (pp. 117–139). Oxford: Blackwell Publishing.

Brinkgreve, C. (2008). Modern ouderschap. In W. Koops, B. Levering, and M. de Winter (eds), *Opvoeding als spiegel van de beschaving: Een moderne antropologie van de opvoeding* (pp. 126–136). Amsterdam: Uitgeverij SWP.

Bröcklin, U. (2010). Gesellschaft beginnt mit Drei. Eine soziologische Triadologie. In *Theorien des Dritten: Innovationenen in Soziologie und Sozialphilosophie* (pp. 189–213). München: Wilhelm Fink Verlag.

Bois-Reymond, M. du (1999). Conflict and negotiation in the family. In I. Sagel-Grande and M. V. Polak (eds), *Models of Conflict Resolution* (pp. 79–95). Antwerpen/Apeldoorn: Maklu.

Bourdieu, P. (1998). *Practical Reason: On the Theory of Action*. Stanford, CA: Stanford University Press.

Bourdieu, P. and L. Wacquant (1992). *An Invitation to Reflexive Sociology*, with Loïc Wacquant. Chicago: University of Chicago Press and Polity Press.

Connell, R. W. and Messerschmidt, J. W. (2005). Hegemonic masculinity: rethinking the concept. *Gender and Society*, 19(6), 829–859.

Connell, R. W. (2009). *Gender: In World Perspective*. Cambridge, UK and Malden, MA: Polity Press.

Coser, L. (1974). *Greedy Institutions: Patterns of Undivided Commitment*. New York: Free Press.

Edwards, R., Ribbens McCarthy, J., and Gillies, V. (2012). The politics of concepts: family and its (putative) replacements. *British Journal of Sociology*, 63(4), 730–746.

Elias, N. (1939). *Ueber den Prozess der Zivilisation. Soziogenetische und psychogenetische Untersuchungen*. Basel: Haus zum Falken.

Elias, N. (1978). *What Is Sociology?* Translated by Stephen Mennell and Grace Morrissey. New York: Columbia University Press.

Elias, N. (2007). *The Genesis of the Naval Profession*, edited and with an introduction by René Moelker and Stephen Mennell. Dublin: University College Dublin Press.

Enloe, C. (2000). *Bananas, Beaches and Bases: Making Feminist Sense of International Politics*. Berkeley, CA: University of California Press.

Enloe, C. (2007). *Globalization and Militarism: Feminists Make the Link*. New York: Rowman and Littlefield Publishers.

Galbraith, J. K. (1983). *The Anatomy of Power*. Boston: Houghton Mifflin.

Gilliam, L. and Gulløv, E. (2014). *Making Children "Social": Civilising Institution in the Danish Welfare State*. https://quod.lib.umich.edu/h/humfig/11217607.0003.103/--making-children-social-civilising-institutions-in-the-danish?rgn=main;view=fulltext.

Greenhaus, J. H. and Beutell, N. J. (1985). Sources of conflict between work and family roles. *The Academy of Management Review*, 10(1), 76–88.

Heider, F. (1958). *The Psychology of Interpersonal Relations*. Hoboken, NJ: John Wiley & Sons.

Hooper, C. (1999). Masculinities, IR and the “gender variable”: a cost-benefit analysis for (sympathetic) gender sceptics. *Review of International Studies*, 25, 475–480.

Kövecses Z. (1990). *Emotion Concepts*. New York: Springer.

Laing, K. D. (2001). *The Politics of the Family*. New York: Routledge.

Lasswell, H. (1936). *Politics: Who Gets What, When, How*. www.policysciences.org/classics/politics.pdf.

MacDermid Wadsworth, S. and Southwell, K. (2011). Military families: extreme work and extreme “work-family.” *The ANNALS of the American Academy of Political and Social Science*, 638, 163–183.

Messerschmidt, J. W. (2016). *Masculinities in the Making: From the Local to the Global*. Lanham, MD: Rowman and Littlefield.

Moelker, R. (2003). Elias, maritime supremacy and the Naval profession: on Elias’ unpublished studies in the genesis of the Naval profession. *British Journal of Sociology*, 54(3), 373–390.

Moelker, R., Nöll, J., and Weger, M. de (2009). *Krijgsmacht en samenleving*, 3rd edn. Amsterdam: Boom.

Moelker, R., Andres, M., Bowen, G., and Manigart, P. (2015). Introduction. In R. Moelker, M. Andres, G. Bowen, and P. Manigart (eds), *Military Families and War in the 21st Century. Comparative Perspectives* (pp. 3–21). London: Routledge.

Moskos, C. C. (1977). From institutions to occupation. *Armed Forces and Society*, 4(1), 41–50.

Segal, M. W. (1986) The military and the family as greedy institutions. *Armed Forces and Society*, 13(1), 9–38.

Swaan, A. de (1982). Uitgaansbeperking en uitgaaansangst. Over de verschuiving van bevelshuishouding naar onderhandelingshuishouding. [A ban on going out may lead to fear for the streets. The shift from command household to negotiation household.] In A. de Swaan (ed.), *De mens is de mens een zorg* (pp. 81–115). Amsterdam: Meulenhoff.

Tilly, Ch. (1975). Reflections on the history of European state-making. In Ch. Tilly (ed.), *The Formation of National States in Western Europe* (pp. 3–83). Princeton, NJ: Princeton University Press.

Woodward, R. and Winter, T. (2007). *Sexing the Soldier: The Politics of Gender and the Contemporary British Army*. London: Routledge.

Wouters, C. (2007). *Informalization: Manners and Emotions since 1890*. London: Sage.

2 Invisibilized invisible

Third-party symbolic violence and the partial militarization of UK military spouses/partners

Kevin Spruce

For my brothers

Who fell to rise no more

Introduction

This chapter investigates the day-to-day experiences of military spouses,[1] through the lenses of Pierre Bourdieu's social theories (Bourdieu, 1977, 1985, 1989, 2001, 2002). The methods used are Bourdieusian in nature (collaborative/cross-discipline, relationships) and intent to seek explanations of the descriptive data by focusing on where *opposites*[2] meet and overlap. Where opposites collide, they will lead to new and progressive knowledge. This is supported by Bourdieu's reviewing a collaboration of other theorists' perceptions/frameworks of Jean Piaget (1896–1980), Lev Vygotsky (1896–1934), and John Dewey (1859–1952), to develop an *agent-centered* approach to learning (see Hammond et al., 2001). By linking the disciplines of sociology, psychology, philosophy, and politics (where they meet and overlap), I was able to investigate the *relationships* within social spaces between agents and social fields, which offered an insight into the subjective (habitus) and objective (social construct) impacts on each other (Bourdieu, 1985). For example, the thematic analysis of the data highlighted an overwhelming need/desire to *conform and comply* to unwritten rules, resulting in spouses' practices and thoughts that will impact on a serving member's career. The method included focusing on the primary unit of analysis (*spouses' experiences*), and then directing the analysis focus toward the secondary unit of analysis, being the relationships between agents and social fields, developing a critical realist view (see Joseph, 1998), of the development of an agents' *habitus*, which (in line with Bourdieu's concepts) "*avoids both the demoralising structuralist position that structures reproduce themselves and are all powerful*" (*ibid.*: 83). The aim of the study is to understand the change from the spouse being the victim of dominance and control, to becoming complicit in their own domination.

As this book is an *international* cooperation, and a collaboration between military and civilian perspectives of the *military*, there follow brief outlines of method; an overview of the British Armed Forces (BAF); an introduction to Bourdieu's Social Theory; followed by sections on family, findings and themes, and a conclusion.

Method

Participants

Participants in this study were 12 former military spouses: six Army, two Royal Navy, and four Royal Air Force; three spouses of commissioned officers, and nine spouses of non-commissioned officers. Seven of them (58 percent) were married before the age of 20 years, the other five (42 percent) married between 20 and 30. All participants married into the services, and post service five of them (42 percent) were divorced. Half of the participants experienced their spouse on active deployments (war zones) and five experienced training deployments. Participants were recruited via adverts placed on social media. Sixteen applications were received; however, four applicants were rejected; two had no links to the military; one had already been interviewed (gave a false name), and one dropped out (no information).

Procedure

Qualitative semi-structured interviews were conducted, by phone (11 participants) due to varied geographical locations, or face to face (1); each lasting between 75 and 110 minutes. Interviews were recorded and transcribed (with consent). Each participant was informed they could withdraw consent at any time up to the handing in of the project. Thematic analysis included listening to recordings (3), listening to recordings with notes (1), and then reading the transcripts, evolving four superordinate themes: self-identity; helplessness; compliance and conformity; and forced independence (see Family section).

Brief introduction to the British Armed Forces

The nature of the military is different from country to country; for example, Israel has compulsory military service for men and women aged 18 years (Defense Service Law), whereas Britain has an all-volunteer military service for men and women aged 16–17 (with parental consent) and 18–33 years of age for regular forces (Armed Forces Act, 2006). The BAF is unique in Europe in that it allows under-18s to enlist. Attitudes to ground combat roles differ; for instance, Australia and the USA have women in these roles, whereas Britain, at this time, has not. Therefore, a brief introduction to the BAF is necessary to contextualize its international position. The British Armed Forces is an all-volunteer force comprising of three "services": the Royal Navy (RN), the Army, and the Royal Air Force (RAF), and includes Regular and Reservist Forces. The Army and Royal Navy include Specialist Forces (Parachute Regiments and Royal Marines), Special Forces (RN: Special Boat Section (SBS) and the Army: Special Air Service (SAS)). The total strength of the BAF as of October 2017 is 195,730, of which 137,280 are fully trained (military personnel only), and its roles include: human security; national security; conflicts and war (Joint Doctrine Publication 0-01, 2014)—for future developments, see Future Force 2020 and Future Reservist Force 2020.

Brief introduction to Bourdieu's Social Theory

Pierre Bourdieu (1930–2002), a French philosopher, anthropologist, and sociologist (and more), developed his Social Theory to explain phenomena that occur within the social world. Bourdieu set out to achieve this by constructing an integrated theoretical framework, based on concepts of the *relationships* between social practices of an agent (subject), and social constructs (objective), and between agent and agent (Asimaki and Koustourakis, 2014). Bourdieu believed that the relationships between agent/agent, agent/social field, and social field/social field are the areas where explanations of practice and thought are to be found, and utilized this concept through the expansion of the themes of Durkheim and Mauss (social systems of classification), Marx (class relations), and Weber (legitimacy, subjective representations) in developing the themes of his own theory. The investigation of the *relational* links between the above theories assisted Bourdieu in overcoming non-productive arguments, as found in areas of *opposites* (dualisms), i.e., "objectivism" and "subjectivism." The development of concepts such as social spaces/fields, capitals,[3] and symbolic power/violence (see Bourdieu, 1985, 2002), are the cornerstones of his theory, with the concept of the habitus being the junction that links those concepts together (see Bourdieu, 1985). The habitus is the embodied experience of an agent and is a social process that can develop, train, and structure propensities in the agent, which when nurtured by social pressures/commands (Wacquant, 2005) can form beliefs that are deeply embedded within the habitus (within ourselves) (Bourdieu and Passeron, 1977). Therefore, the reactions of an agent during encounters within the social field/space can be made unthinkingly, as the habitus allows the agent's practices and thoughts to become *second nature* (Elias, 1939). Second nature is described as when an agent reacts to an event/experience without the need for thought, such as a boy child being told that "big boys don't cry" (Branney and White, 2008), repeatedly, could automatically repress feelings of future emotion[4] (i.e., wanting to cry) in all relationships, without the awareness of the agent. Reproduction occurs when, unthinkingly, the agent repeats the statement to their children, or simply by their children never seeing them cry; both could reproduce the arbitrary concept that *big boys don't cry* and therefore do not show emotions (Branney and White, 2008). Gillies suggests that the notions of "patriarchy and capitalism" (2003: 5), are similarly reproduced, believing that the central role of socialization within the family passes on the belief, and therefore acceptance of arbitrary gender dominatory and subjectification practices (Gillies, 2003). This suggests that patriarchy and capitalism can be reproduced, achieved without conscious thought, in line with Bourdieu's Social Theory.

Bourdieu's Social Theory views the "social world . . . [as] accumulated history" (1986: 241), and highlights how the *rules* that are determined by the dominant group (for example, the insidious arbitrary *rules of the game* found in a patriarchy[5]) will, over a period of time, be inculcated to form dispositions/second nature, mediated by the habitus (Bourdieu, 1985, 2004), in both men and women. Therefore, it is the development of the habitus that assists the agent in becoming complicit in their own domination, in that the inculcation of the doxa of a social field will normalize the dominatory practices within those doxa. The doxa are created through the arbitrary development of the dominant group's dispositions, therefore creating the *rules of the game*, which the agents who want to succeed are required to inculcate in order to invest, through engagement, in the game. This requires the agent to believe that the doxa of the social field are significant to their success in that social field. Therefore, those who engage in the *game* have to believe that the *profit* promised by the dominant social field is real and available for illusio[6] to occur (see Heidegren and Lundberg, 2010). Illusio is necessary for the game to continue through the agent's investments, and this *belief in the system* is necessary for the agent to engage and to keep investing in the game, in the hope of achieving the *promised* benefits (profits) (Heidegren and Lundberg, 2010). An example of this the military's (or government's) continuous belief that *peace* can be achieved through the use of *violence*. This can be seen as *those who profit from* war needing to develop *rules* for the *investors* (engaged or potential—i.e., military/government/service personnel) to believe they will gain the promised benefit. This will keep those *investors* investing in the *game*. Therefore, the inculcation of the dominant group's *rules of the game* hides the real nature of the dominant group's objective (economic capital), and the continuation of the *game* relies on the *recruitment and retention* of agents that have a *need* to be successful in that field. It is that *need* that directs their habitus toward *accumulating* profit, by believing the promises are real and achievable. Therefore, it is the dominant group that creates the "selected . . . principles of [the] construction of the social space" (Bourdieu, 1985: 724), which include the agent playing to the *rules*, focussing the agent on the tasks of accumulating the *scarce resources* in the social field (Bourdieu, 1985, 1986). Basically, the *rules of the game* become the *natural attitude* of the agent (Bourdieu, 2004)—as mentioned previously, the *second nature*; therefore, the agent unknowingly becomes a source of the reproduction of those *arbitrary rules*, thereby engaging in their own domination (Bourdieu, 2001). Burawoy suggests that it is the game that "obscure[s] the conditions of their own playing through the very process of securing participation" (2012: 189). The agent's focus is on *securing participation* and, therefore, away from the *nature* of the game, which develops a skewed "sense of the[ir] position . . . in social space" (Bourdieu, 1985: 728). O'Leary and Chia suggest that this process leads to an "underlying code of a culture" (2007: 2), invested to make "lasting, useful relationships that can secure material or symbolic profits" (*ibid.*: 22). The type of investments (accumulation of capital) determine the agent's "chances of success" (Bourdieu, 1986: 241). Bourdieu suggests that this process, once the agent becomes complicit, is *symbolic violence* (1985, 1986, 2001, 2004). Thapar-Björkert describes *symbolic violence* as "impervious, insidious and invisible" (2016:); therefore, to investigate its presence requires the identification of its *outcomes*. Further research in this area can offer insights into "the gaps between the ways in which gendered violence is 'lived'" (Morgan and Thapar-Björkert, 2006: 443), and its ability to "accompany or precede physical violence"[7] (*ibid.*).

The next section offers an insight into the dynamics of the family, where the spouses' experiences occurred—highlighting the complexity and traditional nature of military marriages.

Families

"The dynamics and structures found in those groups called families in our society may not be evident in those groups called families in other places and times" (Laing, 1971: 3). As can be seen, Laing believes that family dynamics (patterns of relating to, or interactions between, family members) within two differing spaces are not homologous in nature (Laing, 1971). He recognizes the importance of *relationships* between agents and suggests that research should aim itself at "relations, not simply objects" (Laing, 1971: 11). Bourdieu and Wacquant state similarly that "what exist in the social world are relations—not interactions between agents" (1992: 97); therefore, this research investigated the *relationships of power*, within/between social spaces, within the social fields of the Ministry of Defence (MoD), military, and spouses. Palmer suggests that military families are "relatively unique" (2008: 205), and Lagrone described military families as having "authoritarian fathers, depressed mothers, and out-of-control children" (1978, cited in Palmer, 2008: 205),[8] and Klein further describes the patriarchal nature of the military in this way: "military service can be described as a rite of passage to male adulthood, teaching toughness, and trying to eliminate what is regarded to be effeminate" (1999, cited in Hale, 2008: 306). The idea that the *rules of the game* influence the habitus is supported by Helen Parr in her book *Our Boys: The Story of a Paratrooper*, in which she reports that when "a female journalist following the Paras in 1990 asked one Sergeant what happened to vegetarians in the Army. 'They die, ma'am' was his reply" (2018: 67) This inculcated arbitrary masculine attitude influenced the development of a toxic environment (to females and effeminate males), by inculcating practices (by abiding by the military doxa), reproducing the patriarchal nature found in the MoD/government, described in Parr's book, as "a harsh, conformist, masculine environment" (2018: 67). This shows the *background picture* of the environment that the spouse was forced to *survive* in and *navigate*, through having to negate their own personal (and at times professional) development, by the dominatory practices of the dominant social field, placing the responsibility of their serving spouse's career as a *rule of the game* . By focusing on engaging in the game, the spouses' *focus* directed away from the legitimacy of the *rules of the game* (military doxa), and away from *real* relationship issues, such as relational ambivalence (see Bowlby, 1960; Ainsworth, 1982), shown in the data.

> A bit like Christmas, it's one of those things that you look forward to, and count down to it so much, but when it happens it's a disappointment [nervous laugh] it's like after a week, I am wishing he went away again [nervous laugh]. . .
>
> (Interview 2)

> When he comes home, I feel as though he does not acknowledge the importance of what I have done while he was away, and the stresses I have been under. I feel as though the partner at home is expected to be understanding, and allow the service partner "time to adjust," but we [spouses] do not get afforded any such privilege.
>
> (Williamson, 2009: 16)

In the case of the spouse's enforced development of *personal independence* (separations/deployments), an enforced development of a *matriarchal* family structure seems to be ignored, and the family returns to a patriarchal structure on the return of the *patriarch*; "you know, you get so independent. . . you know, you can fix a plug, change a light bulb or. . . you know. . . things like that. . . it, errm, it was quite stressful because I was thinking 'why are you home because I can do this, errr, meself' [sic]" (Interview 1). This participant stated that it was them that had to change: "it was quite, errr, you know what I mean, it was quite awkward for a few days. . . really got to get used to them being back" (Interview 1). The data highlight changes in the spouses' habitus in the areas of military-esque language, post-service, such as "R&R"[9] for holidays (Interview 1; 2), "quarter"[10] as the family home, and "civvy street."[11] The data show awareness of changes:

> I. . . I. . . I just think, once you been in or a part of what I call a Naval family I personally feel you never get out of it. . . ermmm, I still have that mindset [habitus]. . . I never considered myself as wholly civilian. . .
>
> (Interview 3)

This suggests that the spouses, although not members of the military social field,[12] have had their habitus influenced by the *rules of the game* (military doxa), in the areas of practice, behavior, and language: "those that survive are those who can change to fit in that environment. . . most of us that survived, it looks like we were compliant and we toed the line, we had a lot of strength to rise above the Bravo Sierra [bullshit]" (Interview 7); "I do not think of myself as a civilian, I think of myself as military" (Interview 6); "[I am] Ex-military. . . never a civilian, but not military anymore" (Interview 9); and the use of military terminology many years after their serving spouse left the forces (all interviewees). The lack of *contract* can lead to economic exploitation and oppression forcing people to work for free (Koffman and MacDonald, 2001).

> Kevin, I don't know that I had an expectation. . . I mean I am not employed by them. . . but it would be nice sometimes that my sacrifices were recognized, such as quick unexpected deployments, deployments being extended, family, children. . . I feel that there has not been an acknowledgment of my sacrifice to our life together.
>
> (Interview 10)

Bourdieu states that "objective power relations . . . impose themselves on all who *enter the field* [my emphasis]" (Bourdieu, 1977: 724), and yet it seems that the *power relations* have imposed themselves on the spouses, who have not entered the field, as many seem to believe they *have* been a member of the military social field; "it's like the soldiers, they break them down to build them up as they want them to be. . . and it's the same with the wives, if you want to survive" (Interview 7). The lifestyle of a spouse within a military marriage impacted their expectations, mental health, and well-being, seemingly unrecognized (or ignored) by the dominant social field; "I experienced, errr, a lot of loneliness and sadness at being separated, and therefore my marriage wasn't what I wanted it to be. . . I guess the separation was great at making. . . sadness" (Interview 10). However, in contrast to this *doom-and-gloom* picture, all participants stated it was the best time of their lives, and some stated they wished they were still "in,"[13] and all hold a strong loyalty toward the BAF.

Findings

The military spouse is a civilian, and as so, cannot become a member of the military social field. Moreover, the structure of the military social field is patriarchal, described by one participant as a "shadow of a matriarchy, over shadowed by a patriarchy" (Interview 4), reflecting the overpowering darkness experienced by the spouses—in Bhasin's description: "male domination . . . a system whereby women are kept subordinate" (1993: 3). This oppressiveness of a patriarchal regime is stated in the data: "the biggest problem was long deployments. . . when he came home it was like he wanted to take on that role of looking after me again. . . errmmm, and it was like go away, I done this myself for six months or nine months" (Interview 2). This reflects the nature as being a "system of social structures and practices that dominate, oppress and exploit women" (Interview 2). It is necessary to investigate the *embodied history* of the military social field and the tensions of this field with the MOD in order to explain the descriptive data. The power structure/dynamics between the relations of the dominant social fields (the MoD and the military social field) will offer an insight into the symbolic power between the fields, the *historization* of the military social field's *doxa*, and will assist in identifying the nature of the symbolic power of the military social field. The military social field doxa influences the day-to-day experiences of spouses; therefore, it would be prudent to investigate (briefly) the relationship between the MoD and the military social field. The military social field is controlled and dominated, legitimately and symbolically, by the MoD. The MoD holds legitimate power over the military social field through legislation (Queen's Regulations), political power (National Audit Office, 2015), and symbolic power (being a subset of government) (National Audit Office, 2015). It is the nature of the military's real power (ability to stage a coup d'état) that reflects the *need* for the MoD to have legitimate power to dominate and control the military social field.

The role of the MoD, according to the Recruitment and Retention Report (RRR) (2007–2008), is to fund military acquisitions, including training, recruitment, and retention of trained soldiers. The MoD also decides where, when, and for how long the military is utilized to fulfil the MoD's defence commitments (war, peacetime duties, peacekeeping duties) (National Audit Office, 2015). The relationship includes the MoD being responsible for all aspects of funding (note that the MoD is subordinate to the elected government), suggesting that the dominant capital in this field is economic, and that the structural framework experienced is a triad (see Moelker, Rones, and Andres, this volume, Chapter 1). As the military social field does not accumulate economic capital it would seem fair to suggest that the driving force within the military is cultural capital (training of assets), symbolic capital (rank), and social capital (promotion).[14] The military social field does not accumulate economic capital in its role of carrying out the demands of the MoD—defending the realm—suggesting that the conflicts experienced by spouses, due to separations/deployments, are ordered by the MoD.

The spouses have an unrecognized power that could impact on the status and economic capital of the MoD in their ability to convince the serving member (asset) to leave/not re-enlist, supporting the concept that military marriage is positioned in a triad, where two sides have similar natures (patriarchal) and the third (spouse) is the outsider, whose position normally is weaker and more vulnerable (see Moelker, Rones, and Andres, this volume, Chapter 1). The threat of the outsider cannot be remedied directly as there does not seem to be a direct relationship (therefore no direct power) between the MoD and the spouse; direct violence is out of the question, leaving symbolic violence as appropriate means to dominate and control spouses. The perpetuation of symbolic violence seems to require a three-party system to eradicate the threat that the spouses could present.

This threat seems real in that the BAF have had a deficit of trained assets since 2000 (with a 27-percent deficit in 2018), and the strength of the BAF to date reflects the difficulties in recruiting and retention of military assets, "7,400 fewer than the 2020 target"[15] (Dempsey, 2018; see Future Force 2020, 2002; and Future Reserves, 2020) possibly due to the power and influence of the media, according to the House of Commons Defence Committee's *Fourteenth Report*, which states, "We note that the sometimes negative media coverage about the Armed Forces is detrimental to the public's understanding of the military and places unnecessary pressure on Service personnel and their families" (House of Commons Defence Committee, 2008: 77); according to the Army Families Federation, "media coverage of current operational deployments was mostly negative" (cited in House of Commons Defence Committee, 2008: 26). The impact that the media can have on military recruitment is also highlighted in Nichols' paper on public opinion and the military: "support may have important implications for civil-military relations . . . and recruitment efforts . . . reliant upon a citizenry advising its youth to join the military" (2015: 76).

The military social field has no economic investment in its assets, suggesting that it is more likely that the MoD has a motive to control and dominate the spouses. However, the pressure to conform and comply seems to come from the military social field, according to the data, therefore suggesting the MoD may use the position of the military social field, in utilizing it as a third-party platform, to dominate and control the spouses (but further research is required). The development of the military social field by the MoD offers the opportunity to create symbols of power within the structure of the military social field that could enable it (unconsciously) to carry out dominatory practices regarding spouses. This would direct the blame away from the real source of the domination, the MoD. However, as there is a lack of relationship between the military social field and the spouse, "Families are often left in the dark. *The military* don't realise the implications that mobilisations have on military families [my emphasis]" (RAFFF, 2011). It may be that this process misdirects the spouses' lens away from the source of the domination.

The power relationships can change once the spouse becomes aware and uses their unrecognized power; rather than just being a victim of symbolic violence they could become a reciprocal *source* of symbolic violence. This power could be used as a way to change policy, in relation to the length and frequency of deployments of serving assets, but also as a lever to force the MoD to invest in the development of effective family support structures. This would enable the spouses to become more aware of the impact of the patriarchal nature of military marriages and more likely to recognize the insidious dominatory practices, and therefore less likely to become complicit in their domination. This in turn would highlight some of the main obstacles (domination and control) to their personal development (Sultana, 2012), and to the influence these obstacles can have on their perceived identity and role. The spouses complicity suggests that this *blindness (as opposed to being aware)* can be self-constructed, and can be conscious or unconscious (Bourdieu, 1985), and, if it is conscious (as suggested in the data), then the ability to reflect on their inculcated beliefs is a requirement, meaning that the spouses are the only ones that can free their minds of the notions that assist in the misrecognition of the legitimacy of the power held over them—reflected in the lyrics of "Redemption Song":

> Emancipate yourselves from mental slavery
> None but ourselves can free our minds
>
> (Bob Marley, *Uprising*, 1979)

This would lead to spouses being in a position to choose whether to reject the dominatory practices, increasing agency and freeing their minds of the perceived patriarchal symbols of power that can lead to *mental slavery*.

Discussion and conclusion

To conclude, the data suggest that the spouses' experiences of the pressure to conform and comply through domination/control, and the normalization of the dominatory practices, makes the domination invisible. This can be said to be an outcome of symbolic violence. The literature and the data suggest that military marriage is a toxic environment for intimate relationships; however, divorce trends in the military are suggested to be lower than those in civilian life (see Karney and Crown, 2007; Cretney, 2005). However, according to Pollard et al., the divorce rate in military marriages increases significantly post-service (2012). This change in the trend may be due to the UK military offering incentives such as accommodation, personal security, and security of serving spouse employment, or that the incentives "encourage unions that would not normally be formalized into marriage in a civilian context, and are consequently more fragile upon exit from the military" (Pollard et al., 2012: 3). Therefore, through a Bourdieusian lens the *incentives* can be perceived as symbols of power that can be used to dominate and control spouses' practices and thought. The acceptance of *incentives*, by spouses, as a benefit can misdirect their focus away from the true nature of the incentives as symbols of power, therefore making the domination/control invisible. The increase in divorce rates post-service also suggests that incentives could be a factor in the low divorce rates during service, suggesting that the self-dominating practices of the spouses, and the acceptance of the pressure to conform and comply to military doxa, could be a misrecognition of the nature of the incentives.[16] This misrecognition would be absent post-service, leading to the politics of the patriarchal military marriage becoming visible, to the spouses, as domination and control. The family has been described as a container for emotions (see Moelker, Rones, and Andres, this volume, Chapter 1); however, in this triad, it seems that it is the spouse who is *expected* to be the emotional container for the serving asset. The power and politics of the military marriage are highlighted in the data as a process of managing survival—for the spouse, in their constructed role to manage the serving asset's emotions and well-being (as an unpaid carer) (see Moelker, Rones, and Andres, this volume, Chapter 1). To take Bourdieu's view of social fields where people play the game for scarce resources necessary to survive, and the assumption that spouses do not have access to all capitals, the field is not a level one. The direction of *trading* capitals seems to be one-way traffic—the spouse having to conform and comply with very little true benefit to themselves. The data show that the spouse's acceptance of the nature of their experiences is via helpless acceptance—"it's just the way it is"—and the capitals that they are required to accumulate simply to *survive* the military marriage are useful mainly in the context of the military marriage/military social field. The spouses place their own personal and professional development on hold, for the sole benefit of their military spouse's career, making unrecognized self-sacrifices on the way. This reflects the inculcation of the dominant groups' non-legitimate symbolic power, which when normalized creates blindness to present and future dominatory practices (Moelker, Rones, and Andres, this volume, Chapter 1). Research and the data suggest that there is a perceived need to *stabilize* the military asset, and marriage is suggested to achieve this, suggesting that the role of the spouse is to primarily stabilize the military asset. This exploitation of the spouses is reflected in the unrecognized sacrifices they seem to accept, and the dismissal of their achievements, through their identity being determined by the personhood of their serving spouse ("wife of" name, rank, and number).

The MoD is a political structure, whereas the military social field is mainly apolitical, which can cause tensions within the relationship through misunderstandings.Each member of this triad is dependent on another (the MoD/military social field); however, there are no clear dependencies between some (military social field/spouse). This research offers an insight into the patriarchal-dominated world of the spouses, and suggests that the symbolic violence perpetrated on them is exploitative and insidious, however accepted it may be by many as being their "duty" to conform and comply. The research suggests that the spouses, who become complicit in their own domination, have to rid themselves (by reflection) of the inculcated beliefs that allow them to simply accept their "lot." The research highlights the real power of the spouses in their influence on their serving spouse's decision making process, which could be used to make changes in the toxic nature of military marriage, if, of course, recognized and utilized. Moelker, Rones, and Andres (this volume, Chapter 1), in discussing politics and coalitions, suggest that two groups that are closer to each other leave the third group disadvantaged, and this rings true in the *coalition* of the MoD and the military social field in achieving the domination and control of the spouse through creating symbols of power that make the spouse feel vulnerable and weak, in order for the spouse to become complicit in their own domination, reflecting the extraordinary day-to-day experiences of military spouses.

Suggestions for further research are to include same-sex partners and female military assets (see Meytal Eran-Jona, this volume, Chapter 6). Comparing all military marriage models would be useful in gaining further insights into the nature of, gender differences within, and the power and political relationships of the military marriage. Action research could be used to develop programs to enable the spouses (and potential spouses) to make informed decisions about their own development and welfare. Finally, comparison with other Armed Forces would be useful in highlighting the differences, taking into account differing cultural attitudes and values of different countries.

Notes

1 In this chapter the term "spouses" is used to refer to spouses and partners of military personnel.
2 An example of opposites: qualitative OR quantitative; masculine OR feminine; psychology OR sociology.
3 Bourdieu suggests that the use of economic capital alone (in a capitalist field) falls short of explaining the positions of agents, and states that research should include other capitals such as cultural, social, symbolic (see Bourdieu, 1977; 1985; 1998; 2002).
4 Without realization.
5 Emotion as weakness, linking masculine to strength and feminine to weakness.
6 A tendency (need/reason) to engage in the game, without questioning the game's meaningfulness.
7 In areas such as domestic violence.
8 Research topic impact of frequent relocation, deployment, exposure to combat, and post-traumatic stress disorder (PTSD) on families.
9 Rest and recuperation, usually taken halfway through a deployment.
10 Military accommodation.
11 Non-military.

12 The power the military social field has is grounded in contract law, which is "a legally enforceable agreement giving rise to obligations for the parties involved" (Koffman and MacDonald, 2001), whereas the spouses are not contracted, meaning the spouses are civilians and therefore cannot be members of the military social field.
13 Suggesting the partial militarization of the habitus.
14 It is accepted that the accumulation of these capitals can lead to the accumulation of economic capital.
15 Expected reduction of armed forces personnel of 50 percent of present numbers.
16 Along with the misrecognition of the military social field's power.

References

Ainsworth, S. M. D. (1982). Attachment: retrospect and prospect. In C. M. Parkes and J. Stevenson-Hinde (eds), *The Place of Attachment in Human Behavior* (pp. 3–30). New York: Basic Books.

Archer, M., Decoteau, C., Gorski, P., Little, D., Porpora, D., Rutzou, T., Smith, C., Steinmetz, G., and Vandenberghe, F. (2016). What is critical realism*? Perspectives: ASA Theory Section 2018.*

Asimaki, A. and Koustourakis, G. (2014). Habitus: An attempt at a thorough analysis of a controversial concept in Pierre Bourdieu's theory of practice. *Social Sciences*, 3(4), 121–131.

Bhasin, K. (1993). What is patriarchy? *Kali for Women* (n.p.), New Delhi.

Bowlby, J. (1960). Separation anxiety: a critical review of the literature. *The Journal of Child Psychology and Psychiatry*, 1(4), 251–269.

Bourdieu, P. (1977). *Outline of a Theory of Practice*. Cambridge: Cambridge University Press.

Bourdieu, P. (1985). The social space and genesis of groups. *Theory and Society*, 14(6), 723–744.

Bourdieu, P. (1986). The forms of capital. In J. Richardson (ed.), *Handbook of Theory and Research for Sociology of Education* (pp. 241–258). New York: Greenwood.

Bourdieu, P. (1989). Social space and symbolic power. *Sociological Theory*, 7(1), 14–25.

Bourdieu, P. (2001). *Masculine Domination*. Cambridge: Polity Press.

Bourdieu, P. (2002). *Language and Symbolic Power*. Cambridge: Polity Press.

Bourdieu, P. (2004). The peasant and his body. *Ethnography*, 5(4), 579–599.

Bourdieu, P. and Passeron, J. (1977). *Reproduction in Education, Society and Culture*. London: Sage.

Bourdieu, P. and Wacquant, L. (1992). *An Invitation to Reflexive Sociology*. Chicago: University of Chicago Press.

Branney, P. and White, A. (2008). Big boys don't cry: depression and men. *Advances in Psychiatric Treatment*, 14 (4), 256–262.

Burawoy, M. (2012). The roots of domination: beyond Bourdieu and Gramsci. *Sociology*, 46(2), 187–206.

Cretney, S. (2005). Irretrievable breakdown as the ground for divorce: the Divorce Reform Act 1969. *Oxford Index Online*, Oxford University Press. //oxfordindex.oup.com/view/10.1093/acprof:oso/9780198268710.001.0001.

Dempsey, N. (2018). *UK Defence Personnel Statistics (Briefing paper CBP7930)*. London: House of Commons Library.

Edwards, E. (2015). Poster. www.goodreads.com/quotes/574669-she-stood-in-the-storm-and-when-the-wind-did and.

Elias, N. (1939) *Über den Prozess der Zivilisation. Soziogenetische und psychogenetische Untersuchungen*. Basel: Haus zum Falken.

Future Force 2020 (2002). Downloaded from www.defence.gov.au/publications/docs/f2020.pdf on 22/03/14.

Future Reserves 2020 (2011). Downloaded from www.gov.uk/government/uploads/system/uploads/attachment_data/file/28394/futurereserves_2020.pdf on 22/03/14.

Gillies, V. (2003). *Families and Intimate Relationships: A Review of the Sociological Research*. Families & Social Capital ESRC Research Group Working Paper No 2. London: South Bank University.

Hale, H. C. (2008). The development of British military masculinities through symbolic resources. *Culture & Psychology*, 14(3), 305–332.

Hammond, L.-D., Austin, K., Orcutt, S., and Rosso, J. (2001). *How People Learn: Introduction to Learning Theories*. Stanford, CA: Stanford University School of Education.

Heidegren, C.-G. and Lundberg, H. (2010). Towards a sociology of philosophy. *Acta Sociologica*, 53(1), 3–18.

House of Commons Defence Committee (2008). *Recruiting and Retaining Armed Forces Personnel, Fourteenth Report of 2007–2008*. London: The Stationery Office Limited.

Joint Doctrine Publication 0-01 (2014). *UK Defence Doctrine*, 5th edn. London: Ministry of Defence Publications.

Joseph, J. (1998). In defence of critical realism. *Capital & Class*, 22(2), 73–106.

Karney, B. R. and Crown, J. A. (2007). *Families under Stress: An Assessment of Data, Theory, and Research on Marriage and Divorce in the Military*. Santa Monica, CA: RAND Corporation: MG-599-OSD.

Koffman, L. and MacDonald, E. (2001). *Law of Contract*. Throwbridge: The Cromwell Press.

Laing, R. D. (1971). *The Politics of the Family and Other Essays*. London: Tavistock Publications.

Morgan, K. and Thapar-Björkert, S. (2006). "I'd rather you'd lay me on the floor and start kicking me": understanding symbolic violence in everyday life. *Women's Studies International Forum*, 29(5), 489–498.

Morris, S. (2018, October 25). All roles in UK military to be open to women. *Guardian* (online). www.theguardian.com/uk-news/2018/oct/25/all-roles-in-uk-military-to-be-open-to-women-williamson-announces.

National Audit Office (2015). *A Guide to the Ministry of Defence*. Downloaded from www.nao.org.uk.

Nichols, C. (2015). Public opinion and the military: a multivariate exploration of attitudes in Texas. *Journal of Political and Military Sociology*, 43, 75–105.

O'Leary, M. and Chia, R. (2007). Epistemes and structures of sensemaking in organizational life. *Journal of Management Inquiry*, 16(4), 1–29.

Palmer, C. (2008). A theory of risk and resilience factors in military families. *Military Psychology*, 20(3), 205–217.

Parr, H. (2018). *Our Boys: The Story of a Paratrooper*. London: Penguin.

Pollard, M., Karney, B., and Loughran, D. (2012). Comparing rates of marriage and divorce in civilian, military, and veteran populations. *Journal of Family Issues*, 33(12), 1572–1594.

Queen's Regulations for the Army (1975). *Authored by Ministry of Defence: Amendment 29*. London: The Stationery Office.

RAFFF (Royal Air Force Families Federation) (2011). *Supporting Service Children*. Peterborough: RAF Family Federation.

Segal, M. W. (1986). The military and the family as greedy institutions. *Armed Forces & Society*, 13(1), 9–38.

Sultana, A. (2012). Patriarchy and women's subordination: a theoretical analysis. *Arts Faculty Journal*, 4, 1–18.

Wacquant, L. (2005). *Bourdieu and Democratic Politics*. Cambridge: Polity Press.

Wharton, A. S. (1991). Structure and agency in socialist-feminist theory. *Gender and Society*, 5(3), 373–389.

Williamson, E. (2009). *Pilot Project: Domestic Abuse and Military Families*. Research commissioned by the North East Hampshire Domestic Violence Forum. Bristol: University of Bristol Press.

Wright, E. O. (1993). Explanation and emancipation in Marxism and feminism. *Sociological Theory*, 11(1), 39–54.

3 Dealing with condemnation

Military families and transitional justice in Argentina

Eleonora Natale

Introduction

Depending on the context, some unexpected outcomes of military performance can often lead to unforeseen developments in the politics of military families on the micro and macro level. Adopting the triadic approach outlined in the Introduction of this volume, this chapter looks at contemporary Argentina and analyzes the problematic triangular dynamic between a specific generation of military families, the Armed Forces, and the state. In particular, it recovers the experience of military families that have formed immediately before or during the last dictatorship (1976–1983), showing how this triadic relationship has been affected by the judicial prosecution of former officers for the human rights offenses perpetrated in that period. Drawing on the results of ethnographic study of former officers and their families, this chapter provides an example of how the sometimes-idealistic relationship that links the military institution with its members and the rest of society can radically be transformed by transitional justice.

The objective of the study realized in Buenos Aires in 2015 and 2016 was to explore the families' narratives of both the years of political violence and the current democratic times, and to understand what it meant to be an officer or a military wife during the last dictatorship, and what it means to be a member of a military family of that age in contemporary democratic Argentina (Natale, 2019). After describing the context of the study, the engagement of families in military life in the 1970s is pointed out; then I describe the strategies implemented within the military world that were applied after the trials that impacted the system of reciprocal expectations between the institution and the families. As concluding remarks, the chapter outlines how kinship contributes to embed military power in Argentine society.

Researching kinship

Argentina suffered from political instability and generalized violence since the mid-1960s. After the death of Juan Domingo Perón in 1974 Argentina was shaken by the increasing action of revolutionary guerrilla organizations, which attacked both military and civilian targets. Paramilitary groups were combating communism by spreading terror in the country fomented by the constitutional government of Perón's widow (1974–1976). The Armed Forces took control of a chaotic situation by installing military rule in 1976. Nevertheless, unlike any precedent military intervention, the self-proclaimed *Proceso de Reorganización Nacional* set a well-structured clandestine repressive plan whose target extended from the members of the guerrillas to the whole society: Argentina needed to be "cleaned" of all individuals considered suspect of "subversive" activities and behavior. After seven years of anti-subversive war – as the military called the annihilation of armed and political militants – in which practices of state terrorism and counterinsurgent warfare partly overlapped (Robben, 2006), the regime collapsed under the pressure of a serious economic crisis, increasing demands for justice, and the defeat in the 1982 Malvinas/Falklands war against Great Britain. Once the military junta resigned and called for elections in December 1983, the commission entitled to ascertain the crimes of the dictatorship reported almost 9000 cases[1] of killings, torture, and forced disappearances between 1976 and 1983 (CONADEP, 1984). Despite this overwhelming truth and the unceasing struggle of the human rights organizations formed by survivors and relatives of the victims, any attempt at bringing the responsible to justice failed. Only in 2003 did president Nestor Kirchner proclaim unconstitutional the laws that had guaranteed impunity to the military during 30 years, and opened a cycle of trials for crimes against humanity. Until the present day, about 2000 people have been prosecuted at some point in Argentina for the crimes of the regime; among these, hundreds of former military personnel are now sentenced to federal prisons or house arrest (Ministerio Público Fiscal, 2017).

As a direct result of the abuses perpetrated in the 1970s and the societal impact of the trials and the politics of memory promoted by Nestor and Cristina Kirchner (2003–2015), the military became a quite unpopular actor in Argentina, and lost its historically prestigious position in society. When this research started at the end of 2015, Mauricio Macri, whose political views are different to those of the Kirchners, was elected president of the nation. Wide sectors of the society expressed their concerns about the fate of the progress reached in the field of human rights so far; indeed, even though Macri did not comply with the expectations that his election generated among the families of the accused, who at first hoped for an interruption in the trials, his administration gave some space to the claims of this sector, especially to the organizations formed by relatives and comrades of the prosecuted military. Despite the softer attitude of the judicial power, which granted some benefits to the convicted since Macri became president—for example, by increasing the concessions of house arrest—this change does not seem to affect the social sentiments toward the military. This group is still experiencing stigma and a public condemnation that is not only juridical but also political and moral. The judicial prosecution is affecting the whole pyramid of the Armed Forces, from the vertexes to its basis, and has important consequences for the families of the accused.

At the core of the study is the experience of former officers of the Argentine Army who were cadets in the Military Academy or used to occupy the lower positions in the ranks between the 1960s and 1970s. These men—second lieutenants, lieutenants, and captains—were in their twenties and early thirties just in the harshest phase of the political repression coordinated by the Argentine Armed Forces (1975–1978),[2] when officers from all ranks were called to fight the subversive enemy. Interestingly, these subalterns were typically also in the process of starting a family in those same years. Considering that in those times cadets were not allowed to get married during the four-year training in the Military Academy, the chances that freshly graduated officers started a family straight after the completion of their preparation increased considerably, many of them getting married just at the time when the dictatorship was being gestated.

This tendency implies that the adaptation to the military world and the creation of the family were two simultaneous and interdependent processes for the officers. The focus on kinship is therefore important because it implies changing relations with state and Armed Forces and, because the starting of a family was a moment of growth for participants before and during the years of the dictatorship, representing one of the common threads in their narratives of that period, a crucial moment in the participants' life that overlapped with the darkest years of Argentina's recent past. This chronological coincidence also meant that this generation of military families lived a quite atypical series of events that had long-term repercussions on their position in society and the Armed Forces as an institution.

Understanding the experience of the military family in the 1970s and the trials, and familiarizing with their own categories, language, and meanings, required working with oral sources. Looking at the members of military families' individual narratives, and approaching them as a community made of different subjectivities, is to try to understand how they saw themselves as a collective interacting with other groups that are constitutive of the same social body. I used oral sources from an ethnographic perspective and also analyzed the situation in which the data were produced (Natale, 2019:59). In order to understand the relation between past and present in a narrative, and the reasons why a particular narrative has been articulated in a specific way—how people "compose" their memories (Abrams, 2016; Summerfield, 1998, 2004; Thomson, 1996)—it was then necessary to understand the relationship between interviewer and interviewees, and how the roles have been determined in the context that produced that relationship. The climate of judicial prosecution in which the interviews with the military were conducted definitely had an impact on the participants' fabrication of narratives about the past and the present; this chapter does not aim simply to report their discourse, but rather to deconstruct and reinterpret it.

Aspiring officers and husbands-to-be: the genesis of the Argentine military family

The study analyzed the military family in its dual meaning: on the one hand the *nuclear* military family, formed by the officer, his wife, and children; on the other, the *large* military family, a complex social system formed by the totality of the military families that connects its members in several levels of interdependence. In general, the relationship between the nuclear military family and the institution depends on a system of reciprocal expectations: the Army expects the families to adapt to the challenges of military life to make the career for the officers feasible, while military families in turn expect purpose, protection, and stability from the organization.

The military have never been particularly wealthy in Argentina. Although historically they tended to gravitate around the oligarchy and to protect their interests, they still belong to the middle class, and especially young subalterns had limited means at the beginning of their career in the 1970s. Nevertheless, before the Armed Forces fell into disrepute due to their responsibilities for state terrorism, the prestige of the military family depended on its vocation, on its spirit rather than its wealth; an officer that made the most of his time in the Army achieved society's respect for his family. On top of this, the institution provided the recently formed family with a series of advantages such as an assigned residence, medical insurance in a private hospital, sports and leisure activities for the families, children's summer camps, and so on, all quite appealing benefits for any middle-class family at the time. However, these rewards came along with the disadvantages of military life. One of the main traits of the Argentine military's lifestyle is its high territorial mobility; after graduation, subaltern officers received their first posts usually in remote destinations (where many of them met their wives-to-be) and changed residence every two or three years for as long as two decades. Military families experienced uprooting when they were displaced in the territory, due to the distance from the biological family. Women in particular quite often had to deal with the challenges posed by their husbands' absence, while the man in turn fulfilled the institution's expectations by being at war or spending many weeks in training and operations in the field. Consequently, women had care for the family and the house but could hardly rely on their own parents or siblings, who were often living hundreds of miles away. Military wives then developed collective strategies to deal with daily problematic situations, weaving a sort of "feminine comradeship" similar to the bond that men establish in the barracks.

The distance from the biological family makes the identification with other military families extremely important, to the point that this military-specific kind of kinship gradually replaces the original ties with the biological family based on consanguinity. In most military posts, including in big metropolitan areas, this mechanism is facilitated and reinforced by the institution through the creation of the *barrio militar*, the military quarter, conglomerates of residencies that physically and socially centralize the military population. This separation is also likely to contribute to the deeply rooted dichotomy between civilians and military, fueling the assumption also reflected by many academic studies that the military represent a block intrinsically different to and separated from the rest of the social body (Soprano, 2010).

The political situation of the early 1970s had an impact on the daily routine that most Argentine military families were familiar with, or at least had in mind, when they joined the military world. In Argentina institutional violence has usually been exerted within the national borders and, excluding the 1982 war in the South Atlantic, the country has never been involved in an international conflict in the twentieth century. The possibility of facing a "real" war was quite unlikely to the generation of military wives who participated in the study, and being in the military was first of all a monetarily secure job, a good career for the family within a long-life and respected institution. Nevertheless, the context of unprecedented violence of the 1970s added to the participants' narrations a dark shade that is quite striking.

In the interviews, former officers stressed the exceptionality of the events that led to the military coup in 1976. Rather than the opposition democracy/dictatorship, and the consequent catastrophic impact on liberties and human rights, the officers' time-framing is built on the armed confrontation between the Army and the guerrillas. I argue that participants decided not to focus on the coup of 1976 like most civilians do because they are being condemned for the "excesses" of the regime; moreover, in the 1970s they were subalterns and their lower positions in the ranks impacted their narratives.

Robben (2006: 357) affirms that it was the exaggerated faith of the military chiefs who orchestrated the *Proceso* in their historical mission as protectors of the fatherland that led to extreme consequences. Participants tended to confirm the vision outlined in the studies that look at the violence of the 1970s as a "war of cultures" (Robben, 2005), where the spirit of the nation itself was at stake; they also stressed the unconventional nature of this war, waged against an irregular enemy that required the employment of special tactics; finally, they depicted the war as a fratricidal conflict, a confrontation among young Argentines moved by opposed ideals:

> One improved professionally, because this wasn't a classic war like Malvinas, it was a (counter)revolutionary war, where one killed and got killed. The cadet doesn't train in the Military Academy for this type of war, the war I understood is the conventional war: you are standing there with a uniform, I'm standing here with another, different flags, and we look each other in the eye, uh? Instead the revolutionary war implied getting dirty into this people's mud.
>
> (Julio)

The officers' visions of the 1970s are generally in line with their wives' narratives, although it is more difficult to interpret women's testimonies since they cannot be directly ascribed to the set of values and discourses given to officers during military training. The military and their families, like police personnel and members of the Argentine elite, used to be targets of the guerrillas in the early 1970s. Several participants recount that they had been the object of regular threats, attempts of execution or kidnapping; others lost friends and comrades by the hand of the guerrillas. Due to the irregular nature of the enemy, the battle was blurry and messy, especially for military wives who were unaware of the operations their husbands were involved into. This is an extract from a double interview with a military couple:

Francisco: I didn't want her to know things she wasn't supposed to know.

Emilia: He used to tell me—"You better watch your back when you go to work, because if they [the guerrillas] take you, you're on your own: I won't trade you, not even for a rifle." And I kept going to work. I wanted my family to go on normally, but they used to follow me to my workplace. They used to phone and say: "Are you sure your children are at school?" Our military friends, their wives carried a gun in their bags, but I never wanted to. If you take a gun and there are kids around you, they can be killed too. And what's my experience in guns? If they want to take me, they take me.

It would be rather simplistic to affirm that the wives simply follow their husbands' narrative. On the contrary, data suggest these women were definitely conscious of being a pillar in that same system that expected their subjection; moreover, like their husbands they belonged to the generation at the center of the political confrontation, and were aware that being military family members in the Argentinean 1970s meant taking a side. Therefore, they show a certain commitment to the cause of the anti-subversive war, being ready to play accordingly to their position in both scenarios, the military family and the political arena, the latter leading to dramatic consequences in the 1970s. Military families were a target, indeed, because they represented a specific cultural model, they incarnated values and principles that were at stake, threatened to be subverted. The dispute for this cultural primacy, of which family was an essential figure, dragged the informants in a confrontation that left deep wounds in thousands of Argentine families. And the exercise of violence made the family a real battlefront. In this perspective, military wives played a quite active role that jars with the subjugated condition traditionally assigned to them in the military world.

In sum, in the 1970s officers and their relatives were exposed to the same routine, difficulties, and even the same threats; the climate of uncertainty and its consequences were only possible to share with peers, members of fellow military families. This identification of one military family with another, and their opposition to an unconventional enemy, relied on a consolidated network of kinship as the members of the military world understand it (for example, with comradeship as a sort of constructed brotherhood), and proliferates just because the families' path and the hardship of military life tend to be reproduced on a large scale.

Condemnation and subverted balances: the age of the trials

The standardization of practices, behaviors, and knowledge typical of the Armed Forces implies the potential replacement of one individual with another, and indeed its ultimate sacrifice. On the other hand, according to its mechanism of reciprocal expectations, the institution represented in the field by the commander has to take responsibility for its subordinates' actions, and put their well-being on top of his priorities. This principle bonds the men to the institution, guaranteeing the respect for discipline and hierarchy, and in turn making sacrifice tolerable.

This mechanism transcends the battlefield and extends to the family. The military families that were part of this study sacrificed both in peacetime (moves, uprooting, absence of the husband/father) and in "wartime" (threats, uncertainty, and fear due to the specifics of the 1970s in Argentina). Sacrifice is then intrinsic within military life—in its functions and vocation of service, in its mythology and narrative of heroism—but also circumstantial, since it depends on the context the military and his family is facing in a specific moment. This burden is bearable to the extent to which the military family can share it with others who face the same difficulties, and feel included within a wider framework of functions, principles, and rewards guaranteed by the institution. Nevertheless, whenever this apparently perfect mechanism jams, the tensions within the triadic relation of families-Army-society are released, generating unpredictable outcomes.

The Argentine Army has an interesting history of rebellion and internal conflicts, and had already experienced judicial prosecution before 2003. Once the results of the special commission on forced disappearances went public, the government at first prosecuted and condemned the juntas in 1985 (an achievement that was then frustrated by the pardons granted by President Menem in the early 1990s). The first subsequent attempt of extending the trials to the lower ranks failed due to the repeated rebellion (1987–1990) of a group of subaltern officers known as *Carapintadas*, "painted faces." The rebels aimed to question the leadership of the Army, and asked their superiors to take a position before the trials to guarantee protection to the subordinates who executed orders during the dictatorship; their action was instead interpreted by the media and the largest part of the society as a new attempt of military coup against the democratic order, and undermined the already-deteriorated civil-military relations. The *Carapintadas* mutinies indeed forced the government to promulgate the impunity laws until Kirchner pushed for their abrogation in 2003. Nowadays, in the age of the trials, another kind of insubordination is affecting the generation of officers—now retired—who were subalterns in the dictatorship, the Malvinas war, and the *Carapintadas* mutinies. This kind of rebellion is having a minor impact on the society compared to the mutinies of the late 1980s, but again it risks being dismissed as a symptom of the antidemocratic tendencies of the Argentine military, rather than being interpreted as an indicator of the state of the relationship between families, the Armed Forces, and society in the context of the trials.

Once the trials were reopened and the politics of memory inaugurated, accompanied by 15 years of strong anti-military rhetoric, most military families opted for silence and kept a low-profile attitude; however, others reacted to condemnation by telling their narrative and defending their cause. Not only former officers, but also their wives and even their adult children are committed to this objective. In Argentina these military families' statements about the 1970s are usually defined by the public opinion, the media, and part of the academic world as denial or pro-genocide discourses. But, according to this study, the strategies participants apply are designed to re-position themselves into the new scenario and apply the same social dynamics that have always been in place in the military family, both in peacetime and "wartime."

Being judicially prosecuted by the same state they served, 40 years later, for doing what they think was their job, is not what members of a regular force would expect. Former officers, and to a certain extent their wives, feel like the 1970s are an unfinished business, a permanent war that is still open and that has transposed from the physical to the judicial and political level. The officers reject condemnation, and refuse to admit responsibility for the crimes, resisting what they define a "witch hunt" and proclaiming themselves "political prisoners." However, these officers are powerless in prison; therefore, comrades outside prison fight this last battle for them. They are organized in an association called *Unión de Promociones* (UP). The name brings together one of the characteristics of military life, unity, with its personification, the *promoción*, which in Spanish indicates the group of officers from a same regiment who graduate in a certain year. The association was created in 2005 by a small group of former officers of the Army, worried for the trials to the subalterns. The network gradually extended to the Navy and the Air Force. Its members morally and practically support accused comrades in several ways: they pay weekly visits to the prisons and offer logistic support for the relatives who travel to the penitentiaries; they provide counseling services, bringing the accused and their families in contact with lawyers; and they act as a channel, publishing the prisoners' declarations and letters online. The UP also participates in TV and radio emissions, and organizes debates and public acts on the 1970s, in order to gain visibility and raise consciousness around the matter.

It is important to notice that the UP is not an institutional network authorized by the Armed Forces; it is a spontaneous, informal answer to the lack of support of the institution in relation to the trials. Its operational core counts a small number of retired officers, but its action has a great symbolic value for the convicted military. When the trials started almost 15 years ago the heads of the institution evaded any responsibility and refused to support its subalterns in any aspect of the question. This rejection provoked bewilderment among former officers who felt abandoned. The officers expected the commanders to protect them, and assume responsibilities; the generals, instead, ignored the subordinates. The UP inserts into a gap of unmet expectations of a whole generation of officers and their families, who feel like their service to the nation did not pay off. The trials are an exceptional situation that many Argentine military families have to deal with. Their members react to this hardship in the same way they used to react to the challenges of military life, by putting up a unified front against their detractors. Military wives join this front, some privately and others publicly. By resorting to the tools that many of them used to implement in other forms of social organization, such as charities and groups close to the Church, some wives became activists for the cause of their husbands. They founded their own association, *Asociación de Familiares y Amigos de Presos Políticos en*

Argentina (AFyAPPA; Association of Relatives and Friends of Political Prisoners in Argentina), which collaborates with the UP. One of the military wives who joined AFyAPPA in 2007 declared:

> It's been a tremendous challenge for me, I don't look like a social activist, I dedicated my life to raise my children and to work. I had no experience in politics or anything like that, so I had to learn the hard way. And today I would do anything for this cause. I believe our social class is not ready to fight, to rebel. Of all things in the world, I never imagined one day I would step into a prison to see my husband.
>
> (Victoria)

This renewed network of support incorporates today a new component. The adult children of convicted military participate in the struggle in an association originally called *Hijos y Nietos de Presos Políticos* (HyN; Children and Grandchildren of Political Prisoners).[3] The group was formed in 2008, and counts almost 2000 members all over the country who denounce the irregularities of their fathers' accusations, trying to make their detention a bit more bearable. The heterogeneity within the group—made of sons and daughters born after the end of the dictatorship, but also of older children who do remember the 1970s—brought some contrasts in the way of interpreting the violence: some children try to put into context their fathers' conduct, others tend to justify them due to their position in the ranks; some see them as heroes, while others still prefer not to get involved. The group is conscious that the violence of the past still represents source of divisions, even among military families, and prefers to direct its action toward the resolution of the trials. HyN does not fight to obtain pardons, nor the annulment of the trials. Some particularly open-minded members are even aware about the moral legitimacy of the trials, and the need for this step to be taken in the society's healing process. However, they blame the state and the government for the partial attitude in neglecting the violence perpetrated by the guerrillas in the 1970s, and for what they see as the political nature of the trials (Natale, 2019:244–245).

Although the children officially opt for closing themselves off from the dispute on the 1970s, their struggle is definitely close to the crusade of AFyAPPA and the UP, and it is possible to see a certain convergence of objectives in the activities of these organizations. However, the group managed in the last years to take further distance from the organizations run by military wives and former officers that are commonly branded as reactionary and pro-dictatorship. AFyAPPA and the UP organize their claim from their position "in the front row" during the 1970s, reviving the bonds created in the "battlefield." This is something that children cannot do since most of them were not there. They stress the consanguinity tie with the accused, instead of the commitment to their fathers' cause as they conceived it in the 1970s. As a result, the discourse of the children does not stem from the universe of war, but is constructed in the judicial framework, which is the predominant way Argentines think of the aftermath of the 1970s (Crenzel, 2017).

HyN position themselves not against their fathers' former enemy and their followers (the ex-guerrillas, the left wing, the Kirchners, the human rights movements), but against the Argentine state that once again would be stepping on its citizens' rights by virtue of the political circumstance:

> The Argentine state is lying to the families of the victims of the dictatorship once again, because it lied when it made their relatives disappear, and it is lying again every time it gives them a culprit who is not.[4]

Besides the public role assumed by the organization, the group works as a space of strong emotional support for the families, which find and in turn provide reciprocal aid. Since most children had lost contact with the military community—with the exception of those who entered the Army—and have no direct memory from the 1970s , they lack tools to make sense of the violence and the trials and therefore they want to remain impartial. Even so, they still have to deal with the trials, which are a direct consequence of the violence and their fathers' roles in the military. The members of these military families face a situation that was not contemplated in the pact underlying their entrance into the military world. This study shows that some of them react to this last threat posed by the most unexpected "enemy" (the Argentine state and its judicial power) by following the mechanisms they learned and implemented during their life in the military, and anchoring their movements to kinship, whose articulations persist in time.

Conclusions: kinship, the compass of the military world

This study suggests that condemnation shapes the boundaries of the military families' sociability in current Argentina, and influences the performance of their identity and the redefinition of their relationship with civilians and the institution. The trials triggered diverse reactions and discourses within the military world that reveal not only how military families remember the 1970s and reshape its narrative in the current context, but especially how they make sense of their relationship with the Army they served and the society they belong to. When the military families at the center of this study were born, before and during the dictatorship, its members expected to be respected by the society and protected by the institution precisely because they were military. In their view, instead, they are now being condemned and ignored for the same reason. This diffused perception is affecting their position before the society and the Armed Forces. At the center of their engagement with these two actors there are issues raised by condemnation and a series of unmet expectations that should have determined their place in the world: was the sacrifice of the military family worth it? What is going to happen to the military family now the patriarch is sent to prison instead of being celebrated as a patriot?

The whole family is dragged into discredit with the military. Societal change has meant that the transactions military families entered into did not pay off.

Therefore, the family keep resisting as they always did—each member according to his/her position and tools—in their ultimate military post, the prison, the unexpected result of a professional project that is likely to fail. The military family relies on kinship to make sense of a relationship with the institution that is compromised, since the obligations have been respected only from one side. The relatives articulate their claim against a resentful society on the basis of kinship, an element that becomes a vehicle for meanings and experiences much deeper and wider than the ideological affiliations of the 1970s.

By looking at the action of the relatives of the disappeared during the dictatorship (then organized in the main movements for human rights, like Mothers and Grandmothers of Plaza de Mayo, or *HIJOS*—Sons and Daughters for Identity and Justice Against Oblivion and Silence), and the protest of the relatives of the fallen conscripts in the Malvinas war, Guber (2001: 171) suggests that Argentines tend to make sense of their nationhood by reinventing kinship as "the last irrevocable and legitimate pillar for social organization."[5] According to the results presented in this chapter, the military, which is indeed part of the social body, seems to join this process as it creates organizations legitimized by the presence of wives and especially children of "political prisoners." Kinship seems to represent a sort of neutral, intimate, and supposedly apolitical terrain to conduct the next level of the dispute on the 1970s; it provides a language to put forward an alternative vision of the past that is understandably rejected by society, but might enable it to overcome the political divisions crystallized in the violence of the 1970s. What might sound like a claim for the actions perpetrated during the regime from a group of ex-military nostalgic of the dictatorship is actually an attempt at making sense of an experience that subverted the military family's relationship with an institution that ignores and a society that despises them, by building an alternative framework that is independent of these two spheres, and falls back on the military-specific articulations of kinship.

Notes

1 The commission clarified that this number may be higher since not all cases have been denounced, while the human rights organizations formed by ex-detainees and their relatives claim the amount of the victims of the regime reaches 30,000.

2 In February 1975, the government of Isabel Perón authorized the Argentine Armed Forces' intervention in the region of Tucumán to contrast the rural guerrilla: by decree 261/75 the *Operativo Independencia* was launched, a large-scale operation coordinated by the General Command of the Army to "neutralize and/or annihilate the subversive elements active in the Tucumán province" (Robben, 2005). Once the military regime was established the operation had been extended to the whole country; according to Robben (2006: 367), and as confirmed by participants too, the guerrilla movements were successfully dismantled between 1978 and 1979.

3 The group changed its name in 2016 to *Puentes para la Legalidad*, "Bridges for Legality."

4 Aníbal Guevara, spokesman of the association in a meeting with the civil society organized by the Interamerican Commission for Human Rights (OAS) in Montevideo, October 25, 2017 (*Puentes para la Legalidad*, 2017).

5 My translation from the original.

References

Abrams, L. (2016). *Oral History Theory*. New York: Routledge.

CONADEP (*Comisión Nacional sobre la Desaparición de Personas*) (1984). *Núnca Más. Informe de la Comisión Nacional sobre la Desaparición de Personas*. Buenos Aires: Eudeba.

Crenzel, E. (2017). La verdad en debate: la primacía del paradigma jurídico en el examen de las violaciones a los derechos humanos en la Argentina. *Política y Sociedad*, 54(1), 229–248.

Guber, R. (2001). *Por qué Malvinas? De la causa nacional a la guerra absurda*. Buenos Aires: Fondo De Cultura Económica.

Ministerio Público Fiscal (2017). *Informe estadístico de la Procuraduría de Crímenes contra la humanidad: el estado de las causas por delitos de lesa humanidad en Argentina*. Buenos Aires: Ministerio Público Fiscal. Available at: www.fiscales.gob.ar/wp-content/uploads/2017/03/LH_Informe-Estadistico_2017.pdf (accessed December 26, 2017).

Natale, E. (2019). The Argentine military, the military family and the violence of the 1970s: an ethnographic study of kinship. Ph.D thesis, Keele University.

Robben, A. C. (2005). *Political Violence and Trauma in Argentina*. Philadelphia, PA: University of Pennsylvania Press.

Robben, A. C. (2006). Combat motivation, fear and terror in twentieth-century Argentinian warfare. *Journal of Contemporary History*, 41(2), 357–377.

Soprano, G. (2010). Los militares como grupo social y su inscripción en el Estado y la sociedad argentina. Batallas intelectuales y políticas por la construcción de un objeto de estudio en las ciencias sociales. *Revista Digital Universitaria del Colegio Militar de la Nación*, 22(8), 1–28.

Summerfield, P. (1998). *Reconstructing Women's Wartime Lives: Discourse and Subjectivity in Oral Histories of the Second World War*. Manchester: Manchester University Press.

Summerfield, P. (2004). Culture and composure: creating narratives of the gendered self in oral history interviews. *Cultural and Social History*, 1(1), 65–93.

Puentes para la Legalidad (2017). *Puentes para la Legalidad en reunión con sociedad civil de la CIDH- Montevideo 25/10/2017*. Available at: www.youtube.com/watch?v=M3vRHMG2Oxw (accessed June 22, 2018).

Thomson, A. (1996). *Anzac Memories*. Oxford: Oxford University Press.

4 Tensions and negotiations surrounding the inclusion of female officers in the Brazilian Air Force

Laura Masson

Introduction

This chapter examines the accounts of Brazilian Air Force (BAF) officers in the rank of captain to identify areas of tension, resistance, conflict, and negotiation regarding the new configuration of their professional environment, which currently includes women as coworkers. I analyze the representations, opinions, and myths that arise from the BAF officers' accounts of the integration and performance of women in the Brazilian Armed Forces and particularly in the BAF. It is my intention to show how their perceptions of the incorporation of women into the Armed Forces (who will become military and share workplaces) mobilizes arguments that involve families. The narratives refer both to the bonds in the families where they have grown up (sisters, mothers) and to the relationships in the families they have formed (wives, children).

I would like to propose a hypothesis and a methodological contribution here. My hypothesis is that the disruption of gender relations in the workplace, on the one hand, produces challenges, adaptations, and possible changes in gender relations in the family environment. On the other hand, while challenging the ideal gender identities constructed in families, it also defies the state-supported gender ideology. The methodological proposal is to incorporate into the analysis the emotional reactions that these changes provoke in the officers (in their workplace) and in the members of their families, and to give emotions a legitimate place in the analysis. As Moelker, Rones, and Andres (this volume, Chapter 1) argue, "the triad 'state,' 'armed forces,' and 'family' is interdependent on each other in reproducing a gender-based system of reproduction that is resistant to change because it is deeply rooted in cultural values and norms and transmitted by socialization."

I will use Connell's concepts of *gender regime* and *gender order* for the analysis. Connell (2009) defines the gender regime as the regular set of arrangements about gender of an organization and considers that the gender regimes of these particular organizations are part of wider patterns. She calls these wider patterns the *gender order* of a society. For the author, "The gender regimes of institutions usually correspond to the overall gender order but may depart from it. Change often starts in one sector of society and takes time to seep through into others" (Connell, 2009: 73).

Context

In 1981, the Brazilian Ministry of Aeronautics created the Women's Corps of the Aeronautics Reserve, which included the Women's Corps of Aeronautics Reserve Officers and the Women's Corps of Non-commissioned Officer (NCO) of the Aeronautics Reserve. The first women who joined the Brazilian Air Force enrolled as professionals (information-technology technicians, social workers, speech-language therapists, nutritionists, and psychologists) to enter the Complementary Officer Staff and as technicians (nurses and program technicians) to enter the NCO Staff.

Female Officer Corps applicants had to pass the Adaptation Stage to become second lieutenants in the Aeronautics Reserve. Then the Active Service could call them to serve for an initial period of two years. If the female NCO Corps applicants were successful in the adaptation period, they were promoted to third sergeants of the Aeronautics Reserve (if they were high-school graduates), or promoted to cabo if they had completed elementary school. Then, they could be called to Active Service for an initial period of two years. Each year the Minister of State for Aeronautics fixed the number of vacancies for each post. Nevertheless, the first major change came in 1995 when the Ministry authorized the admission of women to the Brazilian Air Force Academy (BAFA) for the Quartermaster Corps. The second-most important change was when, in 2003, the BAFA created vacancies for women in the Permanent Aviator Officer Staff and the first 20 female cadets began the Air Force Officer Training Course at BAFA. In 2006, 11 female aviators graduated from the Brazilian Air Force. Ten years later, Captain Carla Borges became the first woman to pilot the presidential plane.

The BAF was the first of three forces to revoke the ban on women from entering the Military Academies. The Army and Navy only allowed women into their Military Academies when President Dilma Rousseff modified the legislation by presidential decree in 2012. There are two other aspects that I consider important to highlight about the Brazilian Armed Forces. First, military service continues to be compulsory in Brazil for men. Second, the Brazilian Armed Forces do not currently take part in armed conflicts, though they do participate in numerous peacekeeping missions.

Research strategies

I did my fieldwork at the Brazilian Air Force University (BAFU) in late 2014,[1] where I conducted interviews. Since I did not have access to observations, I do not have information regarding what occurs in everyday practice. I worked with the interviewees' perceptions based on a semi-structured interview guide that included questions about real cases, hypothetical cases, and their experiences as well as those of their comrades.

I directed the interview guide to gather experiences and opinions about the coexistence of men and women in the workplace. I asked about the reasons for their entry into the Armed Forces; opinions about women's entry into the Armed

Forces; experiences while working with women; opinions and experiences about male and female leadership; women in combat roles; whether women improve the Armed Forces; whether the entry of women can be an obstacle to the good performance of the Armed Forces. As the interviews were semi-structured, the interviewees had the possibility to talk about other topics that were not covered in the interview guide. I completed 15 interviews with captains of the Brazilian Air Force (eight men, the majority pilots, and seven women, six from the Complementary Corps—medical division—and one woman from the Quartermaster Corps).[2] The few female pilots in the BAF had not yet been promoted to captain when I conducted the interviews.

The age of the interviewees ranged from 32 to 41 years old. Most of them do not come from military families. Only two mentioned that their fathers were servicemen: a woman—the daughter of a non-commissioned officer—and a man whose grandfather, father, sister, and brother-in-law were also military officers. Another woman has brothers that are in the military. While most do not come from military families, approximately two-thirds of them are married to military staff. Of the women, three were married at this moment to civilian men, three are unmarried, and one of them is part of a dual-military couple (she's a pharmacist and he's a dentist).

Most of their parents are not college graduates. Only two fighter pilots' parents are university graduates. In one case, they are doctors and in another they are engineers. In all other cases, the mothers are teachers or housewives and the fathers are bank employees, teachers, military personnel, a waiter, an engineer and a pilot for a civilian airliner. In general, the families did not object their choice to join the Armed Forces, with the exception of the children of university graduates, who commented that their parents "did not like" their career choice. One woman, whose grandfather was a non-commissioned officer, stated that her family was proud that she was an officer in the Air Force.

Gender, family, and work

The accounts of the interviewed officers narrate of conflicts, difficulties, and tensions, real or imagined, which in many ways include "the family." At the start of the study, gender equality in the workplace provided the main axis of analysis, but later it became a tool to observe the permeability and interconnection between the family environment, work relations, and institutional decisions for the entry of women into the Armed Forces. The gender equality perspective went from being the main focus to being an analytical strategy. As Howard, Risman, and Sprague state in the foreword of a book by Dorothy Smith: "looking through a gender lens allows us to show how our often-unquestioned ideas about gender affect the words we use, the questions we ask, the answers we envision" (Smith, 2005: 10).

Indeed, the answers I got differed from what I expected. The analysis of the stories of everyday experiences, representations, shared myths, and opinions allows me to show how the interviewees overlap, articulate, and mix the roles of the gender regimes of the family, the workplace, and the state in order to think about the place of women in the Armed Forces. Connell (1987: 119) draws attention to the importance of analyzing intermediate levels such as workplaces, markets, and media. She considers that this is where our daily lives are developed and that it is the research on institutions that has changed the way we look at gender. The author also mentions that when the social sciences looked at the intermediate level, they usually chose one particular institution as the carrier of gender and sexuality (Connell, 2009: 119).

In this chapter, I would like to emphasize that not only the Armed Forces act as "gendered institutions," but also families, in the way they articulate their links (Rubin, 1975) and the state as a producer of gender identities (Moore, 1988; Muel-Dreyfus, 1996; Yuval-Davis, 1993). Therefore, to understand gender relations in the workplace, gender relations in families must be incorporated. This involves bringing into the "public space" what has been relegated to the domestic sphere, such as emotions. The exclusively masculine model of the Armed Forces has been historically maintained in a heavily gendered family model, which is apparently also challenged by the entry of women into the Armed Forces (Masson, 2010). Thus, I consider that to comprehend the resistances to the incorporation of military women to the work environment, it is necessary to keep in mind how this change has affected the pervasive images, symbols, and ideologies about femininity and masculinity of the *family regime*.

Availability of the female and male body for work: pregnancy, breastfeeding, and menstrual pains

Some of the interviewed men focused on the female body as a reproductive body and on childcare tasks as the responsibility of women. From this standpoint, they question the relevance of women in the Armed Forces. Some considered that the female body does not have the same "availability" for work as the male body. Because of menstrual cramps, breastfeeding, and pregnancy, for example, women would not be able to fly. On this subject Connell draws attention to the importance of taking into account how closely linked social and bodily processes are in order to understand gender regimes.

The author considers that "gender involves a cluster of human social practices—including child care, birthing, sexual interaction—which deploy human bodies' capacities to engender, to give birth, to give milk, to give and receive sexual pleasure" (Connell, 2009: 68). The "reproductive body" of women in the workplace is considered, in the imaginary of some men, as a "problem" for their professional performance. The way some interviewees think of women's bodies ("limited" or "unavailable bodies" for work) puts a strain on abstract values of equality and challenges the legitimacy of women's rights as mothers. The argument is based on an alleged overload of work for men, due to women's leave for pregnancy, breastfeeding, and absences for alleged menstrual cramps. These opinions are based on stereotypes, not on specific case evaluations, since the incorporation of women into the Air Force is still recent and very few women have joined the Air Force up to the time of the fieldwork. Henry is a pilot and considers that "Women's health, due to the issue of physical effort, is complicated. The times you can count on a man and a woman are different." Duke, for his part, believes that the incorporation of women is very beneficial, but with some limitations:

> What a woman does at the level of the Armed Forces, a man can also do. *However, not everything that men can do, women can do in the same measure*; there are limitations. Despite these limitations, women reach a level similar to that of the men. *However, in some cases, the entire workload falls on the men.* For example, a female pilot is going to be limited when she's pregnant. The excess workload falls on the men, and that isn't fair. It is not an issue of ability, but *she becomes temporarily incapacitated*. . . Take menstruation, for example, she probably won't be able to fly in that state because she's in pain. . .
>
> Women can be pilots just like men, but *they have these particularities such as pregnancy, lactation*, and that is extra work for the rest. *There are wonderful women, but they have these limitations*. I see the men and they don't have leaves of absence, and they also have a family and end up with excess workloads.
>
> (Duke, pilot)

In this case, men complain about a supposed extra workload that results from more permissions granted to the women to attend to "feminine issues," and this requires a greater amount of work and takes time away from their own families.[3] In this interpretation a rivalry is formed between the female officers' family and that of the male officers. One of the women interviewed, who belongs to the "Cuerpo Profesional" (in this case doctors, nurses, dentists, etc.), points at the disruption that a pregnant woman's body implies in the workplace. From personal experience she observes:

> What I saw as difference in the Armed Forces was the issue of pregnancy. *The military does not like pregnant women.* My pregnancies were high-risk, and *they didn't believe it was true*, they thought I should be present. . . I almost lost my baby.
>
> (Sharon, physician)

Until the time of women's entry into the Armed Forces, these roles were confined to the domestic sphere of the military family. When these roles are recognized for military women as rights (maternity leave, reduced hours for breastfeeding, or a leave to take care of their child), the sexual division of labor and the division of domestic and public spaces are clearly challenged. If the institution recognizes the right of military women to "care" through leave or absence, then men argue that this right should also be recognized for them: "they [the men] also have a family." This position not only modifies the gender regime of the institution, but simultaneously questions the gender regime of families. As West and Zimmerman

(1987: 144) show, "It is not simply that household labor is designated as 'women's work', but that for a woman to engage in it and a man not to engage in it is to draw on and exhibit the 'essential nature' of each. What is produced and reproduced is not merely the activity and artifact of domestic life, but the material embodiment of wifely and husbandly roles."

West and Zimmerman (1987: 144) also introduce a question of great relevance to the case of the Armed Forces, which I present here as a rhetorical question: "How does gender get done in work settings outside the home, where dominance and subordination are themes of overarching importance?" In relation to the female body, there are two situations to be considered. On the one hand, as we saw earlier, it is understood from its reproductive characteristics (to engender, to give birth, to give milk) and linked to social practices such as childcare. In this sense, it shows the rejection of the pregnant body for being considered "limited." On the other hand, although other interviewees also regard the female body from this position, they bring in nuance by using reflection. The arguments are the historical changes in the average fertility rate, one's own experience with pregnancy and maternity, and the experience of men and women living together in military academies. One of the interviewees refuted the fact that the men were overworked because the women allegedly left their jobs because of demands for childcare, menstrual cramps, pregnancy, or breastfeeding. Based on her experience, she asserts that:

> *I was pregnant when I was in the Air Force and at no time did I give up my commitments to my activities for that reason. Even when my son was little.* There is no justification for saying, we are not going to have women, that is why. The integration and the benefit you get is greater and even more so if we consider that today it is not like before when women had ten children. Perhaps at that time it was something extremely significant. But today they have one or two children. There is no justification for not letting them in because of this, it would be discrimination.
>
> (Susan, pharmacist)

Another interviewed pilot considers that the challenge of the female body in the workplace is something that arises from men who have not lived with women at the time of their training at the Military Academy. He believes that this perspective is changing and that living with women in the workplace changes the ideology that underpins a dichotomous world.

> *It is obvious that older staff members who did not live with women during the training period [at the Academies] are going to think differently.* We've already entered with them and we have another reasoning. Of them [the older ones], sometimes I hear . . . "uhh, is she far away because she's pregnant? Another one?" Like it's something that bothers them. *Perhaps because they have not yet seen women soldiers in command positions.* If there is still conflict, it is because there are no parameters to measure its performance.
>
> (Brad, pilot)

Both testimonies show how the institutional gender regime is challenged from daily interactions, while these interactions also challenge established assumptions about the "unavailability of female bodies for work" and also challenge the inadequacy of a pregnant body in the workplace.[4] Furthermore, the very construction of the male body as a strong, available, and "not limited" body depends on the sexual division of labor. The construction of stereotypes about male and female bodies is intertwined. Connell (1987: 241) states that "The familiar public/private distinction is part of a process of dichotomizing the world that is the most systematic form of 'purification' attempted by sexual ideology." While pregnant bodies and care tasks remain in the domestic sphere of the military family and do not invade the institution, male bodies can disengage, move away from that role, and build themselves up as strong and available.

Emotions and jealousy: the question of social change

Some interviewees believe that Brazilian society was not yet ready for women to join the Armed Forces. This gap that they detect between what Connell calls gender order and the gender regime causes, according to some interviewees, situations that are difficult to deal with and that create tensions in their daily lives or among comrades. One of the interviewees used the expression "the social side" to refer to the tensions and conflicts generated by the incorporation of women as coworkers for him and his colleagues in their married lives.

> Another problem is the social side. *My wife does not handle the fact that I work with other women well.* She is a nurse, and I tell her: where you work, are there only women? I test your patience because there are doctors, male nurses, or whatever . . . So, *that social part is still very hard,* I think . . . That part is really difficult . . . I talk about her, but *I have many friends who have the same problem.*
>
> (George, pilot)

> For example, if you are going on mission with a woman, your wife won't like it at all. She is not going to be happy at all about that. *We need to evolve a lot so that these things become more natural.*
>
> (André, pilot)

The reference to emotions (specifically their wives' jealousy) as a legitimate argument to point out difficulties, tensions, and negotiations in their daily lives since the incorporation of military women was one of the most unexpected responses during the field work. This illustrates in an exemplary way the interaction between institutional gender regimen and family gender regimen.

In her book *The Purchase of Intimacy*, Viviana Zelizer (2005) shows that allegedly antagonistic worlds such as economics and intimacy are not hostile worlds, as much of the literature on the subject has presupposed and tried to demonstrate. On the contrary, she shows that affection and rationality mix all the time. The author offers a conception of connected lives aimed at promoting overcoming explanations of dichotomies and formulas.[5] If we use Zelizer's perspective of "connected lives," the jealousy of officers' wives becomes a legitimate argument that helps us to understand the difficulties of accepting military women. Catherine Lutz points out that "emotion occupies an important place in western gender ideologies; in identifying emotion primarily with irrationality, subjectivity, the chaotic and other negative characteristics, and in subsequently labeling women as the emotional gender, cultural belief reinforces the ideological subordination of women" (Lutz, 1986: 288).

If we remain in the position of holding the domestic sphere and the labor sphere as pure and separate worlds, the jealousy of officers' wives may be read as an emotional immaturity, an anomaly, or a banality. However, some officers consider this issue a serious one.

In their opinion, this problem would be solved with a change, understood in evolutionary terms, in the order of gender, i.e., at the level of society: "We need to evolve a lot so that these things become more natural." As for the explanation of the jealousy of the officers' wives, I can only cite one testimony, collected in Brazil, in another context where a military wife said that it is not jealousy because of possible infidelity. The problem is that they are women they could admire more than their own wives. They play challenging roles and have more interesting lives than a military wife could have. Jealousy is about professional performance and the place they occupy socially.

Family roles as an explanation for stress and difficulties in the workplace

In this section I analyze the family roles that the interviewees used to refer to the entry and performance of military women in the Air Force. These roles were used both to undermine their professional work and to flatter it. But in both cases the sexual division of labor was reinforced. In the form of myth, family ties (in this case the father-daughter relationship) introduced the idea of "contamination" into the institutional bureaucracy, which is presumed to be rational, objective, and egalitarian.

In the bibliography on Brazilian military sociology there are several studies that address the particularities of military families. I am especially interested in those that show how the rules, hierarchies, and values of the military institution pervade the lives of the wives and children of military men (Chinelli, 2018; Marques Virote de Sousa Pinto, 2018; Rodriguez da Silva, 2018). Interestingly, in this study, I observe an inverse movement to that shown by the abovementioned researchers. In this case, kinship ties and family roles are brought to the military institution to interpret the disruption caused by the presence of women soldiers in the Air Force. I will analyze the reference to the image of the "mother," the "daughters," and the transmission of gender roles in the families of older officers as ways of explaining tensions, misunderstandings, and conflicts.

Woman as a representative image of a "mother"

The comparison of women with mothers was created to belittle women's leadership abilities and their performance on the battlefront as well as to argue in support of the idea that they improve the work environment:[6]

> *It's not that I can't trust a woman as a leader*; the person who is in a position of command is not there for nothing. Surely, she [this person] deserves it, but there's that prejudice. For example, *if I see a woman older than me, I see the figure of my mother*, a delicate figure, and I find myself wanting to protect her no matter what. . . Do you understand?
>
> (Duke)

> For example, in a hospital with female military physicians. *They do not lose their position of leadership, but they create a more family-oriented environment than the men*, who are more focused on their work. It is difficult to perceive that mixture in a man, he's your boss and your father, but in them, *it's half-boss and half-mother. She hits when she has to hit, but she cares when she has to care.*
>
> (André)

The interviewee's portrait of a female leader as a hybrid, half-boss, half-mother entity shows that the position of authority makes her a non-pure person. This image condenses characteristics of each of the worlds to which, according to the interviewees' representation, it belongs: the domestic and the public. Connell sustains that

> The modern liberal state defines men and women as citizens, that is, as equals. But the dominant sexual code defines men and women as opposites and customary ideas about the division of labor in family life define women as housewives and caretakers of children. Accordingly, women entering the public domain—trying to exercise their rights as citizens—have an uphill battle to have their authority recognized.
>
> (Connell, 2009: 73)

One of the questions in the interviews concerned women in combat roles and men's reactions when a woman dies on the battlefield. Here the figure of the mother appears again:

> The affectation of men towards the death of women in combat. . . there is something there may be a psychologist can explain, *the issue of the mother. . . he lost his mother. Women have a maternal side which is going to create a differentiated sentiment, whether you like it or not, she is a different sex.*
>
> (André)

> I don't know. . . *when a woman dies in combat, you might think you're killing a mother*. And the figure of the mother in the education of a child seems to me to have more weight.
>
> (Grace, physician)

Again, it is the figure of the mother that delegitimizes the participation of women in the Armed Forces, in this case in combat roles. Two things can be said. On the one hand, as Enloe (1990) points out, women's participation in the Armed Forces defies a powerful cultural construct according to which "womenandchildren"[7] are the reason men go to war. So, if women are in the war, who are the men defending? On the other hand, the hard core of military identity (and in many cases military promotion) depends on combat service and as long as women are forbidden to perform combat duties, their promotion is formally restricted (Sasson-Levy, 2011: 393). Prohibiting women from deploying in combat is one way of sustaining the sexual division of labor.

The ghost of the "daughters of" as a myth of the opening of the Academy of the Air Force to women

This is a point I want to consider in greater depth since it not only appeared in the interviews but was also an issue mentioned by a historian of the Air Force University. In the testimonies, this concept appears without any real substance because according to their own accounts, the first female pilots were not the daughters of servicemen.

> Many people. . . rumor has it that *women only entered because [he refers to the entry of women into military aviation] the daughters of the most senior officers wanted to get in*, but there wasn't any room for them.
>
> (Henry)

This myth reveals an imaginary dispute between the most senior and junior generations, mediated by gender and kinship: the most senior officers would favor women (their daughters), to the detriment of subaltern males.[8] The presence of women again appears as a polluting element in an institution that recognizes itself as objective and neutral: they "only enter because they are the daughters of." According to the mythical tale, the feelings and emotions that characterize family relationships allow women to enter the Air Force. There is no mentioning in that statement that the institution is not neutral, but masculine. And for that reason, everything feminine can do nothing but contaminate it. Amanda Sinclair, in reference to research on bodies in organizations, mentions that dominance is thus often accomplished via hierarchies of bodily masculinities. To illustrate her argument, she cites research by Barrett (1996) on naval cultures that show that at the top are extremes of physical risk-taking among "fly-boys," to a technical rationality expressed via capabilities, habits, and physical demeanors among supply officers at the bottom. But, despite the bodily hierarchies between males, each masculine bodily subculture finds its position and legitimacy in opposition to the feminine. Each is not-female, which is what matters (Sinclair, 2011: 119–120).

Here the family breaks into the institution to undermine the supposedly equal and meritocratic foundations of the state bureaucracy. The assumption that affections pollute the institutional ethos is convenient, in this case discrediting the place of women aviators.

Traditional gender roles in the family as determining factors in the resistance of higher-ranking officials

Finally, one of the explanations for the difficulties that arise with the presence of female military in the Air Force is the influence that the family education of senior officers, based on a marked division of gender roles, has on their professional performance. One of the interviewees says

> Now not so much, but *I felt that there was a great resistance among the colonels, the most senior officers*. . . The thing is that the entrance of women, whether you like it or not, is very recent, and *the father of that colonel was a person who lived through a regime. . . who was raised by a father whose wife wasn't allowed to speak. And he carried that inside of him*. . . It's not his fault, *it's the environment he grew up in*. So, there was a very strong resistance.
>
> (Paul)

The interviewee's point of view is based on the fact that the gender roles, built up in the context of Air Force officers' families, influence the degree of acceptance of female military personnel. This perception can be reinforced by current studies of military families in Brazil. The study describes military families as pertaining hierarchical and traditional gender roles, especially in the case of high-ranking officers. I will cite as an example the account of a military wife socialized in the early 1960s, relieved by Oliveira de Adão (2018: 36): "even though you put your life aside, you realize that family is much more important. Family ties are much stronger than your own life."

Conclusion

This study shows that gender relations in families cohere to gender relations in the workplace of the Armed Forces. In other words, both the Armed Forces and families are "gendered institutions" and they influence each other. While most of the research on military families shows how the military institution influences families, I have tried to show the impact of "the family" on the institution. The stories show that in the presence of military women in the Armed Forces, the interviewees evoke symbols and ideologies about femininity and masculinity based on family and domestic roles. Family roles within the institution threaten the order and supposed neutrality of the work organization.[9] And the familiar images with which military women are associated make it difficult to recognize their professional performance.

One of the instances where this is evident is in the hypervisibilization of women's bodies. While, as Sinclair maintains (2011: 120) "It's not that men's bodies are not important in leadership, it's that they have been made invisible for particular ideological purposes. Meanwhile, female leader bodies are highlighted and made available for judgment, potentially undermining their claim to leadership." The author reinforces her position by stating "the bodies of leaders are rendered visible (usually in the case of women) and invisible (usually in the case of men) via a pre-existing socially defined body order." This places us in a complex and, only apparently, contradictory situation. While women's bodies are visible (when they are leaders) women's professional performance becomes invisible (or placed second) because they are not supposed to break the glass ceiling or join the armed forces in numbers that jeopardize the status quo of the male hierarchy.

Another point that highlights the tension caused by the presence of women soldiers in the institution is when there is an imbalance in the emotions of the families of their male comrades. Military women not only challenge the sexual division of labor, they challenge socially established and widely accepted gender roles. This puts in check, on the one hand, the identity of men as "warriors" and, on the other, the identity of their wives as women who play a role that is naturally determined. On the other side, military women seem to bring with them the subjectivity, arbitrariness, and other negative characteristics associated with kinship, when they break into the public sphere. Here, "truly egalitarian" treatment appears as a great challenge.

Finally, I would like to point out that despite the resistance that is evident in the stories, most of the interviewees consider that the presence of women in the Armed Forces is already a fact and is inevitable. Inevitability is attributed to social progress. They believe that society is evolving and that the Armed Forces must evolve accordingly. In this sense, the prohibition of women from entering or remaining, according to them, is a position of backwardness.[10]

Notes

1 As a foreign (Argentine) researcher it was not easy to get permission to do my research. After several formal attempts, visits to the University of the Air Force, and meetings with civilian professors and university authorities, I obtained permission to interview officers with the rank of captain studying to complete a mandatory course to be promoted to superior ranks (major, lieutenant colonel, and colonel). The support of one of the civilian teachers was crucial in doing the fieldwork.

2 The names of all interviewees were changed to protect their identity.

3 It is interesting to note that there were no cases of pregnancy among the pilots they know. On the other hand, they explain that the period of greatest activity for pilots is up to 35 years of age (afterwards, the number of flights diminishes, and they begin to take on more administrative activities), which indicates that maternity does not necessarily have to be an obstacle if the women were to have a later pregnancy.

4 It should be noted that women's testimonies are from health corps officers and not from the command corps, so they do not belong to the hard core of the Armed Forces' identity.

5 Zelizer showed that "Economic sociologists studying intersections of economic interchange and intimate ties, in short, long hesitated between hostile worlds and nothing-but formulations. They never arrived at a satisfactory adjudication among such views because the social reality in question requires not a choice between the two, but their transcendence" (Zelizer, 2005: 46).
6 It is interesting to note that in a survey of Argentine military personnel with the objective to identify masculine and feminine prototypes of leadership, respondents mainly identified male leaders with military people belonging not only to the current military population, but also those recognized because of their heroic feats. In relation to female leaders, respondents identified mainly religious people, in the first place Mother Teresa of Calcutta (Lupano Perugini, Castro Solano, and Casullo, 2008).
7 Enloe doesn't separate the words as a literary strategy to show that they always go together.
8 Henrietta Moore notices that "opposition between the sexes is usually constructed, by implication, on the basis of opposition between spouses, and little mention is made, if any, of the other sets of gendered relations, brother/sister, mother/son, father/daughter, which are an equally important part of being a woman or a man" (Moore, 1988: 19).
9 Catharine MacKinnon analyzes how the supposed neutrality of the liberal state is constructed and shows under what circumstances and why she considers the state to be masculine: "the state is male in that objectivity is its norm. Objectivity is liberal legalism's conception of itself. It legitimates itself by reflecting its view of society, a society it helps make by so seeing it, and calling that view, and that relation, rationality" (MacKinnon, 1989: 162).
10 It should be remembered that at the time of the fieldwork the entry of women into the Army and Navy Academies had not yet taken place.

References

Barrett, F. (1996). The organizational construction of hegemonic masculinity: the case of the U.S. Navy. *Gender, Work and Organization*, 3(3), 129–142.

Chinelli, F. (2018). Familia militar: apontamentos sobre uma comunidade performada. In C. Castro (ed.), *A familia militar no Brasil. Transformações e permanências* (pp. 67–88). Río de Janeiro: FGB EDITORA.

Connell, R. W. (1987). *Gender and Power: Society, the Person, and Sexual Politics*. Stanford, CA: Stanford University Press.

Connell, R. W. (2009). *Gender in World Perspective*. Cambridge, MA: Malden.

Enloe, C. (1990). Women and children: making feminist sense of the Persian Gulf crisis. *The Village Voice*, September 25.

Lupano Perugini, M. L., Castro Solano, A., and Casullo, M. M. (2008). Prototipos de liderazgo masculino y femenino en población militar. *Revista de Psicología*, 26(2), 195–218.

Lutz, C. (1986). Emotion, thought, and estrangement: emotion as a cultural category. *Cultural Anthropology*, 1(3), 287–309.

Marques Virote de Sousa Pinto, W. (2018). Construção da subjetividade de mulher de militares: discursos e contexto. In C. Castro (ed.), *A familia militar no Brasil. Transformações e permanências* (pp. 115–132). Río de Janeiro: FGB EDITORA.

Masson L. (2010). Las mujeres en las Fuerzas Armadas ¿qué tipo de integración? In *Género y Fuerzas Armadas: algunos análisis teóricos y prácticos* (pp. 71–78). Buenos Aires: Ministerio de Defensa de la Nación, Fundación Friederich Ebert.

Mackinnon, C. (1989). *Toward a Feminist Theory of the State*. Cambridge, MA: Harvard University Press.

Moore, H. (1988). *Feminism and Anthropology*. Minneapolis, MN: University of Minneapolis, Minnesota Press.
Muel-Dreyfus, F. (1996). *Vichy et l'éternel féminin: contribution à une sociologie politique de l'ordre des corps*. Paris: Seuil.
Oliveira de Adão, M. C. (2018). Projeto e individualismo: considerações sobre a adesão das esposas ao projeto professional dos oficiais do Exército brasileiro. In C. Castro (ed.), *A familia militar no Brasil. Transformações e permanências* (pp. 29–48). Río de Janeiro: FGB EDITORA.
Rodriguez da Silva, C. (2018). Familias na fronteira: experiências de esposas de militares na selva brasileira. In C. Castro (ed.), *A familia militar no Brasil. Transformações e permanências* (pp. 89–114). Río de Janeiro: FGB EDITORA.
Rubin, G. (1975). The traffic in women. Notes on the "political economy of sex." In R. Reiter Rapp (ed.), *Toward an Anthropology of Women*. New York: Monthly Review Press.
Sasson-Levy, O. (2011). The military in a globalized environment: perpetuating an "extremely gendered" organization. In E. L. Jeanes, D. Knights, and P. Yancey Martin, *Handbook of Gender, Work and Organization* (pp. 391–411). Chichester: John Wiley & Sons.
Sinclair, A. (2011). Leading with body. In E. L. Jeanes, D. Knights, and P. Yancey Martin, *Handbook of Gender, Work and Organization* (pp. 117–130). Chichester: John Wiley & Sons.
Smith, D. E. (2005). *Institutional Ethnography: A Sociology for People*. Lanham, MD: Altamira Press.
Stølen, K. A. (1996). *The Decency of Inequality: Gender, Power and Social Change on the Argentine Prairie*. Oslo: Scandinavian University Press.
West, C. and D. H. Zimmerman (1987). Doing gender. *Gender and Society*, 1(2): 125–151.
Yuval-Davis, N. (1993). Gender and nation. *Ethnic and Racial Studies*, 16(4), 621–632.
Zelizer, V. (2005). *A Purchase of Intimacy*. Princeton, NJ: Princeton University Press.

5 The military–family industry

The role of the family in the construction and development of the military profession

Elena Lysak

Introduction

The policies of contemporary countries are largely devoted to the recognition not only of the technical capabilities of the Army, but of human resources as well: women and men who have chosen to serve their country (White Paper on Defense and National Security, 2013). This means that up to now only female and male Army personnel have been taken into account and recognized as actors of the institution. However, there are other actors whose role, although very important, is still neglected: military wives who perform essential work for the functioning of the Army. The marital status of military personnel offers a particular case for reflection when considering the interweaving of work and family in the Army.

Since 1808, the French Army exercised control over the future spouses of soldiers that wanted to get married. Marriage control consisted of monitoring the morality and honor of a young woman and examining her domestic skills. Under the Vichy regime, these requirements were supplemented by the restriction of access to the labor market; thus, according to the Military Marriage Instruction (*Instruction relative au mariage des militaires*; Ministry of Defense, 1942), the officer "shall make a written commitment that, from the date of his marriage, his wife shall cease all remunerated work" (Ministry of Defense, 1942). In France, this hierarchical control for each military marriage existed until the 1970s, only to be finally abolished in 1972. Yet even today it is not uncommon to hear that when marrying a soldier, a woman also marries the Army (Bergere, 2004). Despite growing independence within marital arrangements, the tendency to impose on women the professional status of their husbands is still present in contemporary society.

Today, although the role of wives pertains to the private sphere, it is recognized as indispensable for the functioning of the Army. Public recognition of the presence of women in the career of their husbands transfers this activity from the private sphere to the professional field. Thus, military spouses play the "secondary role" in their conjugal team (Singly and Chaland, 2002) and provide by extension "a free service," by creating the "military as a family" by doing emotional labor (Hochschild, 1983) that is favored by military leaders and explained by the "feminine nature" of these tasks (Avril, 2003).

Moreover, in view of the current situation, the growth of interest in the presence of women in a soldier's career can be observed. For example, in 2010, the Directorate for Human Resources of the French Ministry of Defence carried out a thorough survey regarding family life in the French Army, which aimed to show the conjugal situation of soldiers, their children, and their lifestyles (French Ministry of Defence, 2010). And while statistics indicated that a significant proportion of soldiers have a partner ("seven out of ten"), the existence of this survey also confirms the recognition of the role of wives by the institution itself and by French society (High Military Condition Assessment Committee, 2017).

However, several studies indicate that although visible at the family and institutional level, the functions of spouses in the Army remain socially undervalued, while according to the interviewees, this activity deserved to be considered "a real job" (interview with a French military spouse, a university teacher, conducted on March 13, 2016).

Research question

The purpose of the present reflection is to question the phenomenon of military wives in order to understand to what extent they contribute to the evolution of the military profession within the contemporary Army. To study this group, individuals whose entry into the institution is the result of their marriage with a soldier are interviewed. It is important to note that although there are men in the contemporary Army whose wives are also soldiers by profession, my research is not concerned with them; the present study concerns only women who are officers' wives. Since their husbands are often transferred, one has to look at the professional life of the military wives and ask whether they are able to hold a salaried job. These considerations are valid not only for the field of military sociology, but also for that of work and family.

This study addresses the following question: to what extent does marital life affect the career development of servicemen in France and Russia? More generally the research examines tensions between marital life and career development in the Army.

A comparison between France and Russia

The global context mentioned in the work of several researchers (e.g., Enloe, 1983; Mathers, 2000) and the surveys that have been already carried out encouraged me to compare two countries, France and Russia, in order to identify international commonalities as well as national specificities, and to examine what this confrontation will bring to light. The two countries have many similarities that may not be obvious but are very important when trying to understand the construction of the military institution.

For instance, in France, according to official statistics, the geographical mobility in the Army is three times higher than that of civilians (French Ministry of Defence, 2010). Likewise, in Russia, all officers according to their ranks and positions are encouraged to accept transfers. This obligation is not inevitable but very necessary for the promotion of a military. Thus, transfers become an important part of military careers in France and Russia.

Therefore, the life of military wives is organized according to the postings of their husbands. Both in France and Russia military wives are isolated in two ways. On the one hand they are physically isolated from family and friends; on the other they are excluded from the civilian world because they belong to the military institution.

A further important point when comparing the two countries is the influence of patriotic ideas in the social policy of those countries. For instance, as heir to the Soviet Army, the Russian Army still preserves the traditions of the USSR (star-shaped insignia, the use of the term "comrade" between soldiers). The visible presence of various patriotic organizations, including veterans' associations, is such that there is a strong concentration of sociopatriotic ideas both in the civilian and military society in Russia. Similarly, in France, there is a recurrence of patriotic ideas and of the "traditional society" with some dominant values stemming from religion, family construction, etc. Quite clear in the society at large, this trend is even more visible in government institutions such as the Army.

Thus, a comparison between France and Russia and above all the fact that patriotic values are coming back in society allows me to integrate national analyses within a larger international framework. I shall try to point out similar and differing general trends in the development of military policies. This reflection is based on three surveys conducted in France and Russia from 2014 to 2018. The first was conducted in Russia as part of a study of professional equality between men and women in the Army. I studied the careers of professional military women, and the reasons they invoked to justify their choice to work in the Army (Lysak, 2015). Twenty-three interviews have been conducted with military men and women. The second survey was conducted in France from October 2015 to April 2016. It includes 21 interviews, not only with military wives, but also with officers and leaders of associations in various French regions. As part of this work titled "Military wife: housewife or soldier without a contract?" (Lysak, 2016), I studied the socioprofessional phenomenon of military wives in order to observe their access to the labor market.

Finally, as part of my doctoral thesis in sociology, I conducted a new study in Russia in March 2017. The purpose of this study was to understand how military spouses build their identities based on their marital status, gender, and the professional status of their husbands. In particular, I chose to study the construction of the identity of women in geographically isolated garrisons. I conducted 27 interviews not only with military wives and military soldiers by profession, but also with the officers responsible for the educational and ideological work of the Army. Today, the synthesis of this material collected in previous years brings forth essential ideas about the presence of women in the military career of their husbands. It provides insight into the extent to which a soldier's wife contributes to the achievement of military policies of contemporary societies.

Economic role: supplementing the insufficient salary of the husband

The study of armies of various countries, such as the British Army, for example (Enloe, 1983), shows that, when paid little for their work, soldiers are unable to earn a salary that essentially meets the needs of their families. Moreover, permanent mobility within the Army limits women's access to the labor market, which points to a certain economic precariousness of military families. Compared to civilian incomes official representatives of the French Army confirm a lower level of income for soldiers compared to those of civilians.

Officer, administration and personnel management, French Army:

> According to statistics from the Ministry of Defence, the income of military households is 15 to 20 percent lower compared to that of the French population. Military spouses have lower wages and lower purchasing power compared to couples who do not need to change place of residence. So, if wives want to work—all the better!
>
> (Interview conducted on January 14, 2016)

Similarly, in Russia I note the economic precariousness of military families caused by insufficient income. Even though today precariousness is not specific to military families, this tendency is very visible in the Army among families forced to frequently change their residence. The interviews show that wives are encouraged to work for different reasons.

Military wife, military psychologist, Russian Army:

> We cannot stay at home with the salary he earns. . . I would just like to say that this is not enough for a family with two or three children. Moreover, we are in a modern society; women work even if they have children to raise. Staying at home was more a thing at the time of our mothers. It is therefore necessary to work.
>
> (Interview conducted on March 14, 2017)

The leaders of the Army are aware of this situation, evident for women. The interviews conducted in Russia show that wives are encouraged to find paid work, first by the institution itself. The military command attempts to manage the careers of wives indirectly.

Colonel, Deputy Commander of the Military Brigade, Russian Army:

> Can soldiers' wives work? Of course! And that's good, given the fairly modest income of soldiers. We, as officers responsible for the ideological work, we have to find a job for the wives, which is not always easy. But the military command asks us for reports on the employment of wives, it forces us to find work for all the wives who come to the garrison. For women who are transferred with their husbands.
>
> (Interview conducted on March 14, 2017)

Following the testimonies and statistics mentioned it seems that military wives are submitted to a dual dependence: first on their spouse and second on society as economically precarious persons. According to Hayek's economic theory (1944), in which economic freedom is the ability of members of a society to take independent economic actions, it can be argued that military wives suffer from strong restrictions on their economic liberty.

Army officials confirm that they are trying to find jobs for women (interviews with French and Russian Army officers), but what is more interesting is to look at the type of work offered/accessible to them. According to the officers, two possibilities are offered to wives: to work in the civilian sector or to be hired by the Army. However, the first option is unfeasible because of a lack of job opportunities. Moreover, this possibility is often frowned upon, as women are advised not to work outside the military base so as to not "distance themselves too much from the army" (interview with a military wife conducted on March 14, 2017). Therefore, to solve the financial problem, the second option remains, that is, to integrate into the Army. Yet being a dual-military couple can create serious problems for the family, which will be described in the next section.

Conflict of interest: shifting work interactions into the family

In Russia, more than half of the women in the military are spouses of men who work in the military (Nepochetaia, 2004). Wives of military personnel are offered the opportunity to work in the Army; all they have to do is go to the employment office in order to join the same institution as their husbands: the Army.

Lieutenant-Colonel, Deputy Commander of the Regiment, Russian Army:

> If the wife wants to work—that's good! We constantly have positions to offer in the Regiment. Of course, working in the canteen is not very prestigious for the woman trained as a teacher, for example. But I do say: if she wants a job, we have some in the Army. In this case, she most often becomes a soldier, the colleague of her husband I would say.
>
> (Interview conducted on March 15, 2017)

"Becoming a colleague of her husband" is the main problem for this type of family. Less promoted than men, these women become in most cases the direct subordinates of their husbands. Eventually, the emergence of a conflict of professional interests forces them to find other possible solutions; to make a choice between two undesirable options.

Military spouse, social worker, Russian Army:

> We are hired, but what happens next? Nobody cares! For example, after ten years of service, I became my husband's subordinate—that's a conflict of interest! Now it's either up to me or him to resign. And that's not possible because you need money to live. So, we decided to divorce—it's a fictional separation, but that worries me. I trust my husband but staying alone with two kids—it's no fun at all. No, you see—instead of helping us, they create constraints.
>
> (Interview conducted on March 14, 2017)

On the contrary, in France, women are not allowed to join the Army when they have married a soldier. But in the French Army another type of conflict emerges when the woman wants to keep her professional activity despite the husband's transfers: a family–work conflict (Beghiti-Mahut, 2015). Keeping in mind that these decisions are not always mandatory, the decision to move is rather a choice made by the couple; a soldier can refuse to be transferred, to favor the development of his wife's career.

Military wife, family judge, French Army:

> It's out of the question for me not to work. When I met my husband in 1998, I wondered if it would be possible given his job. Finally, we chose not to move, to stay here. In fact, my husband still refuses to be transferred. Fortunately, it is possible. But, yes, I'm not sure it's always good for his promotion.
>
> (Interview conducted on March 13, 2016)

It is clear that the existence of conflict between family and work operates in favor of the career of the husband, to the detriment of his wife's. The conflict is almost inevitable also because of the many transfers during the career.

Military wife, university teacher, French Army:

> I have wondered about the effect of my presence in my husband's career, because there were probably professional opportunities he had that he did not take because of my work. We never moved from here and one day, one of the former commanders came to me saying that I was breaking my husband's career! But we had decided that with my husband at the beginning, and we will not change our minds, even if it's asked by a leader.
>
> (Interview conducted on March 13, 2016)

The emergence of conflict is obvious: the issue of transfers becomes a constraint for the professional life of women, but at the same time, the choice of the military member not to be transferred can hinder his promotion. However, the interviews highlight that the professional choice results rather from an agreement made between the spouses within the family home. And once again, I perceive a strong presence and impact of women and the family on the military career of soldiers. These results reflect the findings in the American and British Armies (see, for example, Moelker, Andres, Bowen, and Manigart, 2015).

Military familialism: integrating the family model into the professional sector

Furthermore, also based on the work of researchers that have tackled the theme of gender in the Soviet/Russian Army (Mathers, 2000), it can be observed that today in Russia, having a full-time occupation like their husband does not diminish the daily tasks of women. The role prescribed to them by the paternalistic society, that of a mother, is clearly visible in the military sector. During my research, I found evidence of the involvement of wives in the care provided not only to the husband, but also to his subordinates in the military.

Major General, Deputy Commander of the Military District, Russian Army:

> In the Army, we are in family. For example, when the end-of-year party takes place, the Commander must stay with the soldiers in barracks, but must come with his wife, to create a family atmosphere, that's important. And then, who wants to leave his wife alone for the party? So, I confirm—we are in family here, and it's great for everyone.
>
> (Interview conducted on March 17, 2017)

This phenomenon of a "military familialism," observed in the British Army (Enloe, 1983), implicates that wives are providing family care to all the men of the regiment, married and single. Although supported by military leaders, this activity is also institutionalized by women's groups. During my research in France I studied the National Association of Military Women (*Association nationale des femmes de militaires*; ANFEM), whose members confirm this idea.

Member of the National Executive Board of ANFEM:

> There is great solidarity between wives in the Army, as the women are very supportive. Men are quite often absent, so they can rely on each other. But the main thing is that through our actions we can gather everyone together, not only women, but also children, husbands. It's a real family.
>
> (Interview conducted on October 12, 2015)

In other words, the activity of women in this association aims to establish a kind of unification of the family within the Army. This type of organization is well known, even supported by the command.

Officer, administration and personnel management, French Army:

> There is an association, ANFEM, and there is a real solidarity, an individual volunteering of women. With ANFEM, the command maintains links with military spouses. They are steered in their personal and professional projects.
>
> (Interview conducted on January 14, 2016)

In Russia there is also an institution that promotes the maintenance of family ties in the military sector. In 1917, the Soviet government institutionalized the Women's Councils (*Zhensovety*), made up of military wives. These organizations aimed at unifying families within geographically isolated garrisons. It should be noted that the control of these Councils is still, today, the responsibility of the officers in charge of the educational and ideological work of each unit.

Major, Deputy Commander for Ideological and Educational Work, Russian Army:

> Of course, we run this activity, everything the women do in their councils. How could it be otherwise? I have to control them, make them follow the directives of Command. Women organize parties, regimental days, and so on. I offer them the annual work plans to follow and then I receive their reports. It's good and very practical.
>
> (Interview conducted on March 15, 2017)

Thus, through these organizations, wives are involved in the daily life of the various Army units in France and Russia. Furthermore, the observation of this feminine activity allows me to say that military wives support the state's and Army's objectives by providing a surrogate family atmosphere to the military units for free. The work that is involved in creating the military as emotional communities (Rosenwein, 2015) is volunteer work, it is emotional labor (Hochschild, 1983), and it is even to the detriment of the family income because the wives sacrifice their own earning potential. The wives are not only sponsoring the military by free labor, but they are even paying for it.

Strategies and perspectives for the development of the contemporary Army

The interviews revealed that military wives in France and Russia partake in free emotion labor on behalf of the Army (Hochschild, 1983), in providing the military unit with a family atmosphere. Moreover, I have found that the military created a system to extract this emotion labor, because by transferring the soldiers to different postings the wives' only option is to follow and to accept that their own career comes second. Furthermore, it should be emphasized that wives are omnipresent in all stages of a military career. Their influence is noticeable not only as regards to their husbands' professional promotions, but also because of their strong impact within the different military units. As a result, it is clear that the role of women is considered by the military command essential for the effectiveness of the Army.

Finally, in the contemporary world, these wives are militarized by their conjugal status; at the same time, they participate in the global process of militarization. Since a large share of public expenditure goes to international armament markets, private persons are militarized, although they are neither explicit Army agents nor workers in armament-producing companies (Enloe, 2016). Historically, this militarization is never neutral at the individual level; it is based on a gender concept. Within this framework, though women are also playing many important roles, they are used within systems of legitimate violence used to control society. They are not militarized of their own free will, but they are used to cheer up men and to make them feel comfortable during and after wars, to produce the next generations of defenders, and, last, to take the place of men in the Army when there are not enough of them.

Similarly, connecting gendered representation and political rights seems to be the best way to revisit the construction of women's personal and social strategies. Historically, states focused on men's enlistment in compulsory military service. They gave women civil rights. Women's direct access to the Army being limited, they themselves try to find the means to obtain their rights as women citizens. One evidence of this is French women joining the ranks of the Resistance during the German Occupation. This movement of women led to the recognition of economic and political equality between the sexes. In 1944, French women won the right to vote and to be elected. It is a fact that militarization strengthens the new political power of women who become actual citizens and enter the political realm.

Thus, a dual motion is at work: women who are militarized due to the policies of various countries also take part in the militarization process, they make it exist. Based on this observation, I was then able to question the role of women who, due to their marriage to a soldier, are involved in the Army. Clearly, they are then inspired to adopt the values and principles of the Army, to share them personally and within the family (Lysak, 2016). Thus, the contribution of wives to the construction and evolution of the profession of servicemen is evident in armies of the contemporary world. This role continues to grow and must be taken into consideration by Army sociologists. Therefore, considering the situation of military wives, it seems appropriate that in its development strategy, the Army should recognize the role of women whose presence in the military is not established by a professional contract, but by another covenant—that of marriage with a serviceman.

References

Avril, C. (2003). Les compétences féminines des aides à domicile. In F. Weber, S. Gojard, and A. Gramain (eds), *Charges de famille. Dépendance et parenté dans la France contemporaine* (pp. 187–207). Paris: La Découverte.

Beghiti-Mahut, S. (2015). Le conflit vie professionnelle/vie privée et la satisfaction: cas des conjoints de militaires navigants. *Revue Interdisciplinaire Management, Homme(s) & Entreprise*, 18, 3–20.

Bergere, M. (2004). Épouser un gendarme ou épouser la Gendarmerie? Les femmes de gendarmes entre contrôle matrimonial et contrôle social. *Clio. Histoire, femmes et sociétés*, 2(20), 7.

Enloe, C. H. (1983). *Does Khaki Become You?: The Militarisation of Women's Lives*. Boston: South End Press.

Enloe, C. H. (2016). *Faire marcher les femmes au pas? Regards féministes sur le militarisme mondial*. Paris: Solanghets.

Greenhouse, E. (2013). The perfect Nazi bride. *The New Yorker*, September 27. www.newyorker.com/culture/culture-desk/the-perfect-nazi-bride.

Hayek, F. (1944). *The Road to Serfdom*. Chicago: University of Chicago Press.

High Military Condition Assessment Committee (2017). Thematic report of the High Military Condition Assessment Committee (*Rapport thématique de Haute Comité d'Évaluation de la Condition Militaire*). Paris: HCECM.

Hochschild, A. R. (1983). *The Managed Heart: Commercialization of Human Feeling*. Berkeley, CA: University of California Press.

Ministry of Defense (1942). Instruction n°27296.1/gend of 6 October, 1942 relative to the marriage of soldiers of the Gendarmerie. Article III: Special Provisions, SHGN, Memorial of the Gendarmerie, 18ad.61.

Jakubowski, S. (2013). La transformation de l'institution militaire: entre logique organisationnelle, rapport au marché et ré-institutionnalisation par le politique. *Res Militaris*, 3(3), 1–18.

Lysak, E. (2015). *L'égalité professionnelle entre les hommes et les femmes dans l'armée russe*. Dissertation (master's thesis 1 in Sociology), Moscow: Collège universitaire français.

Lysak, E. (2016). *Femme de militaire: mère de famille ou soldat sans contrat?* Dissertation (master's thesis 2). Paris: École des hautes études en sciences sociales.

Mathers, J. (2000). Women in the Russian Armed Forces: a marriage of convenience? *Minerva: Quarterly Report on Women and the Military*, 18, 3–4.

Moelker, R., Andres, M., Bowen, G., and Manigart, P. (2015). *Military Families and War in the 21st Century: Comparative Perspectives*. London: Routledge.

Nepochetaia, N. (2004). *Gendernyi kontrakt zhenshchin na voennoi sluzhbe v Rossii: Istoriia I sovremennost v sotciologicheskom osveshchenii*. Saint-Pétersbourg: unpublished Phd thesis.

French Ministry of Defence (2010). Report on soldiers and their families (*Rapport sur des militaires et leur famille*). Paris: SGA/DRH-MD.

Rosenwein, B. H. (2015). *Generations of Feeling: A History of Emotions*. Cambridge: Cambridge University Press.

Sigmund, A.-M. (2004). *Les femmes du IIIe Reich*. Paris: JC Lattès.

Singly, F. de and Chaland, K. (2002). Avoir le "second rôle" dans une équipe conjugale. Le cas des femmes de préfet et de sous-préfet. *Revue française de sociologie*, 43, 127–158.

Thiolay, B. (2012). *Lebensborn, la fabrique des enfants parfaits: ces Français qui sont nés dans une maternité SS*. Paris: Flammarion.

White Paper on Defense and National Security (Livre blanc sur la défense et la sécurité nationale, LBDSN) (2013). Paris: Directorate of Legal and Administrative Information (Dila).

6 New families in the IDF

Toward diversity in family policies

Meytal Eran-Jona and Dotan Aviram

Introduction

After decades of interest in military families, and vast study exploring military families and the military's impact on spouse and children (Moelker, Andres, Bowen, and Manigart, 2015), we identify a gap in the literature and a lack of research about new forms of families and their encounter with the Armed Forces. Whereas most militaries think of the family in the traditional heteronormative way, mother, father, and children, living together under the same roof, the reality is different and changing. Divorcée families, single-parent families, cohabitation, and same-sex partners are only examples of new family forms that are constantly growing.

Advances in medical technologies and changes in social norms contribute to gradual change in family forms. Perhaps the most fascinating social phenomenon we are witnessing along the last decades is the way technology is changing the family. Getting pregnant and giving birth, which throughout history depended on two partners and a common pregnancy, changes. Technology allows men and women to have children without spouses. Same-sex couples that were doomed to be childless can give birth to children by *in vitro* fertilization and other techniques; women that suffer from health issues and cannot give birth can have a child through substitute mothers. The heteronormative relationship is no longer a precondition for having a biological child. Fertility technologies allow men and women to have children in different ways, using sperm donation, egg donation, substitute parents, and other means.

This research is located in the interface between "new" family forms and the military as a work organization. The research was conducted with cooperation from the IDF Advisor to the Chief of Staff on Gender Issues, and its findings were presented to the advisor, to support the IDF policy planning regarding gender and family issues.

Changes in marriage, parenting, and family life

We live in a time of unprecedented change regarding marriage, parenting, and family life (Abela and Walker, 2014; Staub, 2018). Half-a-century ago, the ideal or common family pattern in the Western democracies was the heterosexual family model. It includes a married man and woman committed to each other and to their children, living under the same roof. It was customary for the man to be the breadwinner, whereas the woman's role was to care for the home and the children. Since this family model was perceived to be the norm it was also embedded in legal arrangement, public policy, and popular culture (Toren, 2003; Luxton, 2011).

Since the middle of the twentieth century, we have witnessed social, economic, and technological processes that have influenced and changed the family structure. The feminist movement and the struggle for equal rights for women led, among other things, to more equality at home, in the workplace, and in society in general. These changes challenged the patriarchal model of family structure in which women's responsibility lies solely in the private sphere and increases women's economic and social independence. Moreover, increasingly, women's earnings have become a necessary part of family income (Abela and Walker, 2014).

The abovementioned processes led to changing roles of men and women combining work and family life. Although decades after the "feminist revolution" in the 1960s, in most cases the burden of care still falls on women, though men are taking up duties in family life and become more involved in childcare (Abela and Walker, 2014; Staub, 2018).

In addition, technological inventions such as the pill and other contraceptives enabled sexual freedom, and the feminist movement propagated the right for abortion. At the same time, technological developments that enabled birth without a spouse (such as *in vitro* fertilization and surrogacy) enabled both genders to become a parent as a single mom or dad or as a same-sex family.

Culturally, and following the changes described above, a number of other significant processes occurred. The ages at which men and women get married and the ages in which women give birth have increased (Pryor, 2014). In addition, the social taboos on divorce and separation of spouses have weakened, and the existence of single-parent families and cohabitation has become more socially acceptable (Noack, Bernhard, and Aarskaug, 2014). In later years, members of the LGBTQ community also began to struggle for their legal and social right to get married, to adopt children, and to recognize that raising children in a same-sex family does not lead to harmful consequences for children (Luxton, 2011; Patterson, Riskind, and Tornello, 2014).

Israel is a familial society with high fertility rates and strong state support for having children. It is one of the most advanced countries in fertility treatments and the state financially supports individuals who ask to become a parent (Luxton, 2011; Achdut, Sofer, and Shelach, 2007).

Although Israel is a conservative society, with a vast influence of religious Jews, the global processes described have influenced Israel and led in the recent decades to a greater diversity in family structures (Toren, 2003).

Divorce and separation

Up until the twentieth century, divorce was not a feature of daily life. When relationships broke down, economic, social, and emotional constraints kept many women locked in their marriage. Divorce was the privilege of the rich, of the clergy, and of men. Those women who did separate and form new partnerships were not able to divorce or to remarry. Only during the twentieth century did divorce become a real option in most countries. Nowadays, large numbers of children across the globe will experience parental separation, the remarriage or repartnering of their parents, and multiple transitions in family living arrangements (Abela and Walker, 2014; Pryor, 2014).

Rates of divorce in the Western world have climbed in the last 75 years. But, there are clear differences in marriage and divorce dynamics between the USA and Europe. In the USA, people marry more, marry younger, divorce more readily, and cohabit less than in other Western countries. The divorce rate (per 1000 population) is 3.5 in the USA, compared to: 2.8 in Denmark; 2.2 in the UK; 1.9 in Australia; 1.7 in Canada and 1.5 in France (Pryor, 2014). The divorce rates in Israel are relatively low, at 1.8, but on the rise (Nahir, 2016).

Evidence accumulated from around the world points to potential negative outcomes for children and their parents, such as economic hardship; continued parental conflict; multiple transitions and changes in household structures and living arrangements; the loss of parental relationships (most often with fathers); one or both partners being unable to make a satisfactory adaptation to the dissolution of the couple relationship; and failure to keep children informed about what is happening and to hear their voice (Abela and Walker, 2014).

Same-sex cohabitation and marriage

People in same-sex relationships are granted more or less equal legal rights and duties as people in heterosexual marriages in more and more countries. This trend started in Denmark in 1989, when so-called registered partnerships were legalized, and the other Nordic countries followed. Registered partnerships were also recognized in the Netherlands in 1998. With few exceptions, people in these registered partnerships have the same legal rights and duties as those in marriages (Noack, Bernhard, and Aarskaug, 2014).

Same-sex marriages have become legal in various Western democracies during the last decade-and-a-half: the Netherlands (2001), Belgium (2003), Canada and Spain (2005), Norway and Sweden (2009), Argentina, Portugal, and Iceland (2010), and all states in the USA (2015). Over 20 countries offer some kind of legal recognition other than marriage (Patterson, Riskind, and Tornello, 2014). In Israel, same-sex couples cannot be legally married and are facing multiple barriers to become parents (they cannot adopt a child and they cannot go through the surrogacy procedure in Israel, but have to go abroad).

Single-parent families

A single-parent family is defined as a household managed by one parent for himself and his children. In our research we focused on women who choose to have children alone without a spouse. In Israel, in the vast majority of cases, the head of the single-parent family is a woman who raises her children alone. For the most part, this group is also the weakest in socioeconomic terms (Achdut, Sofer, and Shelach, 2007).

New family structures and work organizations

Most of the academic research dealing with family and work issues deals with the work–life balance (or imbalance) and the employees' commitment to the organization (Beauregard and Lesley, 2009) from within the context of traditional families. These studies have found that employees report higher commitment to the organization when family-friendly policies are employed (Grover and Crocker, 1995). There are as yet few studies on single-parent families. A study conducted in Ireland about divorced fathers argues that since organizations perceive the family as a responsibility for mothers, fathers who head a single-parent family are not recognized, are not entitled the same rights, and are discriminated against both in the legal system and in state support systems (Mckeown, 2000). However, implications for same-sex families have hardly been studied in the context of work organizations and certainly not in the military context.

Military families

The heteronormative family was perceived by the IDF as a significant component in the state-building project. The ideal military family was a heteronormative household with the man being the breadwinner and the woman having sole responsibility for the private sphere (Eran-Jona, 2008). In accordance with this expectation, the IDF policy, which was expressed in the orders of the IDF General Staff, was written in this spirit. For example, only recently the IDF updated the order regarding pregnancy and parenting policy, stating that the husband can also replace his wife in maternity leave (General Staff Order 36.0406 "Benefits due to pregnancy and parenthood").

According to this approach, the research on family and military service also pertains mainly to heteronormative families. Most of the studies regarding military families were conducted in the American military. The families are perceived as a source of support for the soldiers and are supposed to have an effect on the willingness of those to continue their service. It was also claimed that family support from the Armed Forces contributes to more positive attitudes of soldiers toward the organization (McFadyen, Kerpelman, and Adler-Baeder, 2005).

In recent decades, Western Armed Forces studies examined questions of satisfaction with life in the Army, commitment to military life, identification with military life, and the impact of military service on children's outcomes and development (Moelker, Andres, Bowen, and Manigart, 2015). But the study of new families remains unresearched while changes in family structures in society as a whole are apparent.

Gay and lesbian service in the Armed Forces has been studied before, with a focus on three main aspects: the debate on "Don't Ask Don't Tell" policy in the

US Armed Forces (Belkin and Bateman, 2003); the difficulties gay soldiers face in a hyper-masculine institution (Belkin and Bateman, 2003; Burks, 2011); and aspects of masculine identity and the anti-gay culture within the Armed Forces (Kaplan, 2006). Nevertheless, we know little of the contemporary interface between the Armed Forces and same-sex families (Wesrcott and Sawyer, 2007; Cahill, 2009; Oswald and Sternberg, 2014; Smith and De Angelis, 2015).

The Israeli career personnel and the family

Unlike most contemporary Western democracies, the Israeli military is still based on the conscription model that includes universal compulsory service for all genders. A military career is seen as the continuation of the compulsory service for both men and women. Socially it is held in high esteem because of its national-ideological value, and is not seen as "just another job" (Moskos, 1988). Based on Moskos' theoretic work (1988), institutional and occupational characteristics exist side by side in the Israeli model of career service. This is especially true for combat officers. These officers who come from middle-class backgrounds in Israeli-Jewish society receive respect and social status because their job is perceived as of national importance. Thus, the Israeli case is both similar to and different from prevailing conditions in Western militaries.

Research questions

We were interested in what happens when the "old" hierarchal, bureaucratic, and "greedy" organization is confronted with diverse nontraditional new forms of families. Our research questions were as follows.

1 What is the proportion of "new" forms of families in the IDF?
2 What are the challenges in the encounter between the service members in "new" family forms and the military?
3 What is the military policy toward new families? And what are, if any, the gaps between the family needs and the organizational policies?

Methodology

We conducted 24 in-depth interviews with servicemen and women of three types of families; an overview of the interviewees by family type is presented in Table 6.1.

The research population includes mainly officers (only one female NCO), in the rank of major to colonel, with one to three children. Because the population was hard to target, the snowball sampling method was used. Three different questionnaires were prepared to examine the three groups. All interviews were conducted by the authors (the principle investigators, at the time officers in the IDF Behavioral Sciences Center). All interviews were recorded and transcribed.

We also conducted four interviews with HR managers, responsible for the HR policy design and implementation, both at the Human Resource Branch and at

Table 6.1 Overview of interviewees by family type

	Overall interviewees	*Number of women*	*Number of men*	*Number of children per interviewee*	*Military rank*
Same-sex	8	5	3	1 to 3	Major
Single mothers by choice	8	8	---	1	Major to lieutenant colonel
Divorced	8	6	2	1 to 3	NGO, major to colonel

the Chief of Staff Advisor on Gender Issues, the office that is in charge for the policy regarding gender and family aspects in the IDF. The interviews were analyzed using qualitative methodologies, based on Grounded Theory (Denzin and Lincoln, 1998).

In addition, we examined all the military orders and instructions that address parenthood and family issues and look at the changes implemented in the Ordinance during the past few years.

"New" forms of families in the IDF

Answering the first question proved difficult since social change has not yet been formalized in the bureaucratic system. Thus, within the IDF official registry system, only four types of marital status can be reported: single, married, divorced, or widowed. No other possibility exists in the official manpower registration system. There was no indication of family type of service members that were not officially married, such as same-sex couples that cannot be married officially in Israel or couples who lived in cohabitation without marriage. Therefore we used the available data to answer the question, using an estimation.

Since the IDF is based on compulsory service, there are many young soldiers that serve for a couple of years, in the draft (the obligatory basic service was at the time of the research 24 months for women and 30 for men, and it is now changing). The take-off for the career is not set; therefore, we decided to look at personnel age 27 and up, since at this age most people are already on a career track. The total number of career soldiers aged 27 and up reflects a masculine organization. The proportion of career women is 18 percent, whereas men constitute 82 percent of the whole (most service men and women are young, since age 45 is the average retirement age).

Examining personnel's marital status, the data reflects a very "familial" pattern, since most career personnel age 27 and up are married (77.5 percent overall; male marriage rates are slightly higher than female rates: 78.3 percent compared to 74.3 percent). Almost one-fifth are single and only 2.5 percent are divorced (Table 6.2).[1]

Divorcée families were the only group that we can easily identify in the official military data set. It constitutes 2.5 percent of the military personnel; most of them

Table 6.2 Military personnel age 27+ by gender and family status, total IDF military population (2016)

	Women (%)	*Men (%)*	*Total (%)*
Married	74.3	78.3	77.5
Single	21.5	19.4	19.8
Divorce	3.8	2.16	2.5
Widow/er	0.25	0.08	0.1

(83 percent) have children. In order to find the other "new" families, we looked inside the "single" category in the data set and checked how many single personnel are also parents. The overall singles (age 27 and up) constitute 19.8 percent of the personnel; only 1.12 percent of the overall personnel are single with children. The number of children per single person varies. The data presented in Table 6.3 present the fluctuation of children in single-parent families. Most single moms have one child (73 percent) compared to half of the single dads. But there are also single service members with two to five children.

The group of single men and women with children points to the existence of various family structures that are not "traditional" among the career soldiers: couples living in cohabitation, sole mothers and fathers (who have brought a child into the world alone), single-parent families who have children and live in various cooperative arrangements, and heteronormative couples that choose to live together in alternative arrangements that are not recognized by Israeli law as formal marriage. All these family structures are "hidden" under this category, building on the manpower registration system. We are not able to distinguish between the groups. For comparison, the estimate rate of LGBTQ personnel in the US army is 2 percent (Smith and De Angelis, 2015). Based on these data we estimate that "new" families in the IDF constitute about 3–4 percent of the overall military families, a number equal to hundreds of families (2.5 percent divorced; 1.12 percent single with children).

Table 6.3 Single personnel age 27+ by number of children and gender, total IDF military population (2016)

	Women (%)	*Men (%)*
Single +1–4	100	100
Single +1	73	54
Single +2	21	29
Single +3	6	13
Single +4	--	4

"New families" and the military

The second research questions was: what are the challenges in the encounter between the service members in "new family" forms and the military? To answer this question we will discuss a number of key issues.

Same-sex families

Five men and three women were interviewed. All of them had children in partnership with the current spouse (in various arrangements). From their stories we learn that the transition to parenthood is a challenge that concerned the transition itself, the relationship, and the organizational context. However, the interviews also raised unique issues for same-sex couples in general, and their military career in particular, which we will discuss.

First of all, the interviewees define the stage of "outing" as a significant stage in which they declared to the world, their family members, and themselves their sexual orientation. This stage involved giving up the dream of a heterosexual\"normative" family.

Both men and women reported a personal difficulty in accepting their sexual orientation vis-à-vis the social and personal costs that this preference may charge the individual at the personal, family, and social level. Some noted attempts to "test" and challenge their preference for members of the same sex, and spoke about years of soul-searching until they recognized and accepted it. Those difficulties reflect the conservative nature of the Israeli society, where homosexuality is the object of ridicule and shame in the eyes of many people.

Another issue that was raised is related to parenthood. The interviewees raised a sensitive issue that they were dealing with within their relationship, the question of: Whose child is it? This issue was raised without being asked about it. It reflects the uniqueness of these arrangements as in those families only one spouse can be the biological parent and not both. This situation comprises both legal and emotional complexities; it raises concerns and questions mainly to the person who is not the biological parent, whose status in the children's life is not clear (for example, what will happen to his/her relationship with the child in case of separation from the spouse who is the only biological parent?).

This unique reality can cause a desire of both partners to have their own biological child. For women, the issue is less difficult since both mothers can (theoretically) have children by themselves. For men, it is more complicated since they need a woman to make it happen (whether it is a friend they choose to have a child with, or it is a surrogate mother abroad).

All other issues that same-sex couples raised in the interviews were very similar to those raised by heterosexual families. It was interesting to find among these couples an unequal division of labor at home that sometimes creates tension between the couples (though the division of labor at home was presented to us as a decision that the couple made together). In most cases, the spouse who took on the role of the main caregiver (the "mother") was the one that is not serving in the military. We cannot generalize to the overall population, but the servicemen and women in same-sex families that we met invested more heavily in the career and took on the role of the "father" (like in heterosexual families; Eran-Jona, 2008). In this respect the greedy character of the military seems gender-blind. Whether you are in a same-sex relationship or not, the IDF expects a total commitment of the uniformed partner leaving the care for the children to the primary homemaker. Thus a traditional division of labor is forced upon non-traditional "new families" as well as upon "old family" types.

However, unlike heterosexual couples, we find that in those families, the division of roles at home was more flexible, meaning that both spouses can switch between roles, alternately adopting the mother role, which takes greater responsibility for family work, or the father role, whose career takes precedence. This flexibility seems to facilitate work-life balance in those families.

We also learned that the encounter between same-sex couples and the IDF as an organization is multifaceted. Although there is no structural mechanism of discrimination, nor any overt negative attitudes against homosexuals based on their sexual orientation and lifestyle, the service of homosexuals in the IDF is not always accepted as "normal." Prejudice and discrimination still exist in people's attitudes toward them. It was discussed as characteristic of combat units that are known for their masculine or macho culture and it was also there when people talked about keeping "the secret" from their colleagues and commanders.

Nevertheless, the culture of the rear units, the non-combat headquarters units, is perceived by these servants to be more diverse and tolerant, and even in some cases "gay-friendly."

We found that in general, men experience greater difficulties with their colleagues and commander regarding their sexual orientation. Their sexuality appears to be more challenging for the organizational culture and the perceptions of other soldiers and commanders than the sexuality of lesbian women, which seems to be less threatening. This experience may be related to the fact that the women interviewed served in non-combatant units; that their character is more "civilian" in a way.

The last significant point that was raised by many interviewees was the economic difficulty involved in the process of childbirth, which is more complex for those couples (especially for men) and requires the use of new birth technologies, which are costly.

While the transition to parenthood poses an economic challenge for families in general, the economic cost of becoming a parent is much higher for many same-sex couples. This is the case especially when using surrogate mothers. The procedure is long, very expensive, and has economical and emotional implications. To have a child by a surrogacy procedure is possible for Israeli couples only abroad. The basic cost is about $60,000, and it requires the couple to spend weeks and sometimes months abroad. In some cases, it may take several surrogacy attempts.

Single-mother families (by choice)

We interviewed eight single mothers, who all made the decision to become a mother without a partner when they were in their forties. Career-wise, this is very late, since the average military career ends at the age of 45. For these women, it is the last chance to become mothers, close to the end of their reproductive age (knowing that the status of mother is extremely important in the Israeli-Jewish society).

The findings indicate that being a single mother in the military is a tough mission. It is clear that the demands of military service and military culture, which are masculine in nature and greedy in their demands in their demands, create many difficulties for single moms. Those difficulties are intensified by the fact that they do not have a partner who shares with them the burden of raising children as well as the resulting economic implications.

A major difficulty that was raised by single mothers was to give away the "fantasy" of a "normative" family. All the interviewees talked about their dream of finding a partner, marrying, and having children together, as everyone else does. Giving up this fantasy is described as an emotionally difficult decision. But as we learn from the interviews, this decision also includes a heavy price in terms of their career. It was found that the choice to become a single mom involves not only giving up the fantasy of a having "normal" family, but also giving up the dream of success in their military career. In a demanding organization that rewards workers who are willing to work around the clock and give up family life, mothers are perceived as less devoted to the organization and single moms are valued as less dedicated and less "worthy" of promotion.

As a sole parent, responsibility for the child lies on their shoulders, without a partner to share it. The choice and responsibility to raise a child alone comes with several challenges:

- the *economic* responsibility and the economic burden of raising a toddler;
- the *emotional* challenge of coping alone with fears, illnesses, and making all decisions alone;
- the *organizational-employment* challenge of combining motherhood with a career in a demanding organization without a partner that will share the burden of parenting, and
- the *social* challenge of being confronted with negative views from the social and family environment

One of the most prominent experiences of single mothers was the combination of loneliness and stress. The experience of loneliness is embedded in their personal and familial situation. Moreover, the experience of loneliness and the challenge of parenting adds to a stressful experience that results from a combination of working in a demanding organization and caring for a young child with many needs. Furthermore, the difficulty of coping with the economic challenge of being a sole breadwinner was prominent among this group of women. Since the family expenditure in Israel is relatively high (mainly the housing), some women were forced to give up their past activities or change their way of life in order to converge to the new budget. Some seek support from the family (mainly from the parents, if they can help).

Divorcée families

We interviewed eight divorced personnel, six women and two men, all of whom had children. The findings indicate that there is vast diversity among these servants in the way they experienced their divorce as well as in their experience of the interface with the organization since their divorce; we found differences in the personal experience following the divorce, its causes, and variation in the relationship with the former spouse, the number of children, and their needs, which affected both the way they cope with the divorce and their experience in the organization.

A common feature we found among divorced personnel we interviewed was that all of them experienced divorce as a (normative) crisis of family transition, which happened during their military service. It puts stress on the whole family and creates a need to develop a new equilibrium over time. It has an impact on both parents and children on many levels: emotional, legal, economic, and familial (Ahrons, 1980). Common difficulties that the interviewed women and men experienced were loneliness, the need to take care of the children, and the need to continue their intensive career, without the support from a spouse, physically and emotionally. Alongside the difficulties, there were those who described the divorce as a positive experience, as an opportunity to start over, to take over their own lives, to take care of themselves, and to become a better parent.

At the organizational level, there was no uniform pattern of how the divorce affected individual life in the organization, nor how the organization accepted it. Some felt that the divorce was the key to the organization's recognition of the needs of the family, and that they increased their legitimacy to consider family considerations. Others described the organization as blind to their needs and experienced difficulties in handling their new family status.

In this context, it is worth mentioning the difficulty that arose for divorced men whose children are not under their legal custody. It was claimed that the commanders do not express flexibility and do not take into account those divorced personnel who, despite the fact that the child is not in their custody, are obligated to take care of them more frequently than before.

Overall, the situation of divorced men and women is not perceived by the interviewees themselves or by the organization as unique (perhaps because it is becoming more common in the overall society). The findings indicate that there is no specific organizational policy with regard to divorcees, and the attitudes of commanders to the subject depends on their personal perspectives and personality. It seems that the only issue that gets special organizational attention is custody arrangements, which have legal validity, and are usually supported by commanders.

Thus, the well-being of divorced service men or women depends on the commanders; his/her sensitivity and his/her attitude to the subject is what creates the difference for individuals' work-life balance.

Changing the organizational policy toward diverse forms of families

The interviews with the human resource personnel revealed a distinct gap between the IDF as a bureaucratic system and the IDF as a cultural system. The organization—the bureaucratic system—has changed much and many efforts by the IDF Chief of Staff Advisor for Gender Issues and the HR branch have led to policy changes that help to meet the needs of diverse families and individuals. Following up on those efforts, during the last years, the IDF has implemented a series of new policy changes addressing parenthood in diverse family structures.

One of the important steps in this direction that is relevant for single moms was recognizing a new family status, a status of "an independent parent," meaning an individual who is a parent without a spouse. The decision to adapt this new status emphasizes the understanding that these families have special needs. Independent parents received special attention and benefits; for example, if they serve in an "open" unit (where they come home every day) they are released from the duties that require them to stay in the unit overnight (for example, commander shifts that all other officers have to do).

Moreover, a new order that was lawfully approved in 2015 entitles couples who are not married the same rights that married couples have. Another policy change was the implementation of the "mother working hours" as an option for fathers as well, meaning they could shorten their working hours along the first years of infantry. Fathers and mothers are entitled to work an hour less every day until their smallest child is 5 years old. Another new order allows fathers to take paternity leave during the first six weeks after birth.

But, despite the great progress, it seems that in many ways the organizational policy precedes the organizational culture. We found that alongside the "bureaucratic system" there is another system that influences those service men and women, which we call the "cultural system," and here the story is different. Many interviewees claim that the military finds it very difficult to digest the diverse family forms; it seems that those "new" forms pose a threat to the existing organizational order.

Even though this was not said clearly, the impression that emerged from all the interviews we conducted was,that the military culture is still biased against LGTBQ persons and homophobia still exists in individual perceptions. Moreover, the gender regime in the military is preserved. Despite the change in IDF policy divorced men are not rushing into "mother working hours" and sole mothers are still measured and promoted by the hours they work, and pay a double price for being a mother: giving up both the dream of a normative family and the dream of being promoted to a higher rank.

Conclusion and discussion

The findings show that those serving in the IDF aged 27 and over are usually men, most are married (78 percent), and only a minority (3–4 percent) live in "new family" forms. The "new family" forms we met face unique challenges. For single mothers, the main challenge was emotional and economic, and their parenthood hampers advancement in their careers. In same-sex families, most of the family burden falls on the parent who does not serve in the military, and the main challenges facing the organization were in handling prejudices and struggling with financial difficulties arising from attempted parenthood. Divorced families were all going through a personal crisis and they needed the commander's support and flexibility on reconciling work and family responsibilities.

Our findings reveal what happens when a progressive and attentive HR policy meets a conservative organizational culture. The human resource managers we interviewed were all gender-sensitive and attentive to the needs of new families and they dealt (for a while, before our study took place) with adapting the military's policy to the needs of diverse families and parents.

Most gaps that we have identified along the research were taken under consideration by the Advisor for Gender Issues, which implemented the necessary policy changes almost immediately. But, while admiring the speed with which the IDF adopted a new policy, we discovered an interesting finding that originally did not belong to the core of the study. The efficiency and speed at which a new policy was adopted to help diverse parents and families contradicted the organizational culture, which still has difficulty in accepting differences.

The model of the "ideal servant" has not changed; it remains a man, free of family obligations (usually passed onto his wife) who is required to devote all his time and even his life to the organization (Eran-Jona, 2008). Deviation from this model, for reasons of commitment to the family (in any family model), is costly to the individual. Costs are expressed mainly in terms of promotion. Thus, even if the policy has been updated in a way that helps individual mothers cope with economic or organizational difficulties, organizational culture perceives them as less worthy, as less devoted, and imposes a halt on promotion. In the same way, the official policy supports the needs of gay fathers who want to have a child by a surrogacy procedure, but the organizational culture makes some of them hide their sexual identity out of fear that it will harm their career.

The gap between a bureaucratic system that enhances diversity and moves ahead with the spirit of the time and the conservative individual perceptions and organizational culture indicates, on the one hand, that the organization has taken the initiative to accept the variance, and on the other hand that there is still a long way to go. Policy change is the first step in accepting families of different types, but not a sufficient step. The next step toward inclusion of diverse workers will be to adopt a point of view that does not see their family status or sexual orientation as an obstacle to advancement to senior ranks and challenging positions.

Note

1 All data presented in this chapter were retrieved from the IDF official registration in August 2016. We want to thank the Israeli Defense Forces for the support in this study.

References

Abela, A. and Walker, J. (2014). Global changes in marriage, parenting and family life: an overview. In A. Abela and J. Walker (ed.), *Contemporary Issues in Family Studies*. New York: John Wiley & Sons.

Achdut, N., Sofer, M., and Shelach, S. (2007). *The Program for the Integration of Single Parents in the Labor Market: A Collection of Articles*. Israel: Research and Economics Administration, Ministry of Industry, Trade and Labor (in Hebrew).

Ahrons, C. (1980). Divorce: a crisis of family transition and change. *Family Relations*, 29(4), 533–540.

Beauregard, A. and Lesley, H. (2009). Making the link between work-life balance practices and organizational performance. *Human Resource Management Review*, 19, 9–22.

Belkin, A. and Bateman, G. (2003). *Don't Ask, Don't Tell: Exploring the Debates on the Gay Ban in the US Military*. Boulder, CO: Lynne Rienner Publishers.

Burks, D. J. (2011). Lesbian, gay, and bisexual victimization in the military: an unintended consequence of "Don't Ask, Don't Tell"? *American Psychologist*, 66(7), 604–613.

Cahill, S. (2009). The disproportionate impact of antigay family policies on Black and Latino same-sex couple households. *Journal of African American Studies*, 13, 219–250.

Denzin, N. K. and Lincoln, Y. S., (1998). *Collecting and Interpreting Qualitative Materials*. Thousand Oaks, CA: Sage Publications.

Eran Jona, M. (2015). Organizational culture and military families: the case of combat officers in the Israeli Defense Forces. In R. Moelker, M. Andres, G. Bowen, and P. Manigart (eds), *Military Families and War in the 21st Century: Comparative Perspectives*. London: Routledge.

Eran-Jona, M. (2008). *In Between Military, Family and Gender*. Doctoral dissertation, Tel Aviv University of Missouri, Tel Aviv.

Grover, S. L. and Crocker, K. J. (1995). Who appreciates family-responsive human resource policies: the impact of family-friendly policies on the organizational attachment of parents and non parents. *Personal Psychology*, 48, 271–288.

Kaplan, D. (2006). *The Men We Loved: Male Friendship and Nationalism in Israeli Culture*. New York: Berghahn Books.

Luxton, M. (2011). *Changing Families, New Understandings*. Ottawa: The Vanier Institute of the Family.

Nahir, S. (2016). *Total Divorce Rate in Israel*. Working Paper Series no. 98. Jerusalem: Central Bureau of Statistics – Department of Demography and Census (in Hebrew).

McFadyen, J. M., Kerpelman, J. L., and Adler-Baeder, F. (2005). Examining the impact of workplace support: work-family fit and satisfaction in the US military. *Family Relations*, 54, 131–144.

Noack, T., Bernhardt, E., and Aarskaug W. K. (2014). Cohabitation or marriage? Contemporary living arrangements in the West. In A. Abela and J. Walker (eds), *Contemporary Issues in Family Studies*. New York: John Wiley & Sons.

Moelker, R., Andres, M., Bowen, G., and Manigart, P. (eds) (2015). *Military Families and War in the 21st Century: Comparative Perspectives*. London: Routledge.

Mckeown, K. (2000). *Families and Single Fathers in Ireland*. Dublin: McKeown, Social and Economic Research Consultant.

Patterson C., Riskind R. G., and Tornello S. (2014). Sexual orientation, marriage and parenthood: a global perspective. In A. Abela and J. Walker (eds), *Contemporary Issues in Family Studies*. New York: John Wiley & Sons.

Moskos, C. and Wood, F. (1988). *The Military: More than Just a Job?* Washington, DC: Pergamon-Brasseys.

Oswald, R. F. and Sternberg, M. M. (2014). Lesbian, gay, and bisexual military families: visible but legally marginalized. In S. MacDermid Wadsworth and D. Riggs (eds), *Military Deployment and its Consequences for Families: Risk and Resilience in Military and Veteran Families*. New York: Springer.

Pryor, J. (2014). Marriage and divorce in the Western world. In A. Abela and J. Walker (eds), *Contemporary Issues in Family Studies*. New York: John Wiley & Sons.

Smith, D. and De Angelis, K. (2015). *Setting the Research Agenda: LGB Families in the US Military*. Paper presented at the 110 ASA Conference, Chicago.

Staub, A. (ed.) (2018). *The Routledge Companion to Modernity, Space and Gender*. New York: Routledge.

Toren, N. (2003). Tradition and transition: family change in Israel. *Gender Issues*, 21(2), 60–76.

Wesrcott, K. and Sawyer, R. (2007). Silent sacrifices: the impact of Don't Ask, Don't Tell on lesbian and gay military families. *Duke Journal of Gender Law and Policy*, 14, 1121–1139.

Part II

Organization, soldier, and military family

Negotiating the tensions

7 I just want to be done with it!

Estonian conscripts negotiating the tensions between military, family, and personal agendas

Kadri Raid, Kairi Kasearu, and Tiia-Triin Truusa

Introduction

In the last decades, the underlying social processes in Western societies have been dominated by individualization, marketization, and de-institutionalization. Beck and Beck-Gernsheim (2002) have pointed out that with the increasing individualization in society, freedom of choice gives everyone a chance to design one's own lifecourse, but at the same time it means that more and more aspects of life must be planned, negotiated, and personally effectuated, as shown by the changes in the main life transitions. Young people remain living with their parents for longer (Mencarini et al., 2010). They start families and have children later (Mills et al., 2011). The proportion of young people who do not study or work increased in the EU during the financial and economic crisis (Eurostat, 2017). All of these changes demonstrate that the lifecourse is less institutionalized, and that the main classical institutions—the family, the educational system, and the labor market—are more flexible than ever before. However, there are some institutions in Estonia, such as the military, which could still be described as relatively stable, hierarchical, and institutionalized. Nolte (2003) has compared the European military law systems and concluded that across countries, there are great variations in civilianization of the Armed Forces. One of the clear and visible differences is compulsory military service. In the post-Cold War era, a large majority of countries in Europe abolished or suspended conscription, but the changes in geopolitical threat perception and difficulties with recruitment into an all-volunteer force have led Lithuania and Sweden to reinstate conscription.

In this chapter, we will use the "triad" (this volume, Chapter 1) as our theoretical framework to look at the individual in the military, and his relationships with the family and society. Our triangle relates to three levels: the micro, the meso, and the macro level. We argue that during the last decades, the society and family have changed and become more fluid but the military has stayed quite traditional. In other words, two sides of our triangle have moved toward de-institutionalization but one has remained institutionalized. In this changed situation, it is important to understand how conscripts in contemporary Estonia are adapting to being conscripts during their compulsory military service period. Family and societal expectations play an important role in successfully completing the conscription.

We combine this theoretical conceptualization with approaches from the lifecourse theory and the ideas of structural ambivalence. We follow the notion that contradictions in norms, values, or statuses can lead to ambivalence. In this case, the contradictions for conscripts may emerge at different levels as the flexibility or inflexibility of institutions can be conflicting, limiting, or competing; for instance, if we look at the classical approach of the family and military as greedy institutions (Segal, 1986), we observe institutions competing for time and attention of individuals. Also contradictions emerge in one's personal life plans and the structural opportunities and obligations that one has; for example, compulsory military service competes with the contemporary drive to continuously add new skills and knowledge to one's life portfolio. Arguably the military could be considered as adding to one's skills, also usable in one's civilian life, which is something that we will also touch upon in our chapter. In both cases, the contradictions in norms, values, or statuses can cause the ambivalence.

The purpose of this chapter is to analyze how young men in Estonia adapt in an environment where tensions are created between conflicting expectations for agency in directing and sequencing life events and the obligation to fulfill their military duty. In order to do that we raise the following research questions.

1 How do conscripts elaborate on their own agency upon entering the compulsory military service?
2 How is agency of the recruits associated with satisfaction in the middle of the conscription period?
3 How is satisfaction with service influenced by the perceived support of family and other close relationships?

The mostly flexible triangle

In order to understand how Estonian conscripts are trying to negotiate the demands of fast-paced modern life, geared toward being in the right place at the right time to create opportunities for personal development and compulsory service, we developed this chapter based on lifecourse theory, a paradigm that guides research on human lives and studies phenomena at the nexus of development trajectories and social change. According to Elder Jr. et al. (2003), lifecourse theory has five general principles: (1) *The principle of life-span development*: human development and ageing are lifelong processes; (2) *The principle of agency*: individuals construct their own lifecourse through the choices and actions they take within the opportunities and constraints of history and social circumstances; (3) *The principle of time and place*: the lifecourse of individuals is embedded and shaped by the historical times and places they experience over their lifetime; (4) *The principle of timing*: the developmental antecedents and consequences of life transitions, events, and behavioral patterns vary according to their timing within a person's life; 5) *The principle of linked lives*: lives are lived interdependently and sociohistorical influences are expressed through this network of shared relationships. Lifecourse theory steers research away from age-specific studies toward the recognition of individual choice and decision making. It also enhances the understanding that human lives cannot be adequately represented when removed from relationships with significant others. Therefore, in the context of military service while studying conscription, it is also important to take into account conscripts' families and the overall societal context.

Traditionally, people's lifecourses have been quite standardized and people could rely upon certain rules in making decisions in their lives (Beck and Beck-Gernsheim, 2002). For instance, it was known that after reaching adult age and leaving school, people continued studies and/or went to work, found a life partner, got married, and then started a family. Conventionally, one had little freedom of choice and possibility to deviate from this rather well-established sequence of life events. Nowadays, the sequencing is less fixed; it has become normal for individuals to continually readjust the sequence of their life events according to the opportunities that emerge. For instance, after graduating, one does not have to decide directly what specialty to study or what job to look for. One may take time off and decide whenever one is ready. Or one may study one field and hold a job and later choose a different one. Due to these changes and structural constraints, such as high housing prices, young people today also live longer in the same household with their parents and do not become independent as soon as they have reached adulthood (Mencarini et al., 2010). This also means that they postpone starting their own family.

The de-institutionalized society amid conditions of globalization and individualization contains contradictory values. The institution of family has also changed. Traditional rules of ascription no longer determine the family bond. Beck and Beck-Gernsheim (2002) state that family and close relationships are becoming more of an elective relationship, an association of individual persons who each bring their own interests, experiences, and plans into the relationship and who each are subject to different controls, risks, and constraints. Therefore, it is, contrary to the past, necessary to devote much more effort into the solidarity of these different biographies. The question is how to hold the relationships together. The family bond thereby becomes more fragile and runs a greater risk of collapse. In this regard, the family has turned into a more elective relationship. That does not mean that relationships between members of family are less important. Balancing the relationships becomes the cornerstone of family solidarity. Elective relationships increase the need to constantly tend the bonds, helped along by the technologically augmented fast and easy ways of staying in contact, such as Facebook, Instagram, and other social media platforms. These trends bring along a certain degree of insecurity because the persistence of relationships can be harder to establish while being away from one's partner in an environment that restricts the use of personal time. Moreover, marriage and cohabitation by themselves are not institutions that guarantee lasting relationships. More important are the strength of the relationship and mutual trust.

In this changed situation, the institution of the military has remained much the same, despite the structural changes militaries have undergone. Armed forces still are strongly hierarchical, with external unifiers such as uniforms, insignia, and specific traditions. Military culture is also different from what is considered the norm in civil society, a culture that stresses such qualities as unity, discipline, and sacrifice (Rahbek-Clemmensen et al., 2012). Basic training in particular is considered to be the time when young men are stripped of their civilian selves and are encouraged, poked, and prodded into becoming soldiers. Fairly strict limitations are placed on personal freedoms and time. In Estonia, according to battalions' internal regulations, the conscripts have limited use of devices such as phones. Conscription and being away from the family and/or partner diminishes the possibilities to invest emotional capital in private relationships on a daily basis and, unless specifically promoted within the military system, they also have a harder time assembling a life portfolio.

In the context of conscription, literature recognizes the military as either a positive turning point or as a disruptive event in the lifecourse (Wilmoth and London, 2013). We argue that social influence and structural constraints play an important role in designing future conscripts' attitudes about conscription. In particular, the attitudes of close relationships such as family ties affect how conscription is perceived, especially if the compulsory nature of conscription limits the alternatives people have in their life. The planning and decision making of individuals, within the particular limitations of their world, can have important consequences for future trajectories (Elder Jr. et al., 2003). In lifecourse theory, the principle of timing lifecourse stresses that the same events or experiences may affect individuals in different ways depending on the moment they occur in the lifecourse (George, 1993). Moreover, the personal perception of the life event is influenced by how many are affected. This brings in the notion of social justice. In Estonia, for instance, approximately one-third of the male birth cohort is drafted (Kasearu, 2018). Furthermore, the very meaning of the event can change at different developmental stages (Wheaton, 1990). For example, it might be easier for a young person to become a conscript before entering the labor market because then he does not have to put his career on pause. The Estonian conscription system allows, to a certain extent, the planning of the specific time of when one wants to serve. Upon turning 17, one can apply to being drafted into service at a certain time period. For example, if one has decided to apply to a university but wishes to complete military service before studies, one can apply to do service at the most suitable time. The system is not perfect; it may happen that the recruit is not drafted at the time that he applied for.

As a society, Estonians value personal freedom, self-realization, and success; they also hold in high esteem patriotism and contributing to the nation and statehood. These principles are at odds and difficult to follow simultaneously because joining conscription means giving up one's personal freedom, habitual everyday life, and friends and family for an extensive period of time. Therefore, the attitudes of who we call "significant others" might contribute to making adaptation easier or harder for young people.

The ambivalence-inducing Estonian context

In Estonia, the conscript service period is either 8 or 11 months and by law all male citizens between the ages of 17 and 27 are called up for selection (Military Service Act, 2013). However, not all call-up selectees will end up doing their military service. A large percentage will be exempted from military service for various reasons, first and foremost for medical reasons. Those permanently exempted make up 24 percent and those temporarily exempted comprise 44 percent of selectees. Also, the attrition rate during service is quite high, about 20 percent (Defence Resources Agency, 2016). It must be added that health reasons are almost the only way to get exempted from military service, because Estonia, unlike for example Norway and Sweden, does not practice a soft version of conscription where the theoretical obligation serves more as a prompt to volunteering (Österberg, 2017). The discussion in Estonia has focused on the health of conscripts, almost disregarding other issues such as the support of the family and the changing dynamics of civilian society. Estonia, in a situation where large percentages of birth cohorts are not drafted, might be faced with unintentional polarization of society. Interestingly enough, the public is very supportive of conscription: in 2017 in Estonia, 63 percent considered it to be absolutely necessary and 29 percent said it was relatively necessary (Kivirähk, 2017b). However, at the same time there are no structural incentives for completing the conscription service. Employers do not consider it to be an advantage if one has completed one's conscription period. Universities do allow for one additional academic year off, but do not offer credit points or other types of credits. One of the possible reasons that conscription is considered important might be as a good chance for young men to learn skills that are also important in civilian life, for instance, first aid, time planning, and self-discipline. However, it probably has more to do with the idea that the military is seen as a rite of passage that turns boys to men. However, the support is highest among those over the age of 60 (over 83 percent). Among the youngest age group, those under the age of 30—those themselves subject to be drafted—the support is a little over 50 percent (Kivirähk, 2017a). Moreover, qualitative research points to ambivalent feelings among young men concerning their conscript service and from a personal point of view they say they are hard-pressed to see any personal value in it (Susi, 2017). This indicates that even when the overall public opinion about conscription is very supportive, young men themselves are not so much willing to participate. On the one hand, young men feel that it is their obligation to join as conscripts and society also expects them to do it. On the other hand, they feel that they have to give up their freedom. These kinds of mixed feelings are called ambivalence.

Robert K. Merton was one of the first scholars who brought the concept of ambivalence to sociology. Previously, this concept was mainly used in psychiatry and treated as a phenomenon that emerges on the individual level, meaning simultaneously held opposing feelings based on countervailing normative expectations and ideas about how individuals should act. Thus, the sociological approach to ambivalence points out that these "mixed feelings" are responses to structural social relations expressed with the ongoing negotiation of contradictions. It means that the sociological approach to ambivalence turns attention to the potential external or societal sources of ambivalence. According to Merton (1976: 5), ambivalence

> focuses on the ways which ambivalence comes to be built into the structure of social statuses and roles. It directs us to examine the processes in the social structure that affect the probability of ambivalence turning up in particular kind of role-relations.

Research methodology

A considerably important step to boost research on different issues concerning conscripts in the Estonian Defence Forces (EDF) took place in 2016; in cooperation with the Centre for Applied Studies of the Estonian Military College and the Centre of Excellence for Strategic Sustainability at the University of Tartu, a longitudinal research questionnaire for conscripts and reservists was designed. The survey is part of an ongoing human resources research project in the EDF. The questionnaire includes topics such as attitudes and experiences about conscription, opinions about society, security, and the EDF, individual values, health and health behavior, learning skills, and motivation.

All the conscripts are given the opportunity to participate in the survey. Conscripts can decline participation without any consequences to them or their service period. The survey is digital, using LimeSurvey software. The survey also includes a few open-ended questions, which were quite well responded to and brought up very different and important aspects of conscripts' reasons for volunteering for the service, and problems and fears concerning the service. The data were gathered via tablets in the units where conscripts train. Codes (different from their personal ID codes) were assigned to the conscripts, so that longitudinal data can be connected to the same person, but the person cannot be identified by the researchers. The data is analyzed anonymously.

The data used in this chapter is from the 2016–2017 pilot study that was carried out in two survey waves among the conscripts that started their service either in July 2016 (11-month service) or in October (8-month service). The waves of surveying during the service took place in the first month after basic training (month 3–4) and during the last month. The first wave of the longitudinal study had 2677 respondents (response rate 90 percent); whereas the second wave comprised of 2084 respondents (Table 7.1). The overall longitudinal sample from two waves is 1908. In our chapter, we combined quantitative and qualitative analysis. We use open-ended survey questions to analyze the individual agency and perceived support from the family as the conscripts describe it, and then predict how the conscript's agency and family support are related to his satisfaction with military service.

In the quantitative analysis of data we initially used descriptive analysis and then applied logistic regression analysis. For deeper interpretation of quantitative

Table 7.1 Estonian conscript survey 2016 pilot, data file V03[1]

	2016 July draft	*2016 October draft*	*Total*
Drafted	1785	1171	2956
Wave I (first month)	1600	1077	2677
Transferred into the reserves before wave II[2]	234	148	382
Longitudinal data waves I + II	1189	719	1908

[1]We have not included women in our data set as there were fewer than ten of them in the sample.

[2]§ 56: Termination of conscript service:

(2) The commander of the conscript service unit shall release the conscript from conscript service before the expiry of the conscript service term if during the conscript service period:

(1) the conscript does not comply with or temporarily does not comply the health requirements for a person liable to mandatory duty to serve in the Defence Forces on the basis of the decision of the medical commission of the Defence Forces. (Military Service Act, RT I, 10.07.2012, 1).

results, we added the descriptive quotes from qualitative thematic analysis of the open-ended questions. Open-ended answers were first coded line-by-line, then categorized through axial coding. We performed qualitative analyses in order to get a better understanding of individuals' motives and attitudes regarding conscription. Those conscripts who volunteered for the service were asked: "Why did you decide now to volunteer for the service?" The axial coding of qualitative data produced two main categories: "life planning" and "taking time out." Also, respondents were asked "What are your personal feelings and fears related to the service?" Axial coding of qualitative data revealed five categories that were of major concern for conscripts during the first wave of questioning: "adjustment to the military way of life," "health-related issues," "economic issues," and the two categories that were particularly strong were "identity" and "agency." The category of "adjustment to the military way of life" includes statements that describe the issues connected to the physical space, where conscripts share dorms and washrooms with many, do not have many opportunities to be alone, and feel that the institutional culture with its hierarchies is difficult to adapt to. "Health-related issues" concern fatigue, injuries, psychological stress, and accidents. "Economic issues" deal mainly with economic loss that conscripts experience due to the service period—either because they cannot continue working, are unable to meet debt payments, or are unable to support their family as is needed. The most prominent categories of "identity" and "agency" deal with adaptation issues that differ somewhat from adjustment to the military organization. These categories describe the personal changes taking place and also the feelings of loss of agency and the ability to take decisions concerning oneself.

For the quantitative analysis, we examined the following dependent and independent variables.

Dependent variable: Conscripts' satisfaction with their service in the third or fourth month (wave II) of service was gauged with a single-item measure.

Conscripts were asked to indicate how satisfied they are with their conscript service at the moment on a four-point categorical scale ranging from "not satisfied at all" to "completely satisfied." For the purposes of logistic regression analysis, we used the dummy variable (1 = satisfied; 2 = not satisfied).

Independent variables

Agency in drafting process. We created a new variable on the basis of whether the conscript applied for service (volunteered) or was drafted, and his attitude toward conscript service if it was on voluntary basis. On the basis of this information, we formed four types of conscripts: (1) "active volunteers" (AV) are conscripts who volunteered for the service and would volunteer as well if conscription was not compulsory; (2) "active non-volunteers" (NaV) are conscripts who volunteered for the service, but would not volunteer if the conscription was not compulsory; (3) "passive volunteers" (PV) are conscripts who were drafted, but would volunteer for conscription if military service was not compulsory; (4) "passive non-volunteers" (NpV) are conscripts who were drafted and who definitely would not volunteer for military service.

Perceived attitude of significant others. To assess perceived attitude of significant others, respondents were asked to indicate at the beginning of the service (wave I) how parents, partner (girlfriend, cohabiting partner, spouse), and colleagues/schoolmates feel about the fact that he/she was drafted (1= good; 4 = bad).

We control for a standard set of variables, which previous research suggested being associated with satisfaction in general. We asked for conscripts' *age* (indicated by three categories: 18–19 years old; 20–22 years old; and 23 and older) and *level of education* (indicated by three categories: basic (up to the ninth grade in general or vocational school), secondary (secondary education, vocational qualification on the basis of secondary education), tertiary (vocational maturity certificate, BA-level education, MA- or higher-level education). We distinguished four types of *main activities before service*: studying; working; studying and working; not studying, not working. The abovementioned variables were added to the model as categorical variables and the last category was chosen as the reference category. Finally, *ethnicity* was included as a dummy variable (Estonian, non-Estonian).

Results

The majority of conscripts are 20–22 years of age and most of them have obtained at least secondary education and have an Estonian ethnic background. Forty-five percent were employed before the service and one-third of the respondents were studying; another 14 percent combined work with study. According to agency in the drafting process, half of the conscripts belong to the group called "passive non-volunteers" (those who were drafted and would not volunteer), followed by "active non-volunteers" and "active volunteers." The smallest group is that of

Table 7.2 Descriptive statistics (N = 1600, those who completed both waves of the survey)

		N	*%*	*% satisfied*	*Cramer V*
Age	18–19 years old	466	29.1	66.1	0.054
	20–22 years old	961	60.1	60.1	
	23–27 years old	173	10.8	61.8	
Education	Basic	358	22.4	63.4	0.018
	Secondary	1122	70.1	61.9	
	Tertiary	120	7.5	60.0	
Ethnicity	Estonian	1366	85.4	63.9	0.092***
	Non-Estonian	234	14.6	51.3	
Main activity before service	Studying	534	33.4	61.4	0.031
	Working	714	44.6	62.6	
	Working and studying	223	13.9	59.6	
	Not studying, not working	129	8.1	65.9	
Agency in drafting process	Active volunteers	306	19.1	78.8	0.255***
	Active non-volunteers	320	20.0	57.2	
	Passive volunteers	168	10.5	84.5	
	Passive non-volunteers	806	50.4	53.0	
Perceived attitude of parents toward conscription	Well	709	44.3	72.6	0.241***
	Rather well	605	37.8	60.0	
	Rather bad	286	17.9	40.2	
Perceived attitude of partner (girlfriend, spouse, cohabiting partner)	No partner	566	35.4	65.4	0.184***
	Well	159	9.9	77.4	
	Rather well	261	16.3	70.1	
	Rather bad	614	38.4	51.6	
Perceived attitude of schoolmates or work colleagues	No schoolmates/colleagues or can't say what their attitude is	387	24.2	58.9	0.235***
	Well	299	18.7	74.6	
	Rather well	466	29.1	71.9	
	Rather bad	448	28.0	46.2	
Satisfaction with the service at three to four months of service	Satisfied	168	10.5		
	Rather satisfied	825	51.6		
	Rather not satisfied	413	25.8		
	Not satisfied	194	12.1		

"passive volunteers," who could be characterized as those who prefer conscription and would come to serve even if the service were on a voluntary basis, but currently they are drafted, which could be seen as limited agency. Table 7.2 indicates that most of the conscripts perceive that their parents evince a supportive attitude toward conscription but their partner's attitude is somewhat negative. A total of 62 percent of conscripts are satisfied with their service at the three- to four-month mark and 38 percent tend not to be.

Agency explained

Looking at the reasons behind volunteering, the "active non-volunteers" (NaV) emphasize the need to plan their life and choose the time of service themselves. They want to combine the service with their other life plans and try to arrange the sequence of their life events. "The time between high-school and university seemed the best possible time to do it [fulfil the conscription duty]; you can't really escape it anyway and before finding a job, it would have been a tad too inconvenient" (NaV). "The least painful time in between other life plans" (NaV). Beside work and studies, starting a family is also one of the life events seen as an obstacle to reconcile in the future the conscript service and family life. "It is better to do it while still young—no family that would have gotten in the way" (NaV).

Among "active volunteers" (AV) the same reasons are highlighted, but from a slightly different perspective. Namely, one reason is the uncertainty toward the future—they are not sure whether to continue study and what speciality to choose or start to find a job. In this case the conscript service could be seen as the possibility to take time off and make further plans. "Because I did not know if and what to study, or to find a job for a while" (AV). "Just graduated from a vocational school and wanted to be done with it (conscription) as soon as possible, also because I was not sure what to do with my life" (AV). These quotes illustrate the importance of agency as a factor also for "active volunteers," but at the same time agency is not applied with the intent to manage and combine the structural and institutional precepts in one's life. Rather it could be seen as a way to bridge the situation of personal uncertainty and lack of further life plans.

In the "active volunteers" segment, there are also some who see their future career in the military and perceive conscription as the first step toward becoming a professional military service member. "Decide to come myself, as in the future I see one of the possibilities for me to continue on at the Defence College" (AV).

If the volunteered conscripts' explanations for their own behavior could be seen as the performance of individual agency on the basis of different reasons, the non-volunteers perceive their situation as structurally forced and experience total loss of their agency. The perception of conscript service among non-volunteers could be described as the feeling of being pulled out from ordinary life. "Time stops during conscription. We are effectively separated from the rest of the world and this is scary. The rest of the world moves on while we are here" (PvN). "I had to decline several good job offers, hence my very negative and critical stance towards the defense forces" (PvN).

More precisely, there is a fear of losing personal freedom, arresting personal development, hindering the achievement life goals and forgoing qualifications. "I feared, and still fear, that I might be missing out on a lot; it is difficult to see how others are marching toward their goals and I have to take a break in reaching my objectives and goals" (NaV). "Difficult to look after my firm, from here. I will probably go bankrupt before I get out of here" (PvN). "I am a professional surfer, but if I can't train for 11 months then I can just start taking it as a hobby" (PvN). These quotes allow us to understand that even though conscription duty can be fulfilled as soon as possible after turning 18, it does not necessarily improve satisfaction with the service. This means that these conscripts have often taken on responsibilities and obligations prior to being drafted that they need to fulfill in a civilian world; they are seeing their conscript service as an event that is disruptive to their lifecourse and they just want to be done with it.

Association between agency and satisfaction with the service

Analysis of open-ended questions brought up the pattern of conscripts' agency in the beginning of the service. In the next step, we analyzed how agency is related to the conformation with the service measured by satisfaction. The satisfaction with service varies according to the type of conscript (Figure 7.1). The share of those satisfied is the highest among active volunteers and passive volunteers ($\chi^2 = 166.7$; $df = 9$, $p < 0.001$). It means that the effect of attitudes is stronger ($\chi^2 = 35.9$; $df = 3$; $p < 0.001$) compared to the effect of action ($\chi^2 = 310.9$; $df = 9$; $p < 0.001$). Namely, not depending on whether the individual was drafted or not, the actual attitude toward conscript service is significantly associated with satisfaction in the fourth month of service. The proportion of satisfied conscripts is highest among those who were not volunteers in their actions, but their attitude is very supportive toward conscript service. The share of satisfied conscripts is the lowest among "passive non-volunteers."

In Figure 7.2, the association between satisfaction, partner's attitude, and agency in the drafting process is described. Univariate ANOVA showed that there were differences in satisfaction according to the agency in drafting process

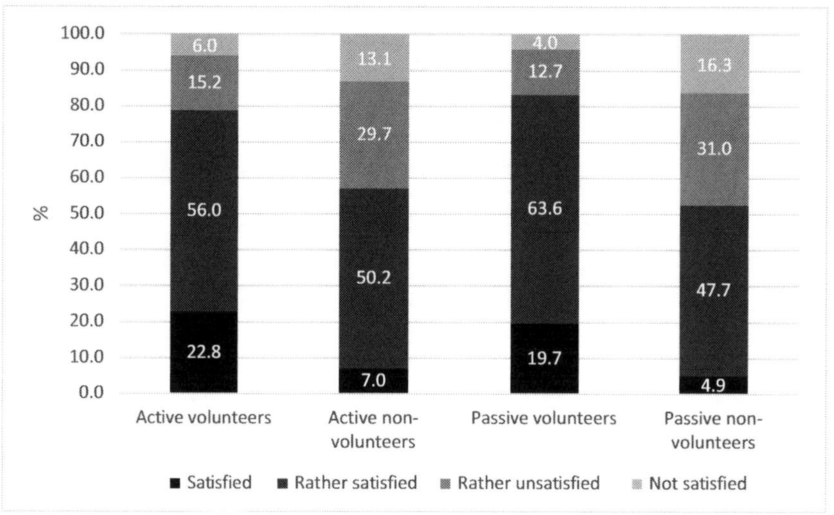

Figure 7.1 Satisfaction with the conscript service by form of drafting (individual agency regarding conscription), percent

(F (3, 1682) = 51.7; $p < 0.001$) and partner's attitude toward conscription (F (3, 1682) = 24.5; $p < 0.001$). However, the effect of attitude of a partner on the conscript's satisfaction with the service is only significant among "passive non-volunteers" (F (3, 866) = 11.5; $p < 0.001$). It clearly suggests that conscripts who are devoted to Army service in the first place give less weight to the attitude of a partner (girlfriend, spouse), or at least it is not related to their satisfaction with the service. The negative influence of partner's attitude is related to the fears that conscripts may have. One of the most persistent convictions circulating among conscripts was connected to close relationships. Many believed that they would break up with their girlfriend or boyfriend during the conscription service. This is illustrated quite well by quotes such as the following: "Over 70 percent of conscripts go through a breakup with their partner or girlfriend during conscription" (NpV). "There isn't enough time to connect with my girl and this may lead to a breakup. This has happened to most of my friends who have been through their conscript service" (NpV).

Logically enough, the few conscripts who had established their own families prior to being drafted expressed the most concern with regard to their family. "It is difficult for my life partner while I am on 'vacation' here" (NpV).

Figure 7.3 represents the association between satisfaction, attitude of the parents, and agency in the drafting process. It shows that the perceived attitude of parents has a similar effect on the conscripts' satisfaction with service—if parents are supportive and their attitude is perceived to be positive, the conscripts are somewhat satisfied with the service, but if the attitude is perceived as negative, then the satisfaction is lower (F (2, 1605) = 61.5; $p < 0.001$). However, only the "active non-volunteers" are demonstrating a pattern where the parents' attitude

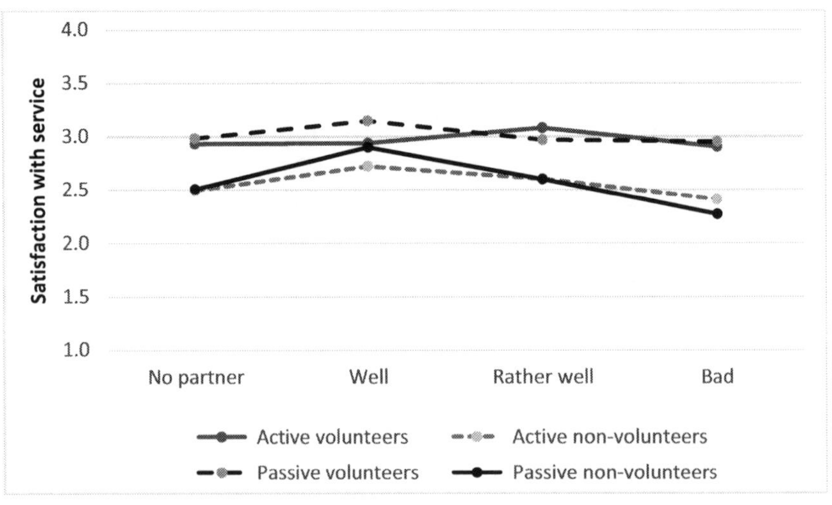

Figure 7.2 Mean score of satisfaction (1 = not satisfied; 4 = satisfied) by form of drafting and perceived attitude of partner (girlfriend, cohabiting partner, spouse)

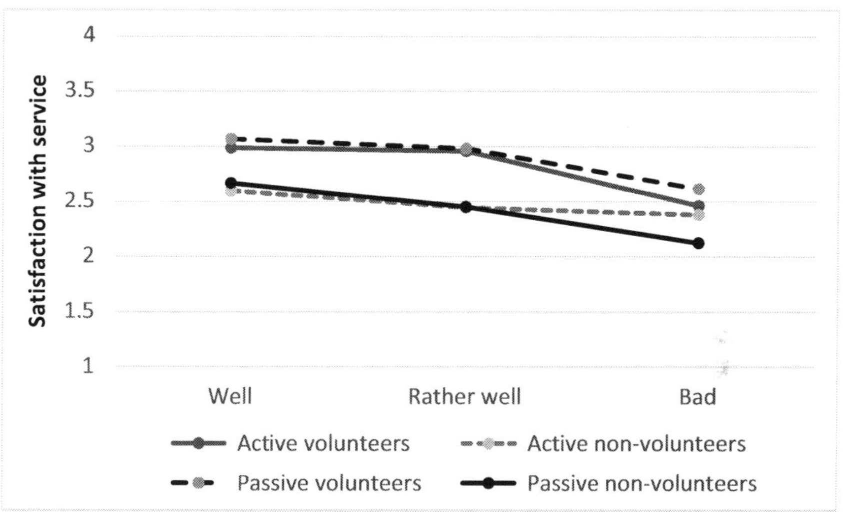

Figure 7.3 Mean score of satisfaction (1 = not satisfied; 4 = satisfied) by form of drafting and perceived attitude of parents' support toward conscription

toward satisfaction with service has a weak effect. Thus, one's agency to choose the time of service is apparently negotiated within the family and even if the parents are not very supportive of the conscript service, it is seen as a pragmatic step, and therefore the variation of satisfaction is low.

In general, this reveals that if the attitude of parents is perceived as non-supportive, the differences in satisfaction with service across volunteers and non-volunteers disappear. The significance of parents in the process of drafting is thus borne out.

The qualitative answers bring forth the tensions young men can face when drafted into service; however, regarding their parents, the main concern was that they are missing them, which could be seen as a universal fear for the long-term separations. "I am afraid I will forget my mother's face" (NaV).

The predictors of satisfaction with service

A logistic regression analysis was conducted to predict if a conscript is satisfied with his conscript service.[1] In the first step, only the sociodemographic background variables were added to the model. The analysis clearly indicated that satisfaction with service does not vary according to the conscripts' age, educational level, or main activity before the service. This suggests that there is no direct effect of these sociodemographic background variables on satisfaction with the service; only ethnicity was a significant predictor; that is, Estonians are more likely than non-Estonians (i.e., mainly Russian speakers) to be satisfied with the service.

Table 7.3 Predictors of satisfaction with the service: logistic regression (N = 1600)

		B	*SE*	*P*	*Exp (B)*
Ethnicity	Estonian	0.42	0.16	0.008	1.52
	Ref: non-Estonian				
Agency in drafting process	Active volunteers	0.77	0.17	0.001	2.17
	Active non-volunteers	−0.11	0.14	0.453	0.89
	Passive volunteers	1.28	0.23	0.001	3.59
	Ref: passive non-volunteers				
Perceived attitude of parents toward conscription	Well	0.72	0.17	0.001	2.06
	Rather well	0.44	0.16	0.006	1.55
	Ref: rather bad				
Perceived attitude of partner (girlfriend, spouse, cohabiting partner)	No partner	0.18	0.13	0.180	1.19
	Well	0.38	0.24	0.117	1.46
	Rather well	0.24	0.17	0.167	1.27
	Ref: rather bad				
Perceived attitude of schoolmates or work colleagues	No schoolmates/colleagues or do not know their attitude	0.16	0.15	0.290	1.18
	Well	0.34	0.21	0.096	1.41
	Rather well	0.65	0.16	0.001	1.91
	Ref: rather bad				

In the next step (see Table 7.3), we added to the model attitude of significant others and the variable measuring the agency in drafting process (χ^2 (12) = 195; $p = 0.001$; Nagelkerke $R^2 = 0.156$). It reveals that agency is a significant and strong predictor of satisfaction with the service. Conscripts who are so-called "active volunteers" are 2.5 times more likely to be satisfied with the service compared to those who are "passive non-volunteers." Moreover, the "passive volunteers" are more satisfied with the service than are the "passive non-volunteers." Looking at the influence of parents' and partners' attitudes on satisfaction with service, we see that parents are more influential than partners. If the parents' attitude is perceived supportive in the beginning of the service, then the conscript is more likely to be satisfied with his service. However, the effect from the partner's side is not so clear. If schoolmates and work colleagues hold a supportive attitude toward the conscription, this will also significantly increase the likelihood of being more satisfied with the conscription in the middle of the service.

Discussion and conclusions

This chapter focused on the question of how young men in Estonia adapt in an environment where tensions are created between conflicting expectations for agency in directing and sequencing life events and the obligation to fulfill their military duty, and how this tension is either relieved or stressed through relationships with partners or family.

The traditional institutions in today's Western societies have become more flexible, and less adherent to norms and rules previously governing them and people's lifecourses. Life in the West is also characterized by over-abundance of choice and the cult surrounding success, so the concept of compulsory military service can easily be interpreted as disruptive. The obligation to serve can create ambivalence within the individual—ambivalence that can be seen on different levels. On the one hand, there is structural ambivalence, which goes hand-in-hand with acceleration of societal time—the expectations of choosing a smooth and successful life path versus conscription as a lifecourse disruption. This points to the fact that in the Estonian society conscription has not been incorporated into the lifecourse of individuals, despite its compulsory nature. It is also tied to the societally perceived role of the military as a strong guarantee of state sovereignty, but as an institution that can do little for the individual's personal development and gain. The results of this study indicate that young men put less emphasis on their personal gains from military service and seem to concentrate more on the negative aspects of their military service—being away from their family and putting their life on hold. The data that were collected during the respondents' military service have a positive bias (Walker, Skowronski, and Thompson, 2003).

Previously, family specialists, researchers, and professionals have been more focused on deployment-induced family separation and how to support the family of professional military service members. This study shows that the favorable attitudes of the family, in particular parents (which might be explained by the age of the conscripts), are of significant importance for conscripts' satisfaction with military service. This is supported by the Swedish experience, where completed military service is well regarded in the society by both employers (Dandeker, Wessely, Iversen, and Ross, 2006) and parents. Österberg (2017) in his research showed that parents supported their children in joining the Preparatory Military Training Program. In Estonia, attitudes toward conscription are ambivalent because of the enduring Soviet military legacy (Nugin, 2016). Thus, they might not feel enough positive support from their families.

Results showed that agency plays a fairly significant role, but more revealing is what underlines the decisions that lead to taking the initiative. Those that fill out a personal application for starting their conscription service at a particular point in time have done so for very different reasons. Beck and Beck-Gernsheim (2002) stress that designing one's own lifecourse means also taking responsibility for it. It corresponds to an image of society in which individuals are not passive reflections of circumstances but active shapers of their own lives, within varying degrees of limitations. However, people vary greatly in their sense of self-efficacy and control over the direction of their lives. We divided conscripts into four groups according to their agency in drafting process: (1) active volunteers: they consciously plan their life path and aim to order the sequence of life events in the manner that they deem best for themselves. They see conscription as an inevitability—a structural dictate that has to be fulfilled, but preferably at the time that most suits them. (2) Active non-volunteers: they have also filled out a personal application for starting their conscription period but the reasons behind their display of agency are different. A small part of them is interested in a career in the military. A significantly larger part of this group is made up of those who take conscription as a chance to prolong the period of "mulling things over," before they have to take a decision on what is the direction they want to take in life. (3) Passive non-volunteers: they have not filled out a personal application for starting their conscription service— those who are not displaying agency, they have passively waited for the summons to be drafted, perhaps even hoping to fulfil 27 years of age, marking the end of their call-up selectee status, effectively making them no longer eligible for conscription service. (4) Passive volunteers: they also have not taken the initiative to enlist, but they are not against conscription service; rather, they favor it or perhaps the draft summons came at a time that suited them. As Elder Jr. et al. (2003) brought out, they plan and make choices in their lives within the particular limitation of their world. Thus, the profiles of conscripts are quite different.

The Estonian Defence Forces and Estonian society need to open up the discussion of how to understand conscription and what it means being a conscript in contemporary Estonia. The larger societal debate is necessary not only for the sake of conscripts, but also because Estonia adheres to a comprehensive defense paradigm that is a whole-society approach to defense. Specific soldiering skills are in the purview of militaries, but at the same time conscripts will learn more than purely combat-type skills—they also acquire abilities and knowledge that can be transferred into their civilian lives, and society needs to figure out how to make use of these and how to gain from these skills. In addition, there are also NATO forces stationed in Estonia and there is little discussion in this context what is the aim of conscription service in this new framework. Though it is probably clear to those who work within the defense organization, most conscripts do not have parents or close personal contacts with people in the system. As was shown in the beginning of the chapter, support for the conscription system is weaker among younger age groups, who will be parents to future conscripts, yet this is the age group that has adapted to the fast-paced, portfolio-building, constant-relationship-tending way of life. These parents in turn will be faced with ambivalent feelings, on the one hand perhaps supporting conscription and on the other not seeing the value for their own children, which in turn will make the mandatory conscript service more difficult for their children once they reach the age of service.

Note

1 The independent variable is satisfaction with the service, measured as a dummy variable: 1 = satisfied; 2 = not satsified. In the logistic regressioon model, we predict the liklehood of being satisfied compared to being not satisfied.

References

Baker, M. (2006). *Translation and Conflict: A Narrative Account*. London: Routledge.

Beck, U. and Beck-Gernsheim, E. (2002). *Individualization*. London: Sage Publications.

Dandeker, C., Wessely, S., Iversen, A., and Ross, J. (2006). What's in a name? Defining and caring for "Veterans." The United Kingdom in international perspective. *Armed Forces & Society*, 32(2), 161–177.

Defence Resources Agency. (2016). *Aruanne kaitseväekohustuse täitmisest ja kaitseväeteenistuse korraldamisest 2016*. Retrieved from /www.kra.ee/kodanik-ja-riigikaitse/uuringud-ja-aruanded.

Elder Jr., G. H., Kirkpatrick Johnson, M., and Crosnoe, R. (2003). The emergence and development of life course theory. In J. T. Mortimer and M. J. Shanahan (eds), *Handbook of Life Course*. New York: Kluwer.

Eurostat (2017). *Statistics on Young People Neither in Employment Nor in Education or Training*. Retrieved from http://ec.europa.eu/eurostat/statistics-explained/index.php/Statistics_on_young_people_neither_in_employment_nor_in_education_or_training .

Ferguson, H. (2001). Social work, individualization and life politics. *The British Journal of Social Work*, 31(1), 41–55.

George, L. K. (1993). Sociological perspectives on life transition. *Annual Review of Sociology*, 19, 353–373.

Kasearu, K. (2018). Militaarsotsioloogiline sissevaade: Ajateenistus Eesti Kaitseväes. *Sõjateadlane. Estonian Journal of Military Studies*, 6, 7–21.

Kivirähk, J. (2017a). *Avalik arvamus ja riigikaitse*. Retrieved from www.kmin.ee/sites/default/files/elfinder/article_files/avalik_arvamus_ja_riigikaitse_marts_2017.pdf.

Kivirähk, J. (2017b). *Avalik arvamus ja riigikaitse*. Retrieved from www.kmin.ee/sites/default/files/elfinder/article_files/avalik_arvamus_ja_riigikaitse_oktoober_2017.pdf.

Martin, A. J. (2010). Should students have a gap year? Motivation and performance factors relevant to time out after completing school. *Journal of Educational Psychology*, 102, 561–576.

Mencarini, L., Pailhé, A., Solaz, A., and Tanturri, M. (2010). *Two Generations at Home: The Time Cost of Young Adults Living with their Parents in France and Italy*. Retrieved from www.carloalberto.org/assets/working-papers/no.179.pdf.

Merton R. K. (1976) *Sociological Ambivalence and Other Essays*. New York: The Free Press.

Military Service Act (2013). Retrieved from www.riigiteataja.ee/en/eli/ee/519092014003/consolide/current.

Mills, M., Rindfuss, R. R., McDonald, P., and Velde, E. te (2011). Why do people postpone parenthood? Reasons and social policy incentives. *Human Reproduction Update*, 17(6), 848–860.

Nugin, R. (2016). Re-constructing a transition generation: the 1970s cohort. In R. Nugin, A. Kannike, and M. Raudsepp (eds), *Generations in Estonia: Contemporary Perspectives on Turbulent Times* (pp. 282–317). Tartu: University of Tartu Press.

Nolte, G. (2003). *European Military Law Systems*. Berlin: De-Gruyter Rechtswissenschaften Verlags-GmbH.

Österberg, J. (2017). Preparatory military training: an experiment in integrating minorities in the Swedish Armed Forces. *Res Militaris*, 5, 1–12.

Rahbek-Clemmensen, J., Archer, E. M., Barr, J., Belkin, A., Guerrero, M., Hall, C., and Swain, K. E. O. (2012). Conceptualizing the civil–military gap: a research note. *Armed Forces & Society*, 38(4), 669–678.

Rosa, H. (2013). *Social Acceleration: A New Theory of Modernity*, trans. J. Trejo-Mathys. New York: Columbia University Press.

Segal, M. W. (1986). The military and the family as greedy institutions. *Armed Forces & Society*, 13(1), 9–38.

Susi, J. (2017). *Kõrgharidust omandavate noormeeste arvamused ajateenistusest* (Thesis). Tartu Ülikool. Retrieved from http://dspace.ut.ee/handle/10062/56778.

Walker, W. R., Skowronski, J. J., and Thompson, C. P. (2003). Life is pleasant and memory helps to keep it that way! *Review of General Psychology*, 7(2), 203–210.

Wheaton, B. (1990). Life transitions, role histories, and mental health. *American Sociological Review*, 55(2), 209–223.

Wilmoth, J. M. and London, A. S. (2013). Life course perspectives on military service: an introduction. In J. M. Wilmoth and A. S. London (eds), *Life Course Perspectives on Military Service*. New York: Routledge.

8 Military lifestyle stressors and social support in the well-being of military families

Sanela Dursun, Zhigang Wang, and Lesleigh Pullman

Introduction

In the most recent survey of Canadian Armed Forces (CAF) spouses[1] (Wang and Aitken, 2015), the top five challenges facing CAF families were spousal employment (43 percent), primary healthcare (37 percent), relocation due to military service (32 percent), financial stability (30 percent), and childcare (19 percent).[2] These results are notable not only because of the high ranking of relocation, but also because relocation can contribute to or exacerbate the other four stressors.

The extent to which these stressors influence the well-being of military families is unclear, however, because many military spouses exhibit a high level of well-being despite these challenges. Supportive relationships are important coping resources, enhancing an individual's well-being in the face of stressful experiences (Wills, 1985). For people with support, fewer situations should tax or exceed their resources and, consequently, less stress should be experienced. Even when people do experience stress, having strong support to rely on should make effective coping more likely and, thus, the experience of negative psychological or health outcomes less likely.

The study reported here examined the extent to which the stressors identified by CAF spouses influenced their well-being and the role of social support as both a predictor of well-being and as a buffer against stress–strain relations.

Relocation and military family well-being

The literature shows that geographical relocations generally have a negative influence on the well-being of military spouses. Both national and international relocations significantly predict psychological well-being, physical well-being, and life satisfaction among military spouses (Burrell, Adams, Durand, and Castro, 2006).

The negative impact on spouses' well-being may be traced to the many disruptions relocation brings in its wake. Military service requires that military families geographically relocate every few years. Hosek, Asch, Fair, Martin, and Mattock (2002) reported that military families are three times as likely as civilians to move out of the county within a year. Female spouses of CAF members are more likely to move provincially compared to spouses of police, federal public servants, and other civilians (Dunn, Urban, and Wang, 2010). Because postings occur at the discretion of the military's organizational and operational needs, the military decides when a family will be posted, where it will be posted, and the length of time it will spend there. Once notified of a posting, the military family will have to make a number of important decisions related to the new posting: selling and purchasing a residence, traveling to the new location, and physically moving the household. The highly disruptive influence on family life is therefore compounded by the limited influence families have over the destination, timeframe, and duration and by the convergence of stressors as the family adjusts to many significant changes at the same time (Wamboldt, Steinglass, and Kaplan De-Nour, 1991).

In short, military postings require military families to continually leave behind old communities, homes, friends, schools, daycares, jobs, and peer circles and adjust to new ones, all within a short span of time. Of the many complex secondary effects that arise from a geographic relocation, however, spousal employment, financial impact, access to healthcare, and the re-establishment of a stable social network may contribute the most to the negative impact of relocation. The following sections will examine each of these stressors and consider the influence they have on spousal well-being.

Spousal employment

In a recent survey of military spouses' quality of life, many identified spousal employment as a significant challenge associated with the military lifestyle (Wang and Aitken, 2015). Surveys of military personnel and their families have consistently found that not being in the labor force is more common among military spouses than civilian spouses, that unemployment rates are higher among military spouses, and that their employment incomes are lower (Harrell, Lim, Castaneda, and Golinelli, 2004). These results hold even when controlling for various sociodemographic differences between military and civilian spouses (Dunn, Urban, and Wang, 2010).

Numerous factors have been identified as predictive of employment issues for military spouses, including being younger, less experienced, less educated, living in rural areas, and having young children in the home (e.g., Dunn, Urban, and Wang, 2010; Schwartz, Wood, and Griffith, 1991). Some of these factors are specific to the military environment, including being married to a service member of lower rank, living in a military dwelling, and experiencing separations as a result of deployments (Buddin and Do, 2002; Schwartz, Wood, and Griffith, 1991).

Much of this literature shows that the frequency of residential relocations has a significant effect on the employment status and income of military spouses (Meadows, Griffin, Karney, and Pollak, 2015). Indeed, residential relocation is associated with as much as a 10-percent increase in unemployment for military spouses and, among military spouses who are working, as much as four fewer hours worked per week (Cooke and Speirs, 2005). Frequent relocations also mean that military spouses spend less time at each job they have, and thus are unable to reap the benefits associated with seniority. It is not surprising, therefore, that military spouses are paid less per hour than civilian spouses (Harrell, Lim, Castaneda, and Golinelli, 2004). The number of relocations a military family experiences has been found to be associated with increased rates of involuntary unemployment among military spouses (Cooke and Speirs, 2005).

Spousal difficulties to secure and sustain gainful employment impact their well-being. Gray (2015) found that military spouses who were employed exhibited better mental health and more life satisfaction than military spouses who were not employed. Similarly, Easterling (2005) found that being both involuntarily and voluntarily unemployed was detrimental to military spouses' psychological well-being (as measured by depression scores). A systematic review by Blakely, Hennessy, Chung, and Skirton (2012) highlighted the importance of spousal employment for the relationship satisfaction of military personnel. Decreased marital satisfaction and well-being may be in part due to financial hardships caused by unemployment.

Financial stability

A significant number of military families experience financial strain and even distress (Deaks et al., 2000). The most recent financial survey found that military families were, on average, more in debt than comparable Canadian families (Wang and Ouellete, 2017). Studies of US military personnel have also found that a substantial percentage (15–29 percent) of military personnel experience stress related to their financial situation (Defense Manpower Data Center and Research Surveys and Statistics Center, 2016).

While military families experience similar financial stressors as other families (Skimmyhorn, 2016), they also face a number of unique financial stressors related to the military lifestyle (Weber and Weber, 2005). These financial stressors include frequent relocations, the challenge of spousal employment, the incidental effects of separation and deployment, pronounced health and childcare expenses, and the varying cost of housing (Daigle, 2013). Deployment can also substantially impact the financial stability of military families. When a military partner is deployed, the military spouse often assumes sole responsibility for childcare. For military spouses who are in the labor force, this may mean that they are forced to work fewer hours or accept a position (often of lower pay) that has flexible hours. While military members do receive a higher wage during deployment, this may not be enough to account for the changes to their spouse's employment and income (Booth and Lederer, 2012).

Financial instability in military families is negatively associated with general well-being and marital satisfaction among military spouses. It is also positively associated with symptoms of depression (Thoresen and Goldsmith, 1987). Similarly, financial satisfaction, defined as satisfaction with standard of living, household income, and ability to cope with financial obligations, is positively associated with well-being in military spouses (Rosen, Ickovics, and Moghadam, 1990).

Access to healthcare

Unlike the military members, Canadian military families do not receive medical care from the CAF. Canadian military families depend on the same provincial healthcare services as other Canadians for almost all of their healthcare needs. Like many Canadians, military families often find it difficult to secure family doctors and specialist practitioners. Waiting lists can be long, especially in smaller centers where demand routinely exceeds the supply of healthcare professionals. The difference from most Canadians, however, is that many military families experience this problem repeatedly as a result of relocations. Moreover, military families often have a heightened need for effective healthcare, for instance, due to the strain caused by the deployment of a military partner.

Research has shown that continuity of care is essential to quality healthcare and that it is associated with better health outcomes (Van Walraven, Oake, Jennings, and Forster, 2010). Among military spouses, continuity of care and patient satisfaction were significantly lower as the number of relocation moves and providers increased (Gleason and Beck, 2017).

Social support

Social support is a key component in the mental health and well-being of military spouses (Skomorovsky, 2014). It is a significant predictor of a healthy lifestyle among military spouses (Padden, Connors, Posey, Ricciardi, and Agazio, 2013) and of their resilience (Wang and Aitken, 2015). However, frequent relocations separate spouses from their families and friends, which can heighten feelings of loneliness and isolation and separate them from social support (Bowen, Mancini, Martin, Ware, and Nelson, 2003). Once the family is relocated, maintaining the previous social network and/or developing a new one may be difficult (Copeland and Norell, 2002). Nonetheless, despite relocation difficulties, social support is important in promoting the well-being of military spouses (Blakely, Hennessy, Chung, and Skirton, 2014). Support from other military spouses and formal support programs provided by the military may lessen the stress of relocation (Kirkland and Katz, 1989).

An open question remains, however, about how social support benefits well-being. Social support has been postulated both as a main effect that influences psychological well-being (Cohen and Wills, 1985) and as a moderator of the relation between encountering stressors and psychological well-being (Antonovsky, 1974). The main-effect model states that perceived social support is beneficial to the health and well-being of individuals, irrespective of the amount of stress they are experiencing. It has been suggested that well-being, in this case, may simply be the by-product of individuals carrying out their social roles (Thoits, 1986). In contrast, the stress-buffering model postulates that perceived social support benefits individuals primarily during times of high stress by bolstering and restoring self-esteem and sense of belonging during.

Both the main-effect (Elal and Krespi, 1999) and the stress-buffering models (Parry and Shapiro, 1986) have received empirical support, but the validity of either model appears to depend on such factors as the sources of social support and the nature of the stressors and strains (Ganster, Fusilier, and Mayes, 1986). In the military context, Fields, Nichols, Martindale-Adams, Zuber, and Graney (2012) found that while spouses with probable generalized anxiety disorder (GAD) reported having less social support and worse overall health than those screening negative for GAD, social support did not moderate this relationship. Similarly, while social support predicted well-being and depression among military spouses, it did not buffer the effect of deployment stress on psychological well-being (Skomorovsky, 2014).

Although social support is an established protective factor in psychological functioning, its role in mitigating the effects of stress and strain for military spouses has been less examined. Accordingly, this study tested which of the two models—the main (i.e., additive) or buffering models—best captured the relation between social support and military lifestyle stressors in their effect upon spousal well-being. In addition, the study tested which stressors were the strongest predictors of various well-being indicators.

Participants and procedures

Data for the current study were collected from the Quality of Life Survey (QOL), an anonymous survey of spouses and common-law partners of CAF Regular Force members administered by Director Military Personnel Research and Analysis in Ottawa, Canada. An invitation to participate was originally mailed to about 8000 military spouses (stratified by their military partner's rank and the military environment). About 23 percent of spouses completed the survey, yielding a sample size of 1822 (see Wang and Aitken, 2015 for a more detailed description of the study sample and procedure).

For our study, 909 civilian female spouses who had experienced at least one residential move were included in the analyses. Participants were, on average, close to 40 years old ($M = 38.86$; $SD = 9.23$). Over 80 percent of participants (81.4 percent) in this sample had completed at least a college or CEGEP diploma,[3] and about 80 percent (78.8 percent) lived in and owned civilian properties.

Measures

The QOL survey measured a variety of unique aspects associated with the military lifestyle that have been identified as significant sources of stress for military personnel and their families and the social support they perceived.

Employment difficulties. Spouses were asked to respond the following statements, regardless of whether they were employed: My spouse/partner's military career has had a positive impact on my employment or career; My employment or career has not been affected by my spouse/partner's military career; I have made some employment or career sacrifices because of my spouse/partner's military career; I am unemployed or my career has been severely affected by the demands or my spouse/partner's military career. Responses were measured on a five-point scale ranging from 1 (*strongly disagree*) to 5 (*strongly agree*).The first two were reverse-scored so higher scores were associated with more employment difficulties. The mean of the four questions created the total score for spousal employment difficulties.

Primary healthcare difficulties. Participants were asked whether there was a time in the past 12 months that they felt they needed healthcare but did not receive it. Participants' responses were used as the indicator of healthcare difficulties (no = 0, yes = 1). About 30 percent reported experiencing difficulties in accessing healthcare, while about 70 percent did not report any difficulty.

Relocation difficulties. To assess the difficulties associated with household relocations, participants were asked how difficult it was to re-establish 13 different services/lifestyle characteristics following a residential relocation (e.g., medical services, employment, housing). Each item was scored on a three-point scale ranging from 1 (*not at all difficult*) to 3 (*extremely difficult*), and the mean response across the 13 items created the total score for relocation difficulty.

Financial stress. Respondents were asked to rate their agreement with three statements ("I have enough money to pay my bills each month," "I have incorporated savings into the family budget," and "I have some extra money set aside in case of an emergency") on a six-point scale ranging from 1 (*strongly disagree*) to 6 (*strongly agree*). These items were adopted from the Support and Resiliency Inventory—Financial Management (Bowen and Martin, 2011). The responses were reverse-scored so higher scores were associated with more financial stress. The mean response across the three items created the total score for financial stress.

Perceived social support. Perceived social support was measured using the Revised Social Provisions Scale (Cutrona and Russell, 1987). This scale measures perception of presence or absence of different types of support. The 12-item scale consists of six subscales: attachment, social integration, reassurance of worth, reliable alliance, guidance, and opportunity for nurturance. Responses ranged from 1 (*strongly disagree*) to 4 (*strongly agree*). The responses were summed to create a total score for each respondent, with higher scores indicating greater perceived social support.

Satisfaction with life. Life satisfaction was measured with the five-item Satisfaction with Life Scale (Diener, Emmons, Larsen, and Griffin, 1985). Respondents indicated their extent of agreement with each statement (e.g., "In most ways my life is close to ideal") on a five-point scale ranging from 1 (*strongly agree*) to 5 (*strongly disagree*). The mean rating across all items will be used as the overall scale score.

Psychological well-being. Psychological well-being was measured using a single item, which asked participants to rate the quality of their mental health from 1 (*poor*) to 5 (*excellent*). Higher scores were associated with better psychological well-being.

Physical well-being. Physical well-being was measured using a single item, which asked participants to rate the quality of their physical health from 1 (*poor*) to 5 (*excellent*). Higher scores were associated with better physical well-being.

Analyses

For each indicator of well-being (i.e., life satisfaction, psychological well-being, and physical well-being), we conducted a hierarchical multiple linear regression to assess the extent to which the stressors identified by CAF spouses influenced their well-being and the role of social support, as both a predictor of well-being and as a buffer of stress-strain relations. In the first block of the regression we added the following difficulty variables: spousal employment difficulties, primary healthcare difficulties, relocation difficulties, and financial stability. In the second block of the regression, we added social support. In the third block of the regression, we added the interaction between social support and each of difficulty variables. The continuous difficulty variables and social support were mean centered prior to being entered into Block 1 and Block 2 of the regression and prior to creating the interactions that were entered into Block 3 of the regression to avoid issues of multicollinearity (Aiken and West, 1991).

Statistical assumption violations[4] (e.g., non-normality and heteroscedacity of residuals) forced us to use robust linear regression, which uses bootstrapping to produce robust standard errors (SE) and significant tests (1000 bootstrap samples; see Salibian-Barrera and Zamar, 2002). In order to control for family-wise error rate, false discovery rate correction (Benjamini and Hochberg, 1995) was used to obtain p-values. Standardized and unstandardized regression coefficients (i.e., β and B) are also reported.

Means and standard deviations (*SDs*) for all the continuous measures used in this study are shown in Table 8.1. Correlations between the four stressors ranged from small (0.11) to moderate (0.41). Further, social support was correlated with each of the stressors, ranging from 0.08 to 0.24. Finally, the well-being indicators correlated among each other, ranging from 0.32 to 0.54 (see Table 8.2).

Table 8.1 Descriptive statistics for continuous measures

Measures	*Item*	*Range*	M	SD	*Cronbach's alpha*
Employment difficulties	4	1–5	3.87	0.93	–
Relocation difficulties	13	1–3	1.94	0.43	–
Financial difficulties	3	1–6	2.62	1.40	0.88
Social support	12	12–48	38.48	5.92	0.88
Life satisfaction	5	5–35	24.03	7.03	0.91
Psychological well-being	1	5	3.40	1.03	–
Physical well-being	1	5	3.51	0.98	–

Table 8.2 Binary correlation between measures

Measures	*1*	*2*	*3*	*4*	*5*	*6*	*7*
1 Employment difficulties	–						
2 Relocation difficulties	0.41**	–					
3 Financial difficulties	0.14**	0.22**	–				
4 Primary healthcare difficulties	0.11**	0.25**	0.11**	–			
5 Social support	−0.08*	−0.24**	−0.23**	−0.19**	–		
6 Life satisfaction	−0.32**	−0.39**	−0.34**	−0.19**	0.45**	–	
7 Psychological well-being	−0.16**	−0.26**	−0.19**	−0.18**	0.37**	0.49**	–
8 Physical well-being	−0.03	−0.21**	−0.25**	−0.17**	0.28**	0.35**	0.54**

$^*p < 0.05$, $^{**}p < 0.01$.

Results

Predictors of military spouses' well-being

Several hierarchical multiple linear regressions were conducted to investigate the stressors and social support to predict military spouses' well-being.

Life satisfaction. The results (Table 8.3) show that difficulty variables accounted for 26 percent of the variance in military spouses' life satisfaction, and social support accounted for an additional 11 percent of the variance after controlling for four difficulty variables associated with the military lifestyle ($\Delta R^2 = 0.11$; F (1, 801) = 138.36; $p < 0.001$). Further, more spousal employment difficulties ($\beta = -0.20$; $p < 0.01$), more relocation difficulties ($\beta = -0.18$; $p < 0.01$), and more financial difficulties ($\beta = -0.18$; $p < 0.01$) were found to be associated with less life satisfaction among military spouses. Higher levels of social support ($\beta = 0.35$; $p < 0.01$) were found to be associated with more life satisfaction. Primary healthcare difficulties ($\beta = -0.05$; $p > 0.05$) were not found to make a significant unique contribution to military spouses' life satisfaction. The strongest predictor of military spouses' life satisfaction was social support that military spouses perceived, following by employment difficulties, financial difficulties, and relocation difficulties.

Psychological well-being. The results (Table 8.4) demonstrate that difficulty variables accounted for 11 percent of the variance in military spouses' psychological well-being, and social support accounted for an additional 8 percent of the variance, after controlling for four difficulty variables associated with the military lifestyle ($\Delta R^2 = 0.08$; F (1, 806) = 76.66; $p < 0.001$). In addition, more relocation difficulties ($\beta = -0.16$; $p < 0.01$) and more financial difficulties ($\beta = -0.08$; $p < 0.05$) were found to be associated with poor psychological well-being among military spouses, and higher levels of social support

($\beta = 0.29$; $p < 0.01$) were found to be associated with better psychological well-being. Employment difficulties ($\beta = -0.05$; $p > 0.05$) and primary healthcare difficulties ($\beta = -0.05$; $p > 0.05$) were not found to make a significant unique contribution to military spouses' psychological well-being. The strongest predictor of military spouses' psychological well-being was perceived social support, followed by relocation difficulties and financial difficulties.

Physical well-being. The results (Table 8.5) indicate that difficulty variables accounted for 10 percent of the variance in military spouses' physical well-being, and social support accounted for an additional 4 percent of the variance after controlling for four difficulty variables associated with the military lifestyle ($\Delta R^2 = 0.04$; F (1, 808) $= 38.45$; $p < 0.001$). Moreover, more relocation difficulties ($\beta = -0.15$; $p < 0.01$) and more financial difficulties ($\beta = -0.16$; $p < 0.01$) were found to be associated with poor physical well-being among military spouses, and higher levels of social support ($\beta = 0.21$; $p < 0.01$) were found to be associated with better physical well-being. Employment difficulties ($\beta = 0.07$; $p > 0.05$) and primary healthcare difficulties ($\beta = -0.07$; $p > 0.05$) were not

Table 8.3 Robust multiple regression: life satisfaction

	B	*SE*	*β*	
Block 1				
Employment difficulties	−1.41	0.26	−0.18	**
Relocation difficulties	−4.06	0.61	−0.24	**
Financial difficulties	−1.25	0.16	−0.25	**
Primary healthcare difficulties	−1.43	0.56	−0.09	*
Block 2				
Employment difficulties	−1.56	0.24	−0.20	**
Relocation difficulties	−2.98	0.55	−0.18	**
Financial difficulties	−0.92	0.15	−0.18	**
Primary healthcare difficulties	−0.80	0.51	−0.05	
Social support	0.41	0.04	0.35	**
Block 3				
Employment difficulties	−1.59	0.25	−0.21	**
Relocation difficulties	−2.98	0.55	−0.18	**
Financial difficulties	−0.92	0.15	−0.18	**
Primary healthcare difficulties	−0.75	0.52	−0.05	
Social support	0.39	0.04	0.33	**
Social support x employment difficulties	0.05	0.04	0.04	
Social support x relocation difficulties	0.00	0.09	0.00	
Social support x financial difficulties	0.01	0.03	0.01	
Social support x primary healthcare difficulties	0.07	0.08	0.04	

Note. With the exception of the variable *primary healthcare difficulties*, which is a dummy variable, all the variables reported in the table are mean-centered.

*$p < 0.05$, **$p < 0.01$.

found to make a significant unique contribution to military spouses' physical well-being. The strongest predictor of military spouses' physical well-being was perceived social support, followed by financial difficulties and relocation difficulties.

The moderating role of social support

Several hierarchical multiple linear regressions were conducted to assess whether social support moderated the effect that military lifestyle difficulties had on the well-being of military spouses. The results showed that the interaction terms between social support and difficulties added to the regression model on each of the three well-being variables did not significantly improve the regression model (life satisfaction: $\Delta R^2 < 0.01$; F (4, 797) = 0.90; $p > 0.05$; psychological well-being: $\Delta R^2 = 0.01$; F (4, 802) = 1.40; $p > 0.05$; physical well-being: $\Delta R^2 < 0.01$; F (4, 804) = 0.99; $p > 0.05$). Further, none of the interaction terms were statistically significant in each of the three models. These results indicate that social support did not moderate the effect that difficulties associated with the military lifestyle had on military spouses' well-being.

Table 8.4 Robust multiple regression: psychological well-being

	B	*SE*	*β*	
Block 1				
Employment difficulties	−0.04	0.04	−0.03	
Relocation difficulties	−0.53	0.10	−0.22	**
Financial difficulties	−0.10	0.03	−0.14	**
Primary healthcare difficulties	−0.19	0.09	−0.09	*
Block 2				
Employment difficulties	−0.05	0.04	−0.05	
Relocation difficulties	−0.40	0.09	−0.16	**
Financial difficulties	−0.06	0.03	−0.08	*
Primary healthcare difficulties	−0.12	0.08	−0.05	
Social support	0.05	0.01	0.29	**
Block 3				
Employment difficulties	−0.05	0.04	−0.05	
Relocation difficulties	−0.39	0.09	−0.16	**
Financial difficulties	−0.06	0.03	−0.09	*
Primary healthcare difficulties	−0.09	0.08	−0.04	
Social support	0.04	0.01	0.25	**
Social support x employment difficulties	−0.01	0.01	−0.03	
Social support x relocation difficulties	−0.01	0.01	−0.03	
Social support x financial difficulties	0.00	0.00	0.00	
Social support x primary healthcare difficulties	0.03	0.01	0.09	

Note. With the exception of the variable *primary healthcare difficulties*, all the variables reported in the table are mean-centered.

*$p < 0.05$, **$p < 0.01$.

Table 8.5 Robust multiple regression: physical well-being

	B	*SE*	*β*	
Block 1				
Employment difficulties	0.08	0.04	0.08	
Relocation difficulties	–0.42	0.09	–0.18	**
Financial difficulties	–0.14	0.02	–0.20	**
Primary healthcare difficulties	–0.21	0.07	–0.10	*
Block 2				
Employment difficulties	0.07	0.04	0.07	
Relocation difficulties	–0.33	0.09	–0.15	**
Financial difficulties	–0.11	0.02	–0.16	**
Primary healthcare difficulties	–0.15	0.07	–0.07	
Social support	0.03	0.01	0.21	**
Block 3				
Employment difficulties	0.07	0.04	0.07	
Relocation difficulties	–0.33	0.09	–0.15	**
Financial difficulties	–0.11	0.02	–0.16	**
Primary healthcare difficulties	–0.16	0.07	–0.07	
Social support	0.04	0.01	0.24	**
Social support x employment difficulties	0.00	0.01	0.02	
Social support x relocation difficulties	–0.02	0.01	–0.06	
Social support x financial difficulties	0.00	0.00	–0.01	
Social support x primary healthcare difficulties	–0.01	0.01	–0.02	

Note. With the exception of the variable *primary healthcare difficulties*, all the variables reported in the table are mean-centered.

*$p < 0.05$, **$p < 0.01$.

Discussion and conclusion

This study examined the extent to which military life stressors influence spousal well-being and the role of social support. Our findings show that military lifestyle stressors, such as employment difficulties, relocation difficulties, financial stress, and healthcare access, play important and independent roles in the well-being of military spouses. These findings broaden our understanding of the stressors experienced by military spouses and their impact on spouses' well-being.

Specifically, we found that residential relocations due to military service and financial stress significantly predicted military spouses' life satisfaction, psychological well-being, and physical well-being. These results confirm previous findings that show residential relocations negatively impact military spouses' well-being (e.g., Burrell, Adams, Durand, and Castro, 2006).

We found that access to primary healthcare predicted military spouses' life satisfaction, psychological well-being, and physical well-being. The relation between these indicators of well-being and access to healthcare was weak or non-existent once social support was added to the model. One reason might be our binary measure of primary healthcare difficulty, which may not reflect military spouses' real challenges in accessing primary healthcare.

We found that employment difficulties significantly predicted life satisfaction, but not the other well-being indicators. The reason could lie in the constructs under investigation. Psychological and physical well-being are typically impacted by a combination of severe stressors, and the impact of employment difficulties may not be as strong as other stressors. Satisfaction with life, on the other hand, as a judgment, may be a summative result of a person's experiences, and it could be influenced by employment difficulties. The measure of employment difficulties in our study reflects the negative impact of the military lifestyle on spousal employment—military spouses have to make some employment or career sacrifices or are even unemployed because of their partner's military career.

We found that social support significantly predicted all three well-being indicators, a finding consistent with previous research on the relation between social support and military spousal well-being (Wang and Aitken, 2016). The results suggest that the influence of perceived social support on well-being indicators is positive and that social support functioned as a main effect, not a stress buffer, a finding inconsistent with studies that found social support moderating the relation between stress levels and well-being among children and adults (Moak and Agrawal, 2009; Peltonen, Qouta, El Sarraj, and Punamäki, 2010) and military members (Smith et al., 2013). We may not have found a moderating effect because we did not measure the stress levels military spouses experienced when they faced various difficulties associated with the military lifestyle. Instead, we measured the levels of difficulties associated with the military lifestyle; similar research did not find a moderating effect of social support either (Skomorovsky, 2014). Another possible reason for lack of moderating effect is that we did not match specific support dimensions with specific stressors. Our measure of social support was a generic measure of the degree to which spouses' social relations provided various dimensions of social support. In contrast, the matching hypothesis posits that the type of support (e.g., emotional, instrumental) most effective in a particular situation depends on the stressor prevalent in that situation (Cohen and McKay, 1984). Although the optimal matching hypothesis offers an eloquent explanation of when buffering is likely to occur, supporting evidence is still mixed (Burleson, 2003).

We found that perceived social support contributed to military spouses' well-being, regardless of the amount of stress they experienced. Over and above the variance in well-being indicators explained by the stressors, social support explained a further (and generally greater) amount of variance in a positive direction. The absence of significant interaction effects between stressors and social support suggests that social support does not need to be mobilized by the presence of these difficulties to be effective. In a sense, main effects are more important than buffering effects because they always offer benefits (Rees, Hardy, and Freeman, 2007). In our study, the proportion of variance in most well-being indicators explained by the main effects of social support was around 10 percent, which represents a medium effect size.

Our study has several implications for military organizations. If spouses who are dissatisfied with their employment situation, financial status, and access to healthcare resulting from frequent relocation discourage their partners from remaining in the military, relocation moves may contribute to lower military retention rates and may require increasing compensation and bonuses to maintain the force. Thus, our findings contribute to our understanding of the reasons for a compensation differential for military service members (beyond the physical hazards and difficult working conditions).

Maximizing the impact of support for military families requires identifying the sources of stressors for military spouses and the processes they use to deal with them. Interventions for military spouses could take the form of support-building to assist spousal well-being. For example, providing social support to spouses of military personnel at a stressful time—such as during relocations—would help prevent the development of psychological health problems.

Several important limitations should be considered when interpreting the results of this study. First, the generalizability of the results may be limited because the response rate to the survey was relatively low (23 percent). Second, the cross-sectional design of this study prevented us from disentangling causal relations between difficulties due to military lifestyle and the well-being indicators. Indeed, it is possible that spouses who have better mental and physical health are more skilled at dealing with difficulties and at constructing social networks and seeking out support in times of need (e.g., Sharkansky et al., 2000). Longitudinal research on spouses through the military lifecycle is needed to understand the causality underlying these effects. Third, in evaluating the relations between spouses' military lifestyle stressors and their well-being, it may be useful to consider individual difference variables that evolve from earlier life experiences, such as previous traumatic stress experiences. Previous stressor encounters can make an individual more vulnerable to psychopathology upon subsequent stressor encounters.

Notes

1 CAF spouse refers to the civilian spouse or common-law partner of a CAF member.
2 This chapter did not examine the childcare stressor due to the limitations of the data collected.
3 CEGEP (*Collège d'enseignement général et professionnel*) is a post-secondary preparatory program offered in high schools in the province of Quebec.
4 Multicollinearity was not an issue because the indicators of tolerance and variance inflation factor (VIF) were in the safe ranges.

References

Aiken, L. S. and West, S. G. (1991). *Multiple Regression: Testing and Interpreting Interactions*. Thousand Oaks, CA: Sage.

Antonovsky, A. (1974). Conceptual and methodological problems in the study of resistance resources and stressful life events. In B. S. Dohrenwend and B. P. Dohrenwend (eds), *Stressful Life Events: Their Nature and Effects* (pp. 245–258). New York: Wiley.

Benjamini, Y. and Hochberg, Y. (1995). Controlling the false discovery rate: a practical and powerful approach to multiple testing. *Journal of the Royal Statistical Society*, B57(1), 289–300.

Blakely, G., Hennessy, C., Chung, M. C., and Skirton, H. (2012). A systematic review of the impact of foreign postings on accompanying spouses of military personnel. *Nursing & Health Sciences*, 14(1), 121–132.

Blakely, G., Hennessy, C., Chung, M. C., and Skirton, H. (2014). The impact of foreign postings on accompanying military spouses: an ethnographic study. *Health Psychology Research*, 16(3), 73–77.

Booth, B. and Lederer, S. (2012). Military families in an era of persistent conflict. In J. H. Laurence and M. D. Matthews (eds), *The Oxford Handbook of Military Psychology* (pp. 365–380), Oxford; New York: Oxford University.

Bowen, G. L., Mancini, J. A., Martin, J. A., Ware, W. B., and Nelson, J. P. (2003). Promoting the adaptation of military families: an empirical test of a community practice model. *Family Relations*, 52(1), 33–44.

Bowen, G. L. and Martin, J. A. (2011). *The Support & Resilience Inventory for Civilian Spouses (SRIO-CS, 2011)*. Chapel Hill, NC: Bowen & Colleagues, Inc.

Buddin, R. and Do, D. P. (2002). *Assessing the Personal Financial Problems of Junior Enlisted Personnel*. RAND National Defense Research Institute. Santa Monica, CA: RAND. Retrieved from www.rand.org/pubs/monograph_reports/MR1444.html.

Burleson, B. R. (2003). Emotional support skill. In J. O. Greene and B. R. Burleson (eds), *Handbook of Communication and Social Interaction Skills* (pp. 551–594). Mahwah, NJ: Erlbaum.

Burrell, L. M., Adams, G. A., Durand, D. B., and Castro, C. A. (2006). The impact of military lifestyle demands on well-being, army, and family outcomes. *Armed Forces & Society*, 33(1), 43–58.

Cohen, S. and McKay, G. (1984). Social support, stress, and the buffering hypothesis: a theoretical analysis. In A. Baum, S. E. Taylor, and J. E. Singer (eds), *Handbook of Psychology and Health: Vol. 4. Social Psychological Aspects of Health* (pp. 253–268). Hillsdale, NJ: Lawrence Erlbaum Associates, Publishers.

Cohen, S. and Wills, T. A. (1985). Stress, social support, and the buffering hypothesis. *Psychological Bulletin*, 98(2), 310–357.

Cooke, T. J. and Speirs, K. (2005). Migration and employment among the civilian spouses of military personnel. *Social Sciences Quarterly*, 86(2), 343–355.

Copeland, A. P. and Norell, S. K. (2002). Spousal adjustment on international assignments: the role of social support. *International Journal of Intercultural Relations*, 26(3), 255–272.

Cutrona, C. E. and Russell, D.W. (1987). The provisions of social relationships and adaptation to stress. *Advances in Personal Relationships*, 1(1), 37–67.

Deaks, M. A., Rockwell, D., Gaines, C., Helba, C., Wright, L. C., Williams, K. (2000). *Tabulations of responses from the 1999 Survey of Spouses of Active Duty Personnel: Programs and services, employment, family, economic issues, and background* (Pub. No. 2000-013). Arlington, VA: Defense Manpower Data Center.

Defense Manpower Data Center and Research Surveys and Statistics Center (2016). *Status of Forces Surveys of Active Duty Members (2013 and 2014 SOFS-A): Briefing on Leading Indicators, Military OneSource, Financial Health, Family Life, Access to Technology, Impact of Deployments, and Permanent Change of Station (PCS) Moves*. Arlington, VA: Author.

Daigle, P. (2013). *On the Homefront: Assessing the Well-being of Canada's Military Families in the New Millennium*. Special Report to the Minister of National Defence. Ottawa: Office of the Ombudsman, National Defence and Canadian Forces. Retrieved from www.ombudsman.forces.gc.ca/assets/OMBUDSMAN_Internet/docs/en/mf-fm-eng.pdf.

Diener, E., Emmons, R. A., Larsen, R. J., and Griffin, S. (1985). The Satisfaction with Life Scale. *Journal of Personality Assessment*, 49(1), 71–75.

Dunn, J., Urban, S., and Wang, Z. (2010). *Spousal/Partner Employment and Income (SPEI) Project: How do Canadian Forces Spouses Compare?* [Director General Military Personnel Research and Analysis Technical Memorandum 2010-028]. Ottawa: Defence Research and Development Canada.

Easterling, B. A. (2005). *The Invisible Side of Military Careers: An Examination of Employment and Well-Being among Military Spouses* (unpublished doctoral dissertation). University of North Florida, Jacksonville, FL. Retrieved from https://digitalcommons.unf.edu/cgi/viewcontent.cgi?article=1424&context=etd.

Elal, G. and Krespi M. (1999). Life events, social support and depression in haemodialysis patients. *Journal of community and Applied Social Psychology*, 9(1), 23–33.

Fields, J. A., Nichols, L. O., Martindale-Adams, J., Zuber, J., and Graney, M. (2012). Anxiety, social support, and physical health in a sample of spouses of OEF/OIF service members. *Military Medicine*, 177(12), 1492–1497.

Ganster, D. E, Fusilier, M. R, and Mayes, B. T. (1986). Role of social support in the experience of stress at work. *Journal of Applied Psychology*, 71(1), 102–110.

Gleason, J. L. and Beck, K. H. (2017). Examining associations between relocation, continuity of care, and patient satisfaction in military spouses. *Military Medicine*, 182(5/6), e1657–e1664.

Gray, L. A. (2015). *Exploring Dimensions of Well-Being among Spouses of Active Duty Service Members* (unpublished doctoral dissertation). Virginia Commonwealth University, Richmond, VA. Retrieved from https://scholarscompass.vcu.edu/cgi/viewcontent.cgi?article=4719&context=etd.

Harrell, M. C., Lim, N., Castaneda, L. W., and Golinelli, D. (2004). *Working around the Military: Challenges to Military Spouse Employment and Education*. RAND National Defence Research Institute. Santa Monica, CA: RAND. Retrieved from www.rand.org/pubs/monographs/2004/RAND_MG196.pdf.

Hosek, J., Asch, B., Fair, C., Martin, C., and Mattock, M. (2002). *Married to the Military: The Employment and Earnings of Military Wives Compared to those of Civilian Wives*. RAND National Defence Research Institute. Santa Monica, CA: RAND. Retrieved from www.rand.org/pubs/monograph_reports/MR1565.html.

Kirkland, F. R. and Katz, P. (1989). Combat readiness and the Army family. *Military Review*, 49, 63–74.

Meadows, S. O., Griffin, B. A., Karney, B. R., and Pollak, J. (2015). Employment gaps between military spouses and matched civilians. *Armed Forces & Society*, 42(3), 542–561.

Moak, Z. B. and Agrawal, A. (2009). The association between perceived interpersonal social support and physical and mental health: results from the national epidemiological survey on alcohol and related conditions. *Journal of Public Health*, 32(2), 191–201.

Owen, R. and Combs, T. (2017). Caring for military families: understanding their unique stressors. *Nurse Practitioner*, 42(5), 27–32.

Padden, D. L., Connors, R. A., Posey, S. M., Ricciardi, R., and Agazio, J. G. (2013). Factors influencing a health promoting lifestyle in spouses of active duty military. *Health Care for Women International*, 34(8), 674–693.

Parry, G. and Shapiro, D. A. (1986). Social support and life events in working class women: stress buffering or independent effects? *Archives of General Psychiatry*, 43(4), 315–323.

Peltonen, K., Qouta, S., El Sarraj, E., and Punamäki, R. L. (2010). Military trauma and social development: the moderating and mediating roles of peer and sibling relations in mental health. *International Journal of Behavioral Development*, 34(6), 554–563.

Rees, T., Hardy, L., and Freeman, P. (2007). Stressors, social support and effects upon performance in golf. *Journal of Sports Sciences*, 25(1), 33–42.

Rosen, L. N., Ickovics, J. R., and Moghadam, L. Z. (1990). Employment and role satisfaction: implications for the general well-being of military wives. *Psychology of Women Quarterly*, 14(3), 371–385.

Salibian-Barrera, M. and Zamar, R. H. (2002). Bootstrapping robust estimates of regression. *Annals of Statistics*, 30(2), 556–582.

Schwartz, J. B., Wood, L. L., and Griffith, J. D. (1991). The impact of military life on spouses' labor force outcomes. *Armed Forces & Society*, 17(3), 385–407.

Sharkansky, E. J., King, D. W., King, L. A., Wolfe, J., Erickson, D. J., Stokes, L. R. (2000). Coping with Gulf War combat stress: mediating and moderating effects. *Journal of Abnormal Psychology*, 109(2), 188–197.

Skimmyhorn, W. L. (2016). *The Financial Welfare of Military Households: Descriptive Evidence from Recent Surveys*. Office of Economic and Manpower Analysis, Department of Social Sciences, United States Military Academy. West Point, NY. Retrieved from www.usma.edu/sosh/SiteAssets/SitePages/Faculty/Publications/FINRA-Paper-2014.pdf.

Skomorovsky, A. (2014). Deployment stress and well-being among military spouses: the role of social support. *Military Psychology*, 26 (1), 44–54.

Smith , B. N., Vaughn , R. A., Vogt , D., King , D. W., King, L. A., and Shipherd, J. C. (2013). Main and interactive effects of social support in predicting mental health symptoms in men and women following military stressor exposure. *Anxiety, Stress, & Coping*, 26, 52–69.

Thoits, P. A. (1986). Social support as coping assistance. *Journal of Consulting and Clinical Psychology*, 54(4), 416–423.

Thoresen, R. J. and Goldsmith, E. B. (1987). The relationship between Army families' financial well-being and depression, general well-being, and marital satisfaction. *Journal of Social Psychology*, 127(5), 545–547.

Van Walraven, C., Oake, N., Jennings, A., and Forster A. J. (2010). The association between continuity of care and outcomes: a systematic and critical review. *Journal of Evaluation in Clinical Practices*, 16(5), 947–956.

Wamboldt E. S., Steinglass, P., and Kaplan De-Nour, A. (1991). Coping within couples: adjustment two years after forced geographical relocation. *Family Process*, 30(3), 347–361.

Wang, Z. and Aitken, N. (2016). The role of social support in military spousal resiliency. In S. Dursun, S. Urban, and W. Dean (eds), *Family Well-Being and Military Readiness*. Kingston, ON: CDA Press.

Wang, Z. and Aitken, N. (2015). *Impacts of Military Lifestyle on Military Families: Results from the Quality of Life Survey of Canadian Armed Forces Spouses* (Director General Military Personnel Research and Analysis Scientific Report DRDC-RDDC-2016-R012). Ottawa, ON: Defence Research and Development Canada.

Wang, Z. and Ouellet, E. (2017). *Top-line Results for the 2017 Military Member/Family Finances Survey*. Presented to the Chief Military Personnel, 24 November 2017. Ottawa, ON: Defence Research and Development Canada.

Weber, E. G. and Weber, D. K. (2005). Geographic relocation frequency, resilience, and military adolescent behavior. *Military Medicine*, 170(7), 638–642.

Wills, T. A. (1985). Supportive functions of interpersonal relationships. In S. Cohen & S. S. Leonard (eds), *Social Support and Health* (pp. 61–82). San Diego, CA: Academic Press, Inc.

9 The influence of work–family experiences during military deployment on organizational outcomes

Helen Pluut and Manon Andres

Introduction

Although work–family conflict is a universal phenomenon (Allen, French, Dumani, and Shockley, 2015), the specific dynamics of work–family issues are likely to be shaped by national culture (Powell, Francesco, and Ling, 2009) and may even reflect the specific challenges of the industry or sector. The military poses a unique set of demands on employees and their families, including frequent and long-term family separations due to training, military deployments, and postings, which increases the likelihood of work–family conflict (Adams, Jex, and Cunningham, 2006). The military and the family are described as greedy institutions (Segal, 1986) and have always been connected. Military employees are embedded in both institutions; they negotiate terms and conditions of work with the military and they negotiate the boundaries between work and non-work with their families. Tensions in the military–employee–family triad (see the framework put forward in this volume and described in more detail in Chapter 1) are assumed to affect all parties involved, yet here we are particularly interested in how work–family tensions affect organizational outcomes. That is, conflict between the military and the family may be greater today than in the past (De Angelis and Segal, 2015) and this creates challenges for the military in attracting and retaining personnel.

The notion of family-relatedness of work decisions (Greenhaus and Powell, 2012) implies that partners may have considerable influence on an employee's work decisions, such as reenlisting with the Navy (see also Huffman, Casper, and Payne, 2013). Not surprisingly, then, the military—as a greedy institution—wants both service members and their families to be committed to the institution (Bourg and Segal, 1999). Despite a growing body of research on military families, little is known about family members' attitudes toward the military. This chapter is guided by the following overall research question: *how do tensions between work and family affect employees' and their families' attitudes toward the military*? We aim to answer this research question through a study among deployed Navy personnel and their stay-at-home partners.

Theoretical background

Work-to-family conflict and organizational outcomes

By its very nature, military deployment entails a form of work-to-family conflict because individuals are separated from their families and opportunities for communication are limited (Andres, Moelker, and Soeters, 2012). Evidently, this puts considerable strain on Navy personnel and their families. We propose that Navy personnel who experience work-to-family conflict will be less likely to reenlist and stay with the Navy, and we focus on overall satisfaction and organizational identification as attitudes that may explain why Navy personnel would decide to stay with or leave the organization.

First, it is likely that people attribute blame to the domain that is the source of conflict and subsequently will develop negative attitudes toward the domain that causes the conflict. This notion has been referred to as the source attribution perspective (Shockley and Singla, 2011). In the case of work interfering with family, it might very well be, as Shockley and Singla (2011: 864) noted, that "an individual is likely to . . . be dissatisfied with the work because it caused the conflict to occur, rather than the family role, which is merely a victim of the interference." Thus, we expect that those service members who experience high work-to-family conflict will be less satisfied with the Navy and will identify less strongly with the Navy compared to those who experience low work-to-family conflict.

Second, negative attitudes toward the Navy will reduce the likelihood that a service member wants to reenlist. Overall satisfaction with the job has consistently been found to correlate with both turnover intentions and actual employee turnover (Cotton and Tuttle, 1986; Griffeth, Hom, and Gaertner, 2000; Tett and Meyer, 1993; see Kelly et al., 2001, for a study among Navy mothers). Moreover, organizational identification has been found to predict lower turnover intentions (Van Dick et al., 2004). Thus, we predict that satisfaction and identification with the Navy are negatively associated with turnover intentions among Navy personnel. The preceding arguments imply that higher turnover intentions among personnel who experience high rather than low levels of work-to-family conflict can be explained (are mediated) by negative attitudes toward the Navy.

> *Hypothesis 1: Work-to-family conflict reported by Navy personnel positively predicts turnover intentions via reduced satisfaction and identification with the Navy.*

Family-to-work conflict and organizational outcomes

It is not uncommon during deployment for family concerns to intrude on the workplace. We propose that family-to-work conflict experienced during a military deployment may affect the work quality of Navy personnel. Family-to-work conflict makes it more likely for people to experience off-task thoughts and engage in unintended behaviors (Demerouti, Taris, and Bakker, 2007). It can lead to employees failing to recall work procedures, not remembering whether they turned off work equipment, not noticing postings, or not fully listening to instructions and getting distracted easily. These are examples of what has been referred to as cognitive failures (Broadbent, Cooper, FitzGerald, and Parkes, 1982; Wallace and Chen, 2005). In one of the few studies focusing specifically on workplace cognitive failures, Lapierre, Hammer, Truxillo, and Murphy (2012) observed that family interference with work was positively related to increased cognitive failures at work.

We posit that Navy personnel who experience high levels of family-to-work conflict during deployment might be more prone to experiencing cognitive failures at work. Thinking or worrying about what happens at home may limit the attention they can devote to their work, setting them up for mistakes. Importantly, cognitive failures may make people frustrated and the work experience less satisfactory because people will perceive they are unsuccessful in their goal pursuit (Lent and Brown, 2006). Meta-analyses indicate that job satisfaction is associated with lower turnover intentions (see Cotton and Tuttle, 1986; Griffeth, Hom, and Gaertner, 2000; Tett and Meyer, 1993). Hence, we predict that family-to-work conflict is associated with higher turnover intentions because those individuals who experience more family-to-work conflict show higher levels of cognitive failures at work and therefore have lower job satisfaction.

> *Hypothesis 2: Family-to-work conflict reported by Navy personnel positively predicts turnover intentions via cognitive failures during deployment and the associated reduced job satisfaction.*

The role of support in relation to work-to-family conflict

Social support is a much-emphasized concept in the work–family literature (Kossek, Pichler, Bodner, and Hammer, 2011; Van Daalen, Willemsen, and Sanders, 2006). In the current study, we focus on the team as a source of workplace social support during deployment because Navy personnel are highly dependent on team members with whom they work and live together on the ship. Importantly, we focus on social support that is specifically targeted at facilitating the employee's ability to manage work–family issues. Kossek and colleagues (2011) found that work–family-specific forms of supervisor and organizational support were more strongly related to work–family conflict than general forms of support. Here, we focus on Navy personnel's perceptions of the degree to which their teams are seen as family supportive and we study this type of support in relation to both work-to-family conflict and family-to-work conflict.

We propose that the experience of being part of a team that offers work–family support may buffer the relationship between work-to-family conflict and negative attitudes toward the Navy. The availability of work–family support in the workplace is reflective of a family-friendly organizational culture (Premeaux, Adkins, and Mossholder, 2007). In a similar way to how supportive supervisors will lead an employee to perceive the organization as supportive (Shanock and

Eisenberger, 2006; Kossek, Pichler, Bodner, and Hammer, 2011), we believe that a work–family supportive team climate is related to perceptions of organizational support. This should help Navy personnel to take a more positive outlook on the Navy despite the experience of work-to-family conflict. Thus, work-to-family conflict may lead to negative attitudes to the Navy through a process of placing blame and retaliation, yet if the individual feels supported in the work–family interface, this may reduce reactivity to negative work–family experiences.

> *Hypothesis 3: Work–family team support buffers the detrimental effects of work-to-family conflict on satisfaction and identification with the Navy.*

The role of support in relation to family-to-work conflict

When individuals feel supported at work, in that they can share their concerns about their family and get advice on family matters, it is easier for them to leave their troubles behind and psychologically detach from home. A family-supportive team climate allows for the discussion of any problems that may otherwise form a distraction while working. In addition to preventing cognitive interference, showing empathy to a person with family concerns may reduce emotional strain that may interfere with work performance (Beauregard, 2006). Thus, we hypothesize that family is less likely to interfere with work if employees receive more work–family team support.

> *Hypothesis 4: Work–family team support diminishes levels of family-to-work conflict.*

The partner's perspective

We propose that partners' attitudes toward the Navy are highly influenced by the degree to which they feel that the work of the service member interferes with their family lives. The job of Navy personnel involves frequent and long-term family separations and a person may feel that their partner's job in the Navy is incompatible with their family life. In line with the source attribution perspective, they may in turn ascribe more negative cognitions to their partner's employer. Specifically, we expect that higher levels of work-to-family conflict (in the eyes of the partner) reduce the level of how satisfied the partner is with the Navy and the degree of identification with the Navy. Moreover, we expect that higher levels of work-to-family conflict make it difficult for the partner to accept job-induced separations as part of their life. Finally, work-to-family conflict will lead an individual to form a more negative opinion on whether the Navy is a good career choice for their partner. Thus, similar to our argument for Navy personnel, we hypothesize that higher levels of tensions in the work–family relationship negatively affect partners' attitudes toward the organization.

> *Hypothesis 5: Partners' views of work-to-family conflict are negatively associated with their attitudes toward the Navy.*

A person can draw support from different sources during their partner's assignment abroad—for instance, family and friends—yet the Navy also organizes support for families. In a similar way to how social support available on the ship may reduce reactivity to work–family issues in deployed Navy personnel, support provided to partners may influence the relationship between work-to-family conflict and their attitudes toward the Navy. If partners are satisfied with the support organized by the Navy, it stands to reason—on the basis of social exchange theory (see Peeters, Ten Brummelhuis, and Van Steenbergen, 2013)—that they want to reciprocate the efforts made by the Navy by evaluating this organization more positively, in spite of the fact that they attribute any work–family tensions to their partner's work for the Navy. Specifically, we expect that perceived organizational support moderates the relationship between partners' views of work-to-family conflict on the one hand and their satisfaction and identification with the Navy as well as their acceptance of separation and evaluation of a Navy career on the other hand.

> *Hypothesis 6: Perceived organizational support buffers the detrimental effects of partners' views of work-to-family conflict on their attitudes toward the Navy.*

Method

Sample and procedure

Data were collected among deployed military personnel of the Dutch Navy and their partners at home. It was communicated that the research focused on the relation between work and family and aimed at investigating the experiences of Navy personnel and the home front. The survey data stem from multiple ships that participated in the study. The researchers brought the surveys on-board to the commander in chief before a ship would leave on a mission. The commander in chief distributed the surveys among the military personnel one month before returning home; an accompanying letter was enclosed, which explained the purpose of the study and emphasized confidentiality. The completed surveys were returned anonymously in a box on-board the ship, which was handed over to the researchers immediately after the ship returned from its mission. At the same time as the surveys were distributed among military personnel on-board, personnel's partners received a survey at their home addresses. Our sample consists of 351 Navy personnel (a response rate of 46 percent), of which 89 were not in a committed relationship. A total of 125 partners completed the survey (a response rate of 57 percent). We could match survey records for 86 military couples.

The Navy personnel were predominantly male (89 percent) and, on average, they were 31 years old ($SD = 9.03$), ranging from 19 to 53. The majority of them (75 percent) were in a committed relationship, 25 percent were not (and defined other persons than a partner as their families); 40 percent had children. Almost all partners were female (93 percent) and they were on average 35 years old

(*SD* = 8.78), varying from 19 to 54. Little more than half of them (58 percent) had children. A large majority of the partners (87 percent) had paid employment, of which 26 percent also worked or had worked within the Ministry of Defense.

Employee survey

With few exceptions, the surveys contained validated scales, which were translated from English as the survey was administered in Dutch.

Work-to-family conflict. We used the five-item Work–Family Conflict Scale developed by Netemeyer, Boles, and McMurrian (1996) to assess the extent to which the work of Navy personnel interferes with family in general (e.g., "The demands of my work interfere with my home and family life"). Responses were given on a five-point Likert scale ranging from 1 (*strongly disagree*) to 5 (*strongly agree*). The Cronbach's alpha was 0.88.

Family-to-work conflict. Five items from the SWING (Geurts et al., 2005) were adapted to assess the extent to which family interfered with work during the current mission of Navy personnel (e.g., "I do not feel like working because I miss my partner/family"). Responses were given on a five-point Likert scale ranging from 1 (*strongly disagree*) to 5 (*strongly agree*) and the Cronbach's alpha was 0.86.

Satisfaction with Navy. We used two items to assess how satisfied Navy personnel were with their job at the Navy: "All things considered, how satisfied are you with the Navy?" and "How satisfied are you with the family life you can have when employed at the Navy?" Answers were given on a scale from 1 (*very dissatisfied*) to 5 (*very satisfied*). The Spearman-Brown coefficient (see Eisinga, Te Grotenhuis, and Pelzer, 2013) for this two-item scale was 0.60.

Identification with Navy. We used a single-item graphic scale developed by Shamir and Kark (2004) for the measurement of organizational identification. Respondents were presented with seven pairs of circles with varying degrees of overlap, from 1 (*no overlap*) to 7 (*complete overlap*). One circle represented the respondent and the other the Navy. Respondents were asked to choose the pair of circles that best represented their current relationship with the Navy. The higher the overlap between circles, the higher the identification with the Navy.

Cognitive failures. We used the eight-item Cognitive Failures Questionnaire-for-others by Broadbent, Cooper, FitzGerald, and Parkes (1982) to assess Navy personnel's level of cognitive exhaustion during deployment. We adapted the items to reflect self-reported failures and also shortened the items. Respondents were asked how they had felt during their current deployment (e.g., "I found it difficult to concentrate on anything"). Answers were given on a five-point Likert scale ranging from 1 (*strongly disagree*) to 5 (*strongly agree*). The Cronbach's alpha for this scale was 0.94.

Job satisfaction. Navy personnel's job satisfaction was assessed with five items from the Brayfield and Rothe (1951) measure (e.g., "Most days I am enthusiastic about my work). Responses were given on a five-point Likert scale ranging from 1 (*strongly disagree*) to 5 (*strongly agree*). The Cronbach's alpha was 0.85.

Turnover intentions. We used three often-used items on turnover intentions from prior research among military families (e.g., Andres, Moelker, and Soeters,

2012): "I often think about leaving the Navy," "I will probably look for a new job in the next year," and "I would like to stay in this organization until I retire." Ratings were obtained on a five-point Likert scale ranging from 1 (*strongly disagree*) to 5 (*strongly agree*). The Cronbach's alpha was 0.80.

Work–family-specific team support. We used the three items from Kossek, Colquitt, and Noe (2001) to assess a family-supportive work climate. We adapted these items to fit a team setting (e.g., "In our team, it is generally accepted that people share concerns about their family"). Answers were given on a five-point Likert scale ranging from 1 (*strongly disagree*) to 5 (*strongly agree*). The Cronbach's alpha was 0.82.

Partner survey

Work-to-family conflict. We administered the same scale to partners at home as we did to employees, with slight adjustments, to assess partners' perceptions of how the naval job interferes with their family life (e.g., "The demands of my partner's job interfere with our home and family life"). The Cronbach's alpha was 0.85.

Satisfaction with the Navy. Similar to Navy personnel, but with slight adaptions, we assessed partners' satisfaction with the Navy: "All things considered, how satisfied are you with the Navy?" and "How satisfied are you with the family life you can have when your partner is employed at the Navy?" The Spearman-Brown coefficient for this two-item scale in the partner sample was 0.58.

Acceptance of separation. We used four self-constructed items to assess the extent to which partners were able to accept the fact that their partner is often away from home because of the naval job (e.g., "I accept that sailing is part of my partner's work"). Answers were recorded on a five-point Likert scale ranging from 1 (*strongly disagree*) to 5 (*strongly agree*) and the Cronbach's alpha was 0.84.

Opinion on the Navy as a career choice. A self-constructed one-item measure was used to assess partners' opinion about their partner working at the Navy. Answer categories ranged from 1 = *I consider the Navy a good career choice* to 3 = *I do not mind* to 5 = *I want my partner to leave as quickly as possible.*

Perceived organizational support. We developed two items that asked partners to what extent they were satisfied with the support made available to them during the absence of their partner. One item focused on support organized by the Navy, the other on support organized by home front groups. Answers were given on a five-point Likert scale and the Spearman-Brown coefficient for this two-item scale was 0.85.

Results

Analyses

We examined the data among Navy personnel and partners separately. Descriptive statistics (i.e., means, standard deviations, and intercorrelations) are presented in Tables 9.1 and 9.2.

Table 9.1 Descriptive statistics, Navy personnel

	Variable	Mean	SD	*1*	*2*	*3*	*4*	*5*	*6*	*7*
1	Work-to-family conflict	3.04	0.84	1						
2	Family-to-work conflict	2.55	0.76	0.43***	1					
3	WF-specific team support	3.65	0.62	−0.13*	−0.14*	1				
4	Cognitive failures	2.04	0.74	0.17**	0.51***	−0.24***	1			
5	Job satisfaction	3.70	0.61	−0.31***	−0.40***	0.24***	−0.48***	1		
6	Satisfaction with the Navy	3.17	0.74	−0.49***	−0.39***	0.16**	−0.29***	0.58***	1	
7	Identification with the Navy	4.15	1.40	−0.23***	−0.29***	0.17**	−0.26***	0.47***	0.52***	1
8	Turnover intentions	2.61	0.96	0.25***	0.24***	−0.10	0.26***	−0.51***	−0.58***	−0.57***

Note. WF = work–family.

* $p < 0.05$. ** $p < 0.01$. *** $p < 0.001$.

Table 9.2 Descriptive statistics, partners

	Variable	Mean	SD	*1*	*2*	*3*	*4*	*5*
1	Work-to-family conflict	3.21	0.85	1				
2	Support by the Navy	3.61	0.80	−.30**	1			
3	Satisfaction with the Navy	3.60	0.68	−.54***	.46***	1		
4	Identification with the Navy	3.60	1.49	−.31***	.32***	.44***	1	
5	Opinion on the Navy as a career	2.01	0.96	−.40***	−.34***	−.37***	−.34***	1
6	Acceptance of separation	3.99	0.78	−.46***	.34***	.52***	.32***	−.39***

First, we used data only from the Navy personnel sample (N = 351) to test our hypothesized model in Figure 9.1. We used path analysis in AMOS version 22 to test the interrelations in the hypothesized model simultaneously. We specified covariances between the exogenous variables in our model and further allowed the error terms of the variables "satisfaction with the Navy" and "identification with the Navy" to covary as these constructs may have common sources of unexplained variance. Second, we used data from the partner sample (N = 125) to test our hypothesized model in Figure 9.2. For testing interactions, we centered the predictor variables prior to computing the product term.

To assess congruence with the data, we report the chi-square value (χ^2) and both incremental and absolute fit indices. The model depicted in Figure 9.1 does not show an acceptable fit to the data as reflected by the chi-square value, χ^2 (20) = 246.8, $p < 0.001$, and fit indices (NFI = 0.73; CFI = 0.73; RMSEA = 0.18), which is not surprising given the comprehensiveness of our model (see also Bagozzi and Edwards, 1998). The model in Figure 9.2 was saturated and thus no meaningful fit statistics can be provided. We are not interested in model fit per se but rather in the significance of hypothesized paths and explained variance in our dependent variables. In the model for Navy personnel, our predictors explained 38.3 percent of total variance in scores on turnover intentions. For partners of Navy personnel, our predictors accounted for explained variances in the various attitudes toward the Navy

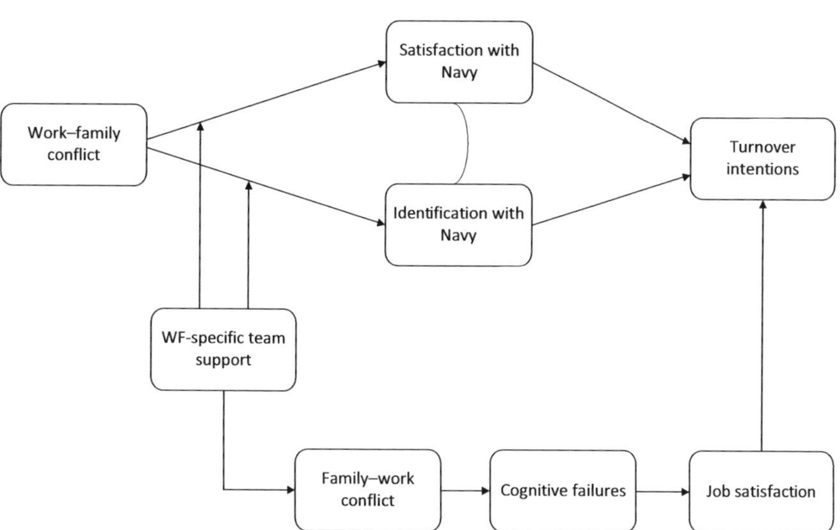

Figure 9.1 Hypothesized model for Navy personnel

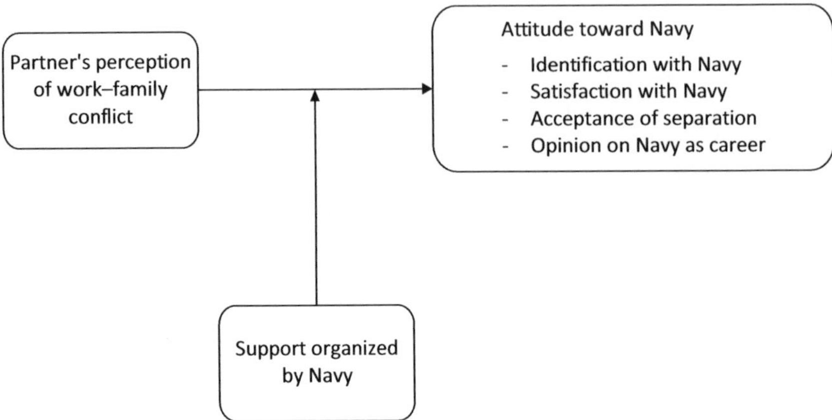

Figure 9.2 Hypothesized model for partners of Navy personnel

ranging from 18 percent for identification with the Navy to 40.9 percent for satisfaction with the Navy.

Test of hypotheses

The results for Navy personnel are shown in Table 9.3. We found that work-to-family conflict was negatively associated with both satisfaction with the Navy ($\beta = -0.50$; $p < 0.001$) and identification with the Navy ($\beta = -0.22$; $p < 0.001$). In turn, satisfaction and identification with the Navy were negatively associated with turnover intentions ($\beta = -0.34$; $p < 0.001$; and $\beta = -0.34$; $p < 0.001$, respectively). In support of hypothesis 1, mediation tests conducted using "RMediation" (Tofighi and MacKinnon, 2011) indicated that work-to-family conflict had a significant indirect effect on turnover intentions among Navy personnel. The indirect effect estimate for work-to-family conflict through satisfaction with the Navy was 0.178, 95-percent CI [0.098, 0.273]. The indirect effect of work-to-family conflict through identification with the Navy was estimated at 0.08 with a 95-percent CI of [0.039, 0.127].

We found a significant interaction between work-to-family conflict and work–family-specific team support in predicting satisfaction with the Navy ($\beta = 0.12$; $p < 0.05$; Figure 9.3) and identification with the Navy ($\beta = 0.11$; $p < 0.05$; Figure 9.4), supporting hypothesis 3. Moreover, we found that work–family-specific team support was associated with lower levels of family-to-work conflict ($\beta = -0.14$; $p < 0.05$), which supports hypothesis 4.

Family-to-work conflict was positively associated with cognitive failures during deployment ($\beta = 0.51$; $p < 0.001$), which in turn were associated with reduced job satisfaction ($\beta = -0.48$; $p < 0.001$). Finally, turnover intentions were higher

Table 9.3 Results from path analysis, Navy personnel

Path from	*To*	*Unstandardized path coefficient*	*SE*	*Critical ratio*
Work-to-family conflict	Satisfaction with the Navy	–0.44***	0.04	–10.52
Work-to-family conflict	Identification with the Navy	–0.36***	0.09	–4.13
WFC x WF-specific team support	Satisfaction with the Navy	0.15*	0.06	2.40
WFC x WF-specific team support	Identification with the Navy	0.28*	0.14	2.03
Satisfaction with the Navy	Turnover intentions	–0.41***	0.06	–6.77
Identification with the Navy	Turnover intentions	–0.22***	0.03	–6.84
WF-specific team support	Family-to-work conflict	–0.16*	0.06	–2.55
Family-to-work conflict	Cognitive failures	0.50***	0.05	10.96
Cognitive failures	Job satisfaction	–0.40***	0.04	–10.25
Job satisfaction	Turnover intentions	–0.28***	0.06	–4.49

Note. WFC = work-to-family conflict. WF = work–family.

* $p < 0.05$. *** $p < 0.001$.

Table 9.4 Results from path analysis, partners

Path from	*To*	*Unstandardized path coefficient*	*SE*	*Critical ratio*
Work-to-family conflict	Satisfaction with the Navy	–0.35***	0.06	–6.04
Work-to-family conflict	Identification with the Navy	–0.39**	0.15	–2.61
Work-to-family conflict	Opinion on the Navy as a career	0.36***	0.10	3.85
Work-to-family conflict	Acceptance of separation	–0.35***	0.07	–4.78
WFC x support by the Navy	Satisfaction with the Navy	0.11†	0.06	1.83
WFC x support by the Navy	Identification with the Navy	0.34*	0.16	2.11
WFC x support by the Navy	Opinion on the Navy as a career	–0.08	0.10	–0.79
WFC x support by the Navy	Acceptance of separation	0.08	0.08	1.04

Note. WFC = work-to-family conflict.

† < 0.10. * $p < 0.05$. ** $p < 0.01$. *** $p < 0.001$.

among those who were less rather than more satisfied with their jobs ($\beta = -0.19$; $p < 0.001$). A test of serial mediation using Hayes' PROCESS indicated that family-to-work conflict indirectly influenced turnover intentions via cognitive failures and job satisfaction. This indirect effect was estimated at 0.12 with a 95-percent CI of [0.08, 0.18]. Hence, also hypothesis 2 was supported.

Table 9.4 shows the results for partners of Navy personnel. Results indicated that partners' views of work-to-family conflict were negatively associated with satisfaction with the Navy ($\beta = -0.44$; $p < 0.001$), identification with the Navy ($\beta = -0.22$; $p < 0.01$), and acceptance of separation ($\beta = -0.39$; $p < 0.001$). Moreover, opinions about the Navy as a career choice were more negative among those partners who perceived higher levels of interference with family life ($\beta = 0.32$; $p < 0.001$). Thus, hypothesis 5 was fully supported. Support organized by the Navy was positively associated with all attitudes toward the Navy, namely satisfaction ($\beta = 0.30$; $p < 0.001$), identification ($\beta = 0.22$; $p < 0.05$), acceptance of separation ($\beta = 0.21$; $p < 0.01$), and opinion on the Navy as a career choice ($\beta = -0.23$; $p < .01$), but did not reduce reactivity to work-to-family conflict in all instances. We found that the interaction between partners' views of work-to-family conflict and support organized by the Navy was significant in predicting identification with the Navy ($\beta = 0.18$; $p < 0.05$; Figure 9.5); in other words, support buffered the detrimental effect of work-to-family conflict perceptions on identification, as hypothesized. However, the interaction between partners' views of work-to-family conflict and support organized by the Navy was only marginally significant in predicting satisfaction with the Navy ($\beta = 0.13$; $p = 0.068$) and support organized by the Navy did not buffer the relationships between work-to-family conflict on the one hand and acceptance ($\beta = 0.08$; $p = 0.298$) and opinion ($\beta = -0.06$; $p = 0.431$) on the other. Thus, we found only partial support for hypothesis 6.

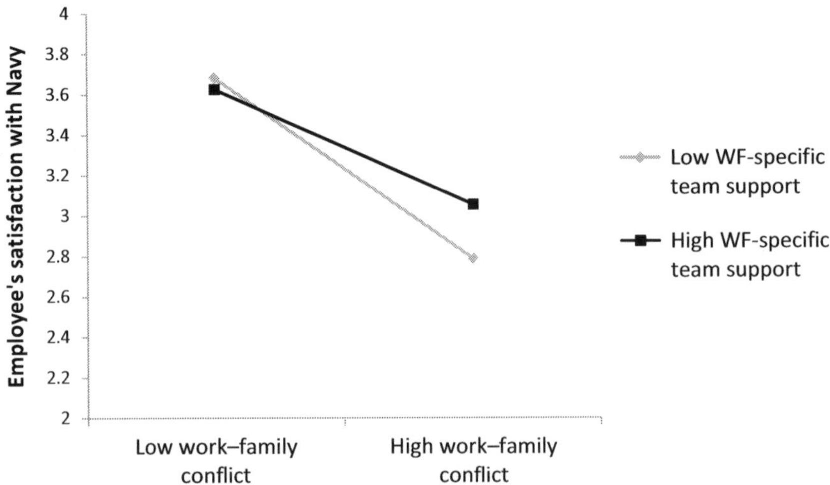

Figure 9.3 The interactive effect between work-to-family conflict and work–family-specific team support in predicting employees' satisfaction with the Navy

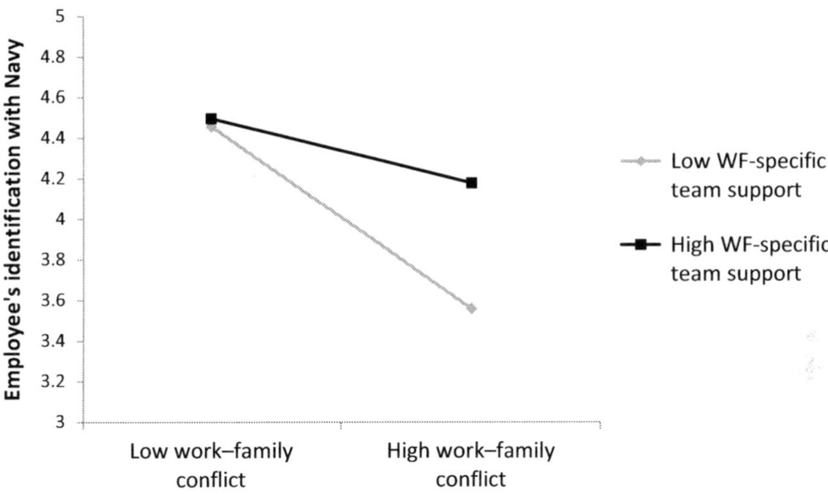

Figure 9.4 The interactive effect between work-to-family conflict and work–family-specific team support in predicting employees' identification with the Navy

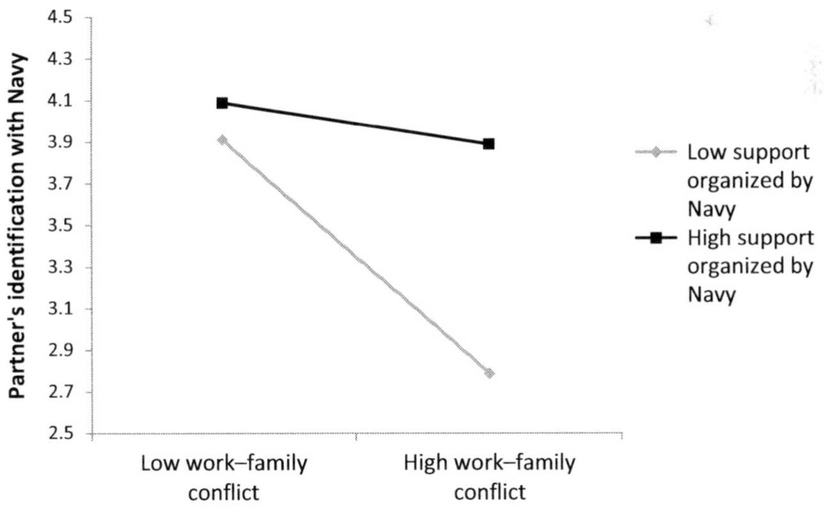

Figure 9.5 The interactive effect between work-to-family conflict and support organized by the Navy in predicting partners' identification with the Navy

Discussion

This study examined tensions in the military–employee–family triad and goes beyond prior research among military families in several important ways. While most research has primarily addressed the effects of military life and job demands on family dynamics and well-being, we have focused on organizational outcomes. Moreover, empirical work–family research in military contexts—in particular during operational conditions—is scarce and little is known about family members' attitudes toward the military. We have sampled the experiences of both service members and their partners during a deployment and have examined various attitudes toward the military. Our study demonstrates that work–family experiences during deployment are critical in determining attitudes toward the military and intentions to reenlist.

Both work-to-family conflict and family-to-work conflict increased the odds of turnover of military personnel, either because employees developed negative attitudes toward the Navy or because they could not function optimally at work and thus enjoyed the naval job less. Moreover, partners who felt that the naval job interfered with their home and family life were more likely to develop negative attitudes toward the Navy. Importantly, our findings also suggest that employers that are considered family friendly may face lower levels of turnover of service members. The benefits of support provided by team members and the organization are reciprocated by employees and their partners with positive attitudes toward the Navy, despite the experience that work interferes with family life, which may be inevitable in times of deployment. We conclude that perceived organizational work–family support is a powerful mechanism in the military–employee–family triad to improve attitudes and thus lower turnover intentions.

Practical implications

A key implication of our findings is that the military should be equally interested in the degree to which work interferes with family as in the degree to which family interferes with work, in order to prevent cognitive failures at work, negative attitudes, and ultimately high turnover, which all induce considerable organizational costs. Given that Navy personnel are away from their families during deployment, they are highly dependent on their team members on the ship. In order to reduce (reactivity to) work–family tensions, it is critical that the team is able to establish a family-supportive climate. The military should ensure that Navy personnel feel psychologically safe to discuss any family matters and share concerns about their families on-board the ship. To this end, it is recommended that supervisors exhibit behaviors that are supportive of family, including role modeling behaviors that demonstrate how service members can successfully manage family separations, as supervisor support for family may be a key antecedent or subcomponent of family-supportive work climates (Hammer, Kossek, Yragui, Bodner, and Hanson, 2009).

Another implication that follows from our study is that any imbalance or tension in the work–family interface may result in changes to the status quo (i.e., intentions to leave the Navy) by which the service member attempts to restore the balance and attain a more positive outcome for the family. Thus, the experiences and attitudes of family members are an important factor for the military to pay attention to. To address the needs of stay-at-home families, the Navy can offer support during the absence of service members, organize home front groups, provide information on its website and social media, and facilitate communication between Navy personnel and their partners during sailing. The level of satisfaction with such initiatives is an important determinant of partners' attitudes toward the Navy, including the evaluation of whether the naval job is a good career choice for their partner.

Limitations and future research

Caution is warranted in drawing conclusions about causality in the relationships that we studied as our data stem from a cross-sectional research design. We suggest that future researchers test our model in a longitudinal fashion. Specifically, we recommend measurement of some of our constructs prior to, during, and after a job-induced family separation, to assess any fluctuations over the course of a deployment. This would offer a better understanding of the work–family experiences of both service members and their families. A second limitation of our study is that it does not shed light on what initiatives by the Navy or what behaviors of team members are seen as family supportive. We recommend future researchers to use scales that assess specific support behaviors (see e.g., Hammer, Kossek, Yragui, Bodner, and Hanson, 2009).

Our argumentation on the benefits of social support did not take into account that individuals differ in their segmentation preferences (Chen, Powell, and Greenhaus, 2009); some try to keep work and family life separate most of the time, while others will talk as much as possible about their family and personal issues with their co-workers. Although we stick with our premise that the military should establish family-supportive team climates on their Navy ships, it should be noted that conversations about family matters may go against the segmentation preferences of some employees. Moreover, even for those who prefer to discuss family matters with colleagues, social support is associated with disadvantages, such as rumination (Boren, 2014), which may lead to cognitive failures and other forms of work impairment. In moving forward, it would be a valuable endeavor to gain further insights into the complexities of offering social support to military personnel and their partners.

References

Adams, G. A., Jex, S. M., and Cunningham, C. J. L. (2006). Work–family conflict among military personnel. In C. A. Castro, A. B. Adler, and T. W. Britt (eds), *Military Life: The Psychology of Serving in Peace and Combat. Volume 3: The Military Family*. Westport, CT: Praeger.

Allen, T. D., French, K. A., Dumani, S., and Shockley, K. M. (2015). Meta-analysis of work-family conflict mean differences: does national context matter? *Journal of Vocational Behavior*, 90, 90–100.

Andres, M., Moelker, R., and Soeters, J. (2012). The work-family interface and turnover intentions over the course of project-oriented assignments abroad. *International Journal of Project Management*, 30, 752–759.

Bagozzi, R. P. and Edwards, J. R. (1998). A general approach for representing constructs in organizational research. *Organizational Research Methods*, 1, 45–87.

Beauregard, T. A. (2006). Predicting interference between work and home: a comparison of dispositional and situational antecedents. *Journal of Managerial Psychology*, 21, 244–264.

Boren, J. P. (2014). The relationships between co-rumination, social support, stress, and burnout among working adults. *Management Communication Quarterly*, 28, 3–25.

Bourg, C. and Segal, M. W. (1999). The impact of family supportive policies and practices on organizational commitment to the Army. *Armed Forces & Society*, 25, 633–652.

Brayfield, A. H. and Rothe, H. F. (1951). An index of job satisfaction. *Journal of Applied Psychology*, 35, 307–311.

Broadbent, D. E., Cooper, P. F., FitzGerald, P., and Parkes, K. R. (1982). The cognitive failures questionnaire (CFQ) and its correlates. *British Journal of Clinical Psychology*, 21, 1–16.

Chen, Z., Powell, G. N., and Greenhaus, J. H. (2009). Work-to-family conflict, positive spillover, and boundary management: a person-environment fit approach. *Journal of Vocational Behavior*, 74, 82–93.

Cotton, J. L., and Tuttle, J. M. (1986). Employee turnover: a meta-analysis and review with implications for research. *Academy of Management Review*, 11, 55–70.

De Angelis, K. and Segal, M. (2015). Transitions in the military and the family as greedy institutions: original concept and current applicability. In R. Moelker, M. Andres, G. Bowen, and P. Manigart (eds), *Military Families and War in the 21st Century: Comparative Perspectives* (pp. 22–42). London: Routledge.

Demerouti, E., Taris, T. W., and Bakker, A. B. (2007). Need for recovery, home-work interference and performance: is lack of concentration the link? *Journal of Vocational Behavior*, 71, 204–220.

Eisinga, R., Te Grotenhuis, M., and Pelzer, B. (2013). The reliability of a two-item scale: Pearson, Cronbach, or Spearman-Brown? *International Journal of Public Health*, 58, 637–642.

Geurts, S. A. E., Taris, T. W., Kompier, M. A. J., Dikkers, J. S. E., Van Hooff, M. L. M., and Kinnunen, U. M. (2005). Work-home interaction from a work psychological perspective: development and validation of a new questionnaire, the SWING. *Work & Stress: An International Journal of Work, Health, & Organisations*, 19, 319–339.

Greenhaus, J. H. and Powell, G. N. (2012). The family-relatedness of work decisions: a framework and agenda for theory and research. *Journal of Vocational Behavior*, 80, 246–255.

Griffeth, R. W., Hom, P. W., and Gaertner, S. (2000). A meta-analysis of antecedents and correlates of employee turnover: update, moderator tests, and research implications for the next millennium. *Journal of Management*, 26, 463–488.

Hammer, L., Kossek, E. E., Yragui, N., Bodner, T., and Hanson, G. (2009). Development and validation of a multidimensional scale of family-supportive supervisor behaviors (FSSB). *Journal of Management*, 35, 837–856.

Huffman, A. H., Casper, W. J., and Payne, S. C. (2013). How does spouse career support relate to employee turnover? Work interfering with family and job satisfaction as mediators. *Journal of Organizational Behavior*, 35, 194–212.

Kelley, M. L., Hock, E., Bonney, J. F., Jarvis, M. S., Smith, K. M., and Gaffney, M. A. (2001). Navy mothers experiencing and not experiencing deployment: reasons for staying in or leaving the military. *Military Psychology*, 13, 55–71.

Kossek, E. E., Colquitt, J. A., and Noe, R. A. (2001). Caregiving decisions, well-being, and performance: the effects of place and provider as a function of dependent type and work-family climates. *Academy of Management Journal*, 44, 29–44.

Kossek, E. E., Pichler, S., Bodner, T., and Hammer, L. B. (2011). Workplace social support and work-family conflict: a meta-analysis clarifying the influence of general and work-family-specific supervisor and organizational support. *Personnel Psychology*, 64, 289–313.

Lapierre, L. M., Hammer, L. B., Truxillo, D. M., and Murphy, L. A. (2012). Family interference with work and workplace cognitive failure: the mitigating role of recovery experiences. *Journal of Vocational Behavior*, 81, 227–235.

Lent, R. W. and Brown, S. D. (2006). Integrating person and situation perspectives on work satisfaction: a social-cognitive view. *Journal of Vocational Behavior*, 69, 236–247.

Netemeyer, R. G., Boles, J. S., and McMurrian, R. (1996). Development and validation of work-family conflict and family-work conflict scales. *Journal of Applied Psychology*, 81, 400–410.

Peeters, M. C. W., Ten Brummelhuis, L. L., and Van Steenbergen, E. F. (2013). Consequences of combining work and family roles: a closer look at cross-domain versus within-domain relations. In J. G. Grzywacz and E. Demerouti (eds), *New Frontiers in Work and Family Research* (pp. 93–109). East Sussex: Psychology Press.

Powell, G. N., Francesco, A. M., and Ling, Y. (2009). Toward cultural-sensitive theories of the work-family interface. *Journal of Organizational Behavior*, 30, 597–616.

Premeaux, S. F., Adkins, C. L., and Mossholder, K. W. (2007). Balancing work and family: a field study of multi-dimensional, multi-role work-family conflict. *Journal of Organizational Behavior*, 28, 705–727.

Segal, M. W. (1986). The military and the family as greedy institutions. *Armed Forces & Society*, 13, 9–38.

Shamir, B. and Kark, R. (2004). A single-item graphic scale for the measurement of organizational identification. *Journal of Occupational and Organizational Psychology*, 77, 115–123.

Shanock, L. R. and Eisenberger, R. (2006). When supervisors feel supported: relationships with subordinates' perceived supervisor support, perceived organizational support, and performance. *Journal of Applied Psychology*, 91, 689–695.

Shockley, K. M. and Singla, N. (2011). Reconsidering work-family interactions and satisfaction: a meta-analysis. *Journal of Management*, 37, 861–886.

Tett, R. P. and Meyer, J. P. (1993). Job satisfaction, organizational commitment, turnover intention, and turnover: path analyses based on meta-analytic findings. *Personnel Psychology*, 46, 259–293.

Tofighi, D. and MacKinnon, D. P. (2011). RMediation: an R package for mediation analysis confidence intervals. *Behavior Research Methods*, 43, 692–700.

Van Daalen, G., Willemsen, T. M., and Sanders, K. (2006). Reducing work-family conflict through different sources of social support. *Journal of Vocational Behavior*, 69(3), 462–476.

Van Dick, R., Christ, O., Stellmacher, J., Wagner, U., Ahlswede, O., Grubba, C., Hauptmeijer, M., Höhfeld, C., Moltzen, K. Tissington, P. A. (2004). Should I stay or should I go? Explaining turnover intentions with organizational identification and job satisfaction. *British Journal of Management*, 15, 351–360.

Wallace, J. C. and Chen, G. (2005). Development and validation of a work-specific measure of cognitive failure: implications for occupational safety. *Journal of Occupational and Organizational Psychology*, 78, 615–632.

10 "Happy wife, happy soldier"

How the relationship between military spouses and the military institution influences spouse well-being

Rachael Gribble, Laura Goodwin, Sian Oram, and Nicola Fear

Introduction

The family and the military are both "greedy institutions" (Segal, 1986), demanding great dedication, commitment, time, and energy from service personnel and leading to potential conflict between work and family life. The demands of the military often extend beyond service personnel to include their family members, with the disruptions of relocation, separations and reunions, and deployment common experiences for many military families (Padden and Posey, 2013; Link and Palinkas, 2013; Beevor, 1990). The increased stress and pressure spouses of Service personnel can experience as a result of these events have been associated with poorer mental health and well-being among this population (Link and Palinkas, 2013; Verdeli et al., 2011; Figley, 1993; Booth et al., 2007; Wood, Scarville, and Gravino, 1995; Drummet, Coleman, and Cable, 2003; Burrell, Adams, Durand, and Castro, 2006; Padden and Posey, 2013).

Conflict can also arise because of the experiences and perceptions military spouses have of the military institution itself and the perceived encroachment of the demands of the military into daily family life. US military spouses living on or near military bases have reported experiencing social pressure from within the military community to provide a range of unpaid, informal support activities, such as organizing community events and supporting other military spouses, that are often related to their husband's position in the military hierarchy (Harrison and Laliberte, 1994). Those not conforming to these roles and the idealized identity of a "good military wife" may face social sanction and exclusion (Enloe, 2000). While social pressure to perform these roles is determined in part by cultural norms from within the military community, these are maintained and underpinned by military procedures that rely on spouses to provide these informal support services to help build a supportive and cohesive community (Horn, 2010; Harrison and Laliberte, 1997; Hyde, 2016). This is an example of Papanek's proposed "two-person single career," which postulates that female spouses of men in certain occupations assume a role within their husband's career because of informal and formal demands from his employer that aim to ultimately benefit the institution (Papanek, 1973). As well as spouses becoming incorporated into their husband's careers via these roles, military policies such as access to bases and military-provided services also bond spouses to their husbands and, by proxy, to the military hierarchy (Weinstein and Mederer, 1997; Enloe, 2000; Horn, 2010). However, at the same time, military policies and procedures that rely on personnel as the point of contact allow the military to exert power and control over spouses despite their civilian status, ensuring they maintain only a peripheral connection to the institution while at the same time allowing the military to rely on their unpaid support (Enloe, 2000; Finch, 1983; Harrell, 2001; Harrison and Laliberte, 1994).

These expectations and pressures highlight the tensions spouses can experience regarding the demands and boundaries of the military organization and the family and the role of the service personnel as both employee and family member. However, these tensions vary by context. The military's most obvious authority over family life is exhibited through accompanied postings, where personnel are relocated because of a change in their job role or a promotion. Just under a quarter of military families report relocating between military base and communities for reasons associated with military service in the last year (Ministry of Defence, 2017). Such relocations can cause difficulties for military spouses trying to find and maintain employment (Gribble, 2017a) and there are increasing concerns about the impact of the educational attainment of children from military families (Office for Fair Access, 2018). Unlike other European countries, approximately 60 percent of UK military families live in Service Family Accommodation (SFA) centered on or near military bases and provided by the Ministry of Defence (Ministry of Defence, 2017); this is highest among the Army (68 percent) and Royal Air Force (56 percent), whose proximity to the military means that spouses are more likely to be subject to expectations from within the community. Because of their proximity to the military and their relationship with service personnel, military spouses in the UK may also experience similar demands from the military and the military community. UK military housing provides not only a home for military families but establishes a community through which military families can access both formal military support through welfares services as well as informal support from other members of the community. Spouses in the UK, especially those of personnel within non-commissioned officer ranks, straddle this divide, providing formalized support services alongside welfare by organizing events such as weekly coffee mornings as well as informal support for the wives of the personnel within their husbands' chain of command.

Although such gendered expectations may be dissipating in light of changing family roles and structure within civil society, they are still evident within recent US research (Durand, 2000; Knobloch and Wehrman, 2014; Enloe, 2016). With only one prior UK study exploring the relationship between spouses and the military (Higate and Cameron, 2004), it is unclear how UK military spouses experience the military institution and to what extent their experiences may influence their well-being. This chapter addresses this gap in the literature by exploring experiences of the relationship between UK military spouses and the military institution during relocation and the perceived influences on spouse well-being.

Methods

Study background

The findings from this chapter are based on part of a larger study of the health and well-being of UK military spouses and partners (Gribble, 2017b). Prior research identified the need for further research regarding the impact of relocation on the mental health and well-being of spouses (Blakely, Hennessy, Chung, and Skirton, 2012); therefore, the qualitative component of this study focused on, but was not limited to, the influence of spouse experiences of military relocations on well-being.

Participants and procedure

Participants were drawn from the King's Centre for Military Health Research (KCMHR) Children of Military Fathers' study (Iversen, Fear, Rowe, and Burdett, 2014). Spouses who consented to follow-up were eligible to participate if they were the spouse of:

- a currently serving member of the UK Armed Forces who had experienced at least one military relocation in the last five years; or
- a former member of the UK Armed Forces who had experienced at least one military relocation in the five years prior to personnel leaving service.

Participants were selected according to service personnel rank as prior research had noted differences in the expectations on US spouses of officers and non-officers to perform roles in the US military community (Harrell, 2001; Enloe, 2000). Ethical approval for this study was granted by the King's College Ethics Research Committee (Am08-Am09).

Semi-structured telephone interviews were conducted from January to July 2015 to explore the relationship between spouses and the military institution.[1] Spouses were asked about their experiences of employment, relationships, social connections during military relocations, their experiences with the military as an institution, and their perceptions of how these experiences influenced their well-being. This chapter discusses findings relating to their perceptions and experiences of the military institution only.

Influences on well-being were determined by spouse descriptions of positive or negative emotional responses to their experiences at the time or discussion of *a priori* themes of well-being identified from the literature (identity, agency/autonomy, and incorporation). Pseudonyms were used and potentially identifying information removed. Quotations are verbatim, with fillers/non-verbal elements removed to improve readability.

As this study focused predominately on experiences of relocation, 19 interviews were completed with women married to members of the most mobile service branches, the British Army or Royal Air Force (RAF). Personnel were of sergeant rank or above. All participants had children and had previously lived within service accommodation on or near military bases; six were currently living on or near a military base. Further details can be found in Table 10.1.

Table 10.1 Qualitative study participants

Rank	*Age group (years)*	*Pseudonym*	*Service branch*	*Husband has left Service*	*No. years married*	*Total no. of accompanied postings*	*Overseas accompanied postings*	*Occupational area*
NCO	30s	**Courtney**	RAF	No	5–9	< 5	Yes	Teacher
		Mary	Army	Yes	10–14	< 5	Yes	Health services
		Allison	Army	No	10–14	5–9	Yes	Educational support
		Dee	Army	No	15–19	5–9	Yes	Educational support
	40s	**Molly**	Army	No	5–9	< 5	No	Educational support
		Gina	RAF	No	10–14	< 5	Yes	Teacher
		Janet	Army	Yes	15–19	< 5	Yes	Health services
		Linda	Army	Yes	20+	5–9	Yes	Stay-at-home parent
Officer	30s	**Jennifer**	Army	No	10–14	5–9	No	Educational support
		Louise	RAF	Yes	10–14	5–9	No	Self-employed
	40s	**Toni**	RAF	No	10–14	< 5	No	Teacher
		Anna	Army	No	10–14	5–9	No	Health services
		Joan	Army	No	15–19	5–9	Yes	Health services
		Kathleen	Army	No	20+	5–9	Yes	Stay-at-home parent
		Kim	Army	No	20+	5–9	Yes	Military charity
		Suzy	Army	No	20+	10+	Yes	Financial services
	50s	**Carrie**	Army	Yes	20+	5–9	Yes	Self-employed
		Kristen	Army	Yes	20+	10+	Yes	Educational support
		Melissa	RAF	No	20+	10+	Yes	Corrections services

NCO = non-commissioned officer of sergeant rank or above

Data were analyzed using Framework analysis, a method for organizing and identifying themes and sub-themes within qualitative data (Lacey and Luff, 2009; Spencer, Ritchie, Ormston, O'Connor, and Barnard, 2003; Ritchie and Lewis, 2003). Themes and sub-themes were checked by a second coder (AR). Feedback from representatives of the Army Families Federation (AFF), a military family charity that advocates for Army families in the UK,[2] was used as a form of participant validation. Differences according to rank (officer/non-officer) were explored and discussed where relevant.

The influence of spouse experiences of the military institution on well-being

Three themes were identified that illustrate how spouses perceived their relationship with the military institution and the influences on well-being (Figure 10.1); *identity, agency*, and *connectedness*.

Identity

Assuming rank

While the extent to which Service personnel rank is extended to spouses has changed over time, it still remains a central means for characterizing and organizing the military community (Drummet, Drummet, Coleman, and Cable, 2003; Rosen and Moghadam, 1989; Hall, 2011). Experiences of gendered expectations to perform informal, unpaid roles associated with their husband's position within the community were prominent among participants.

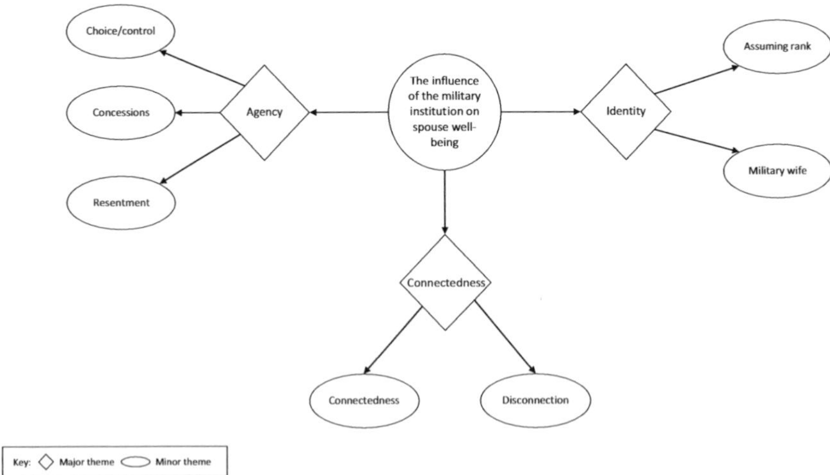

Figure 10.1 Thematic diagram of the influence of partner experiences of the military institution on well-being

> I took it on myself to . . . look after the other wives . . . I think I felt that because of [husband]'s rank that I had to. . . it was kind of an expectation that I should do it really as the [NCO's] wife.
>
> (Mary, 30s; NCO, Army, transitioned)

Some participants did not believe such roles were suited to their personalities and described feelings of anxiety and reluctance about performing these roles due to a lack of self-confidence and an unwillingness to be a focal point in the community.

> There's part of me that felt a little bit daunted by it, I've never done anything like that before. There's also part of me that doesn't like to be in the spotlight. . . I was a little, little scared. You know there is that kind of "Oh my God! Will I do a good job like she did?"
>
> (Joan, 40s; officer, Army)

The ability of spouses to balance the different identities assigned to them may impact on mental health and well-being. Thoits' Identity Accumulation Theory (Thoits, 1983) postulates that multiple role identities can influence the psychological and emotional well-being of individuals by providing resources that can be drawn on to reduce or prevent distress. However, incompatible role demands can lead to negative effects on health and well-being (Owens, Robinson, and Smith-Lovin, 2010). The timing of expectations regarding social roles may be an important factor in spouse well-being. One participant described her first accompanied posting as a new mother to an area where she knew no-one, shortly after which her husband was deployed. The strong social pressures she was experienced to provide support for other officer wives, combined with the stressors of motherhood and moving and concern about her husband, resulted in this posting being a time of emotional stress. "When [I was] feeling at my very, very lowest ebb. . . that was when I was the CO's wife!. . . being absolutely at the lowest point inside, but then having this. . . outer image of. . . being there for everyone else" (Anna, 40s, officer, Army).

As such roles had particular social identities attached to them, by performing them, spouses "*assumed rank,*" becoming incorporated into their husband's identity and adopting a similar standing within the military hierarchy (Finch, 1983; Jervis, 2011; Harrell, 2001). Taking on these roles and therefore taking on their husband's identity could result in uncertainty among spouses about replicating the rank system within the wider military community and the potential impact of this on their relationships with other spouses.

> We did it! But under pressure. . . because we were the Officers' wives they thought that we should be leading them . . . we didn't feel it was appropriate or why should we have to do it just because we're an officer's wife . . . you're conscious that the soldiers' wives are probably looking at you and thinking "Well, who does she think she is?"
>
> (Suzy, 40s; officer, Army)

Military wife

Some participants discussed how negative encounters with representatives of the military and particular military practices and policies bound them to their husband. Participants viewed these encounters as reminders of their status as separate from personnel as full and valued members of the community, leading to a sense of "otherness" and division from the institution, diminishing their independent identity and incorporating them into the identity of "military wife."

Such experiences are similar to those discussed in the prior UK study (Higate and Cameron, 2004) and suggest that institutional practices contain to maintain the dependency of spouses on personnel some ten years later. One spouse described an interaction with a housing officer who refused to continue talking to her when she became upset about a problem with their service accommodation and only spoke to her husband:

> It was breath-taking, I just thought "I can't believe people speak to people like this!"... There is this attitude which permeates, especially out here at camp, that is really you're not your own person. You're "wife of"... even the title dependent... it's fairly derogatory really, in my opinion. "UK dependent" is what you're called!
>
> (Gina, 40s; NCO, RAF)

While such patriarchal views within the military were acknowledged as rare, they are not uncommon, and have been reported in UK studies of spouses (Jervis, 2011; Higate and Cameron, 2004). Such marginalization or expressions of power by the military via its representatives were also experienced by spouses in more overt ways. Previous research has demonstrated how spouses who resisted social norms to adhere to the expectations of being a "good wife" may face social sanction from within the military community (Enloe, 2016); censure may not only be applied to spouses but also to their husbands through the loss of potential promotions (Goldstein, 2001; Harrison and Laliberte, 1997). Although acknowledged as a rare occurrence, one participant explained how a campaign to prevent the closure of a community facility resulted in the husbands of the spouses involved being informally cautioned by their commanding officer. This paternalistic threat of sanction led to deliberate changes to this spouses' behavior to align herself with what she perceived would be viewed as more befitting for an officer's wife in order to protect her husband's career.

> I feel constrained in what I can say and do because there are people of the mind-set in the military that if your wife doesn't behave and stay in line in the way they think they should, their husband's career will suffer... surely there's no other organization that behaves like that.
>
> (Toni, 40s; officer, RAF)

Agency

Choice/control and concessions

While accompanied postings could be a source of enjoyment and adventure for some spouses, others viewed them as relinquishing *choice/control* of family life to the military, with little opportunity to resist or delay relocation.

> There have been times when it's . . . a little bit, sort of, stressful. It's just not being in control of the planning, really. "Oh, by the way you're going to move to such-and-such an area" where you've got no control at all, being told where you're going to move to, and not having a choice. That, I think, is one of the hardest things.
>
> (Gina, 40s; NCO, RAF)

> You get settled in your way of life, like, you know, we've been here over three years and, you know, you go along and you're doing your thing and then its "Ok, now you're off again!" It's really, it's hard!
>
> (Allison, 30s; NCO, Army)

Other participants described their lack of agency in terms of the passive "choices" and *concessions* made to try and negotiate the restrictions of military life. For many, this involved opting to send their children to boarding school[3] to provide social and educational stability for their children, directly calling into conflict their roles as mothers and (military) wives. For those who had a strong sense of being a "good mother," separating their family by sending their children away to school was seen as sacrificing part of their role as a mother and difficult to resolve against this ideal, resulting in feelings of uncertainty and guilt or more serious effects on well-being.

> I prided myself on being a good mum when they were younger and [sending them away has] been quite hard. . . I've missed out a bit on their childhood because they've not been here. . . I panic every now and again and think "Have I done the right thing?"
>
> (Suzy, 40s; officer, Army)

> [I was] not depressed by any stretch of the imagination, but I was quite low because I had to leave my two older sons with their father. . . they're part of my family unit and I wanted them to live with me. . . but I didn't feel I could enjoy [the posting] because we weren't living as a family unit.
>
> (Molly, 40s; NCO, Army)

The uncertainty some spouses experienced in relation to whether or not they were adequately performing the role of mother due to their children's physical absence from the family home suggests these participants may be experiencing a form of *ambiguous loss* as a result of confusion and ambiguity about family boundaries and roles due to the separation of family groups (Boss, 2004). Such losses can result in poorer psychological well-being and feelings of hopelessness about the absence, as might be demonstrated by spouses who perceive a lack of agency regarding such decisions. While similar expressions of distress were reported among UK spouses regarding this decision (Jervis, 2011), few discussed this, possibly as on overseas postings boarding school is one of the few options available to military families who want to provide stability for their children's education during these accompanied postings.

Resentment

As in prior research (Jervis, 2011), the perceived lack of agency among spouses was reported to lead to feelings of resentment toward the military as a result of a perceived lack of institutional support or negative encounters with representatives of the military.

> The Army'll say, oh you know, "A happy wife, a happy soldier". . . happy wife! And it's not like that at all, is it? No, it's not . . . it's not like that all! Family comes very, very, very low down on the priorities list.
>
> (Molly, 40s; NCO, Army)

> [The military] can take a decision I don't like and I've just got to suck it up! . . . They're taking decisions in my home that affect my children . . . that they're not entitled to take, but I'm supposed to just accept that . . . you're just expected to just let your husband talk for you. . . the fact that I wasn't allowed a voice. Yes I'm angry about that . . . it's not on!
>
> (Toni, 40s; officer, RAF)

However, unlike previous studies, resentment and blame were also expressed by several participants toward Service personnel because of the concessions spouses were required to make because of their husband's career and the perceived lack of power spouses felt they had.

> You're very resentful quite a lot of the time. Resentful of the job and resentful of not being able to do things because of his job . . . cross that maybe you were at home with the children all the time and obviously you haven't got your family support up there.
>
> (Mary, 30s; NCO, Army, transitioned)

> I take it out on my husband a bit. I blame him, it's all his fault! . . . He just accepts it. He knows that I don't mean it. And obviously he quite understands it.
>
> (Dee, 30s; NCO, Army)

Such perceptions may have long-term implications for relationships, particularly when related to relocation, with marital tensions and marital satisfaction negatively associated with geographical mobility (Bellou and Gkousgkounis, 2015; Ebenrett, 2002). This may be heightened among spouses who feel unable to negotiate the impact of military life on their career and family life.

Connectedness

For the military institution, relying on spouses to perform unpaid and gendered labor allows them to provide community cohesion and social support (Harrison and Laliberte, 1997), particularly during times of deployment (Hyde, 2016). While some spouses were reluctant to take on assigned identities, for example, by performing unpaid roles, there could be benefits in doing so. For spouses, the activities associated with these roles provided access and membership to an important social group generated by the presence of the military and an avenue for establishing reciprocal networks of support and understanding. Such support is important in preventing depression and improving psychological well-being among military spouses (Green, Nurius, and Lester, 2013; Sudom, 2010; Wang, Nyutu, Tran, and Spears, 2015), as well as higher retention of Service personnel (Burrell, Durand, and Fortado, 2003; Joseph and Afifi, 2010).

> It was fairly obvious that, you know, if you do lots of really good things and it was lots of fun and I think on the whole the regiment really benefitted from it . . . I was part of that community and so, you know, me, my kids, my family all benefitted from it.
>
> (Joan, 40s; officer, Army)

However, certain military policies and a lack of engagement with families not living on-base could lead to spouses feeling disconnected from the military community. Participants housed off-base due to a shortage of appropriate military housing explained how the perceived physical and social barriers between them and the military community led to a sense of isolation and exclusion from the community, even among those who were critical of the military institution and its expectations on them.

> [The current posting is] kind of the worst of both worlds really. You're not in a military community . . . the military community is, you know, 45 minutes away . . . I'm sure that actually there's a very strong community there, but I'm not part of it . . . there's actually no support there to help [us] be part of that.
>
> (Joan, 40s; officer, Army)

Similar perceptions of disconnection have been expressed by spouses experiencing unaccompanied postings. With the proposed Future Accommodation Model, which suggests changes to the provision of Service Family Accommodation (SFA),[4] including increasing private renting and home ownership, such responses indicate that the military will need to pre-empt some of these issues families might experience as a result of geographical dispersion to prevent poor well-being among the military community.

Conclusion

This is one of the few UK studies to examine the relationship between UK military spouses and the military institution. While there are limitations regarding the involvement of female spouses of Army and RAF Service personnel of officer and senior non-commissioned officer (NCO) rank only, this study provides much-needed understanding of the tension between the military and family life from the point of view of spouses and the possible influences on well-being.

The findings indicate that tensions between the boundaries of the military and the family, and the participation of Service personnel in both institutions, can influence the well-being of UK military spouses. The military institution is perceived to exert control over spouses and their families through institutional practices and cultural norms that challenge spouse identity and agency but that support military families through the community that is created. Social expectations for spouses to "assume rank" by performing informal, unpaid roles within the community because of their husband's position indicate that the two-person single career is still evident within the UK military community. Interactions with representatives reliant on military policies and procedures were viewed as bonding spouses to their husband's identity and expectations, diminishing and constraining their independence and incorporating them into the pre-defined identity of "military wife." Participants described a perceived lack of agency and power because of the control the military wields over daily life and postings decisions. Unsuccessful attempts by spouses to negotiate these restrictions and perceived power the military had over their family life could lead to resentment toward the military but also within their own relationship with their husband. Yet despite the conflicts between spouse identity and agency and their experiences with the military, they received a sense of connectedness and support for spouses through the community it maintained. The extent to which spouses accept or do not accept this trade-off may alter following changes to military housing provision in the UK but should be an important consideration in future military policy and research.

Notes

1 For further information on other topics discussed during this study, see Gribble (2017a).
2 See www.aff.org.uk for more information.
3 School where children live, returning to the family home at weekends or during the school holidays.
4 See www.gov.uk/government/collections/mod-future-accommodation-model for further information.

References

Beevor, A. (1990). *Inside the British Army*. London: Chatto & Windus.

Bellou, V. and Gkousgkounis, G. (2015). Spouse-and service-related antecedents of officers' commitment: the case of the Greek Army. *Armed Forces & Society*, 41, 440–459.

Blakely, G., Hennessy, C., Chung, M., and Skirton, H. (2012). A systematic review of the impact of foreign postings on accompanying spouses of military personnel. *Nursing & Health Sciences*, 14, 121–132.

Booth, B., Segal, M., Bell, D., Martin, J., Ender, M., Rohall, D., and Nelson, J. (2007). *What We Know about Army Families: 2007 Update*. Family and Moral Welfare and Recreation Command, US Army. www.army.mil/fmwrc/documents/research/WhatWeKnow2007.pdf.

Boss, P. (2004). Ambiguous loss. Research, theory and practice: reflections after 9/11. *Journal of Marriage and Family*, 66, 551–566.

Burrell, L., Adams, G., Durand, D., and Castro, C. (2006). The impact of military lifestyle demands on well-being, Army, and family outcomes. *Armed Forces & Society*, 33, 43–58.

Burrell, L., Durand, D., and Fortado, J. (2003). Military community integration and its effect on well-being and retention. *Armed Forces & Society*, 30, 7–24.

Drummet, A., Coleman, M., and Cable, S. (2003). Military families under stress: implications for family life education. *Family Relations*, 52, 279–287.

Durand, D. (2000). The role of the senior military wife—then and now. In J. Martin, L. Rosen, and L. R. Sparacino (eds), *The Military Family: A Practice Guide for Human Service Providers* (pp.73–86). Westport, CT: Praeger Publishers.

Ebenrett, H. (2002). *The Impact of Military Mobility Requirements on German Soldiers and Their Families*. International Applied Military Psychology Symposium. Bundeswehr Institute for Social Research.

Enloe, C. (2000). *Maneuvers: The International Politics of Militarizing Women's Lives*. Berkeley and Los Angeles: University of California Press.

Enloe, C. (2016). *Globalization and Militarism: Feminists Make the Link*. Lanham, MD: Rowman & Littlefield Publishers.

Figley, C. (1993). Coping with stressors on the home front. *Journal of Social Issues*, 49, 51–71.

Finch, J. (1983). *Married to the Job: Wives' Incorporation in Men's Work*. London: George Allen & Unwin.

Goldstein, J. (2001). Heroes: the making of militaryzed masculinity. In J. Goldstein (ed.), *War and Gender: How Gender Shapes the War System and Vice Versa*. Cambridge: Cambridge University Press.

Green, S., Nurius, P., and Lester, P. (2013). Spouse psychological well-being: a keystone to military family health. *Journal of Human Behavior in the Social Environment*, 23, 753–768.

Gribble, R. (2017a). *Employment among UK Military Spouses and Partners* (Report prepared for the Army Families Federation). London: King's Centre for Military Health Research/Army Families Federation.

Gribble, R. (2017b). *What's It Like to Have a Partner in the UK Armed Forces? Influences on the Mental Health and Well-Being of Women*. Degree of Doctor of Philosophy, King's College London.

Hall, L. (2011). The importance of understanding military culture. *Social Work in Health Care*, 50, 4–18.

Harrell, M. (2001). Army officers' spouses: have the white gloves been mothballed? *Armed Forces & Society*, 28, 55–75.

Harrison, D. and Laliberte, L. (1994). *No Life Like It: Military Wives in Canada*. Toronto, ON: Lorimer.

Harrison, D. and Laliberte, L. (1997). Gender, the military, and military family support. In L. Weinstein and C. White (eds), *Wives and Warriors: Women and the Military in the United States and Canada*. Westport, CT: Bergin & Garvey.

Higate, P. and Cameron, A. (2004). Looking back: military partners reflections on the traditional military. *Journal of Political and Military Sociology*, 32, 207–218.

Horn, D. (2010). Boots and bed sheets: constructing the military support system in a time of war. In L. Sjoberg and S. Via (eds), *Gender, War and Militarism*. Santa Barbara, CA: Praeger Security International.

Hyde, A. (2016). The present tense of Afghanistan: accounting for space, time and gender in the processes of militarisation. *Gender, Place & Culture*, 23, 857–868.

Iversen, A., Fear, N., Rowe, S., and Burdett, H. (2014). *Children of military fathers with PTSD*. King's College London, London: U.S. Army Medical Research and Material Command.

Jervis, S. (2011). *Relocation, Gender and Emotion: A Psycho-Social Perspective on the Experiences of Military Wives*. London: Karnac Books Ltd.

Joseph, A. and Afifi, T. (2010). Military wives' stressful disclosures to their deployed husbands: the role of protective buffering. *Journal of Applied Communication Research*, 38, 412–414.

Knobloch, L. and Wehrman, E. (2014). Family relationships embedded in United States military culture. In C. Agnew (ed.), *Social Influences on Romantic Relationships*, 1st edn. Cambridge: Cambridge University Press/Cambridge Books Online.

Lacey, A. and Luff, D. (2009). *Qualitative Data Analysis*. The NIHR RDS for the East Midlands/Yorkshire & the Humber.

Link, P. and Palinkas, L. (2013). Long-term trajectories and service needs for military families. *Clinical Child and Family Psychology Review*, 16, 376–393.

Ministry of Defence (2017). *UK Tri-Service Families Continuous Attitude Survey Results 2017* [Online]. Ministry of Defence. Available at: www.gov.uk/government/uploads/system/uploads/attachment_data/file/632455/Tri-Service_Families_Continuous_Attitude_Survey_2017_Main_report.pdf (accessed March 26, 2018).

Office for Fair Access (2018). *Topic Briefing: Students from Military Service Families*. Office for Fair Access. https://webarchive.nationalarchives.gov.uk/20180511111620/https://www.offa.org.uk/universities-and-colleges/guidance/topic-briefings/students-from-military-service-families/.

Owens, T., Robinson, D., and Smith-Lovin, L. (2010). Three faces of identity. *Annual Review of Sociology*, 36, 477–499.

Padden, D. and Posey, S. (2013). Caring for military spouses in primary care. *Journal of the American Academy of Nurse Practitioners*, 25, 141–146.

Papanek, H. (1973). Men, women, and work: reflections on the two-person career. *American Journal of Sociology*, 78, 852–872.

Ritchie, J. and Lewis, J. (2003). Carrying out qualitative analysis. In J. Ritchie and J. Lewis (eds), *Qualitative Research in Practice: A Guide for Social Science Students and Researchers*. London: Sage.

Rosen, L. and Moghadam, L. (1989). Can social supports be engineered? An example from the Army's unit manning system. *Journal of Applied Social Psychology*, 19, 1292–1309.

Segal, M. (1986). The military and the family as greedy institutions. *Armed Forces & Society*, 13, 9–38.

Spencer, L., Ritchie, J., Ormston, R., O'Connor, W., and Barnard, M. (2003). Analysis: principles and processes. In J. Ritchie and J. Lewis (eds), *Qualitative Research in Practice: A Guide for Social Science Students and Researchers*. London: Sage.

Sudom, K. (2010). *Quality of Life among Military Families: Results from the 2008/2009 Survey of Canadian Forces Spouses*. Personnel and Family Support Research. Toronto, ON: Defence R&D Canada. www.cfmws.com/en/AboutUs/MFS/FamilyResearch/Documents/DGPRAM/Quality%20of%20Life/QOL_Survey_Spouses.pdf.

Thoits, P. (1983). Multiple identities and psychological well-being: a reformulation and test of the social isolation hypothesis. *American Sociological Review*, 48, 174–187.

Verdeli, H., Baily, C., Vousoura, E., Belser, A., Singla, D., and Manos, G. (2011). The case for treating depression in military spouses. *Journal of Family Psychology*, 25, 488–496.

Wang, M., Nyutu, P., Tran, K., and Spears, A. (2015). Finding resilience: the mediation effect of sense of community on the psychological well-being of military spouses. *Journal of Mental Health Counseling*, 37, 164–174.

Weinstein, L. and Mederer, H. (1997). Blue Navy blues: submarine officers and the two-person career. In L. Weinstein, and C. White (eds), *Wives and Warriors: Women and the Military in the United States and Canada*. Westport, CT: Bergin & Garvey.

Wood, S., Scarville, J., and Gravino, K. (1995). Waiting wives: separation and reunion among Army wives. *Armed Forces & Society*, 21, 217–236.

11 Balancing act

The demands of family, military service, and civilian employment for reservists

Joanna E. Anderson and Irina Goldenberg

Introduction

In Canada, as in many other countries, the Armed Forces include a reserve component. The Canadian Armed Forces (CAF) Primary Reserve is a primarily part-time force that supplements the full-time Regular Force in operations at home and abroad. Reserve taskings and deployments are voluntary.[1] The part-time, voluntary nature of most reservists' military service means that many members hold civilian employment as well. Thus, although the macro, meso, and micro level tensions that apply to Regular Force members (as outlined in Chapter 1) also apply to reservists to varying degrees, the most salient triadic tensions may emerge from a trio of responsibilities uniquely applicable to reservists: family, military service, and civilian work. Tensions between these responsibilities primarily impact the member at the meso (organizational) level, pulling him or her in different directions as they compete for time and commitment.

In this chapter, the authors examine evidence for the existence and impact of meso level tensions between these three factors. This examination includes, first, a review of existing research, both Canadian and international. It reveals numerous ways in which meso level tensions between family, military service, and civilian work manifest. We then present new data from the CAF Primary Reserve to investigate the possibility that, when conflicts between members' three sets of responsibilities arise, they may be inclined to reduce the tension by eliminating the pull from the military organization: that is, by leaving the Reserves. Finally, we consider another way in which tensions might be reduced without eliminating any of the sources—a more productive solution for a member and military organization who would presumably prefer to maintain their working relationship. Specifically, we examine whether support from the organization to reservists' families has a positive impact on their work–life balance and likelihood of staying.

Tensions between military and civilian employment

To a much greater extent than their Regular Force counterparts, reservists hold potentially conflicting roles as citizens and soldiers (Griffith, 2005), largely because a large proportion of Reserve Force members are employed in civilian jobs outside of the CAF. The importance and difficulty of balancing these roles has been identified in existing research, with qualitative research from the UK and USA indicating that some reservists see their service as "incompatible with a private-sector job" (Wenger, Orvis, Stebbins, Apaydin, and Syme, 2016: 56) and that "the civilian employer or career was a significant barrier to maintaining Reserve service" (Parry et al., 2016: 61).

Specifically, employers in the UK described reserve duty as equally disruptive as maternity leave or jury service (though less disruptive than sickness); in particular, they noted absences for military training and deployment as key disadvantages of employing a reservist (Lack and Vannozzi, 2014; Parry et al., 2015). This was found to be particularly consequential for small organizations and in cases where the reservist had specialized skills that were difficult to replace. Many of the reservists and employers interviewed for Parry and colleagues' study indicated that absences related to reserve duties negatively impacted the performance of the organization or team. Even self-employed reservists may incur significant hardship related to the tensions between their military service and civilian work, in that they cannot obtain financial compensation for lost work time as others can (Ministry of Defence, 1998). These studies all indicate the strain that reserve service places on civilian employment—strain that may be difficult to resolve.

Relatedly, other studies have shown that reservists' civilian career progression may be negatively impacted by their military service, particularly if they deploy (Dandeker et al., 2010). Born and Koundakjian (2013) found that nearly one in six reservists in Canada who had been deployed reported that their civilian positions had been eliminated when they returned from deployment. Similarly, almost a third of UK reservists who were deployed reported a loss of "seniority, promotion opportunity, responsibility, or income" (Harvey et al., 2011: 669). Serious consequences of reserve service are infrequent but very deleterious on the rare occasions they occur; for example, Anderson (2017) reported that 4 percent of CAF reservists believed their reserve service had caused them to be fired, 5 percent to be denied promotion, and 8 percent to be refused employment.

Further, tensions between military service and civilian work are not unidirectional. Research suggests that civilian employment also impacts the accomplishment of reservists' military duties. For instance, reservists returning from deployment may be unable to complete post-deployment screening due to difficulty taking additional time off work (McKee and Powers, 2008). Reservists with civilian employment have also reported significantly more difficulty completing required courses and training than those without such obligations, and many indicated that inability to take time off from their civilian jobs was the reason for missing the training (Anderson, Koundakjian, and Pettalia, 2015).

The findings thus far clearly indicate that tensions exist between reserve service and civilian work. At the same time, it is important to note that some employers describe reservists as assets to the workforce (Lack and Vannozzi, 2014). Parry et al. (2015) identified a number of benefits UK employers obtain from employing reservists, including transferable skills and training that would otherwise have to be provided and paid for by the civilian employer. That said, it appeared that employers often failed to recognize the relevance of benefits stemming from military training or employment (Parry et al., 2015).

What is the impact of the tension between military service and civilian employment on reservists? Studies suggest that it is consequential for reservists' general attitudes, perceptions, and well-being. Although reservists with civilian employment have actually reported greater normative commitment (i.e., feelings of duty or obligation to the military organization) and identification as a reservist than those without (Anderson et al., 2015), differences between military and civilian work and organizational cultures can create internal conflict and challenges in terms of adaptation (Griffith, 2005; McKenzie and Healy-Morrow, 2006).

Most crucially, previous analyses conducted in the Canadian context provide initial evidence that tensions between military service and civilian employment may spur some members to leave the Reserve Force. Namely, a 2014 study found that conflict with a civilian job was a common reason for releasing from the Primary Reserve, reported by close to a third (29.3 percent) of employed reservists (Koundakjian, 2014). Although the data from that study—as well as the current one—cannot speak to the relative likelihood of leaving a civilian job versus reserve service in the event of irreconcilable tensions, they at least suggest that for a notable proportion of members, reserve service will be the "weakest link"—that is, the first role to be dropped. Later in the chapter, we consider additional data to speak to this possibility.

Tensions between family and work

Mirroring their statements about civilian employment, participants in qualitative research have suggested that having a family is a barrier to remaining in the Reserve Force (Dandeker et al., 2010; Parry et al., 2016), or even that reserve service is "incompatible with family life" (Wenger, Orvis, Stebbins, Apaydin, and Syme, 2016: 56). However, research on the tensions between reservists' military and family obligations is relatively lacking, particularly in contrast to the literature on civilian employment. This is problematic in that the provision of effective programs and policies is predicated on understanding the specific needs and challenges faced by reservists' families (Clever and Segal, 2013). Much of the existing research on reservists' families centers on the effects of deployment or mobilization (Basham and Catignani, 2018). Notably, Lomsky-Feder, Gazit, and Ben-Ari (2008) emphasize that reserve family dynamics are uniquely affected by the fact that reservists frequently transition between types of service (i.e., part-time and full-time) and/or mobilization. They describe reservists as "transmigrants" to reflect the frequency and ubiquity of such transitions. This flux in demands and circumstances require significant adaptation on the part of the reservist and his or her family, producing tension between these aspects of a reservist's life.

Given the time and effort dedicated to military service by reservists, their spouses often have to make up the difference at home, for example, with a larger share of household chores and childcare (Basham and Catignani, 2018; Dandeker, Greenberg, and Orme, 2011; Nataraj Kirby, Grissmer, Williamson, and Naftel, 1992).

Indeed, Basham and Catignani have even observed that some reservists actively use their reserve obligations as an excuse to reduce their family responsibilities. This unbalanced division of labor at home is likely to be more readily accepted if reserve service is valued and supported by the reservist's significant other. If, on the other hand, service is seen as a "hobby" or "extra-curricular activity," significant others are generally less keen to assume a greater share in terms of household and childcare responsibilities (Basham and Catignani, 2018). That said, the study showed that family members often do support and even encourage reservists' military service, often because they recognize the importance of this service to the reservists' personal fulfilment. Nevertheless, this study also found that most reservists' significant others, even those supportive of reserve service, preferred that the reservist spent more "spare time" with the family than on reserve duty. In short, these studies provide evidence of the tensions between military and family life for reservists.

What is the impact of the tension between military service and family life on reservists? Extant research indicates that family well-being is a key factor in reservists' decisions to stay in or leave the military (Catignani and Basham, 2014; Comptroller and Auditor General/National Audit Office, 2007). For example, previous research in the Canadian context identified conflict with family life as the fourth-most common reason for leaving the CAF (Koundajakian, 2014). In addition, family responsibilities are often cited as the most important factor influencing deployment decisions among reservists (Dandeker, et al., 2010; Fraser and Powers, 2009; Nataraj Kirby, Grissmer, Williamson, and Naftel, 1992). Later in this chapter, we describe analyses that further explore the importance of conflict between family and the other "organizations" in a reservist's life.

Maintaining the triad: three-way tensions

As described above, it is clear that tensions can arise between reservists' military service and the other central organizations in their lives: civilian employment and family. However, to the extent that we characterize reservists' meso level responsibilities as a triad, as described in Chapter 1, it is crucial to consider the balance of all three simultaneously. Some existing research has considered reserve service, family, and civilian work conjointly; however, as noted above, much of that work focuses on deployment and mobilization (Basham and Catignani, 2018). For instance, in the context of a large-scale study on reservists' ability to re-integrate after deployment, Werber et al. (2013) emphasized that both family well-being and career aspects are key to understanding reintegration success, and further, that these tend to be interrelated. This research demonstrated that the success of reserve families' reintegration was impacted by several factors, including the spousal relationship and his or her civilian employment status and reintegration.

Deployments are major life events and research on their effects is clearly important, but reservists are predominantly part-time and their military obligations most often include training, readiness preparation, and professional development in garrison (Basham and Catignani, 2018; Chief of the Defence Staff, 2015).

Currently, there is a dearth of research on the effects of balancing the requirements of military service, civilian employment, and family obligations in the face of these routine commitments. This is an important yet relatively unexplored area. For instance, some of Parry et al.'s (2016: 60) participants "explained that the pressure of balancing the RF [Reserve Force], a civilian career and a family would be too much to maintain," and that they were able to maintain their reserve commitments for now only because they did not have families. Further supporting this point, the most significant challenge identified in an international review of reservist attrition and retention was the need to balance military and civilian responsibilities, particularly civilian employment and family and personal relationships (Hadziomerovic and Simpson, 2013). It has further been suggested that attaining optimal balance is becoming increasingly difficult given that many families now depend on two incomes and that civilian jobs increasingly entail evening and weekend work shifts and longer hours (Basham and Catignani, 2018).

Existing research suggest that when faced with the challenge to "do it all," some reservists drop or postpone reserve obligations in order to prioritize more pressing family and work commitments (Basham and Catignani, 2018; Parry et al., 2016), which again suggests to us that the Reserve Force may be the first institution to be dropped if triadic tensions become too high. For example, Connelly (2013: 26) cites a member of the UK's Reserve Force (formerly called the Territorial Army [TA]) saying that "TA priorities are family, work, and then TA." Other research suggests that because reserve service often needs to be managed in the dual context of family and civilian employment, reservists are cognizant of whether their time is used effectively, their training is optimal and efficient, and their service requirements are reasonable and meaningful (Lomsky-Feder, Gazit, and Ben-Ari, 2008).

In this chapter, we specifically focus on reservists whose commitments are threefold, including military service, civilian employment, and a family. We consider the entire experience of being a reservist in the CAF, which may include deployments or long-term taskings, but is mostly made up of routine commitments like training and professional development. Namely, we consider the question of what happens when members are not satisfied with the balance of meso level factors. Do they become less satisfied with their service or less committed to the organization? Most crucially, does an inability to resolve these tensions increase their likelihood of leaving military service, as previous research suggests? Finally, we also consider whether CAF programs aimed at reducing tensions between military service on the one hand and family or civilian employment obligations on the other are successful in that goal.

Data and analyses

The data presented in this chapter come from the *CAF Reserve Force Retention Survey* (RFRS). The RFRS is a comprehensive, omnibus survey administered every three years to members of the CAF Primary Reserve. The most recent administration was completed online by a stratified random sample of 3669 reservists between November 2015 and January 2016 (Anderson, 2017). Strata were based on rank, type of service (part-time, full-time, mixed), and environment (air, land, sea).[2] The response rate was 36.9 percent and the overall margin of error was ± 1.5 percent, with 95-percent confidence. All estimates provided in this chapter are weighted, to better reflect the overall Primary Reserve population.

The survey included dozens of measures related to reserve service, civilian work, and family (see Anderson, 2017, for details). Some of the constructs considered in this chapter include job satisfaction (Ironson, Smith, Brannick, Gibson, and Paul, 1989), affective commitment (Meyer, Allen, and Smith, 1993), leave intentions (Anderson, 2017: 13–14), work–family conflict (Netemeyer, Boles, and McMurrian, 1996), satisfaction with work–life balance (Anderson, 2017: 17), and perceptions of organizational support to families (Goldenberg, 2012).

The Primary Reserve: population and sample

In the CAF, the Primary Reserve comprises approximately 30,000 members and is a primarily part-time force whose mandate is to supplement the full-time Regular Force in operations at home and abroad. Reservists belong to the same environments as members of the CAF Regular Force, including the Canadian Army, the Royal Canadian Navy, and the Royal Canadian Air Force, and can also be part of the Legal Reserve or the Health Services Reserve. Employment as a reservist is voluntary and for an undefined period of time. In the CAF, reservists are classified into one of the following types of service: Class A (part-time non-operational employment), Class B (full-time non-operational employment), or Class C (full-time operational employment). Although reservists can, and often do, transition between these classes of service, approximately 70 percent of Primary Reservists are part-time, Class A at any given time (Anderson, 2017; Born and Koundakjian, 2013). In this chapter, we focus on those prototypical, part-time members of the Primary Reserve and do not include in our analyses members whose service is exclusively full-time; the latter group is more comparable to a member of the Regular Force than the typical reservist.[3] In the remainder of the chapter, references to members include only those who have served as Class A (part-time) for at least part of the preceding 12-month period. This group represents a substantial majority (84 percent) of the Primary Reserve population.

As already noted, many Canadian reservists have multiple commitments to juggle. The most crucial and common are families (particularly those with dependent children) and civilian employment. The most recent data indicates that approximately 36 percent[4] of part-time Primary Reserve members in the CAF have dependent children[5] to support. More than two-thirds (69 percent) of members with children hold civilian employment as well. These members, with their trio of responsibilities, are the focus of our analyses. The characteristics of our sample are presented in Table 11.1.[6] On average, these members are 41.4 years old and have served for 16.9 years. Most (88.2 percent) are married or in common-law relationships and 87.2 percent are part of dual-income households (i.e., have partners who work). Most (90.4 percent) hold full-time (versus part-time) civilian employment. Approximately a quarter (27.3 percent) are officers.

Table 11.1 Sample characteristics

Characteristic	*Estimate* (SE)
Mean age	41.4 (0.4)
Mean years of servic in the CAF	16.9 (0.4)
% Married/common-law	88.2 (1.5)
% Dual-income households	87.2 (1.6)
% With full-time civilian job	90.4 (1.3)
% Officers (vs. NCOs)	27.3 (0.3)

N = 810

Evidence of triadic tensions

General work–family conflict

The data from the RFRS reflect the multiple strains and pulls on the time of reservists with families and civilian careers. First, tensions between work (including both military and civilian obligations) and family responsibilities were assessed with an adapted version of Netemeyer, Boles, and McMurrian's (1996) work–family conflict scale. The five items revealed substantial tensions, as shown in Table 11.2. For instance, most members (70.8 percent) indicated that their work at least sometimes interfered with their home and family life. Most (73.1 percent) had also changed personal plans to accommodate work duties.

Whereas the work–family conflict scale captures tensions arising largely from competition for time or resources, additional tension may arise directly from the family or civilian workplace, if the other individuals involved in the reservist's

Table 11.2 Work–family conflict

Item	*Mean* (SE)	*% Agree**
Due to work-related duties, I have to make changes to my plan for personal activities	4.09 (0.07)	73.1
The demands of my work interfere with my home and family life	3.96 (0.06)	70.8
The amount of time my job(s) take up makes it difficult to fulfill personal responsibilities	3.78 (0.06)	60.2
Things I want to do at home do not get done because of demands my job(s) put on me	3.73 (0.06)	59.4
My job(s) produce strain that makes it difficult to fulfill my personal obligations	3.46 (0.06)	49.4
Scale composite	3.80 (0.05)	

1 = *strongly disagree*, 2 = *disagree*, 3 = *somewhat disagree*, 4 = *somewhat agree*, 5 = *agree*, 6 = *strongly agree*

*Includes responses labeled 4 through 6

life do not support their attempts to balance multiple roles. To get at this, the RFRS included items measuring reservists' perceptions of their spouse's and civilian employer's attitudes toward their reserve service. Most were fairly positive, with only a minority indicating that their spouse (13 percent) or employer (13 percent) was unfavorable toward their reserve service. Thus, our data suggest that this source of tension may be relatively uncommon for CAF reservists; however, it is potentially important for those few.

Career progression

We also considered tensions related to specific military obligations. Whereas previous research broadly suggests that it can be challenging for members with families to find time for the activities necessary to progress in one's reserve career (Basham and Catignani, 2018), the present analyses expand on these findings. Results showed that almost a third (32 percent) of members' military careers had been held up because of difficulty getting a career course. Notably, an inability to get time off from one's civilian job was among the most common causes of career delay (57 percent), as was conflict with family or social obligations (31 percent). These items provide explicit evidence of the tensions between reservists' triad of responsibilities.

Deployments and full-time assignments

As previously noted, deployments are relatively rare occurrences for reservists, yet they are an important aspect of service, as are short-term, full-time assignments. It is through deployments and full-time assignments that the Reserve Force actively supports and supplements the Regular Force. Respondents to the RFRS were asked whether they had turned down a deployment or full-time assignment in the past five years and, if so, for what reasons. Among reservists with family and civilian employment obligations, those were the two most common reasons for turning down these key aspects of service: specifically, family/social obligations were a factor for 65 percent of members who turned down a deployment and 63 percent who turned down a full-time assignment; being unable to take time off work was a factor for 58 percent of members who turned down a deployment and 59 percent who turned down a full-time assignment. At the same time, the majority of members indicated interest in deployments and full-time assignments,[7] suggesting that reservists generally want to fulfill or expand their military role, but conflict with other aspects of their lives may prevent them from doing so.

Consequences of triadic tensions

Qualitative and self-reported findings from multiple studies suggest that reservists think of family and civilian employment obligations as major reasons for leaving the military (Hadziomerovic and Simpson, 2013; Parry et al., 2016; Wenger, Orvis, Stebbins, Apaydin, and Syme, 2016). In this study, we similarly found that, among the many members who have civilian employment in addition to a family, the three most commonly reported reasons for leaving the Primary Reserve were the impact of their reserve duties on their civilian job (indicated by 26 percent), their children (25 percent), and their spouse or partner (21 percent).

Using linear regression, we also statistically examined the impact of work–family conflict on several key outcomes. First, members who reported more work–family conflict tended to be less satisfied with their overall work–life balance ($R^2 = 0.37$).[8] In turn, that dissatisfaction with work–life balance was associated with lower overall job satisfaction ($R^2 = 0.15$) and affective commitment to the Reserve Force ($R^2 = 0.05$), as well as stronger intentions to leave the Primary Reserve ($R^2 = 0.04$). These findings support the self-reported reasons for leaving described in the current and previous research. Together, they point to the importance of attaining a balance among the three sources of conflict in reservists' lives, as it appears that when triadic tensions get too strong, some reservists will reduce them by abandoning their military service. In the next section, we consider other ways of reducing triadic tensions, for the benefit of reservists and the military organizations they serve.

Reducing triadic tensions by improving support

It is clear that reservists who balance reserve service, family life, and civilian employment face major challenges. Therefore, it is essential to ensure that the support they receive from the Armed Forces, meant to assist with that balancing act, is effective. The true criticality of that support is outlined in this section.

To the extent that reservists experience conflict between their military service on the one hand, and their family and civilian employment obligations on the other, providing support in one or the other of the non-military domains may reduce the tensions and allow members to maintain all three. The CAF offers a variety of programs like this, including outreach to civilian employers and support for families. Having already shown that reservists experience conflict between the three main organizations in their lives (military, family, civilian employment) and that those triadic tensions have important consequences for job satisfaction, affective commitment, and leave intentions, the final goal of this chapter is to investigate whether attempts to reduce the conflict between military service and civilian employment or family obligations can be successful.

Support to civilian employers

Previous research suggests that reservists with employers who are more supportive of reserve activities are less likely to leave the CAF as compared to reservists with less supportive employers (Anderson et al., 2015; Nataraj Kirby, Grissmer, Williamson, and Naftel, 1992). For example, it has been observed that more favorable attitudes on the part of civilian employers minimize the conflict reservists feel with respect to managing these sometimes-competing employment roles, and are associated with greater employer support to attend drills, annual training, and other reserve obligations (Nataraj Kirby, Grissmer, Williamson, and Naftel, 1992).

The CAF offers the Reservist Assistance Program (RAP) to "prevent conflicts between Reservists and employers and assist in resolution when necessary" (National Defence and the Canadian Armed Forces, 2016). The RFRS included items measuring respondents' awareness of, use of, and satisfaction with the RAP. In theory, to assess whether the RAP mitigates tensions between military and civilian work, one would examine the association between use or satisfaction and work–family conflict and leave intentions. However, in this case, the answer is quite clear: only an estimated 0.2 percent of reservists have used this program, which is too few to examine correlations. It is also too few to determine whether the program could be effective, yet it would seem, almost by definition, not to be especially effective at the present time, perhaps simply due to lack of awareness. Why that is the case is a matter for future research, but estimates indicate that 55 percent of members are at least slightly aware of the RAP, so there may be barriers to access that are preventing people from using it.

Support to reservists' families

Military institutions have increasingly recognized family well-being as central to the well-being of military members and to the health of the force as a whole. As such, there has been an increased emphasis on policies and programs related to military families in recent years, including the families of reservists (Department of National Defence, 2017). However, it is worth noting that it can be more difficult to provide services and resources to support reservist families. They tend to be more geographically dispersed and less often living in proximity to a military base as compared to Regular Force families (Werber Casteneda, 2008; Dandeker et al., 2010; Werber, 2013). In addition to diminished access to military services and resources, this geographical dispersion also results in reservists' families being more isolated from others in the military community (Clever and Segal, 2013; Comptroller and Auditor General/National Audit Office, 2007; Ministry of Defence, 1998). This can have a variety of effects unique to reservist families, such as children of reservists being the only ones in their school to have a parent in the military or on deployment (Clever and Segal, 2013).

Given these factors, it is particularly important to examine current levels of satisfaction with family support and whether it is effective in reducing the tensions that reservists experience. As shown in Table 11.3, on average, members with children and civilian jobs are somewhat satisfied with the support available to their families ($M = 3.93$). For instance, most members (70.1 percent) indicate that support for families is available through their units. Further, almost three-quarters (72.9 percent) agree that their families are able to access the support provided by Military Family Resource Centers (MFRCs), and 54.2 percent agree that the support from MFRCs meets their family's needs. Overall, however, there is evidently some variation in how the different aspects of family support are perceived. It appears that access to support is better than the current ability of that support to cover a family's needs.

Table 11.3 Perceptions of family support

Item	*Mean* (SE)	*% Agree**
My family is able to access the support provided by a Military Family Resource Centre (MFRC)	4.10 (0.07)	72.9
My family will receive enough support from the MFRC if I am deployed	3.97 (0.09)	67.8
Support for my family is available from my unit	3.95 (0.07)	70.1
My family will receive enough support from my unit if I am deployed	3.88 (0.09)	66.8
My family is able to access the support provided by my unit	3.86 (0.07)	66.2
The support available to my family from my unit covers my family's needs	3.67 (0.08)	60.9
The support available to my family from the MFRC covers all my family's needs	3.55 (0.09)	54.2
Scale composite	3.93 (0.06)	

1 = *strongly disagree*, 2 = *disagree*, 3 = *somewhat disagree*, 4 = *somewhat agree*, 5 = *agree*, 6 = *strongly agree*

*Includes responses labeled 4 through 6

We next examined the impact of family support on several key outcome variables. Most importantly, the more support members report receiving for their families, the less work–family conflict they reported ($R^2 = 0.11$). This finding suggests that it is possible for organizations to ameliorate some of the tensions between the triad of responsibilities reservists often hold.

In addition, family support is strongly predictive of key psychological variables related to overall well-being: namely, overall job satisfaction ($R^2 = 0.13$) and affective commitment (i.e., emotional attachment; Meyer, Allen, and Smith, 1993) to the Reserve Force ($R^2 = 0.14$). That is, to the extent that members see the CAF's family support as accessible and comprehensive, they tend to be more satisfied overall with their jobs as reservists and to feel emotionally connected to the Reserve Force. For instance, among members who were at least somewhat satisfied with family support, 94 percent were also satisfied with their jobs overall and 92 percent were affectively committed. Among members who were at least somewhat dissatisfied with family support, a significantly lower 78 percent were satisfied with their jobs overall and 73 percent were affectively committed.

The ultimate indication of family support's importance is its effect on attrition, and members who report better family support are less likely to intend to leave the Primary Reserve within three years ($R^2 = 0.06$). For instance, among members who were at least somewhat satisfied with family support, 16 percent were likely to leave within three years, whereas among members who were at least somewhat dissatisfied with family support, a significantly higher 32 percent were likely to leave.

It is well-documented in previous research that job satisfaction (Anafarta, 2015; Kuo, Lin, and Li, 2014; Malik, Waheed, and Malik, 2010) and affective commitment (Griffeth, Hom, and Gaertner, 2000; Luchak and Gellatly, 2007) often play a mediating role in retention; here as well, positive perceptions of family support are linked to better overall job satisfaction and affective commitment to the Reserve Force. In turn, overall job satisfaction and affective commitment are linked to leave intentions (R^2s = 0.20 and 0.13, respectively), such that more satisfaction and commitment are associated with lesser intentions to leave. Additional analyses indicated that perceived family support indirectly impacts on attrition.[9]

With regard to the other indicator of work–family tensions discussed above, spousal attitude, family support was important again. Members who reported more family support from the CAF had spouses with more favorable attitudes toward their reserve service ($R^2 = 0.09$). This suggests, in conjunction with the preceding analyses, that receiving family support from the CAF is critically important for reservists with families and civilian employment to balance. Members who do not feel they receive enough family support experience more work–family conflict, are less satisfied with their jobs, less emotionally committed to the organization, and more likely to leave.

These findings align with theorizing about the difficulty of balancing multiple roles and responsibilities. Our data provide converging evidence that having a family and a job places strain on members as they have to balance the competing demands and that, if that balance is not attained, members may abandon their reserve service. It is therefore important to note our final set of analyses, which indicate that an organization that supports the reservist's family effectively can alleviate some of those stresses, strengthening and supporting their ability to maintain the balance of triadic tensions.

Discussion

In this chapter, we have considered existing Canadian and international research and presented new findings on the topic of reservists' need to balance a triad of responsibilities: family life, military service, and civilian employment. Although existing research indicates the importance of family and civilian employment to reservists, there are few quantitative investigations to date that have simultaneously examined all three parts of the triad.

The results presented herein, from the *CAF Reserve Force Retention Survey*, are intended to provide a deeper dive into this issue, highlighting some of the specific tensions and examining how they can be relieved. Notably, this research demonstrated that although tensions between military service, civilian employment, and family life are real and impactful, providing support to reservists' families can substantially reduce those particular tensions. That is, specifically supporting reserve families appears to change the balance of tension and conflict, such that maintaining military service becomes more feasible.

The results presented in this chapter provide strong impetus for military organizations, including the CAF, to continue to improve and expand the support that they provide to the families of reservists. Further development is needed in the research domain as well. The majority of past research on military families has typically excluded reservists; thus, there is room for a far better understanding of the unique needs of reservists and their families, particularly in relation to balancing multiple demands. Perhaps most useful in this regard would be longitudinal research to follow reservists and their families through transitions between classes of service as well as deployment to better understand both the dynamic nature of military life and the specific family and employment needs of reservists at different points in time (Clever and Segal, 2013). Further, most research that has been conducted on reserve families has been from the perspective of the reservists themselves, perhaps because reserve families are a difficult population to access (Connelly, Hennelly, Smith, Morrison, and Fear, 2016). Research focusing directly on reserve families is lacking, but is critical to fully understanding and ameliorating challenges faced by these military spouses and children.

The present analyses were unable to directly assess the effectiveness of the CAF's programs supporting the civilian employers of reservists, although they do exist. The extremely low rates of use observed in this study suggest a problem with how the program is advertised or made available. Although determining the barriers is beyond the scope of our available data, this should be examined in future research. To the extent that any parallel can be drawn between offering support to reservists' families and civilian employers, increasing the use of these programs to levels similar to family support programs could have a noticeably positive impact on retention in this important military component.

Reserve forces are integral to the operational effectiveness of most NATO and partner nations' Armed Forces. Indeed, many Armed Forces are expanding their reserve forces' size and/or functions (Bury, 2017; Department of Defence, 2017; Ministry of Defence, 2013; Parry et al., 2016). As discussed in this chapter, understanding and supporting the unique circumstances of reservists, particularly with respect to the common need to balance military service with family and civilian employment responsibilities, is critical to enabling reserve force participation.

Notes

1 Except under extenuating circumstances.
2 For more detail about the sampling methodology, see Anderson (2017).
3 For instance, only 8 percent of them hold civilian employment.
4 The fact that this number is relatively low may be indicative of the perception described in the introduction that serving in the Reserve Force is not conducive to having a family. Relatedly, a US study found that former Regular Force members who were unmarried and childless were more likely to join the Reserves than others were (Wenger, Orvis, Stebbins, Apaydin, and Syme, 2016).
5 Henceforward referred to as children. This group, as it was measured and defined on the RFRS, includes all children supported financially by the member, whether they live at home or not.

6 Members with spouses or partners but no dependent children (approximately 18 percent of the population of interest) were not included in the current analyses. It is worth noting, however, that most of the findings reported in this chapter show a similar but weaker pattern if members with spouses but no dependent children are included.

7 An estimated 70 percent of reservists in our sample would welcome an opportunity to deploy, and 80 percent would prefer to have at least one full-time assignment per year.

8 It is recommended that, in reading this report, an R^2 of 0.01 be considered a small effect, 0.04 a medium effect, and 0.10 a large effect. These recommendations are based a meta-analysis of effect sizes specific to the organizational behavior literature conducted by Paterson, Harms, Steel, and Credé (2015). They observed the distribution of effect sizes r in the literature. An R^2 of 0.0144 corresponds to the 25th percentile of the distribution ($r = 0.12$), an R^2 of 0.04 to the 50th percentile (i.e., the median; $r = 0.20$), and an R^2 of 0.0961 to the 75th percentile ($r = 0.31$).

9 This analysis was conducted using the Sobel test (Goodman, 1960; Sobel, 1982) because the complex sample makes modern procedures like bootstrapping difficult to perform. As described in the body text, family support significantly predicted both job satisfaction and affective commitment. Second, overall job satisfaction and affective commitment were tested as simultaneous mediators. Each mediator significantly predicted leave intentions controlling for family support and the other mediator ($ps < 0.002$). The Sobel test statistic was significant for both overall job satisfaction ($z = -5.47$; $SE = 0.02$; $p = 5 \times 10^{-8}$) and affective commitment ($z = -2.99$; $SE = 0.02$; $p = 0.003$), indicating mediation by both variables.

References

Anafarta, N. (2015). Job satisfaction as a mediator between emotional labor and the intention to quit. *International Journal of Business and Social Science*, 6, 72–81.

Anderson, J. (2017). *The 2015 Reserve Force Retention Survey: Descriptive Results for the Primary Reserve* (Director General Military Personnel Research and Analysis Scientific Report DRDC 2017-XXX). Ottawa, ON: Defence Research and Development Canada.

Anderson, J., Koundakjian, K., and Pettalia, J. (2015). *Balancing the Demands of Civilian Life as a Primary Reservist*. Scientific Letter -DRDC-RDDC-2015-L177. Ottawa, ON: Director General Military Personnel Research and Analysis.

Basham, V. M. and Catignani, S. (2018) War is where the hearth is: gendered labor and the everyday reproduction of the geopolitical in the army reserves. *International Feminist Journal of Politics*, 20(2), 153–171.

Born, J. and Koundakjian, K. (2013). *Well-Being of Reservist Families: Analysis of the 2012 CAF Primary Reserve Retention Survey*. Scientific Letter. Ottawa, ON: Director General Military Personnel Research and Analysis Scientific Letter.

Bury, P. (2017). Recruitment and retention in British Army reserve logistics units. *Armed Forces & Society*, 43, 608–631.

Busby, C. (2010). *Supporting Employees who Deploy: The Case for Financial Assistance to Employers of Military Reservists*. Technical Report CD Howe Institute: Toronto.

Catignani, S. and Basham, V. (2014). *Sustaining Future Reserves 2020: Assessing Organisational Commitment in the Reserves*. ESRC-FR20 Partnered Research Launch.

Chief of the Defence Staff (2015). *Reserve Strategy 2015: Strengthening the Primary Reserve*. Memorandum published by Chief Reserve and Cadets 1052-4-02.

Clever, M. and Segal, D. R. (2013). The demographics of military children and families. *The Future of Children*, 23, 13–39.

Comptroller and Auditor General/National Audit Office (2007). *Reserve Forces - Thirty-sixth Report of Session 2006–07*. London: The Stationery Office.

Connelly, V. (2013). *Cultural Differences between the Regular Army and the TA as Barriers to Integration*. Paper prepared for Director Personnel Capability. United Kingdom.

Connelly, V., Hennelly, S., Smith, J, Morrison, Z., and Fear, N. (2016). *Support to the Families of Reservists: An Investigation of Needs, Current Provision, and Gaps*. London: Defence Human Capability Science and Innovation Central Department of National Defence.

Dandeker, C., Eversden-French, C., Greenberg, N., Hatch, S., Riley, P., van Staden, L., et al. (2010). Laying down their rifles: the changing influences on the retention of volunteer British Army Reservists returning from Iraq, 2003–2006. *Armed Forces and Society*, 36(2), 264–289.

Dandeker, C., Greenberg, N., and Orme, G. (2011). The UK's Reserve Forces: retrospect and prospect. *Armed Forces & Society*, 37, 341–360.

Department of National Defence (2017). *Strong, Secure, Engaged: Canada's Defence Policy*. Ottawa: DND.

Fraser, K. and Powers, S. (2009). *Canadian CF Primary Reserve Study 2008: Survey design, sampling procedures, and top-line results* (Report number: DGMPRA TN 2009-017). Ottawa, ON: Defence Research and Development Canada, Director General Military Personnel Research and Analysis.

Goldenberg, I. (2012). *The Canadian Forces Retention Survey: Methodological Refinements in Preparation for the 2012 Administration* [Director General Military Personnel Research and Analysis Technical Memorandum 2012-007]. Ottawa, ON: Defence Research and Development Canada.

Goodman, L. A. (1960). On the exact variance of products. *Journal of the American Statistical Association*, 55, 708–713.

Griffeth, R.W., Hom, P.W., and Gaertner, S. (2000). A meta-analysis of antecedents and correlates of employee turnover: update, moderator tests, and research implications for the next millennium. *Journal of Management*, 26, 463–488.

Griffith, J. (2005). Will citizens be soldiers? Examining retention of Reserve Component soldiers. *Armed Forces & Society*, 31, 353–383.

Hadziomerovic, A. and Simpson, S. (2013). *Attrition and Retention among Military Reservist Groups: A Literature Review*. Contract Report DGMPRA CR 2013-015. Ottawa, ON: Director General Military Personnel Research and Analysis.

Harvey, S. H., Jones, M., Hull, L., Jones, N., Greenberg, N., Dandeker, C., Fear, N., and Wessely, S. (2011). Coming home: social functioning and the mental health of UK Reservists on return from deployment to Iraq or Afghanistan. *American Journal of Epidemiology*, 21, 666–672.

Ironson, G. H., Smith, P. C., Brannick, M. T., Gibson, W. M., and Paul, K. B. (1989). Construction of a job in general scale: a comparison of global, composite, and specific measures. *Journal of Applied Psychology*, 74, 193–200.

Koundajakian, K. (2014). *The 2012 Canadian Armed Forces Primary Reserve Retention Survey: Descriptive Results* [Director General Military Personnel Research and Analysis Technical Memorandum 2014-004]. Ottawa, ON: Defence Research and Development Canada.

Kuo, H. T., Lin., K. C., and Li, C. (2014). The mediating effects of job satisfaction on turnover intention for long-term care nurses in Taiwan. *Journal of Nursing Management*, 22, 225–233.

Lack, A. and Vannozzi, T. (2014). *SaBRE Awareness & Attitudes Monitor Wave 10*. Presentation. Jigsaw Research.

Lomsky-Feder, E., Gazit, N., and Ben-Ari, E. (2008). Reserve soldiers as transmigrants: moving between the civilian and military worlds. *Armed Forces and Society*, 34, 593–614.

Luchak, A. A. and Gellatly, I. R. (2007). A comparison of linear and nonlinear relations between organizational commitment and work outcomes. *Journal of Applied Psychology*, 92, 786.

Malik, O. F., Waheed, A., and Malik, K. (2010). The mediating effects of job satisfaction on role stressors and affective commitment. *International Journal of Business and Management*, 5, 223–235.

McKee, B. and Powers, S. A. (2008). *The Canadian Forces Reserve Force Study 2008: Focus Group Report* [Centre for Operational Research and Analysis DRDC CORA TN 2008-051]. Ottawa, ON: Defence Research and Development Canada.

McKenzie, W. and Healy-Morrow, I. (2006). Global deployment of reserve soldiers: a leadership challenge. *Human Dimensions in Military Operations – Military Leaders' Strategies for Addressing Stress and Psychological Support*, 13-1–13-8. Meeting Proceedings RTO-MP-HFM-134, Paper 13. Retrieved March 23, 2012 from http://ftp.rta.nato.int/public//PubFullText/RTO/MP/RTO-MP-HFM-134///MP-HFM-134-13.pdf.

Meyer, J. P., Allen, N. J., and Smith, C. A. (1993). Commitment to organizations and occupations: extension and test of a three-component conceptualization. *Journal of Applied Psychology*, 78, 538–551.

Ministry of Defence (1998). *The Strategic Defence Review White Paper*. Research paper 98/91, House of Commons Library.

Nataraj Kirby, S., Grissmer, D., Williamson, S., and Naftel, S. (1992). *Costs and Benefits of Reserve Participation: New Evidence from the 1992 Reserve Components Survey*. Santa Monica, CA: RAND National Defence Research Institute.

National Defence and the Canadian Armed Forces (2016, May 4). *Reservist Assistance Program*. Retrieved April 15, 2018 from www.forces.gc.ca/en/business-reservist-support/assistance-program.page.

Netemeyer, R. G., Boles, J. S., and McMurrian, R. (1996). Development and validation of work-family conflict and family-work conflict scales. *Journal of Applied Psychology*, 81, 400–410.

Parry, E., Morrison, Z., Robinson, D., Snowden, E., Swift, S., Rennick, K., Booth, C., and Connelly, V. (2016). *Awareness, Attraction and Retention of the Reserve Forces: Final Report*. Defence Human Capability Science and Technology Centre. O-DHCSTC_I2_P_T2_048/007.

Parry, E., Robinson, D., McKeown, R., Hinks, R., Mercer, M. Brannon, D., Catherine, R., and Bourne, M. (2015). *Support to the Future Reserves 2020 Programme: Organisational Benefits of Employing Reservists*. Defence Human Capability Science and Technology Centre. UC-DHCSTC_I2_P_T2_027/002.

Paterson, T. A., Harms, P. D., Steel, P., and Credé, M. (2015). An assessment of the magnitude of effect sizes: evidence from 30 years of meta-analysis in management. *Journal of Leadership & Organizational Studies*, 23, 66–81.

Sobel, M. E. (1982). Asymptotic intervals for indirect effects in structural equations models. In S. Leinhart (ed.), *Sociological Methodology* (pp. 290–312). San Francisco: Jossey-Bass.

Wenger, J. W., Orvis, B. R., Stebbins, D., Apaydin, E., and Syme, J. (2016). *Strengthening Prior Service-Civil Life Gains and Continuum of Service Accessions into the Army's Reserve Components*. Santa Monica, CA: RAND Corporation.

Werber, L., Gereben Schaefer, A., Chan Osilla, K., Wilke, E., Wong, A, Breslau, J., and Kitchens, K. E. (2013). *Support for the 21st Century Reserve Force: Insights on Facilitating Successful Reintegration for Citizen Warriors and their Families*. Santa Monica, CA: RAND National Defence Research Institute.

Werber, L., Harrell, M. C., Varda, D. M., Curry Hall, K., Beckett, M. K., and Stern S. (2008). *Deployment Experiences of Guard and Reserve Families: Implications for Support and Retention*. Santa Monica, CA: RAND National Defence Research Institute.

12 Relocating military families in Finland

Anitta Hannola

Introduction

The Finnish Defence Forces (FDF) personnel consists of 12,000 people, 65 percent serving in military positions, including conscripts and reservists. Many of the FDF personnel have a spouse and children. The Finnish family is quite often a dual-earner family, women being employed as often as men. Jobs are usually full-time and half of the female employees have at least a bachelor's degree (Official Statistics of Finland, 2014).

Work in the military and the family as a social institution are both demanding. This has previously been referred to using the concept of "greedy institutions" (Coser, 1974; Segal, 1986). The demands of both the military and the family have changed: soldiers have different missions than in past decades (such as the wars in Iraq and Afghanistan from a US perspective or peacekeeping operations from a Finnish perspective), while families have experienced changes in structure and expectations along with the social roles of men and women (De Angelis and Segal, 2015; Jallinoja, 2000; Sutela and Lehto, 2014). Changes in the conceptualization of the family (Jallinoja, 2000) and in roles within the family (Autio, Leinonen, and Otonkorpi-Lehtoranta, 2011) have strengthened the position of the family. Negotiations within a household with tensions and a shifting power balance affect family relations. Research concerning military families is fundamentally based on the North American research tradition centered around a professional military structure. Further research is necessary to better understand the Finnish military context—what demands do work and family obligations place on employees and how are these challenges solved?

The modern Finnish military cannot be described as Goffman's total institution, being entirely isolated from the outside world, where activities are under authoritarian control and family life is non-existent (Goffman, 1997). Rather than a fenced-off garrison, the limits for military personnel are either symbolic (such as uniform clothing) or immaterial (such as strict confidentiality). Although commitment is voluntary, the institution develops mechanisms of increasing loyalty and commitment (Coser, 1974).

This chapter examines the challenges of combining military work and family life in Finland, based on the concepts of greedy institutions and work–family conflict, which is taken as a by-product of institutional greed. The greediest institution may seek to monopolize an individual's energies and interests or even capture their total personality (Coser, 1974). Also, other social institutions and groups place demands on individuals, through different roles or social pressure (Helkama, Myllyniemi, and Liebkind, 2007). The greediness of military work and the family may often lead to conflicts, and the influence of work on family is particularly pronounced (De Angelis and Segal, 2015; Moelker, Andres, Bowen, and Manigart, 2015; Moelker and Van der Kloet, 2006).

The greedy family

Generally, the unambiguous definition of the family is somewhat problematic. The concept of a military family traditionally refers to a nuclear family (Segal, 1986; Segal and Segal, 2006). In most recent studies, the family may also include an adult soldier's family, stable non-married partners, or same-sex parents (see also Eran-Jona and Aviram, Chapter 6, this volume). An emotional commitment is demanded—members are expected to display affection toward other family members, identify with the family unit, and fulfil family role obligations (Segal, 1986).

Segal (1986) found the family institution being more demanding on military men as more women enter the labor market. De Angelis and Segal (2015) mention that the normatively based division of domestic work has shifted in a more egalitarian direction; new family roles have been adopted and men have wished to increase their domestic activity, particularly as fathers. The dual-breadwinner model has been considered the Finnish norm and discussions over the role of the father have increased. Finnish studies highlight a familistic trend and increased emphasis on family values (Kinnunen, Malinen, and Laitinen, 2009). Home and family life are most appreciated when families have small children (Sutela, 2007). The significance of family life has increased among Finnish men, while the significance of work has stabilized. Men utilize more family leaves and participate more equally in childcare, particularly among public-sector employees (Sutela and Lehto, 2014).

Soldiers and their families emphasize quality of life, and military life is, accordingly, compared to civilian society—life as a soldier is acceptable, but not unconditionally (Andres, Bowen, Manigart, and Moelker, 2015). According to international studies, mandatory relocations can be met with increased reluctance (Weibull, 2009). This may be influenced by the unwillingness of military wives to adapt to the military greediness (Segal, 1986) and of civilian spouses being reluctant to sacrifice their careers to the military (De Angelis and Segal, 2015). Finnish military families no longer typically live in garrisons (Autio, Leinonen, and Otonkorpi-Lehtoranta, 2011) and long distances between work and home are therefore common. The military career in itself is shifting from a devoted calling to a conventional paid profession and fewer partners will be integrated into the military community (Moelker and Van der Kloet, 2006).

The greedy military

The military is greedy due to the normative pressures and obligations it imposes on both military personnel and their families (Segal, 1986). The military demands are rarely negotiable on either an individual or family level (Dandeker, Eversden, Birtles, and Wessely, 2015). The hierarchic command structure and subordination can be considered particularly demanding relative to civilian occupations. Demands also include geographic mobility, periodic separation from the family, residence in foreign countries, and, in extreme cases, the risk of injury or death (Segal, 1986). In Finland, the foreign transfers most commonly include participating in peacekeeping operations or other special tasks.

Relocations and transfers detach family members from their usual social networks and sources of social support. The separations are also exacerbated by long training periods and military exercises. A Canadian study found that conflict between the family and the spouse's work increased with the amount of relocations during a military career (Dursun and Sudom, 2015). Although families adapt to separations, they always require adjustments by the family members (Segal, 1986). The wives of British soldiers reported that relocations offered variety to life and gave wives greater self-confidence. However, they also caused problems, such as disruptions to children's schooling and losses of social networks and wives' employment (Dandeker, Eversden, Birtles, and Wessely, 2015).

Obligatory transfers or relocations can be seen as a particular feature of the FDF. Depending on the task, the rotation is two to six years; peacekeeping rotations are 6–12 months long. The rotation is lengthened so that frequent transfers (less than two years) are only exceptions (HESTRA, 2015). These mandatory—yet temporary—transfers give rise to the phenomenon of widespread work and occupation away from the family. In the FDF context the term relocating employee ("relocatee") reflects rotating officers traveling long distances while their family does not relocate. The relocation concept was acknowledged in the FDF following the structural changes in the 1990s, which resulted in fewer departments and less available accommodation in garrisons.

Traditional military work is increasingly shifting toward a profession with a standard career path, impacting the readiness for commitment and transfers. As the military moves in a more occupational direction, mechanisms for motivating individual participation and commitment must be developed (Segal, 1986), and both the family and the military require stronger commitment and loyalty. This demand for loyalty strengthens through the pressure of two seemingly voluntary institutions—gainful employment and the family (Moelker, Andres, Bowen, and Manigart, 2015).

A recent study by the FDF found that the organizational culture still relies on support from a military employee's family for their military career (Autio, Leinonen, and Otonkorpi-Lehtoranta, 2011). Indeed, it is expected that committed officers work long hours to justify their advancement. The result is absence from home, and officers being less able to provide emotional support and attention than if they consistently lived in the home (Eran-Jona, 2015). Military careers do have a strong unofficial culture in which certain events support or enhance careers or status (Mauno and Kinnunen, 2005).

Work–family conflict

When demands from work and family seem incompatible, it can lead to work–family conflict (Greenhaus and Beutell, 1985; Netemeyer, Boles, and McMurrian, 1996). Conflicts of interest may also stem from individual family members' hopes and aspirations. International literature highlights two distinct constructs in conflicts, in which work-based demands hurt family obligations or vice versa (Netemeyer, Boles, and McMurrian, 1996). Finnish studies found that work impacts family life more commonly and strongly than family life impacts work (Rantanen and Kinnunen, 2005; Sutela and Lehto, 2014; Nieminen, Rantanen, Hietalahti, and Kokko, 2014). Segal (1986) noted that conflict between military requirements and family needs is avoided when the family adapts to the military's demands. Coser (1974) also stated that total commitments might reduce the anxieties springing from competing role-demands.

Studies into performing multiple roles have adopted two perspectives: roles can either strain or strengthen one another. The strain hypothesis includes the negativity of the work–family interaction and highlights the problematic nature of combining different roles (Rantanen and Kinnunen, 2005). A positive organizational approach to families serves to decrease work–family conflict, particularly according to working spouses (De Angelis and Segal, 2015). Conflict can be mitigated with the help of family support provided by the military and of supportive commanders (Moelker and Van der Kloet, 2006). Fewer transfers and a longer time in the same municipality improve spouses' employability, satisfaction, and family adaptation.

Earlier research in the FDF context considers long-distance work and long separations from the family as key stressors for work–life balance. Those with long absences or frequent transfers are particularly likely to experience difficulties. The same is true for single parents, parents of young children, and families attempting to dovetail the careers of two highly educated parents. The question of combining work and the family is crystallized in everyday procedures as the concrete personal circumstances and family-related temporal and locational challenges are not always supported by one another (Autio, Leinonen, and Otonkorpi-Lehtoranta, 2011; Aikkila, 2011).

Research questions

It has been observed that existing research is mostly based on the American professional military model and on deployments. This study examines the work–family interface experienced by Finish relocated military employees and addresses the following research questions.

Who are Finnish relocatees and how do they experience the working climate?

How do relocated military personnel describe the greediness of the family and military work?

How do they describe the conflicts originating from work toward the family?

Method

The primary resource was qualitative material from the work community questionnaire conducted annually by the Army Command. Background questions describe the typical military employee and open-ended questions examine the challenges combining work and family life. This qualitative material clearly represented the relocation phenomenon. The text-based material consisted of 60 pages.

A national working climate questionnaire provided a supplementary resource (Table 12.1). The quantitative questionnaire is carried out annually by the Defence Command. The response scales were five- or seven-staged Likert scales depending on the statement. The statements covered different elements of the work environment, such as "My work in the FDF does not seriously harm my family matters," "My work does not include things that hurt my work motivation," and experiences of work exhaustion and stress. The variable *energy* consists of six individual statements describing the symptoms of fatigue and weariness based on their frequency on a scale of 1 to 7 (1 = never, 7 = daily). In order to compare this variable with the other variables, it was scaled to be five-staged. The variable *workload division* contains two statements that describe the experienced just division of the workload and the sufficiency of regular worktime to accomplish personal tasks. The responses were on a scale of 1 to 5 (1 = completely agree, 5 = completely disagree). The variable *leadership* consists of six variables (scale 1 to 5) asking whether the respondent receives thanks, recognition, encouragement, and support from his immediate superior. The *community spirit* consists of four statements that assess, on a scale of 1 to 5, the spirit between daily co-workers: the positive work environment, their willingness to help and support each other, and the positive relations between them. The variable *employer image* has statements comparing the FDF with other public- and private-sector employers. The assessment was done on a five-staged scale (1 = far superior, 5 = much inferior). The results were analyzed by comparing responses from relocatees with non-relocatees using t-tests, χ^2-tests, and effect size analysis tests (Cohen's D).

The qualitative material (60 text pages) was analyzed using Atlas.ti, an analysis program for qualitative data. Following the process of coding and analysis, the recorded text could no longer be attached to individual respondents, which enabled the examination of the phenomenon based on itself, along with clear abstraction

Table 12.1 The research material

Questionnaire	*Dimension*	*Year*	*N*	*Focus in analysis*
Work community Open-ended questions	Local (MAAVE: the Army Command, located in Mikkeli)	2012–2015	~ 160 annually	Combining the military career and the family
Working climate Likert scale questions	National	2015	9300	Describing the relocating personnel

Table 12.2 The qualitative analysis categories and codes

	Description	*Number of codings*
Family (structure)	----	35
Spouse, husband, wife	---	22
Family time	Insufficiency, lack of	24
Family loyalty	Stable relationships	12
Family commitment	Time and energy devotion	49
Family demands	Obligations, requirements	14
		157
Military work		
Working time	Also commuting	74
Work energy	Energy demanded/produced	9
Work loyalty, commitment	Stability, vocation, discipline	3
Work demands	Obligations, requirements	69
		155
Work–family conflict		83
Strain	Pressures, exhaustion	35
Obligations	Task rotation, forced transfers	42
Flexibility (work hours)	---	59
Financial challenges	Second apartment, traveling costs	42
Additional aspects	Vocation, profession, separation, trust, adjustment	14
		275

and phenomenology. The codes energy, time, loyalty, commitment, and demands received the prefixes "work" or "family" depending on which institution the respondent referred to. Descriptions of family structures were also coded in conjunction with the concept of the family. Commitment and loyalty were seen to have a conceptual difference—commitment reflected the will to devote time and energy and the promise of time together, while loyalty reflected a dependable, stable relationship. Codes and classifications were not considered entirely mutually exclusive; the borders between the two were somewhat fluid. The list of codes remained the same throughout the whole analysis. It is of note that despite the strong American orientation of the theories, concepts related to greediness and work–family conflict could be used in the coding process without difficulty (Table 12.2).

Results

The relocatee and the working climate

The relocatees in this study exhibited a wide range of background characteristics, such as age, gender, time in service, personnel group, and administrative unit.

Relocatees were represented in all personnel groups: officers (38 percent), other military personnel (42 percent) and civilians (20 percent); officers were overrepresented. There were also relocatees in each age group, including those under 24 and over 55 years old. Eleven percent of relocatees were women, being underrepresented. Most relocatees had a long service record of over 20 years, and relocation was more common as time occupied by the FDF increased. However, every tenth (9 percent) relocatee had been in service for five years or less. Although each administrative unit contained relocatees, they tended to cluster in certain units. Army Command had a comparatively high proportion of relocatees, at 34 percent. This observation strengthened the representation and relevance of the MAAVE questionnaire in studying the relocation phenomenon.

Every tenth (10 percent) respondent was a relocatee. Relocatees defined themselves as a person whose responsibility to transfer and/or task rotation mean they need to work, and on weekdays live, in a different municipality from their regular address. Responses of relocatees were compared to the responses of non-relocatees. T-tests showed a few significant differences in mean scores of the study variables (Table 12.3), yet the effect sizes (Cohen's D) showed insignificant statistical power. Relocatees were slightly more negative with regard to energy, division of workload, and employer image. Relocatees were slightly more positive regarding experienced leadership and community spirit.

The individual statements showing the most significant differences are indicated in Table 12.4. Relocatees more often found their regular work hours insufficient relative to their workload. Equality between different personnel groups was experienced somewhat better among relocatees. These differences showed small statistical power, though. Relocatees felt more often that their work caused severe harm to their family life, showing large statistical power. Indeed, half (51 percent) of them responded that work caused some or a lot of harm.

Table 12.3 Differences between relocatees and non-relocatees; combined variables (mean, scale 1–5)

Sum variable	*Internal consistency (Cronbach's α)*	*Relocatees mean (scale 1–5)*	*Non-relocatees mean (scale 1–5)*	*t (df)*	*p-value*	*Cohen's D*
Energy	0.89	3.72	3.78	−1.86 (8600)	0.06	0.07
Workload division	0.51	3.42	3.48	−1.79 (8535)	0.09	0.06
Leadership	0.94	4.16	4.08	2.53 (8106)	0.012	0.07
Community spirit	0.91	4.27	4.18	3.12 (8597)	0.002	0.14
Employer image	0.84	3.53	3.63	3.27 (8575)	0.001	0.12

Table 12.4 Differences between relocatees and non-relocatees; individual variables (mean, scale 1–5)

Variable	*Relocatees mean (scale 1–5)*	*Non-relocatees mean (scale 1–5)*	*t (df)*	*p-value*	*Cohen's D*
My duties are usually executed during regular working hours	3.40	3.65	6.11 (8520)	0.000	0.21
My work in the FDF has not severely harmed my family/private matters (reversed)	**2.82**	**3.84**	**24.00 (8503)**	**0.000**	**0.84**
The equality among different personnel groups is good	3.93	3.72	−5.13 (8545)	0.000	0.19

Respondents to the Army Command questionnaire typically had families (73 percent) and were officers (50 percent). The majority (75 percent) responded that combining work and family was successful or very successful. However, a third (30 percent) felt that living separated made everyday family life more difficult. The combination of work and private life caused mental strain, according to over a third (36 percent) of the respondents. Flexible work times were seen to ease adaptation, with almost all respondents (90 percent) reporting that work could be adjusted based on private needs (Table 12.5). These findings supported the qualitative material.

Table 12.5 Descriptions of the respondents (Army Command work community questionnaire)

		% all respondents
Status: officer		50
Having family (children of age under 18)		73
The respondents with family have succeeded in balancing work and family	Poorly	12
	Successfully	56
	Very successfully	19
Living separated has complicated the everylife of the family	Very much	3
	Moderately	27
Balancing work and family has increased mental pressures	Yes	36
Regarding family needs and demands, I find work time flexible	Yes	90

The soldier's family and family life

The familial demands, greediness, and changes thereof were examined in the text (Table 12.2). The family structure was repeatedly described as a family with children of younger age; a spouse, domestic partner, wife, or husband was also mentioned. Descriptions highlighted so called two-municipality families: some children lived with the mother and some with the father. However, in most cases, the father lived at his work municipality while the mother and children lived at the home municipality. In general, descriptions reinforced the idea of the soldier's family as the classical nuclear family.

Military men described that responsibility for the family's everyday life fell on their wives during the week, particularly in cases children requiring transport to school or hobbies. Even if the father's work was in the same municipality, matching schedules felt difficult. This was impacted by, for example, work trips assigned on short notice or meetings being scheduled outside normal office hours. From the perspective of everyday life, the familial demands were described as being busy due to overlapping family and work obligations or as support for the spouse.

Descriptions related to family time highlighted work-hour flexibility, such as dispersed work, in the FDF as positive. Dispersed work means a work arrangement in which work is done some other place than the normal office. However, it is necessary to work in an FDF unit, for example, in a relocatee's home municipality and the amount of dispersed work days is limited. Opportunities for dispersion were lessened by, for example, a supervisory position or other tasks attaching the worker to the place of employment, and also by particular mandatory meetings arranged for Mondays or Fridays and short-notice work trips.

Family commitment and loyalty manifested in an unwillingness to compromise family matters for the sake of work. Respondents wished to be a part of daily life, living together with their spouse and children and taking responsibility over the future of the family. It was commonly stated that after a relocation and reasonable separation, the family should be reunited and allowed to live together.

Family commitment was described positively in a general sense, yet was also culturally determined. Supporting the family and the mother and spouse was described as a responsibility inherent in fatherhood, but not greediness. Time together, participation in everyday life, and companionship were brought up as positives of familial commitment. Separation was seen to impact the relationship and family negatively; living apart "ate into the relationship" and even divorces were caused by the work–family conflict. The long separations reflected also in the behavior of the children. Despite the long distance, some refused to live apart from the family, and made a daily commute between two municipalities. Indeed, the possibility of going home in the evening was seen as a key benefit of dispersed work.

Work in the military

Greediness connected to military work was described frequently, especially the time-related demands. Respondents described the insufficiency of work hours in times of excessive workload, which resulted in longer intensified workdays, unofficial overtime, and working at home. Several factors reflected negatively on the amount of work and the time spent on work. These were: (excessive) diligence, increased rush, and unexpected changes in schedule or work times. The result was the accumulation of work, increase in tasks due, and more urgency in work; thus, work days became longer and dispersed work was not practically feasible. Off-the-books overtime and evening work had become regular, work times were unclear, and work was done at home. These factors caused both problems in combining work and the family and individual exhaustion. Military exercises and mandatory work-related travel were seen as a necessity. However, respondents wanted to know well in advance the time required for them and long absences were generally felt to challenge the family.

Comments stated that long-distance travel or living in another municipality left far too little time for the family. Multiple respondents began their commute very early in the morning and returned late in the evening, meaning daily absences commonly amounted to 12 hours. Respondents did feel that travel time was their "own" time, yet it was time away from the family regardless. There was a limited chance to spend the evening or night with the family: only 12–18 days in a month, the military father being commonly absent for over two weeks each month. Work trips demanded significant amounts of free time, which was not compensated for. The lack of time was also colored by dissatisfaction over the inability to be physically present in the family's everyday life. The family was seen as a source of energy and strength; however, this was eroded by low amounts of daily presence with them. Indeed, in some individual cases, longer work distances had even caused resignation.

Task rotation and the obligation to transfer are mentioned in contemporary HR documents that apply to all personnel (HESTRA, 2015). In colloquial language and in this research material, these are simply referred to as transfers or, negatively, forced transfers. A forced transfer to an unwanted or excessively distant municipality was seen as unreasonable. However, even unpleasant transfers are considered and workers do not necessarily wish to resign, referring to a high degree of occupational loyalty. Loyalty is also exemplified by the texts stating that a soldier will see their tasks through, perhaps with gritted teeth. The military work itself was still described as important and it was assumed that one entered his career with certain expectations. Those forced to transfer wished to dedicate themselves to their work, even if the transfer caused conflict between work and the family. Respondents wished that employees' individual eagerness for rotation would be considered and short-term transfers avoided.

They stated that work consumed a lot of mental energy due to military exercises, excessive work trips, the high amount and compounding nature of their work, inflated work days, and rush. Respondents commonly mentioned that there was little time for hobbies and family time even though these were seen as sources of renewed energy. Work was described as demanding of all FDF employees: civilians and soldiers, relocatees and local residents. Although military exercises were considered necessary, they also caused challenges for the individual themselves, such as sleep deprivation. Work-related travel was considered most damaging when it was assigned with immediate commands on short notice.

Work–family conflict

The main sources for conflicts were high distances between the work and home municipalities and living away from the family. Living apart was long-term and continuous separation of up to seven years was mentioned. Other described sources of conflict included long work days and excessive workload. The recent FDF reform also initially caused uncertainty, misinformation, and concern for the future.

Only one respondent mentioned that family life interfered with work due to illness in the family. Respondents described that the time-based demands of military work particularly caused issues with household and childcare tasks. They expressed particular concern for their spouses' energy and capability to carry on. Family issues and challenges were also focused on and compounded during weekends, which caused additional pressure. Some descriptions depicted the negative feelings, such as dissatisfaction, self-sacrifice, and melancholy. Under a variety of family pressures, respondents wished for support from their work community and organization.

Respondents described different ways of tackling conflict and its consequences on both an individual and organizational level. They released stress through exercise, time with their family, empowering activities, and hobbies. Relocatees commented that the rotation following their current transfer and separation should allow them to return to their home municipality. The optimal time for task rotation was considered to be two to three years and short temporary transfers were also thought more attractive. The strain of being a relocatee was compounded by financial worries stemming from considerable expenses from their second apartment and travel home. Military organizational support of these expenses must be clear, fair, and equal.

The FDF supports the combination of work and family on an organizational level by enabling flexible working hours, mitigating the conflict of separation (HESTRA, 2015). The respondents had positive experiences with flextime and dispersed work in particular. Flextime allowed for participation in the family life in the middle of the week as well. By utilizing dispersed work, a relocatee can, in an ideal situation, occasionally live at home for an entire week. On both an organizational and particularly a managerial level, attitudes to flexible work times were somewhat accepting. In some cases, specific tasks, the superior's negative attitude, the amount of work, or a manager role precluded the possible dispersed work. Transparency, equity, and fairness in the standards for allowing for or denying flexible work time opportunities were demanded, including among non-relocatees. Cynically, they stated that flextime could not be utilized to decrease work hours, yet it could increase work hours every day.

Conclusions and discussion

Earlier studies on military and family greediness (Coser, 1974; De Angelis and Segal, 2015; Segal, 1986) have examined the subjects from a North American perspective. It has been noted that, on a general level, there are differences between countries in the experiences of the interaction of work and the family and these differences are not entirely explained by differences in research methodology (Rantanen and Kinnunen, 2005). New information was needed on how personnel of the FDF experience the greediness. The military and family greediness were described in the texts as clearly separate but equally significant elements. The conflict on the family resulting from military work—and the obligation to transfer in particular—was clearly reflected in the results. The military also caused other stressors and demands that impacted the family.

Military greediness was clearly demonstrated since the demands of time, energy, commitment, and loyalty (Segal, 1986) were observed. Descriptions repeatedly mentioned the concentration of work, perceived as a part of military greediness: the work is typically done with an increasingly tight schedule imposed by the hierarchical command structure and based on the commands of superiors. Relocatees also felt that their regular work time was insufficient for managing their tasks and described intensification of their work and an increase in work-related pressure, referring to a situation in which work-related strain increases due to rush, uncompleted work, and insufficient personnel (Sutela and Lehto, 2014). Thus, it can be concluded that relocation is connected with negativity regarding the work–family combination and the intensification of work. The causality between these could not be studied because of the cross-sectional research material; there is a need for a longitudinal study.

Earlier research showing a clear connection between working hours and the feeling of work–family conflict (Netemeyer, Boles, and McMurrian, 1996; Nieminen, Rantanen, Hietalahti, and Kokko, 2014; Rantanen and Kinnunen, 2005) was supported by this study. The different demands related to working hours were described: increasing workload, unofficial overtime, taking work home, inflated workdays, and obstacles to utilizing flexible work times. These features caused anxiety, weariness, and stress. The high working hours prevented participation with the family and in household tasks, increasing conflicts. Earlier research has found that military training supports task orientation (Autio, Leinonen, and Otonkorpi-Lehtoranta, 2011), a finding that was also supported in this study. The soldiers reported wishing that they could manage their assigned tasks within a certain time limit. Other studies have observed that an external value system (success, status, and power) as a basis for work orientation is connected to weariness and the conflict between work and the family (Nieminen, Rantanen, Hietalahti, and Kokko, 2014). It was found that, for example, the upward trajectory of an officer's career and the normative pressure to accept personnel transfers may strengthen feelings of conflict.

This study examined relocatees—employees working in the FDF who lived apart from their family due to their obligation to transfer. Relocation was a career phase particularly associated with officers with a long service record. In a Finnish context, the results highlighted personnel transfers, relocations, and other absences from the family resulting from work. Relocatees felt that their work caused severe harm to their family life, at a much higher rate than other FDF personnel. A Finnish study found that a fifth (20 percent) of the fathers of small children felt that their work hurt their family life (Kinnunen et al., 2009); for relocatees the rate was considerably higher (51%).

The conservative organizational culture of the FDF expects families to support a military career (Autio, Leinonen, and Otonkorpi-Lehtoranta, 2011), although developing societal patterns demonstrate an increasing significance of the family. The military career weakening from an institutional calling to "just work" and family relationships increasing in importance, fewer officers want to adapt their family in conjunction with transfers. Potential stressors impacting the family, such as a spouse's employment hardships and the construction of a new social network – which have indeed found to be the negative consequences of transfers (Urban and Martinell, 2012) – were the most common explanations for reluctance to adapt the family. Relocatees' family seldom transferred with the father, concluding that the family had quite strong power position at the meso level.

The challenges of combining work and the family life caused strain, stress and conflict directed especially from work towards the family. Studies found that supportive policy by the Armed Forces and the supportive unit commander lessens the military–family conflict (Moelker and van der Kloet, 2006). The results of this study cannot be generalized. However, they practically suggest that adapting to relocations would be helped by: specific time definitions for any individual transfer, living in the home municipality with the family between transfers, flexible working times and taking into account a relocatee's personal willingness. Negative factors included unclear schedules for transfers, transfers to a remote location or excessively frequently, the supervisor's negativity regarding working time flexibilities, financial worries stemming from living apart and the increased work demands.

The overall strengthening of traditional family values (Kinnunen, Malinen, and Laitinen, 2009; Sutela and Lehto, 2014) gained further support from this study. In the Finnish language, the word "greedy" (*ahne*) carries rather negative connotations, and the negatively experienced family greediness was indeed not mentioned. Conversely, respondents described extremely positive wishes to commit and provide loyalty, time, and energy to their family. Officer fathers found it important to participate in everyday family life and the lack of time was considered negative and harmful. Thus, the familial greed can be considered positively.

The negative impact of military transfers was mitigated by opportunities for more flexible work. The excellence of flexible working times, and dispersed work in particular, was highlighted as they enabled "normal life" and spending more time with the family. Balancing multiple careers with young children was described to be difficult, though not greedy in the Segalian sense. The study reinforced the idea that relocatees are unwilling to adapt the family for their work and the benefit of the family conquers the demands of a military career.

To conclude, the family and the military can both be considered greedy in the Finnish context, although their greediness has changed. Demands related to the family are seen in personnel wanting to be present with their family. Military greediness in the FDF was highlighted in descriptions of personnel transfers, living apart, and generally intensified work with different demands.

The study is limited by its basis in cross-sectional material and the problem-focused frame of analysis. Although the material from work community questionnaires spanned four years, the answers could not be individually identified. Thus, conclusions regarding the change in personal solutions could not be drawn. The descriptions of family greediness were typically authored by a father of a nuclear family; further study should be expanded to include other family structures and other family members. Additional studies should analyze both the conflict originating from the family toward work and especially the value work and the family can provide each other (Nieminen, Rantanen, Hietalahti, and Kokko, 2014). Rather than role conflicts, it would be more fruitful to study role strengthening, as multi-role life has been found to support different facets of life (Kinnunen, Malinen, and Laitinen, 2009). The results from these studies could be implemented in, for example, the norms and procedures of the FDF to support the combination of work and the family.

References

Aikkila, J. (2011). *Työn ja perhe-elämän yhdistäminen nuoren upseerin ammatissa.* Helsinki: Maanpuolustuskorkeakoulu (National Defence University).

Autio, H., Leinonen, M., and Otonkorpi-Lehtoranta, K. (2011). *Työn ja perheen yhteensovittaminen puolustusvoimissa.* MATINE/Tampereen yliopisto, työelämän tutkimuskeskus. Tampere: Tampereen Yliopisto, Työelämän tutkimuskeskus (Tampere University, Work Research Center).

Andres, M., Bowen, G., Manigart, P., and Moelker, R. (2015). Epilogue. In R. Moelker, M. Andres, G. Bowen, and P. Manigart (eds), *Military Families and War in the 21st Century: Comparative Perspectives* (pp. 319–330). London: Routledge.

Coser, L. (1974). *Greedy Institutions: Patterns of Undivided Commitments.* London: The Free Press.

Dandeker, C., Eversden, C., Birtles, C., and Wessely, S. (2015). The British military family. In R. Moelker, M. Andres, G. Bowen, and P. Manigart (eds), *Military Families and War in the 21st Century: Comparative Perspectives* (pp. 107–127).

De Angelis, K. and Segal, M. W. (2015). Transitions in the military and the family as greedy institutions: original concept and current applicability. In R. Moelker, M. Andres, G. Bowen, and P. Manigart (eds), *Military Families and War in the 21st Century: Comparative Perspectives* (pp. 22–42). London: Routledge.

Dursun, S. and Sudom, K. (2015). The well-being of military families: coping with the stressors of military life among spouses of Canadian Armed Forces members. In R. Moelker, M. Andres, G. Bowen, and P. Manigart (eds), *Military Families and War in the 21st Century: Comparative Perspectives* (pp. 128–144). London: Routledge.

Eran-Jona, M. (2015). Organizational culture and military families: the case of combat officers in the Israeli Defence Forces. In R. Moelker, M. Andres, G. Bowen, and P. Manigart (eds), *Military Families and War in the 21st Century: Comparative Perspectives* (pp. 43–56). London: Routledge.

Goffman, E. (1997). *Minuuden riistäjät. Tutkielma totaalisista laitoksista.* 2. painos. Marraskuun liike. Lohja: Mielenterveyden keskusliitto ry (Central Organization for Mental Health.

Greenhaus, J. and Beutell, N. (1985). Sources of conflict between work and family roles. *Academy of Management Review*, 10(1), 76–88.

Helkama, K., Myllyniemi, R., and Liebkind, K. (2007). *Johdatus sosiaalipsykologiaan.* Helsinki: Edita Prima Oy.

HESTRA (2015). *Puolustusvoimien henkilöstöstrategia 2015* (The personnel strategy of the FDF). HK1027. Helsinki: Puolustusvoimat, Pääesikunta (Finnish Defence Force, Defence Command).

Jallinoja, R. (2000). *Perheen aika.* Keuruu: Kustannusosakeyhtiö Otava (Publishing Enterprice Otava).

Kinnunen, U., Malinen, K., and Laitinen, K. (2009) Työn ja perheen yhteensovittaminen: perheiden kokemuksia ja ratkaisuja. In A. Rönkä, K. Malinen, and T. Lämsä (eds.), *Perhe-elämän paletti. Vanhempana ja puolisona vaihtelevassa arjessa* (pp. 125–147). Jyväskylä: PS-kustannus.

Mauno, S. and Kinnunen, U. (2005). Perhemyönteinen organisaatiokulttuuri ja henkilöstön hyvinvointi. In U. Kinnunen, T. Feldt, and S. Mauno (eds), *Työ leipälajina. Työhyvinvoinnin psykologiset perusteet* (pp. 265–286). Keuruu: PS-kustannus.

Moelker, R. and Van der Kloet, I. (2006). Military families and the Armed Forces. In G. Caforio (ed.), *Handbook of the Sociology of the Military*. New York: Springer.

Moelker, R., Andres, M., Bowen, G., and Manigart, P. (2015). Introduction. In R. Moelker, M. Andres, G. Bowen, and P. Manigart (eds), *Military Families and War in the 21st Century. Comparative Perspectives* (pp. 3–21). London: Routledge.

Netemeyer, R., Boles, J., and McMurrian, R. (1996). Development and validation of work-family conflict and family-work conflict scales. *Journal of Applied Psychology*, 81(4), 400–410.

Nieminen, I., Rantanen, J., Hietalahti, M., and Kokko, K. (2014). Heijastavatko työn ja perheen yhteensovittamisen kokemukset yksilön elämänarvoja? *Työelämän tutkimus*, 12(2), 116–136.

Official Statistics of Finland (2014). Työolojen muutokset 1977–2013. Helsinki: Helsingfors. Retrieved from: http://www.stat.fi/tup/julkaisut/tiedostot/julkaisuluettelo/ytmv_197713_2014_12309_net.pdf

Rantanen, J. and Kinnunen, U. (2005). Työn ja perhe-elämän vuorovaikutus. In U. Kinnunen, T. Feldt, and S. Mauno (eds), *Työ leipälajina. Työhyvinvoinnin psykologiset perusteet* (pp. 229–264). Keuruu: PS-kustannus.

Segal, M. (1986). The military and the family as greedy institutions. *Armed Forces & Society*, 13(1), 9–38.

Segal, M. and Segal, D. (2006). Implications for military families of changes in the Armed Forces of the United States. In G. Caforio (ed.), *Handbook of the Sociology of the Military* (pp. 225–233). New York: Springer.

Sutela, H. (2007). Työ, hoiva ja perhe. In H. Sutela and A. Lehto (eds), *Tasa-arvo työn takana. Työmarkkinat 2007* (pp. 60–67). Helsinki: Tilastokeskus.

Sutela, H. and Lehto, A. (2014). *Työolojen muutokset 1977–2013.* Helsinki: Tilastokeskus.

Urban, S. and Martinell, J. (2012). *Relocation Programs and the Impact of Relocation on Families.* Ottawa, ON: Defence R&D Canada, unpublished.

Weibull, L. (2009). *Vi borde också får medalj – Om stöd till militära familjer under utlandstjänstgöring.* Stockholm: Försvarshögskolan.

13 The spirit of community, the Army family, and the impact on formal and informal support mechanisms

Emma Long

Introduction

Evidence shows that the "spirit of community" within the British military community is changing. Servicemen are more likely to regard their profession as a job, rather than a vocation and way of life. Likewise, partners are becoming less involved in creating and maintaining networks of support for each other, their serviceperson, and the military (Deakin, 1994). More Army families are choosing to live away from military patch (i.e., military housing, close to military locations), instead choosing civilian housing/areas to protect the non-serving partner's career and children's education (AFF, 2016). The physical dispersal impacts access to formal family support, services often being made available in and around the base. Additionally, it alters the support networks families are exposed to in their everyday lives, which, coupled with the mental move away from the military, may lead to more families becoming isolated. Research shows that partners who live off-patch feel estranged from the military community, that they have lost part of their identity, and feel excluded from social and information networks (Fossey and Verey, 2013). It is therefore incorrect to equate families moving off-patch with the rejection of the military community and lifestyle—their needs must be acknowledged.

This chapter captures how Army partners access support, considering both those who live on- and off-patch. Two primary questions are addressed: (1) How do partners prefer to seek support when living on/off-patch? (2) What are partners' experiences of accessing formal and social support when living on/off-patch?

This chapter reflects the overall theoretical framework as outlined in Chapter 1 by considering how the Army family (re)organizes itself, at the meso level, when negotiating the demands of the military (deployment) and the family (childcare). During deployment the military family experiences the physical separation of their serving partner—a member of the family triad (military parent, non-military parent, children). This separation alters the family power dynamic, which partners seek to balance by engaging with social networks and employment. Incorporating others into the traditional family triad to increase coping capabilities during deployment is complex and tensions arise. This research evidences the high value partners place on speaking to other partners when coping with and managing military-related stress, yet this is limited due to stigma, concerns surrounding gossip, and possible negative impacts on the serving partners' career. Those living in private accommodation with careers want to be involved within the military community; however, they are more likely to feel isolated and "out of the loop" as welfare offerings and social events are generally organized on-patch. Military welfare organizations need to improve outreach efforts, especially during deployment, and encourage informal support networks, increasing the likelihood of families reaching out if in need.

Patch life

The military community model is based around the military base, where personnel can live on or near to their duty station, with their families, in Service Families Accommodation (SFA). This is known as living "on-patch." Patch life enables easy access to resources such as the Unit Welfare Officer (UWO) and the Army Welfare Service (AWS)—the primary points of contact for families seeking support.

Living on-patch exposes military families to one another by living in close proximity and attending local social events. UWOs and the AWS facilitate social activity within the locality by organizing events including "Coffee Mornings" and seasonal parties. However, practice varies according to the focus/personality of the UWO and interest of the camp, thus some camps become more integrated than others.

More Army families are choosing to live privately, in civilian areas, rather than in SFA (Fossey and Verey, 2013). The annual Tri-Service Continuous Attitudes Survey has shown a gradual decrease in the proportion of Army families living in SFA during the working week (see Table 13.1).

One reason families choose to live off-patch is to protect the non-military partners' career from relocations as many feel they are overqualified for the job they have (AFF, 2016; Centre for Social Justice, 2016; MoD, 2015). In 2014, 68 percent of military partners were, employed increasing to 75 percent in 2016 (MoD, 2016).

Table 13.1 Percentage of Army families living in SFA during the working week (MoD, 2016b; MoD, 2015)

Year	*Percentage*
2010	76
2011	75
2012	69
2013	73
2014	70
2015	71
2016	69

The movement of Army families into civilian areas is likely to increase further due to the Ministry of Defence's (MoD) upcoming Future Accommodation Model (FAM). The model aims to increase the variety of accommodation to be equally attractive to all, irrespective of rank or relationship status (MoD, 2016a). Personnel will be financially supported to live in a house they choose, with the people they choose, helping to balance their career with family needs. As more families choose to live off-patch, more will be distanced from formal welfare and informal support networks with other military families. It is essential that military partner experiences of the various support mechanisms are fully understood on/off-patch, so the formal welfare program may adapt to protect what is highly valued and overcome some of the limitations in its offerings.

Social network, social capital, and social support

Army families face stressors that are unique to the military lifestyle, including periods of separation during lengthy deployments that render partners more vulnerable to depression, loneliness, and anxiety (Theiss and Knobloch, 2014; Asbury and Martin, 2012). Additionally, pile-up of other non-military stressors can impact resilience and coping strategies. Post-deployment, the serving partner may have developed symptoms relating to PTSD, depression, and alcoholism, for example (Houses of Parliament, 2016; Thandi et al., 2015; Williamson, 2012; Fear et al., 2007) and partners often have similar mental health issues (Eaton et al., 2008). Additionally, military life is highly mobile and on average Army families can be relocated every two to three years (AFF, n.d.), disrupting routines, education, and support networks.

According to Rivera and Soderstrom (2010), being embedded within a social network is regarded as contributing to human achievement and action behavior. Social networks develop due to association, affiliation, and affection and are more likely to occur between individuals of similar attributes, especially when attributes are considered rare (Mehra et al., 1998). Homophily reduces the likelihood of misunderstanding and enforces notions of shared experiences, meaning, and understanding (McPherson et al., 2001). Proximity is also a feature of a social network—the closer a group is to other individuals, the more likely they are to develop closer connections (Bidart and Lavenu, 2005). However, due to expansive options of communication media such as social networking sites and web-cam-based technologies, relationships-at-distance can also be translated into practical and moral support (Fine, 2012). Reviewing social networks enables researchers to understand how ties between individuals are made, who they are made up of, and the kinds of relations that are perceived (Smith and Christakis, 2008).

The concept of social capital has been used by many researchers, including Bourdieu (1986), who regarded social capital as the aggregate of the actual or potential resources available to an individual. Building on this concept, Fine (2012) argues that social networks are a key feature of an individual's social capital, enabling social support, attachment, trust, and emotional affliction.

Relationships considered of high social capital are labeled with terminology evocative of belonging such as "family," "friend," or "military family." For Bourdieu, the level of social capital depends on (1) the size of the individual's network and (2) the social capital their network possesses—the more connected one is with others who are highly connected, the higher the level of capital. Therefore, social capital is (re)created through affiliation with others/groups.

Military partners tend to prefer seeking support from informal avenues as opposed to formal mechanisms (Aducci, Baptist, George, Barros, and Goff, 2011; Dandeker, French, Birtles, and Wessely, 2006; Manigart, Lecoq, and Lo Bue, 2015). For military partners, seeking social support is beneficial, and those active in doing so tend to manage separation better (Figley, 1983). Higher levels of social support predict lower levels of stress, regardless of the number of deployments (Van Winkle and Lipari, 2015). A study conducted by Dandeker et al. (2015) found that 96 percent of partners sought support from wider family, 85 percent from friends, yet only 20 percent accessed formal support.

Social capital is not just a property of an individual but also a community. Bowen, Martin, Mancini, and Nelson (2000) argued that a community with shared responsibility amongst and between members, and members' collective competence, could help a community reach key goals. Social capital develops a social energy for collective and individual efforts, fueling the sense of shared responsibility and competence. Social capital is created by sharing information and the trust that may develop. Bowen, Martin, Mancini, and Swick (2015) found that those who report lower levels of depression are more likely to see their community as one that considers the welfare of others, to feel personally empowered, and to view their community as one that comes together for positive community change. Ultimately, it is argued that agencies should do more to encourage and foster informal support networks, increasing community capacity.

A key benefit of being part of a community, as discussed by Bowen, Martin, Mancini, and Swick (2015) using their community capacity model, is that social capital can be gained via information sharing—keeping one another informed. Dandeker et al. (2015) have identified this as one of the primary benefits of military families living within a military community—they felt better informed about news from warzones. News would often come from other partners and also, more formally, UWOs.

However, it is not simply a case of social support existing; what matters is the individuals' perspective of social support. Perspectives are impacted by the perceived access, availability, and quality of these social supports and their ability to navigate between the various nodes of the available network. Manigart, Lecoq, and Lo Bue (2015) argue that for those lacking access to family or friends, the military helps to provide an alternative to this psychosocial support. This may be achieved by improving access to family centers, helping increase the mobility of psychosocial actors, and establishing a network of experienced family members who could support others by offering experience and advice. Such an initiative is problematized when families choose to live off-patch and are less involved in military life.

Methodology

This study, funded by the Economic and Social Research Council, is part of wider PhD research exploring the experiences of partners engaging with various support options during the reintegration process of the serving personnel returning home from combat-related deployment.

This chapter reflects on the results of a focused exploration into the experiences and perspectives of partners' support networks within the context of living on/off-patch; 27 British partners, all of whom lived in England, were interviewed during 2015–2017. Purposive sampling was used, and the study was advertised by posting on social network sites and within community centers in military-welfare locations. Additionally, contact was made by referral from those working in a support capacity. The study was advertised to partners—only wives in heterosexual relationships responded and all but one had children.

The study's qualitative nature and lengthy semi-structured interviews gained detailed accounts of individual experiences. Questions were asked to uncover partner's experiences of (in)formal support on/off-patch. Data was audio recorded, transcribed, and analyzed thematically (using NVivo). Codes were developed via an iterative process that was constantly reviewed as each interview was analyzed, ensuring best-fit. Participants have been assigned pseudonyms and some data has been altered (locations, names of social events), ensuring anonymity.

Results

This section outlines some of the key themes that emerged from the interviews conducted with partners. To answer the first research question, this section outlines the experiences living on/off-patch, specifically outlining partners' reflections on isolation and inclusion in both social events and information networks. To answer the second research question, partners' reflections of engaging with their support network are presented. The two primary avenues that the partners discussed were support sought from their mother and friends (from both within and outside the military community).

Experiences of living "off-patch"

1 Excluded from communication

Research has shown that formal support services struggle to access off-patch communities (AFF, 2016; Fossey and Verey, 2013). The serviceperson must declare their family's home address to the welfare services, and if this does not occur, families will not receive information. Partners living off-patch felt that information does not always reach them and were most concerned about missing advice about deployments, upcoming events, and activities that are available in and around the camp. Lack of communication meant partners felt isolated and excluded from the military community and struggled to develop networks with other partners due to lack of exposure and attendance at social events.

> [UWOs] seem to organize things like day trips out or events . . . obviously these welfare people live near the camp or wherever, and that's where the families live, and they seem to approach them that way, or they're advertising things on camp, or they're on Facebook groups which are closed and private for that specific camp, and obviously we don't get to access them because we don't know about them, . . . you just kind of get left out of all of that, so you don't really know about anything.
>
> (Bronwen)

2 Difficulties with access

For those living off-patch, access to social events and welfare was an issue. Many bases are in remote locations and there is a need to either drive or depend on public transport. Large camps such as Catterick and Tidworth are inaccessible via train. Participants reported being put off from attending social events due to difficulties in transport and having to find childcare. Some participants stated that they depended on their friend driving them.

3 Impact of employment

Some partners living on/off-patch who were employed stated that most events are hosted during the daytime and welfare services are often open during standard working hours. This clashed with their working hours and they were unable to access camp during the advisory services opening hours. Social networking sites were a method that partners used to overcome this barrier; however, limitations were identified, including the lack of anonymity. "Because we don't live on a [patch] estate, and because I work, I have no access to welfare units. The welfare unit opens form nine 'til four, the only access I have is the Facebook page" (Holly).

4 Isolation and exclusion on-patch

It was also felt by those living on-patch that they were not necessarily acknowledged due to the proximity to services and other partners. Some felt neglected by formal welfare and others were not confident that that local community of other military families necessarily meant they had a good support network.

> Oh, I just wanted the Army to acknowledge the fact that I was living on camp on my own with my child and my husband was away . . . I just wanted a feeling in the back of my mind that they knew I was there and they knew my husband was away.
>
> (Rachael)

Support from mothers

For the partners interviewed, the most popular source of support, especially regarding practical issues such as childcare, was their mother. This was the case for partners who lived on/off-patch. Relying on familial support was easier when living locally and a positive relationship is shared. When speaking about receiving both practical and emotional support, participants only referenced their mother as the support-provider. Alternatively, fathers and other male family members were referenced as supportive if they served in the military—thus indirectly providing support because of the context of the partner's upbringing. Partners said that being a military child prepared them for military-related stress and provided them with an opportunity to receive "understanding advice."

> Grandad used to be on leave and they'd [the military] ring him and he'd have to go within two weeks . . . So me grandma has instilled it into me mum and me to be strong independent women, like you don't actually need a man, he's never there . . . and it's one of the best lessons I ever learnt.
>
> (Karianne)

Support from friends

1 Relationships with civilian friends

Generally, if wider family were not easily accessible, partners would opt to seek support from friends. This avenue was more pertinent for those living on-patch, distanced from wider family. Partners often discussed their experiences of speaking with civilian friends (friends who are not married to, or part of, the military), especially with regards to support received surrounding practical issues. Civilian friends were also valued for providing an escape from the military where partners could engage in what they would sometimes refer to as a "normal life." However, it was commonly felt that civilian friends were unable to understand what the partner was experiencing during separation and were met with ambivalence or criticism. Many of their reflections were recounted emotionally and feelings ranged from tolerance to frustration. "Civilians have absolutely no concept in what we go through from a day-to-day basis, they just don't know, the ignorance is overwhelming to be honest" (Lisa).

One partner had settled within a civilian location for an extended period, and she felt this enabled her civilian friends to develop their understandings, which led to a more valuable relationship. "They have got better . . . if their partner's going away they're like oh I feel like I miss him . . . they do limit themselves around me 'cos they're like no it's nothing compared to what you have to go through" (Catherine).

An issue regularly considered by the partners was whether they felt accepted by the civilian community. Eleanor, who lives on-patch, stated that she attends civilian community gatherings such as swimming clubs so that she can integrate with the wider community. Generally, she felt accepted, although she felt that some civilians attached a stigma to partners of being unruly. She felt the military community were scapegoated when negative events occurred within the community, such as "drunken behavior."

2 Relationships with military partners

Those interviewed valued relationships with other military partners due to a feeling of shared experience. Generally, a higher value was placed upon relationships with other military-connected individuals when compared to civilians.

During deployment, these relationships were most valued and utilized for support as partners felt they could depend on others to share advice, experiences, and practical issues, including childcare. Some of the participants living on-patch talked about sharing household duties with other military partners on-patch whilst their partners were deployed. They would cook, clean, and share childcare tasks including walking to school and going to the local park. Additionally, they would share evenings together to stave off loneliness and feelings of being a single parent. Such comradeship and community living was never mentioned by those living off-patch. Instead, the demands of employment helped distract them from worries during deployment. However, this was not effective in the evenings once children were asleep leading to feelings of loneliness.

There were numerous tensions, which limited the cohesiveness of the partner community. First, many partners referenced perceived divisions based on the serviceperson's rank:

> There was one or two wives who wouldn't talk to you 'cos you weren't as high a rank as their husband, they wouldn't talk to you in the school yard and things and you didn't get invited to barbeques and things if you were a junior rank, which I thought was absolutely pathetic.
>
> (Rachael)

Partners perceived that others assumed the serviceperson's rank, and this created hierarchies within the community where it was felt officer's partners judged and excluded those married to non-officers. This perspective was discussed by partners of non-officers, yet officers' partners did not allude to this, instead focusing discussions on their "community role," which they perceived to involve the provision of advice and support to others. One partner said that her identity blurred these boundaries as she was not married to an officer, yet she was a senior manager of an education-related organization. She critically described social situations—such as dinner parties with her husband's senior-ranking officers and their partners—where she was regularly faced with surprise and confusion when describing her employment. Some partners in the cohort stated that there were no divisions and that this assumption was outdated.

Second, the military community is often described as close-knit, which may encourage informal support amongst partners. However, many interviewed described situations where living on-patch facilitated gossip:

> I think it's all just gossipy, bitchy and there's a set group of people that go to the coffee mornings, there's a set group of people that go to choir, and although it's made to look like everyone's welcome, that's not actually the case.
>
> (Valerie)

This was perpetuated by the high mobility that Army families face where they frequently experience the breaking up and remaking of their social support networks. Most of those interviewed compared social experiences on-patch against previous locations and if they had experienced close friendships prior, and their current situation lacked this, negativity would be associated.

Many partners felt that the close-knit nature of the community meant they were unable to keep a secret. For them, this is problematic as they perceive a culture of stigma attributed to being seen not to cope and help-seeking—interviewees presented and perpetuated this stigma by referring to those who sought "too much" formal support as a "welfare case." Help-seeking that was stigmatized was attributed to those considered "too dependent" and not supporting their serving partner, especially if their situation was not perceived to be the worst-case scenario on-patch.

Some of those interviewed were also concerned that the welfare team, living and working on-patch, would also spread gossip and break the rule of confidentiality.

> I think even though you know when you go to welfare [it] is strictly confidential, it's hard to actually let go of that and actually go and see them, there are always doubts . . . they're going to say something in the mess or in the bar or when they're down the pub, because often you've got quite a close-knit community, I think it is very difficult to actually go and access when the people that are in your welfare department are people that you see quite regularly around the patch or around the camp.
>
> (Molly)

Discussion

For those living off-patch, there are issues with accessing informal support. Reasons included a lack of communication and not being informed about social events. Additionally, some struggled to access events or see a UWO due to employment responsibilities and transport difficulties. Those who lived off-patch felt isolated and excluded from what was considered the "core" military community.

Those who live on-patch also reflected upon limitations to their support network. One felt ignored by formal support and did not receive the support she needed. This issue is widespread as evidenced by organizations such as Homestart, who have a contract with the MoD, working with partners who feel isolated from the military community due to issues such as social anxiety. Additionally, many participants perceived the nature of the close-knit society of patch life as facilitating gossip, reducing the likelihood of accessing support if needed. Importantly the concern of gossip, and being branded a "welfare case," was attributed to both the wives' community and the welfare workers. Perhaps elements of stigma associated with help-seeking may be reduced by moving away from patch.

Many of the findings discussed in this chapter are consistent with Gribble's (2017) report on social connections among UK military spouses and the influences on well-being. In her interviews with women married to military personnel, exploring the impact of accompanied/unaccompanied postings, she found that the presence of the military community provided access to a group in which they could seek practical and emotional support and experience "belonging." However, like this study, spouses may experience isolation due to perceived restrictions including the influence of rank/hierarchy. Additionally, Gribble (2017: 23) warns that "there may be implications not only for the well-being of spouses but for military families if a perceived lack of engagement with civilians and reduced access to informal support from other military spouses or partners becomes the norm following the introduction of FAM."

Bourdieu argued that the level of individual social capital depended on the level of social capital held by those they engage with. We can apply this to the partner perspective of the utility of their social network. Military-connected friends and family were perceived as more useful in mitigating the issues faced due to the military lifestyle. In this study, participants only talked about isolation if they felt they were distanced from other military families, as opposed to feeling isolated from the civilian community. This suggests a desire to be connected to the military community, even if the family has chosen to the live off-patch.

Social capital is also a feature of the community, and the higher the level of social capital, the more supportive the community. Formal support services should therefore continue to maintain and increase connectivity within the military community, especially as more families are choosing to live off-patch. Formal welfare should consider increasing outreach efforts by sending out more advice packs, inviting all families to events, extending/adapting opening hours, developing more social activities that accommodate those who work, and creating solutions for those unable to travel.

One way in which formal support could access more families is to increase its online presence, offering advisor and information services. The military currently operates a system called ArmyNet; however, this has a low uptake and was not mentioned by any of the participants. Perhaps a solution to this would be to develop a communication network on platforms in regular use such as Facebook. However, there are various security concerns associated with announcing large congregations of military personnel and their families and publicly posting details that render individuals identifiable. The MoD are engaged in exploring how to advise families about using social media.

Social media are already used by military families to connect with others—both within their immediate community, i.e., "UK Wives and Partners Support Group." Facebook pages allow partners to communicate with others, keeping contact with old friends and introduce themselves when relocating—thus maintaining and extending social capital (Ellison, Steinfield, and Lampe, 2007). Questions relate to services and events on camp and playgroups are organized. By being a part of a group, one can access support at their convenience—overcoming issues of transport and childcare. Therefore, that there is a real opportunity for the formal welfare services to tap into this as a resource, as part of the solution to the currently limited outreach program.

There are various considerations that must be made if military welfare services chose to utilize social media as a platform for advice and encouraging the development of social networks. One would be that the internet is associated with quick responses and thus there would have to be a welfare officer whose job was significantly dedicated to online care, advice, and possibly advertising. One of the benefits of using social media is that many already have profiles, so tapping into this resource will overcome the need to create new profiles and navigate new systems. However, the link to a personal profile may not be appropriate and it removes the opportunity to speak with anonymity. Some of the partners in this study talked about their use of social media, with some saying that they were comfortable posting questions and engaging with others, and some saying that they would prefer to "watch" and not interact. Some partners expressed concern about the utility of Facebook as an option for support as many who engage with the military specific pages were often the younger partners and it was felt that they needed the support more; additionally, one partner stated that "sometimes it gets a bit too bitchy for me" (Eleanor).

Another key consideration is whether the use of the internet can decrease social capital as it may detract from face-to-face interaction due to the increased possibility of miscommunication and misinterpretation. However, Ellison, Steinfield, and Lampe (2007) argue that the use of social media should instead be treated as a supplement to face-to-face interaction, and as such welfare services should regard the use of web-based support as an addition to their current work.

A limitation of the use of social media for individual's looking for support is that people are not always comfortable reaching out. Newman, Lauterbach, Munson, Resnick, and Morris' (2011) study of 14 people suffering significant health concerns explored their utilization of Facebook. The researchers found that users were constantly thinking about their self-presentation online and would be extremely cautious about what they disclosed. It was reported that if interviewees were to post a status update requesting for help, or reporting a negative event in their lives, they received multiple messages of support from both their close friends and those outside of their usual support network. Yet they also talked about their distrust in the sincerity of these messages of support and they were concerned about the possibility of appearing needy. Bolger and Amarel (2007) argue that supportive acts are only effective when such support is given without the recipient's knowledge.

Conclusion

During deployment, Army families experience the physical separation of their serving partner, altering the experience of parenting within households. This research has shown that partners try to fill this space within the family by engaging with informal support to support them emotionally (loneliness) and practically (childcare). This process is complicated by trust and access.

Some families choose to live off-patch within civilian communities, in part to sustain spousal employment opportunities. However, this does not necessarily mean that they want to exist separately to the military community. Therefore, given the possibility that more families will live away from patch due to the FAM, it is essential that formal welfare service are attuned to continuing to develop and maintain support networks between military families. Accessing other military families, who are often in the same position, is important for partners as it is felt that they are more understanding than civilian relationships during times of military-related stress such as deployment. The value of speaking to others who are military connected translates onto wider family relationships too as is evident from the cited value participants placed on having military connected parents, increasing their own resilience and understanding.

There are many outstanding questions to add to this debate. It is yet to be evidenced whether issues can be resolved via increasing social networks. Also, is the fact that so many choose to access informal networks for support evidence of the effectiveness of speaking with others or does it indicate a perceived inadequacy of formal support. Additionally, due to constraints, this chapter has been unable to consider the relationship of gender, militarized cultures, and support-seeking.

References

Aducci, C., Baptist, J., George, J., Barros, P., and Goff, B. (2011). The recipe for being a good military wife: how military wives managed OIF/OEF deployment. *Journal of Feminist Family Therapy*, 23(3–4), 231–249.

Asbury, T. and Martin, D. (2012). Military deployment and the spouse left behind. *The Family Journal: Counselling and Therapy for Couples and Families*, 20(1), 45–50.

AFF (Army Families Federation) (n.d.). *Armed Forces Information*. Available at: www.gov.uk/government/uploads/system/uploads/attachment_data/file/417260/Families_Federation_factsheet_armed_forces_information.pdf (accessed February 23, 2017).

AFF (Army Families Federation) (2016). *The Future of Military Housing*. Available at: www.aff.org.uk/linkedfiles/aff/bigsurveyfullbrieffinal.pdf (accessed February 23, 2017).

Bidart, C. and Lavenu, D. (2005). Evolutions of personal networks and life events. *Social Networks*, 27(4): 359–376.

Bolger, N. and Amarel, D. (2007). Effects of social support visibility on adjustment to stress: experimental evidence. *Journal of Personality and Social Psychology*, 92(3), 458–475.

Bourdieu, P. (1986). The forms of capital. In J. G. Richardson (ed.), *Handbook of Theory and Research for the Sociology of Capital* (pp. 241–258). New York, Greenwood Press.

Bowen, G., Martin, J., Mancini, J., and Swick, D. (2015). Community capacity and the psychological well-being of married U.S. Air Force members. In R. Moelker, M. Andres, G. Bowen, and P. Manigart (eds), *Military Families and War in the 21st Century* (pp. 210–226). London: Routledge.

Bowen, G., Martin, J., Mancini, J., and Nelson, J. (2000). Community capacity: antecedents and consequences. *Journal of Community Practice*, 8(2): 1–21.

Centre for Social Justice (2016). *Military Families and Transition.* Available at: www.centreforsocialjustice.org.uk/UserStorage/pdf/Pdf%20reports/MILITARY-FAMILIES.pdf (accessed on May 17, 2016).

Dandeker, C., Eversden, C., Birtles, C., and Wessely, S. (2015). The British military family: the experiences of British Army wives before, during, and after deployment, their satisfaction with military life, and their use of support networks. In R. Moelker, M. Andres, G. Bowen, and P. Manigart (eds), *Military Families and War in the 21st Century* (pp. 107–127). London: Routledge.

Dandeker, C., French, C., Birtles, C., and Wessely, S. (2006). Deployment experiences of British Army wives before, during and after deployment: satisfaction with military life and use of support networks. In *Human Dimensions in Military Operations – Military Leaders' Strategies for Addressing Stress and Psychological Support* (pp. 38-1–38-20). Meeting Proceedings RTO-MP-HFM-134, Paper 38. Neuilly-sur-Seine, France: RTO. Available from: www.rto.nato.int/abstracts.asp (accessed on February 20, 2018).

Deakin, S. (1994). British civil-military relations in the 1990s. In D. Ashkenazy (ed.), *The Military in the Service of Society and Democracy: The Challenge of the Dual-Role Military* (pp. 121–128). Westport, CT: Greenwood Press.

Eaton, K., Hoge, C., Messer, S., Whitt, A., Cabrera, O., McGurk, D., Cox, A., and Castro, C. (2008). Prevalence of mental health problems, treatment need, and barriers to care among primary care-seeking spouses of military service members involved in Iraq and Afghanistan deployments. *Military Medicine*, 173(11), 1051–1056.

Ellison, N., Steinfield, C., and Lampe, C. (2007). The benefits of Facebook "friends" social capital and college students' use of online social network sites. *Journal of Computer-Mediated Communication*, 12(4), 1143–1168.

Fear N., Iversen, A., Meltzer, H., Workman, L., Hull, L, Greenberg, N., Barker, C., Browne, T., Earnshaw, M., Horn, O., Jones, M., Murphy, D., Rona, R., Hotopf, M., and Wessely, S. (2007). Patterns of drinking in the UK Armed Forces. *Addiction*, 102(11), 1749–1759.

Figley, C. R. (1983). Catastrophes: an overview of family reactions. In C. Figley and H. McCubbin (eds), *Stress and the Family. Volume II: Coping with Catastrophe* (pp. 3–20). New York: Brunner.

Fine, G. (2012). Group culture and the interaction order: local sociology on the meso level. *Annual Review of Sociology*, 38, 159–179.

Fossey, M. and Verey, A. (2013). *Report on Geographically Dispersed Families 2013.* Available at: www.aff.org.uk/linkedfiles/aff/latest_news_information/geographicallydispersedfinalrepro.pdf (accessed February 23, 2017).

Gribble, R. (2017). *Social Connections among UK Military Spouses: The Influences upon Well-Being*. Available at: https://aff.org.uk/wp/wp-content/uploads/2018/03/GRIBBLE-Final-AFF-report-2017-Social-connections-among-UK-military-spouses-the-influences-on-wellbeing.pdf (accessed November 24, 2018).

Manigart, P., Lecoq, V., and Lo Bue, S. (2015). How do military families cope with multiple deployments abroad of loved ones? The case of Belgium. In R. Moelker, M. Andres, G. Bowen, and P. Manigart (eds), *Military Families and War in the 21st Century* (pp. 242–260). London: Routledge.

McPherson, M., Smith-Lovin, L., and Cook, J. M. (2001). Birds of a feather: homophily in social networks. *Annual Review of Sociology*, 27(1): 415–444.

Mehra, A., Kilduff, M., and Brass, D. J., (1998). At the margins: a distinctiveness approach to the social identity and social networks of underrepresented groups. *The Academy of Management Journal*, 41(4), 441–452.

MoD (Ministry of Defence) (2016a). *MoD Future Accommodation Model.* Available at: www.gov.uk/government/collections/mod-future-accommodation-model (accessed February 9, 2017).

MoD (Ministry of Defence) (2016b). *Tri-Service Families Continuous Attitude Survey: 2016.* Available at: www.gov.uk/government/statistics/tri-service-families-continuous-attitude-survey-2016 (accessed February 11, 2017).

MoD (Ministry of Defence) (2015). *Tri-Service Families Continuous Attitude Survey: 2015.* Available at: www.gov.uk/government/statistics/tri-service-families-continuous-attitude-survey-2015 (accessed February 11, 2017).

MoD (Ministry of Defence) (2011). *The Armed Forces Covenant.* Available at: www.gov.uk/government/policies/armed-forces-covenant (accessed May 11, 2016).

Newman, M., Lauterbach, D., Munson, S., Resnick, P., and Morris, M. (2011). *"It's not that I don't have problems, I'm just not putting them on Facebook": Challenges and Opportunities in Using Online Social Networks for Health.* Published in proceedings of the ACM 2011 conference on computer supported cooperative work, pp. 341–350.

Rivera, M. and Soderstrom, S. (2010). Dynamics of dyads in social networks: assortative, relational and proximity mechanisms. *Annual Review of Sociology*, 36, 91–115.

Smith, K. and Christakis, N. (2008). Social networks and health. *Annual Review of Sociology*, 34, 405–429.

Thandi, G., Sundin, J., Ng-Knight, T., Jones, M., Hull, L., Jones, N., Greenberg, N., Rona, R., Wessely, S., and Fear, N. (2015). Alcohol misuse in the United Kingdom Armed Forces: a longitudinal study. *Drug and Alcohol Dependence*, 156, 78–83.

Theiss, J. and Knobloch, L. (2014). Relational turbulence and the post-deployment transition: self, partner, and relationship focused turbulence. *Communication Research*, 41(1), 27–51.

Van Winkle, E. and Lipari R. (2015). The impact of multiple deployment and social support on stress levels of women married to Active Duty servicemen. *Armed Forces & Society*, 41(3), 395–412.

Williamson, E. (2012). Domestic abuse and military families: the problem of reintegration and control. *British Journal of Social Work*, 42(7), 1371–1387.

14 Who *emotionally contained* the deployed military?

Trends in the dependence of former Argentine peacekeepers on their families, Haiti, 2004–2015

Sabina Frederic

Introduction

It was three weeks before the redeployment to Argentina. Two months since the flood caused by hurricane Jeanne left 2000 dead in Gonaïves, this incident proved the most difficult moment for Argentine peacekeepers. It was night already, when shots were heard coming from the courtyard of the Base of the Argentine Joint Battalion (BCA). In the darkness, the soldiers saw First Lieutenant Hernández, who, with a gun in his hand, was shooting in the sky. "He was out of control" said Lieutenant Colonel Suarez, who had been the commander of that BCA. "We managed to contain him," he added. When Henandez could speak he told us the reasons for his anguish. His partner in Argentina had gone with another man. "I decided to repatriate him to Argentina . . . it was not good for the boys that he stayed, and it was not so long to complete the six months," according to the commander.

This experience of the Argentine military in the peacekeeping operation in Haiti indicates the effect that jealousy and abandonment have on a military and the mission. Emotions like anguish, sadness, melancholy, or depression have negative consequences for those who suffer from them and also affect the rest of the battalion. The aim of this study is to explore the repertoire of institutional and interpersonal resources to alleviate, manage, or control the effects of distance in the emotional bond between the peacekeeper and his family. In other words, to understand in what way the military organization and individuals tried to sustain, repair, or reconstitute, or *emotionally contain*, the deployed military that are supposedly affected by separation from their families.

Emotional containment refers to the practice of identifying negative emotions and redirecting them toward well-being and coexistence. It refers to the way in which the military understand the practices of care, affection, listening, and conversation offered to and from their comrades, wives, parents, or friends that sustained their emotional states so that they can perform their tasks with enthusiasm.[1] Psychologists who belong to the Armed Forces and intervene in the pre- and post-deployment phase apply the same concept. Emotional restraint is not just an internal process generated by broader social conditions, in the sense of Norbert Elias (1994); it is also a result of everyday interpersonal emotional work (Hochschild, 1979). Then, in this context, *containment* is a type of practice that provides others with some attention so that whoever received it can feel emotionally supported. During deployment, the absence of friends, spouses, parents, or brothers enhances the role of the commander and comrades, who take upon them the responsibility to keep the staff motivated. But still, if things do not go well in the homes of the deployed military, it is difficult to fulfill their task.

From an analytical point of view, the centrality of emotional sociability in basic military training in Argentina has been demonstrated by Máximo Badaró (2009). He has pointed out the particular role military instructors at the academy played in learning how to manage emotions. Each cadet had a photographic portrait of his family of origin and nostalgia was a valid sentiment approved by the instructors. By enduring the harshness of education in the military academy the cadets demonstrated the sacrifice they made for their family. The incorporation of an emotional and moral repertoire is part of the socialization into the military hierarchy, discipline, and camaraderie. It provided bodily and verbal dispositions to fulfill their duties in scenarios of increasing uncertainty, where one's own lives and those of others (civilians, comrades, enemies) could be at risk. But it also forged a close relationship between that family and the military life, integrating the officer into "the military family," and subsequently leading him to create "his family" that would become part of that.

Some studies have shown the generally negative emotional impact of military operations on soldiers and their families. These analyses have focused on the emotional states of the wives of the deployed military (e.g., Faulk, Gloria, Cance, and Steinhardt, 2012), on the emotional impact on the military produced by contact with a very different cultural population (e.g., Schut, de Graaff, and Verweij, 2014) and post-deployment emotional damage (e.g., Azari, Dandeker, and Greenberg, 2010). Those researchers have attributed emotional impact to the character of post-Cold War military operations, and the changes in families' way of life and their contemporary organization. The scope, intensity, and increasing frequency of deployments in geographically and culturally very distant countries, for periods of six months or more, have had an unprecedented impact on the military and their families. The concept of stress linked to the pathology of postraumatic stress (PTSD) has been predominant in the above-mentioned studies. Generally, they assume that the military manages to develop self-contained emotional states. They show how emotional self-restraint is affected by misery, culture shock, and confrontation with people whose moral standards are different (and in the eyes of the deployed soldiers, reprehensible).

Some authors (Moskos, Williams, and Segal, 2000; Böene, 2003) state that not only has there been a change in the nature of armed conflicts, but also in the relationship between the families of military personnel and the Armed Forces, attributed to the progressive shift from the "institutional model" to the "occupational model" (Moskos, 1977). They point to a growing number of soldiers who decide to live outside military bases and the tendency to keep professional and personal life separate; features also found in the Argentine Armed Forces. The Argentine military endorses the growing separation of the military profession from family life. Regardless of their own beliefs or family organization, they tend to see it as an obvious change in the military institution, which few resist (Frederic, 2013, Frederic and Masson, 2015). But that was not what took place in Haiti. There, traditional mechanisms also worked, while new ones were developed to prevent or respond to family problems during the peacekeeping operation. Rosana Guber (2016) shows that during the Malvinas/Falklands War the traditional principles operated: many of the wives of the former A4B pilots stayed at the military base where their husbands departed, but others returned to their parents' house. Guber highlights the gratitude of one of the pilots for his wife's words when he left to the Falklands, when she told him to take care of fulfilling his duty while she would take care of raising their children (Guber, 2016: 132). For Argentina, Haiti was the largest military deployment undertaken by its Armed Forces since the defeat in the Malvinas/Falklands War, because of the number of military involved over a decade (13,000 troops),[2] the scope of the organization (contingents of 550 soldiers), and the complexity of the situation in that country. It tested deployment logistics, training criteria, and also the emotional and moral disposition of the personnel.

Since the beginning of the twenty-first century, the idea of the "military family" as a large family that gives its members and the institution the power to regulate acceptable and unacceptable ties was challenged in Argentina.[3] This challenge was caused by the changes in the family life of contemporary Argentina, and by the redefinition of the role of the Argentine Armed Forces. Among other things, military women, more recently incorporated to the institution, asked for institutional recognition to divorce and concubinato, because the traditional military regulations still considered them "an irregular family." This classification had a negative impact on military promotion as it was taken into account at the time of rank evaluation. For this reason, some soldiers managed to conceal their private life from the eyes of the institution. On the basis of a gender policy aimed at promoting the rights of military women, the Ministy of Defense applied some policies to promote individuals' autonomy of professional conditions and protect private and family life (Frederic, 2013). The aim was to help prevent family situations from hindering individuals' carreers and to prevent military life from interfering with personal and/or family life. The distinction between "regular" and "irregular" situations was abolished, marriage between officers and non-commissioned officers was allowed, and military personnel's requests to move to military destinations closer to their families tended to be accepted. Nevertheless, families play an important role in sustaining the motivation during peace operations. Research has shown "that the motivation of soldiers during a mission abroad is highly correlated with the well-being of their partners and families at home" (Tomforde, 2015: 87).

Method

The findings of this study are based on the analysis of 50 ethnographic interviews conducted between 2014 and 2015 with servicemen, former members of the BCA located in Gonaïves, and psychologists and instructors in charge of pre-deployment and post-deployment training.[4] Departing from the idea that the performance of deployed soldiers not only depends on the soldier but also on his family, the Argentine Joint Training Center for Peace Operations (CAECOPAZ) developed a specific program aimed at providing emotional security to the military through their families. Its objective was to emotionally support the members of the "military family" during deployment. The program was certified by the International Training Standards of the United Nations, and was mentioned as an Argentine contribution to the international instruction offered to blue helmets before deployment to the MINUSTAH.

Confinement: the military base as a big "pressure cooker"

The emotional challenges imposed on the Argentine peacekeepers by the deployment in Haiti become more clear if we look at the characterization of the base as "a pressure cooker" or a "Big Brother." At the base, called La Roca, lived approximately 500 male soldiers that beheld the BCA. Military women first entered the mission five years after it began and never represented more than 1 percent of the total force. The members of the BCA were fully renewed every six months; 24 battalions had rotated there. From the third BCA it was decided that to improve unit cohesion it was more appropriate that different infantry regiments in Argentina were successively designated as a "core unit." This would also help to have most of the peacekeapers' families geographically more concentrated. Therefore, almost all of the members of the BCA belonged to the Army (60 percent), 30 percent belonged to the Marine infantry, and 10 percent to the Air Force.

When the former blue helmets compared the military base in Gonaïves with a "pressure cooker," they referred to those aspects that amplified the confinement in La Roca. They named: the threat of armed gangs, which intensified political and criminal violence in Gonaïves; the general misery and the city as "a great shanty town"; the absence of recreational places outside La Roca; and finally the hardening of the specific directives of the UN toward the deployed military personnel that, in the second year of the mission, prohibited contact with the local population. Gonaïves had been the epicenter of violence that precipitated the decision to establish MINUSTAH in 2004. In addition, it had no recreational, social, or leisure facilities such as bars, cinemas, theaters, etc. where they could go out after duty and get in touch with people outside the military base. Many noncommissioned officers and officers mentioned the uncomfortable feeling of seeing hungry and abandoned barefooted children around La Roca.

Therefore, the military institution responsible for unit welfare immediatly realized that it was imperative to find "escapes" from the confinement and contact with misery. Finding an "escape valve," a place that provided a recreational release to "let off steam," "relax," and "oxygenate," was for the first battalions as essential as it was difficult. Some former blue helmets compared the military base with a "prison" or a "cloister monastery." Thus, a former blue helmet, at the time of the interview a senior officer of the Joint Chiefs of Staff, remarked:

> For me, the peculiarity of Haiti lies in the fact that one lives locked up for six months. For example, on Sundays or off-days, if you wanted to have a drink or a cup of coffee, there was nowhere to go in Gonaïves. And, look, you can be the most fun person in the world, but after a while the atmosphere finally depresses you, it's very difficult to get along, there are no places where you can disconnect and relax for a while; you simply go from work to the base and vice versa; it becomes really tedious.

Consequently, the absence of entertainment and recreation became one of the concerns of the commanders during the mission. The first option was to find a beach near the military base. At the beginning of the mission this was not a safe area for the troops; it was difficult to reach it because the roads were broken. Even so, they managed to rent a house on the beach five hours from the base. Every week they took a group to rest, along with custody patrol. Security prevented the peacekeepers from leaving the premises or letting prostitutes in.

Thus, the constant exposure of troops to extreme situations, the distance of their wives and loved ones, with almost no means to decompress and relax, dragged them to intolerable tensions. Therefore, in addition to the rotating "escape" to the beach, senior officials urged their staff to make good use of their free time. They were advised to travel, relax, and have fun, to lower their emotional "tensions." They believed the exhausted junior staff sometimes wasted their leisure time, tended to "roll up," "make out," and ended up obsessed with personal matters. As it was forbidden to leave the base during free time, one official recalled: "I insisted that while they were not in active service, and were at La Roca, they would try to relax, take off their uniforms and wear casual clothes: shorts, T-shirts, flip flops, to feel human beings . . . You can not spend all day in uniform and combat boots." Another senior officer remembered that he recommended his troops that, although it could be more expensive, they travel to Argentina to stay with their family, to make the rest of the mission in Haiti more bearable.

Those recommendations reflected a certain expertise of those military with the highest ranks at La Roca—mainly their knowledge and practices of protection and care, which allowed them to identify emotional problems and solutions through which to maintain or recover subordinates' well-being. This feature attributed to the "superior" was typical of the way the Argentine Army understood the command. Commanders had to master risk situations, as well as take responsibility for the emotional and moral state of their troops.

When the MINUSTAH command prohibited any interaction with the local population, the pressure in the "pressure cooker" was rising. For the United Nations, relations with civilians outside the military base, even if there was consent, were subject to disciplinary sanctions since it was considered that the military was in a position of absolute superiority. This prohibition was reinforced after several scandals involving sexual abuse among other contingents. This led to a greater sense of confinement and isolation among the Argentine blue helmets. To counteract these emotional states some BCA leaders organized soccer tournaments in the context of "civic action," which normally helps to gain trust of the local population. When the BCA stopped doing this in the last few years of MINUSTAH, the abandonment of the base found by the last BCA revealed demotivation, loss of cohesion, and a series of painful behaviors, such as alcohol abuse.

As a result, compulsory military leave was crucial in the emotional regulation carried out by the BCA leadership. Normally, the peacekeepers would first take a full week of vacation and, later, 21 successive days. But unlike the mission in Cyprus, in which some had participated, they could not bring their family for vacations in Haiti. Cyprus did not have the complexity of Haiti and was also very close to Europe, which was a source of encouragement for the recomposition of family ties. In Haiti, the available options were: to make short trips to nearby places, to go to Argentina for the duration of the holidays, or to simply stay at the base. In each case, the staff paid their own expenses, which also affected their choices. Haiti meant, for many of them, a significant amount of extra money that could be better used once they returned to Argentina and shared with their family. Therefore, against the suggestions of the bosses, some opted to stay in La Roca, thus risking the impairment of their emotional state.

Given the cost and effort of traveling, as well as the limited possibilities for entertainment in Haitian cities, the daily organization of recreational activities became essential for the management of emotional well-being of the troops and the success of the mission. Sports activities, especially soccer matches, stood out as the most relaxing and popular activities. There were competitions organized to develop and strengthen bonds of camaraderie among service members.

Music activities were also sponsored by the authorities as part of the entertainment and recreation of the troops. The BCA XI, for example, had a band of music, and it became an effective means to bring the troops and the local population closer, with consent of the commander. On several occasions, the former blue helmets, aided by the MINUSTAH authorities, the bishop, and other NGO officials, organized music festivals with artists from Haiti and Argentina. Those events were very successful.

Therefore, instead of friends, brothers, and wives at home, it was military comrades who soldiers turned to when emotional support and care was needed. The bonds forged with the comrades-in-arms were maintained over time. Even if, once in Argentina, they never saw each other again, the intensity of the experiences they shared united them deeply over time.

Regardless of their position in the military hierarchy, or their level of command, the interviewees seemed to use the same strategies to deal, both professionally and personally, with fatigue, nostalgia, anxiety, stress, or difficulties during the peacekeeping mission. The main coping strategies for dealing with these emotional states were: a) to remain physically active and completely dedicated to continuous and regular tasks that would distract them and make them feel "useful," and b) the support and conversations between comrades, without hierarchical distinction, essential to avoid melancholy, isolation, and depression. In each of the cases, the interviewees expressed feelings of empathy and felt morally obliged to intervene and help the companions when they saw them being sad, worried, or lonely. Very often, they helped by inviting their collegues for a talk, a card game, or a cigarette. Thus, identifying other comrades' negative emotional states was a task ubiquitous to the mission for them and the group.

Institutional and personal resources for *emotional containment*: the emotional trackers

Given the confinement as a central feature of the operational environment in Gonaïves, it was necessary to take care of the bonds with blue helmets' families. The commanders of each of the BCAs mentioned the importance of ensuring communications between the troops and their families. The involvement in family affairs of immediate subordinates is a basic routine for Argentine commanders. At the beginning of the mission, only a single satellite phone was available for the 500 troops. As the mission progressed, each peacekeeper hired their own internet and cell phone service. But in any case, communication with the family was conceived as a key factor. The experiences of family left in Argentina were a source of emotions that had an impact on the military, and there were several practices to deal with them before and during deployment, both by the military themselves and by their families, relatives, and the military institution. When former peacekeepers talked about their professional and personal experiences in Haiti, they repeatedly highlighted the impact of family problems on their professional performance. Among other things, they talked about school problems, illnesses, accidents, and the consequent family destabilization that was caused by the absence of the father. But distance also removed the emotional containment provided by the wives of the military to them. This containment, as emotional support, was a sensitive and constant issue because it could hardly be compensated due to the particularities of the daily environment in Gonaïves. That is why communication was considered fundamental.

The regulation of the communication between the deployed personnel and the loved ones that remained in Argentina was one of the main concerns of the military command in Argentina and in Gonaïves, and was expressed in the "lessons learned." Therefore, along with their decision to participate in peacekeeping operations, the military had to report on their family situation in order to prevent problems once in Haiti. The institution, through the commanders of the units deployed in Argentina and the psychologists of the Military Hospital, asked them to report on the health situation of their family members and on relationship conflicts existing within their family. Failure to comply with these requirements could endanger their permanence in the mission (forced repatriation) and could be sanctioned, and even affect future promotions. In this sense, we note a consensus among former military blue helmets on the importance of "putting the house in order," or "leaving the 'ranch' accommodated," as a personal need beyond institutional requirements. One of the certainties shared by them was that "leaving everything in order" meant being able to focus on work, because, as they said, unresolved problems could come back during the deployment. To focus more on their house than on their work was undesired, thus "communication with families" was the key to avoid those situations. Former blue helmets claimed that their wives "were used to taking the reins" and dealing with children and the home while they were in military maneuvers. However, six months in Haiti was different from two weeks of training, which took place close to their homes and did not represent real risks for the troops.

The military and civilian personnel in charge of the welfare of the troops during the mission (psychiatrists and psychologists) considered that emotional work with families, of both the institution and deployed service members, was inseparable from the professional performance. Therefore, the mental health team of the Military Hospital in charge of the pre-deployment phase and the post-deployment diagnosis recommended that peacekeepers "discuss everything in detail beforehand" and warn the family about unexpected situations and uncertainties (as occurred with the floods and the earthquake) that might otherwise cause unnecessary stress and anxiety. One of the psychologists pointed out that: "When the communication between the spouses tends to be bad or insufficient, the unreported problems, such as the health of the children or marital problems, may seem worse." The same could happen when the media dramatized local or national news, causing excessive concerns for both partners.

Promoting and facilitating "good communication" between personnel and their families during the deployment was also part of the duties of the military command in Haiti. Technological improvements at the military base in Gonaïves eliminated long queues for the only satellite phone, and allowed for more agile ways to stay in contact with those who were at home. Midway through the mission, the soldiers could choose to pay a monthly fee to have their own wireless routers, instead of depending on the institution for the internet connection. This allowed them to send emails and use instant messaging with their friends and family in Argentina. In fact, life after they returned home was altered when this happened, as pointed out by those who participated in the initial BCA, who critized those who sunk into the internet, which was at the expense of the camaraderie achieved in the first battalions. The emotional containment turned more to digital communication with those who stayed in Argentina than to personal contact and conversation with comrades.

Assiduous communication was in some peacekeepers' accounts a source of concern and emotional disturbance. Certain stories of their wives awakened jealousy and led some of them decide to reduce communication, to only tell the minimum and indispensable. Wives did the same, in an attempt not to worry them. This is what First Lieutenant Carlos Robles told us:

> I got very bad, she told me about the lawyer. She had gone to see him to certify a document . . . and I became obsessed, I despaired. I started imagining things, and in a few minutes we were already fighting for stupidity . . . So I told her not to tell me everything, to talk less. I said to her "I don't tell you everything either."

Weighing the "military family" and the "family of the military" emotional containment

The families affected by military deployment were supported by military comrades of their spouses or by their families. Friends and comrades were there to help the wives and children, if necessary. Generally, the oldest non-commissioned officer in charge strongly supported his subalterns and acted as a kind of nexus between them and their families in Argentina, including those who did not live in the military base. However, the former blue helmets claimed that they "breathed easier" when their spouses and children stayed with extended family, or lived near them. They tried to move them before deployment to Haiti, often changing residence.

Helena Carreiras (2015) finds a similar situation among the former Portuguese blue helmets deployed in Bosnia, Kosovo, and East Timor. In Portugal, military personnel also considered their families as the key to their professional performance. In spite of this, the Portugese Armed Forces made the military family more and more invisible. Therefore, the emotional containment of those left behind, the family members, depended on the informal support network of the extended family, close friends, and neighbors. Military personnel observed the absence of institutional coverage, but also acknowledged that interference by the military institution in their personal and family life, in fact, would have been a reason for leaving the Armed Forces. In the same way, the former Argentine blue helmets admitted that having their families in the military bases or having more institutional support did not give them greater peace of mind. It was the possibility of having their relatives close to their spouses and children that really relieved or contained them while being deployed.

However, something different happened when the first news of the earthquake in Haiti arrived in January 2010. Here the "military family" was put into effect. Distressed wives of the blue helmets approached the wife of the Lieutenant Colonel, commander of the BCA XI. They went to her house in the military district of the infantry regiment in Argentina, which had become the center that provided the majority of the troops to that contingent. Her immediate response was to contact her husband through Skype, who in turn reassured them and allowed each wife to talk with her husband. While he was passing on the computer to the service members, one by one, so did his wife with the respective wives. This experience seems to indicate that the "military family" continues to operate as an agglutinating entity, while the importance of the "family of the military" grows.

According to the military personnel, the institution's ability to respond by containing family members in exceptional or critical circumstances was not what really reassured them; however, they did not reject it or call for more institutional interventions. They did reject the institutional intervention when the BCA returned three months later than planned due to the Haitian earthquake of 2010. When the soldiers arrived in Buenos Aires, they were not allowed to contact their families, who were waiting for them at the military airport, until they underwent a series of psychological tests. They rejected the measure; the reunion with their families was a priority for them. Many believed that the Argentine Army was more interested in covering its back than worried about the welfare of its soldiers. The Army mental health team saw staff discontent as a misinterpretation of the causes of the measure.

Paradoxically, although military personnel did not call for more institutional interventions, Argentina provided an institutional response considered adequate to the "families of the deployed personnel," offering them permanent support. The institutional resources from 2009 incorporated the value of the "family of the military." The support was gradually developed at the Argentine Center for Joint Training in Peace Operations (CAECOPAZ) and on the impulse of one of the CAECOPAZ psychologists. She found that neither the traditional military community nor the families had sufficient resources to face these types of situations; even though military personnel were prepared, the wives were not.

Although technically the pre-deployment course had to follow the standards established by the Integrated Training Service ITS (United Nations), the domestic version of the course led by CAECOPAZ has tried to validate one of its own "lessons learned": to help guarantee the emotional preparation of the deployed soldier and those left behind, to "minimize the risk of stress," as the CAECOPAZ psychologist and instructor argues in her book (Muzio, 2010). Basically, the book supports the connection between the efficiency of the staff deployed and the absence of stress related to the family. Her book was sponsored by CAECOPAZ and the military authorities, and the work was backed up in such a way that she was in charge of guaranteeing the emotional preparation of the families in the pre-deployment stage. The tasks included the preparation of the families, complimenting the preparation carried out by the leader of the military unit, who selected from among the volunteers the soldiers least likely to interrupt the effectiveness of the mission with personal or family matters. Even so, the CAECOPAZ staff could not extend its activities beyond this pre-deployment stage. Any complex or unexpected family problem that occurred while the military were in Gonaïves was beyond its sphere of influence and should be dealt with by the contingent chief, or the NCO in charge of the subordinate personnel at La Roca in Haiti. As was pointed out, the latter was in charge of inspecting the troops to relieve or detect health or personal problems, such as depressed mood or aggressive behavior. His emotional work, in the sense of Arlie Hochschild (1979), was to detect those who showed signs of emotional disengagement. Those signs led these emotional trackers, who were often guided by comments from other colleagues, to track and trace the existence of problems and to try to act to restore the emotional state of that comrade. There was also a chaplain who contributed to this task of the NCO in charge.

The dramatic experience of the earthquake in 2010 challenged the Joint Chiefs of Staff of the Armed Forces. The resources described above proved not to be sufficient; therefore, in the following rotations a military psychologist was deployed so that emotional support in Gonaïves could be provided continuously. This professional was supplied by the Air Force, being the only institution that had psychologists incorporated into the service. The experience during the earthquake had been very complex, both because of the extension of the deployment, and because of the dramatic situations that many had experienced attending the population in Port-au-Prince. The mental health team of the military hospital was searching for ways of detecting possible disorders of the type of post-traumatic stress (PTSD), without causing more anguish or anger. However, there was no policy to follow up on possible cases of PTSD or other emotional or psychological disorders in peacekeeping operations as it effectively was for veterans of the Malvinas/Falklands War.[5] Even those who went through the most heart-wrenching experiences such as caring for food supplies trucks and being forced to shoot people who were driven by hunger and dispair, or suffered the impact of seeing countless adult and baby corpses, were not diagnosed with post-traumatic stress disorder, nor assisted more than the first weeks after returning from the mission—even though those images followed them and caused them anguish several years after.

Military personnel described their six-month experience in Haiti as new and disruptive, or at least different. Some spoke of the "hidden costs" of the mission to Haiti, such as post-deployment divorces or marital problems. Many experienced family distress caused by the prolonged separation and distance, particularly related to the reunion and reintegration into daily family life. The monetary reward did not compensate the emotional fatigue of the deployment and the hardship of their wives. Haiti tested the "military family" as well as the "family of the military."

Conclusion

Haiti was different from other peacekeeping operations not just because it was the most complex military operation after the Malvinas/Falkland War, performed in times of democracy, but also because of the impact of the operational environment on military personnel, their families, and the "military family." Undoubtedly, the forced isolation and restrictions of the "Big Brother," represented by the "pressure cooker," posed unprecedented challenges. The Hatian experience demonstrates that the model of the "military family" was challenged, while the model of the "family of the military" became deeply strengthened in practice to contain the emotions of deployed servicemen.

The narratives show the emotional dependence of military personnel on their families. Also, they show how personnel compensate the lack of emotional containment of their families, and how to safeguard against the problems of the "family of the military" breaking in during the mission. Consequently, the emotional work was performed by the trackers of negative feelings. Before the deployment, the emotional trackers were psychologists. During the deployment, non-commissioned officers and senior officers took over the role of the emotional trackers. Clearly, they decided on the rules that distinguished right from wrong feelings. Also, it was emotional work to reestablish emotional states apt for military performance during deployment.

During the ten-year duration of MINUSTAH, the military institution strengthened the assistance and emotional support for peacekeeper families, not making them invisible, as happened in the Portuguese case (Carreiras, 2015). Strengthening the category of the "family of the military" as an object of institutional attention was a way of dealing with the weakness of the "great military family" and the consequent tensions between the military profession and the family (De Angelis and Segal, 2015), expressed during the deployment in MINUSTAH. The performance in Haiti demanded a set of personal arrangements in Argentina to take care of peacekeepers' families. But above all, it required a set of emotional tasks between superiors and subordinates, between comrades and the mental health team, designed to compensate the emotional support usually provided by wives.

Notes

1 The relevance of the emotional component was highlighted and problematized in articles that dealt with the effects on it produced by the "cultural other" in military operations, when the cultural contrast was perceived as radical (Schut, de Graaf, and Verweij, 2014; Azari, Dandeker, and Greenberg, 2010)

2 The total deployed military was 13,000, but around 10,000 went to Gonaïves in successive BCAs; the remaining 3000 were either in the Military Hospital or in the United Nations Staff, with both units located in Port-au-Prince. This city was charged with the responsibility to deploy the Force Command and the Brazilian battalion, the country that led the Mission.

3 The challenge to the "military family" that occurred in Argentina is not a general tendency in all Latin American countries, as was shown in recent studies about the Brazilian Army (Castro, 2018; Rodriguez da Silva, 2018).

4 I did not interview female former military blue helmets deployed at the BCA in Gonaïves. There were very few that went to the MINUSTAH, a total of around 30 out of 10,000 males deployed to the BCA at Gonaives. They began to be deployed in 2009, in a number of around five NCOs, which in 2011 increased to ten NCOs and two officers. There were women from the beginning of the mission at the Military Hospital located in Puerto Principe, all of them nurses, biochemists, or doctors.

5 According to other authors, PTSD can result from peace operations precisely because of its characteristics, which require a high level of interaction with people who live in dramatic situations and high levels of poverty (Azari, Dandeker, and Greenberg, 2010). Dismissing this type of disorder is the result of the fact that its diagnosis obliges the state to recognize disability pensions, in this case psychological.

References

Azari, J., Dandeker, C., and Greenberg, N. (2010). Cultural stress: how interactions with and among foreign populations affect military personnel. *Armed Forces & Society*, 36(4), 585–603.

Badaró, Máximo (2009) *¿Militares o Ciudadanos? La formación de los oficiales del Ejército Argentino*. Buenos Aires: Prometeo.

Böene, B. (2003). La professionnalisation des armées: contexte et raisons, impact fonctionnel et sociopolitique. *Revue Française de Sociologie*, 44(4), 647–693.

Carreiras, H. (2015). The invisible families of Portuguese soldiers: from colonial wars to contemporary missions. In R. Moelker, M. Andres, G. Bowen, and P. Manigart (eds), *Military Families and War in the 21st Century. Comparative Perspectives* (pp. 261–277). New York: Routledge.

Castro, C. (2018). A tradicional familia militar. Autobiografía de mulheres de militares. In C. Castro (ed.), *A familia militar no Brasil: transformacoes e permanencias* (pp. 15–28). Rio de Janeiro: FGV Editora.

De Angelis, K. and Segal, M. W. (2015). Transitions in the military and the family as greedy institutions: original concept and current applicability. In R. Moelker, M. Andres, G. Bowen, and P. Manigart (eds), *Military Families and War in the 21st Century. Comparative Perspectives* (pp. 22–42). New York: Routledge.

Elias, N. (1994). *The Civilizing Process*. Oxford: Blackwell.

Faulk, K. E., Gloria, C. T., Cance, J. D., and Steinhardt, M. A. (2012). Depressive symptoms among US military spouses during deployment: the protective effect of positive emotions. *Armed Forces & Society*, 38(3), 373–390.

Frederic, S. and Masson, L. (2015). Profession and the military family in the Argentine Armed Forces: generational differences and socio-cultural changes. In R. Moelker, M. Andres, G. Bowen, and P. Manigart (Eds), *Military Families and War in the 21st Century. Comparative Perspectives* (pp. 73–83). New York: Routledge.

Frederic, S. (2013). *Las trampas del pasado. Las fuerzas armadas y su integración al estado democrático en Argentina*. Buenos Aires: Fondo de Cultura Económica.

Guber, R. (2016). *Experiencia de Halcón. Los escuadrones de la Fuerza Aérea Argentina que pusieron en jaque a la flota británica en Malvinas*. Buenos Aires: Sudamericana.

Hochschild, A. (1979). Emotion work, feeling rules and social estructure. *American Journal of Sociology*, 85, 551–575.

Moelker, R., Andres, M., Bowen, G., and Manigart, P. (2015). Introduction. In R. Moelker, M. Andres, G. Bowen, and P. Manigart (eds), *Military Families and War in the 21st Century. Comparative Perspectives* (pp. 3–21). New York: Routledge.

Moskos, C. (1977). From institution to occupation. *Armed Forces & Society*, 4(1), 41–50.

Moskos, C., Williams, J. A., and Segal, D. (eds) (2000). *The Postmodern Military: Armed Forces after the Cold War*. New York: Oxford University Press.

Muzio, M. I. (2010). *La participación en Operaciones de Mantenimiento de Paz e impacto en el ámbito familiar: tratando de enfrentar el desafío*. Buenos Aires: Editorial Dunken.

Rodriguez da Silva, C. (2018). Familias na fronteira: experiencias de esposas de militares na selva brasileira. In C. Castro (ed.), *A familia militar no Brasil: transformacoes e permanencias* (pp. 89–114). Rio de Janeiro: FGV Editora.

Schut, M., Graaf, M. C. de, and Verweij, D. (2014). Moral emotions during military deployments of Dutch forces: a qualitative study on moral emotions in intercultural interactions. *Armed Forces & Society*, 41(4), 616–638.

Tomforde, M. (2015). The emotional cycle of deployment. In R. Moelker, M. Andres, G. Bowen, and P. Manigart (eds), *Military Families and War in the 21st Century. Comparative Perspectives* (pp. 87–106). New York: Routledge.

15 Standing strong in the context of organizational and family demands

A measure of USAF civilian spouse fitness[1]

Gary L. Bowen, Todd M. Jensen, and James A. Martin

Introduction

Beginning with the terrorist attacks by the Islamic terrorist group al-Qaeda on the United States on September 11, 2001, America's military members and their families have experienced a continuous series of combat deployments, as well as a corresponding high military operational tempo across all service branches and seemingly unrelenting duty demands (Bowles et al., 2015). Consequently, both practitioners and scholars have been interested in exploring the interface between military and family life challenges (Bowen, Jensen, and Williams, 2017; Jensen and Bowen, 2017), and the subsequent functioning and well-being of individuals and families, with an appreciation for the bidirectional nature of these military-family life influences. Although much attention has been placed on the military member at the center of military and family institutions, an inclusive approach to promoting family and individual resiliency will require a broader focus on the families of service members, including their civilian spouses and children (Eaton et al., 2008; Hengstebeck, Meadows, Griffin, Friedman, and Beckman, 2016). Moreover, efforts are warranted to develop or tailor interventions and initiatives that foster fitness and resiliency among civilian spouses, who represent central figures in the meso or organizational level triad of the military member, family, and work organization.

Past research has revealed that civilian spouses of military members often face unique challenges. For one, civilian spouses (especially spouses of active-duty members) are generally embedded in a military context with unique rules and guidelines—a context that can require some adjustment, especially when families are stationed overseas (Crouch, Adrian, Adler, Wood, and Thomas, 2017; Eaton et al., 2008). In addition, due to frequent military reassignments, family relocation can result in disruptions in the civilian spouse's labor-market appeal, employment status, and earning potential (Castaneda and Harrell, 2008; Cooke and Speirs, 2005; Hosek and MacDermid Wadsworth, 2013).

When military members deploy, civilian spouses take on new roles and responsibilities in various life domains, which can place civilian spouses at a heightened risk of emotional distress or general strain (Chandra et al., 2011; Eaton et al., 2008; Lester et al., 2010). Civilian spouses also often experience stress in response to the onset and persistence of deployment-related mental health concerns among their active-duty partners (Donoho, Riviere, and Adler, 2017). Consequently, there is some evidence that civilian spouses report similar rates of mental health concerns as their military partners (Eaton et al., 2008). From a role theory perspective, civilian spouses might experience role conflict, or the demands and expectations of multiple roles being at odds with each other; role ambiguity, or unclear or ill-defined role expectations; and role strain, or excessive stress related to any one particular role (Robbins, Chatterjee, and Canda, 2012). Moreover, from a work-family conflict perspective (Perry-Jenkins and MacDermid Wadsworth, 2017), civilian spouses may experience stress as a result of competing demands placed on them from both military and family spheres.

Importantly, civilian spouses typically demonstrate notable strengths, such as a relatively greater willingness than their military partners to pursue and access behavioral health treatment services (Eaton et al., 2008). Moreover, turning to the experiences of the United States Air Force (USAF) specifically, some civilian spouses are invited by commanders to participate in spouse leadership efforts (known in the USAF as the *Key Spouse Program*), which affords them opportunities to provide direct support to peers and families, helping to foster a sense of community among family members, and forging stronger bonds between unit leaders and families. As a result, *Key Spouses* are especially positioned at the nexus of the military and family institutions, with implications for family functioning and individual well-being. From a work-family facilitation perspective (Perry-Jenkins and MacDermid Wadsworth, 2017), any responsibilities civilian spouses have that are associated with the military sphere could be conceptualized as a work-related role, which, if performed successfully, promotes performance enhancement in other settings or roles, such as in the family sphere. Such work-family facilitation might be especially salient for *Key Spouses* when roles in the military and larger-community spheres are successfully performed, leading to a positive spillover in the family sphere (and vice versa). In the pursuit of building a fit and resilient military, an ongoing focus on the resiliency of military spouses is warranted. This should include further study of initiatives at the unit and higher command levels within and across the service branches to design, implement, promote, and measure the impact of unit and community strategies to enhance resiliency between and among military spouses.

Relatedly, the USAF officially launched its Comprehensive Airman Fitness (CAF) program on March 30, 2011 (Gonzalez, Singh, Schell, and Weinick, 2014). In 2014, CAF program requirements were extended and broadly defined the term *airman* as including military members, civilian employees, and family members (USAF, 2014). Somewhat similar in focus and form to the earlier US Army Comprehensive Soldier Fitness program (CSF; Casey, 2011), the CAF framework highlights four core fitness components: mental, physical, social, and spiritual.

Unlike the US Army, which made assessment of the CSF a priority from the program's inception (Peterson, Park, and Castro, 2011), the USAF did not initiate systematic work to develop and validate an empirical assessment of CAF. According to a 2015 RAND report (Meadows, Miller, and Robson, 2015), USAF leaders intended to use metrics from existing data sources for CAF assessment rather than burden the USAF population with additional data collections. However, we could identify only one subsequent example of such work (Ipsos Public Affairs, 2013).

In response to USAF policy guidance that calls for valid and reliable metrics to be used by commanders and community support coordinators to monitor fitness (USAF, 2014), Bowen, Jensen, and Martin (2016a, 2016b) proposed and validated a 12-item measure of CAF and demonstrated the instrument's invariance across three USAF components: active-duty personnel, National Guard/Reserve members, and civilian employees. The results indicated the four individual CAF-latent constructs supported the construct of a total CAF score. As predicted, the second-order construct of total CAF was associated with a statistically significant increase in individual resiliency, which was self-assessed with three items addressing military member's successful role performance in meeting the challenges of military life, performing assigned duties successfully, and meeting personal responsibilities (e.g., family life roles). Focusing on resiliency as an outcome is consistent with current policy guidance to promote and sustain "a fit, resilient, and ready force" (USAF, 2014: 3).

The present investigation extends the work of Bowen et al. (2016a, 2016b) by proposing and testing a similar measure of CAF for civilian spouses of USAF active-duty members. The 12-item spouse measure was validated empirically through confirmatory factor analysis of the four fitness components and an overall or *total fitness* measure of CAF. The construct validity of the measure was examined in the context of a spouse resiliency measure developed by an USAF-sponsored *Family Resiliency Working Group*, which defined spouse resiliency as "the extent to which spouses know and use their individual and community resources, experience a meaningful connection to the Air Force, and meet the challenges of military life" (Bowen and Martin, 2011a: 3).

As alluded to earlier, a focus on spouse fitness and its relationship to resiliency is particularly appropriate in the context of the challenges that contemporary life poses for military families, including challenging duty requirements, frequent deployments, periodic relocation, and the general stress inherent to military duties and associated service life—all of which can significantly disrupt the lives of family members (US Department of Defense, 2015; Segal, Lane, and Fisher, 2015). In today's USAF, 46 percent of active-duty members are married to civilian spouses (Air Force Personnel Center, 2016), and considerable USAF-sponsored research reinforces the contribution of civilian spouses to the success of active-duty members in meeting mission demands (Bowen, 1986; Spera, 2009). The validation of a metric for assessing civilian-spouse fitness has important implications for USAF leaders, policymakers, and practitioners charged with understanding, promoting, and supporting CAF, as well as for researchers interested in evaluating policy and program interventions to promote fitness. Moreover, reliable and valid measures of intended outcomes are critical to evidence-informed policy and practice as well as intervention research (Fraser and Galinsky, 2010; Mullen, 2004).

Support and resiliency inventory

The SRI is a brief (15–20 minutes), self-administered, web-based assessment tool that examines respondents' perceptions of the sources of informal and formal support in their lives, their individual fitness, their positive behaviors toward self and others, and their success in adapting to life challenges and meeting the responsibilities of military life and duty. Completion of the SRI is voluntary, and the information provided is anonymous (Bowen and Martin, 2011b, 2015).

The development and initial pilot-testing of the SRI was sponsored by the USAF Space Command Family Matters Office (2004–2007) in support of the USAF unit services outreach strategy (Orthner, Bowen, and Mancini, 2003). During its initial development, the SRI was known as the Unit Assets Inventory, with parallel versions for USAF members and their civilian spouses. From 2008 to 2013, the SRI was used USAF-wide as part of the Airman and Family Services Division's Community Readiness Consultant Practice Strategy (Bowen, Martin, Liston, and Nelson, 2009). In 2013, sponsorship for the SRI shifted to HQ AF Resilience Division for use by community support coordinators, who became at that time the "specialist and facilitator" for CAF at the installation level (USAF, 2014: 7). USAF sponsorship of the SRI ended in 2015 (although the content of the SRI instrument is available from the authors).

In 2011, the SRI for civilian spouses was revised, in part, to better capture the evolving concept of CAF (Bowen and Martin, 2011a). In the current version, 12 items assess the four domains of AF fitness (three items per domain). This developmental process has involved some trial and error, including exploratory data analysis used to examine various combinations of items in the context of the nominal definitions of the four fitness components (see Table 15.1).

Other than exploratory analysis conducted on the SRI (Bowen and Martin, 2011a), the conceptual integrity of the measure for civilian spouses has not received sufficient empirical attention, and USAF policy guidance now requires "CAF metrics/indicators derived from defined measures and self-reported data provided in community-based Air Force surveys [that can be] used to provide commanders a view of the comprehensive fitness of an organization" (USAF, 2014: 11). An important next step will be to establish that the four fitness measures, and the concept of a total fitness score, actually represents more than just an indication of a statistically significant change in resiliency. Indeed, the goal is to establish that a change in these fitness scores reflects an important difference in actual and

Table 15.1 US Department of the Air Force definitions of four fitness domains

Fitness domain	*Definition*
Mental fitness	The ability to effectively cope with unique mental stressors and challenges
Physical fitness	The ability to adopt and sustain healthy behaviors needed to enhance health and well-being
Social fitness	The ability to engage in healthy social networks that promote overall well-being and optimal performance
Spiritual fitness	The ability to adhere to beliefs, principles, or values needed to persevere and prevail in accomplishing missions

Source: US Department of the Air Force (2014, April 2). *Comprehensive Airman Fitness (CAF): Air Force Instruction 90-506* (pp. 15–16). Washington, DC.

meaningful resiliency outcomes. Validating a total fitness score in this way would provide a particularly efficient way to measure fitness in empirical research and a simple way to display results for military leaders, policymakers, and practitioners.

Hypothesized model

Figure 15.1 illustrates the hypothesized model tested in this investigation. The model shows 12 observed variables associated with four first-order latent fitness factors (mental, physical, social, and spiritual). Table 15.1 includes definitions of these components (USAF, 2014). With the exception of the social domain, the indicators for each fitness component are identical to the active-duty member measure of total fitness (Bowen et al., 2016a); however, rather than focusing on particular sources of support (e.g., friends), the spouse version addresses broader aspects of community support and the spouse's ability to receive support from others in the community. The model shows a second-order factor structure in which the four first-order latent fitness factors load onto a higher-order latent factor, total fitness.

The construct validity of the total fitness measure is examined with the addition of a competency-based resiliency measure, which is defined as a latent factor with five observed variables. This assessment of resiliency is similar to the majority of studies of military family resilience that assess outcome proxies for resilience (Wright, Riviere, Merrill, and Cabrera, 2013). In Figure 15.1, total fitness is expected to have a direct and positive influence on resiliency, which is consistent with the Resiliency Model of Role Performance (Bowen and Martin, 2011b).

Methods

Data source

Following institutional review board authorization from the Office of Human Research Ethics at the primary author's university, we used data collected during February and March 2011 from a voluntary, anonymous survey of participants in the *Key Spouse Program*. The *Key Spouse Program* is a USAF commander's program for civilian-spouse volunteers that supports airmen and their families during deployments, separations, and emergencies (USAF, 2013). As noted previously, *Key Spouses* provide peer-to-peer support, work to strengthen communication between unit leaders and families, and promote a sense of community. Each installation's Airman and Family Readiness Center is responsible for the training and support of *Key Spouse* participants. Although no empirical evidence is available, in the context of their position and their identification by unit leaders, it is assumed that these spouses are regarded as among the most committed and best-adjusted civilian spouses.

In the present study, *Key Spouses* across 62 bases from 10 major USAF Commands were identified and asked by a local base point-of-contact to pilot-test the Support and Resiliency Inventory designed specifically for Civilian Spouses (SRI-CS; Bowen and Martin, 2011c). For administration convenience, Reserve Command and

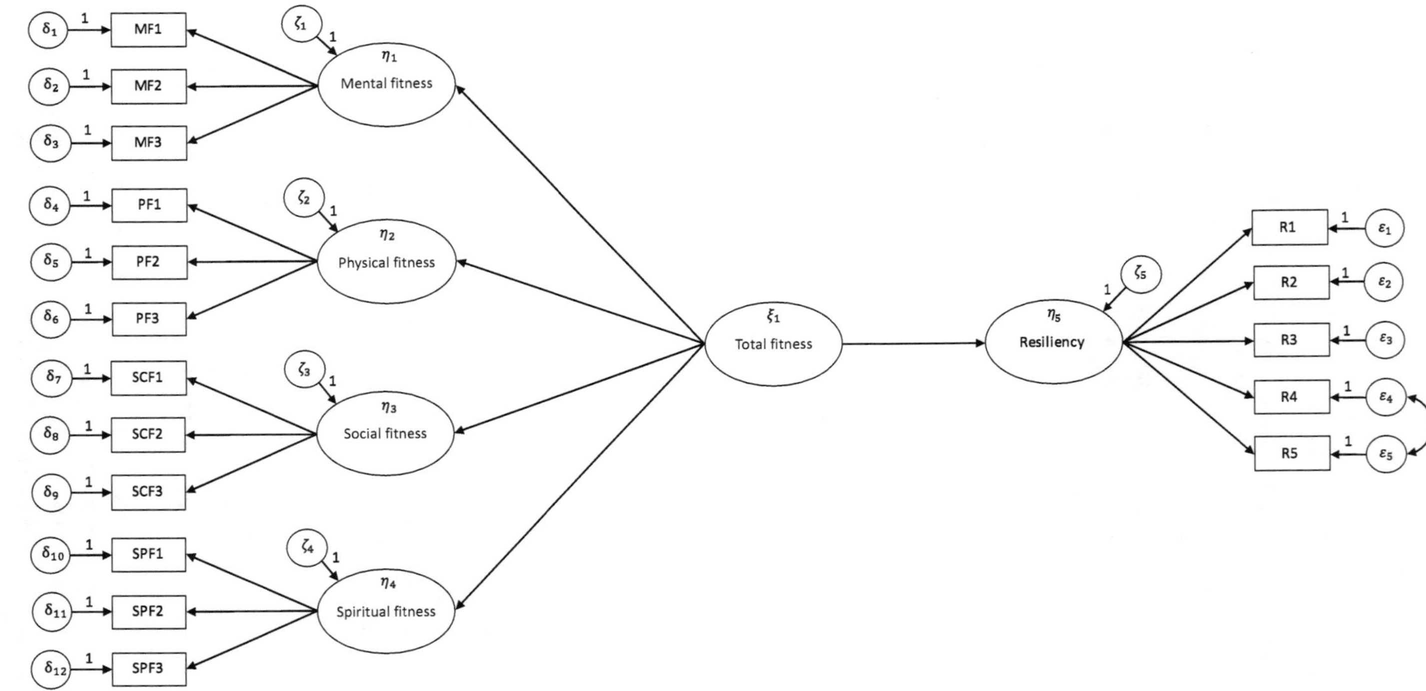

Figure 15.1 Hypothesized model

Note: For metric calibration, the variance/error variance of first- and second-order factors are fixed to 1.

joint bases where the USAF is not the lead service were not asked to participate in the pilot test. *Key Spouses* were selected for the pilot test given their USAF experience; that is, they were considered to be in the best position to evaluate the revised SRI-CS.

All items corresponding to the support, fitness, and resiliency measures were worded in a positive, proactive direction to focus on positive knowledge, attitudes, and behaviors rather than the negative. The SRI-CS represented a continued evolution of the original military model and the associated instrumentation. By drawing on the Resiliency Model of Role Performance (Bowen and Martin, 2011b), it further emphasizes positive synergy between individual assets and social connections in promoting resiliency among USAF members and their families.

Sample

Overall, more than 3000 USAF *Key Spouses* were identified at the 62 bases (12 bases did not report *Key Spouse* numbers), and 1104 of these spouses participated in the pilot test, yielding an estimated participation rate between 25 and 30 percent. Notably, 14 bases had participation rates of 40 percent or higher and eight bases had participation rates of 15 percent or less. Because we do not know the actual number and profile of *Key Spouses* at the participating bases, caution must be given to any extrapolation of these data to all USAF *Key Spouses*.

Participants assented to complete the SRI-CS. During the pilot test, all participants at a given installation used the same passcode to access the web-based SRI-CS. Survey administration took place from February 28 to March 10, 2011; one installation was provided a brief extension because of a miscommunication of the instructions and passcode.

Of the 1104 *Key Spouse* respondents, a small proportion were men (2 percent) and 5 percent self-identified as the spouse of someone other than an active-duty member. Given the small numbers, these subgroups were excluded, yielding an analytic sample of 981 female *Key Spouses* married to active-duty USAF members. As expected because of *Key Spouses'* special status, approximately half (49 percent) of the respondents were married to officers, and the remaining 51 percent were married to more senior enlisted members. The modal respondent had been married six years or more (72 percent), had children living at home (94 percent), and was not employed for pay outside the home (62 percent). Nearly one-in-five (19 percent) of those with children in the home reported having a child with special needs (i.e., a physical, mental, emotional, or developmental disability; a serious or chronic medical problem, such as asthma or cancer; or a child enrolled in the Exceptional Family Member Program). More than 80 percent of respondents lived with their USAF spouse in the contiguous United States, and one-in-five respondents (22 percent) reported their military spouse was currently deployed.

Measures

The SRI-CS used 12 items to assess the four first-order constructs in the CAF measurement model: mental fitness (three items: MF1, MF2, MF3), physical fitness (three items: PF1 PF2, PF3), social fitness (three items: SCF1, SCF2, SCF3), and spiritual fitness (three items: SPF1, SPF2, SPF3). Five additional items measured a construct of resiliency (R1, R2, R3, R4, R5). In the context of similar wording at the beginning of the survey item (i.e., “Successfully meet”), we hypothesized an error correlation between items R4 and R5 (see N. Bowen and Guo, 2012, for justification). Each item associated with CAF was assessed using a six-point scale, ranging from *strongly disagree* (0) to *strongly agree* (5). Each item associated with resiliency was assessed using a 100-point continuum to measure the percentage at which the respondents felt the item described them, ranging from *not at all* (0) to *completely* (100). This continuum follows the argument by DeVellis (2012) regarding the advantages of allowing greater variation in response. Additionally, this response scale offers advantages for web-based administration, such as using a radio button for dragging across the scale. Descriptive statistics for these items are presented in Table 15.2, item content is shown in Table 15.3, and a correlation matrix is presented in Table 15.4. Alpha coefficients for the summary measures ranged from a low of 0.84 for resiliency to a high of 0.95 for spiritual fitness.

Table 15.2 Variable and sample description for the full sample (N = 981)

Variable and item labels	*N*	*Mean*	SD	*Skewness*	*Kurtosis*	*Min.*	*Max.*	*Missing values*
Resiliency variables								
R1	981	80.68	16.79	−1.85	7.87	0	100	0.00%
R2	981	72.08	22.17	−1.08	3.82	0	100	0.00%
R3	981	80.84	20.20	−1.68	5.95	0	100	0.00%
R4	981	88.42	14.53	−3.21	17.43	0	100	0.00%
R5	981	88.91	12.81	−3.64	23.04	0	100	0.00%
Fitness variables								
Mental Fitness								
MF1	981	4.25	0.82	−1.32	5.70	0	5	0.00%
MF2	980	4.36	0.71	−1.10	4.68	0	5	0.10%
MF3	979	4.37	0.71	−1.31	6.42	0	5	0.20%
Physical fitness								
PF1	980	3.97	0.83	−0.86	4.34	0	5	0.10%
PF2	981	3.64	1.19	−0.77	3.16	0	5	0.00%
PF3	980	3.94	0.87	−0.80	4.01	0	5	0.10%
Social fitness								
SCF1	981	4.15	1.09	−1.73	6.15	0	5	0.00%
SCF2	981	3.85	1.26	−1.18	3.91	0	5	0.00%
SCF3	979	3.75	1.34	−1.04	3.38	0	5	0.20%
Spiritual fitness								
SPF1	956	4.71	0.52	−1.91	7.58	0	5	2.55%
SPF2	955	4.70	0.54	−1.86	7.38	0	5	2.65%
SPF3	944	4.63	0.61	−1.63	5.35	0	5	3.77%
Sample characteristics								
Parent or stepparent (1 = yes)	981	0.83						0.00%

Military installation residence (1 = yes)	976	0.45	0.51%
Paygrade	981		0.00%
E1–E6		0.31	
E7–E9		0.20	
O1–O3		0.15	
O4 and higher		0.34	
Age	980		0.10%
Younger than 26 years		0.08	
26–35 years		0.46	
36 and older		0.46	

Table 15.3 Observed indicators for each first-order latent construct

Construct/item label	*Description*
Resiliency (α = 0.84)	
R1	Know about military and/or local civilian community resources
R2	Effectively use military and/or local civilian community resources
R3	Experience a meaningful connection to the military
R4	Successfully meet the challenges of the military life
R5	Successfully meet the overall responsibilities associated with the various roles that you have in your life (e.g., spouse, parent, son/daughter, community member, employee/student, and so forth)
Mental fitness (α = 0.92)	
MF1	I look forward to beginning each day
MF2	I maintain a positive outlook on life
MF3	I enjoy most days
Physical fitness (α = 0.88)	
PF1	I maintain a healthy diet
PF2[a]	I exercise on a regular basis
PF3	I maintain a healthy lifestyle
Social fitness (α = 0.94)	
SCF1	I have positive relationships with others in the community in which I reside
SCF2	I experience a feeling of belonging in my relationships
SCF3	I can depend on others in the community in which I reside for help or assistance, if I request it
Spiritual fitness (α = 0.95)	
SPF1	I have a guiding set of principles or beliefs
SPF2	I attempt to live in accordance with a guiding set of principles or beliefs
SPF3	I draw strength from a set of guiding principles or beliefs when I face life challenges

Note: All fitness dimensions range from *strongly disagree* (0) to *strongly agree* (5). Resiliency ranges from *not at all* (0 percent) to *completely* (100 percent).

[a] The Centers for Disease Control and Prevention define minimum regular exercise as 150 minutes per week of moderate-intensity aerobic activity, as well as muscle strengthening activities two or more times per week. Survey respondents were provided with this definition.

Table 15.4 Correlation matrix of observed indicators

	1	*2*	*3*	*4*	*5*	*6*	*7*	*8*	*9*	*10*	*11*	*12*	*13*	*14*	*15*	*16*
Resiliency																
1 R1																
2 R2	0.69 *															
3 R3	0.57 *	0.61 *														
4 R4	0.53 *	0.41 *	0.55 *													
5 R5	0.45 *	0.36 *	0.41 *	0.73 *												
Mental fitness																
6 MF1	0.11 *	0.15 *	0.26 *	0.26 *	0.31 *											
7 MF2	0.15 *	0.21 *	0.30 *	0.31 *	0.32 *	0.77 *										
8 MF3	0.10 *	0.16 *	0.26 *	0.29 *	0.34 *	0.79 *	0.81 *									
Physical fitness																
9 PF1	0.08 *	0.09 *	0.10 *	0.14 *	0.17 *	0.37 *	0.35 *	0.37 *								
10 PF2	0.05	0.09 *	0.10 *	0.10 *	0.16 *	0.34 *	0.30 *	0.32 *	0.66 *							
11 PF3	0.07 *	0.13 *	0.15 *	0.16 *	0.22 *	0.43 *	0.41 *	0.42 *	0.80 *	0.75 *						
Social fitness																
12 SCF1	0.15 *	0.20 *	0.26 *	0.23 *	0.18 *	0.30 *	0.30 *	0.33 *	0.20 *	0.19 *	0.22 *					
13 SCF2	0.16 *	0.21 *	0.29 *	0.21 *	0.15 *	0.31 *	0.31 *	0.34 *	0.18 *	0.19 *	0.19 *	0.84 *				
14 SCF3	0.16 *	0.21 *	0.29 *	0.19 *	0.15 *	0.32 *	0.30 *	0.34 *	0.17 *	0.17 *	0.18 *	0.81 *	0.87 *			
Spiritual fitness																
15 SPF1	0.13 *	0.16 *	0.16 *	0.20 *	0.15 *	0.26 *	0.31 *	0.30 *	0.22 *	0.17 *	0.23 *	0.18 *	0.18 *	0.18 *		
16 SPF2	0.12 *	0.16 *	0.15 *	0.19 *	0.14 *	0.25 *	0.32 *	0.29 *	0.23 *	0.18 *	0.24 *	0.16 *	0.18 *	0.17 *	0.92 *	
17 SFP3	0.12 *	0.16 *	0.20 *	0.17 *	0.14 *	0.31 *	0.34 *	0.34 *	0.25 *	0.22 *	0.26 *	0.20 *	0.23 *	0.22 *	0.83 *	0.85 *

Note: *$p < 0.05$. Analysis included non-missing data (N = 942 to 981). All variance inflation factor scores across items were below 8 in the context of a supplemental analysis, indicating no issue with multicollinearity.

Analysis

We began by examining the distributional properties of each of the 12 CAF items in the hypothesized model. All skew index values for these items were less than 2 (average = –1.29), and all kurtosis index values were less than 8 (average = 5.17). These values indicated the distributions of our CAF items were not severely problematic (Curran, West, and Finch, 1996; Kline, 2011). We estimated a correlation matrix with the inclusion of all observed indicators to assess inter-item associations. Because some inter-item correlations were relatively high (> 0.80), we ran a supplemental analysis to assess the presence of multicollinearity. Results from a regression model in which a composite scale of resiliency was regressed on all exogenous observed indicators yielded variance inflation factor scores less than 8 for each indicator, confirming that our models were not significantly burdened by multicollinearity. All univariate and bivariate analyses were conducted in Stata 13.0 (StataCorp, 2013).

Our subsequent analysis consisted of two key components: (a) confirmatory factor analysis by which we tested the suitability of a second-order factor structure for CAF compared with a first-order factor structure, and (b) an analysis of the influence of CAF on resiliency to gauge the construct validity of CAF among *Key Spouses*. We used structural equation modeling in Mplus 7.11 (Muthén and Muthén, 2012) to conduct these substantive analyses. Before estimating the models, we randomly partitioned the full sample (N = 981) into a model-development subsample (n = 491) and a model-validation subsample (n = 490). The development subsample was used for initial model-building, tests of alternative factor structures, and construct validation. The validation subsample was used to reanalyze the data and confirm results.

The following criteria of model fit were used to evaluate how well our specified models fit the input data matrix: root mean square error of approximation (RMSEA) and its upper-bound 90-percent confidence interval (CI) $\leq$ 0.08 (Browne and Cudeck, 1993), Tucker-Lewis Index (TLI) $\geq$ 0.95, and comparative fit index (CFI) $\geq$ 0.95 (Hu and Bentler, 1999). Because chi-square difference tests are highly sensitive to sample size, we followed the guidelines extended by Cheung and Rensvold (2002) and examined change in model CFI as an additional indication of significant change in model fit. Model changes/constraints were considered statistically negligible if the change in CFI was smaller than or equal to –0.01 (i.e., ΔCFI $\leq$ –0.01). We used a maximum likelihood (ML) estimator; however, we reanalyzed our final model with maximum likelihood estimation with robust standard errors (MLR) to assess the extent to which our analyses might be sensitive to the distributional properties of the observed indicators. Missing data (less than 0.06% across all observed indicators) were handled with full-information maximum likelihood estimation (Enders, 2010).

For the confirmatory factor analysis, we began by analyzing a first-order factor model with four fitness constructs specified for mental, physical, social, and spiritual domains. We used a jigsaw-piecewise technique, whereby model fit and measurement parameters were assessed one construct at a time (Bollen, 2000).

Because we hypothesized a higher-order total fitness construct would drive variation across each of the four fitness components, we tested a second-order factor model in which the four first-order factors loaded onto a higher-order construct. Because model difference tests indicated both factor structures were statistically indistinguishable, we selected the second-order factor model because it matched our hypothesis and provided a more parsimonious fit with the data. We subjected the second-order factor model to construct validation. Preliminary calculations indicated that all analytical models were over-identified and sufficiently powered (N. Bowen and Guo, 2012; MacCallum, Browne, and Sugawara, 1996). All adjustments to the model were specified in the hypothesized model (as shown in Figure 15.1). The final model was re-estimated using the full sample.

Results

Factor structure and construct validation

Table 15.5 displays the model fit indices associated with the first-order and second-order factor models for the development (Model 1A and Model 2A) and validation subsamples (Model 1B and Model 2B). Results indicated the second-order factor structure was statistically indistinguishable from the first-order factor structure in both subsamples (i.e., $\Delta CFI = 0.000$; $\Delta\chi^2(2) = 0.821$, $p > 0.05$ and $\Delta CFI = 0.000$; $\Delta\chi^2(2) = 2.777$, $p > 0.05$ for the development and validation subsamples, respectively). These results supported our hypothesis that first-order fitness constructs can be conceptualized as part of a larger construct representing total fitness among *Key Spouses*. Model fit indices for the second-order factor model were $\chi^2(50) = 81.584$, $p = 0.003$; RMSEA = 0.036 [upper-bound 90-percent CI: 0.050]; TLI = 0.992; CFI = 0.994 and $\chi^2(50) = 102.538$, $p < 0.001$; RMSEA = 0.046 [upper-bound 90-percent CI: 0.059]; TLI = 0.986; and CFI = 0.990 for the development and validation subsamples, respectively.

Table 15.5 displays the model fit indices associated with the structural model in which the second-order CAF was predictive of resiliency. The results indicated the structural model fit the data well for both the development and validation subsamples. Results associated with the development subsample indicated that all estimated parameters were significant at the $p < 0.001$ level, and total fitness was positively associated with resiliency ($b = 0.399$, $\beta = 0.371$). Specifically, a one-unit increase in total fitness was associated with a 0.4-unit increase in resiliency, and 13.8 percent of the variance in resiliency was explained by the total fitness construct. These results were confirmed with the validation subsample, as all estimated parameters in the validation model were significant at the $p < 0.001$ level and total fitness was similarly associated with resiliency ($b = 0.444$, $\beta = 0.406$); 16.5 percent of the variance in resiliency was explained by total fitness in the validation-sample model. More details associated with model parameters for the development and validation sample models are available upon request.

Table 15.5 First- and second-order confirmatory factor analysis and construct validation with development (N = 491) and validation subsamples (N = 490)

Model	*N*	*Para-meters*	χ^2	df	p-*value*	*RMSEA*	*Upper-bound CI*	*TLI*	*CFI*	$\Delta\chi^2$	df	*sig.*	*ΔCFI*	*Comparison*
Development subsample														
Factor structure														
Model 1A: First-order factor structure	491	42	80.763	48	0.002	0.037	0.051	0.992	0.994					
Model 2A: Second-order factor structure	491	40	81.584	50	0.003	0.036	0.050	0.992	0.994	0.821	2	n.s.	0.000	Model 1A
Construct validation														
Model 3A: Structural model	491	57	321.688	113	< 0.001	0.061	0.069	0.962	0.968					
Validation subsample														
Factor structure														
Model 1B: First-order factor structure	490	42	99.761	48	< 0.001	0.047	0.060	0.986	0.990					
Model 2B: Second-order factor structure	490	40	102.538	50	< 0.001	0.046	0.059	0.986	0.990	2.777	2	n.s.	0.000	Model 1B
Construct validation														
Model 3B: Structural model	490	57	296.832	113	< 0.001	0.058	0.066	0.966	0.971					
Full sample (N = 981)														
Model 4: Second-order structural model	981	57	431.286	113	< 0.001	0.054	0.059	0.970	0.975					

Note: n.s. = non-significant. $\Delta\chi^2$ = change in chi-square; ΔCFI = change in CFI; *df* = degrees of freedom; CI = confidence interval; RMSEA = root mean square error of approximation; TLI = Tucker-Lewis Index; CFI = comparative fit index.

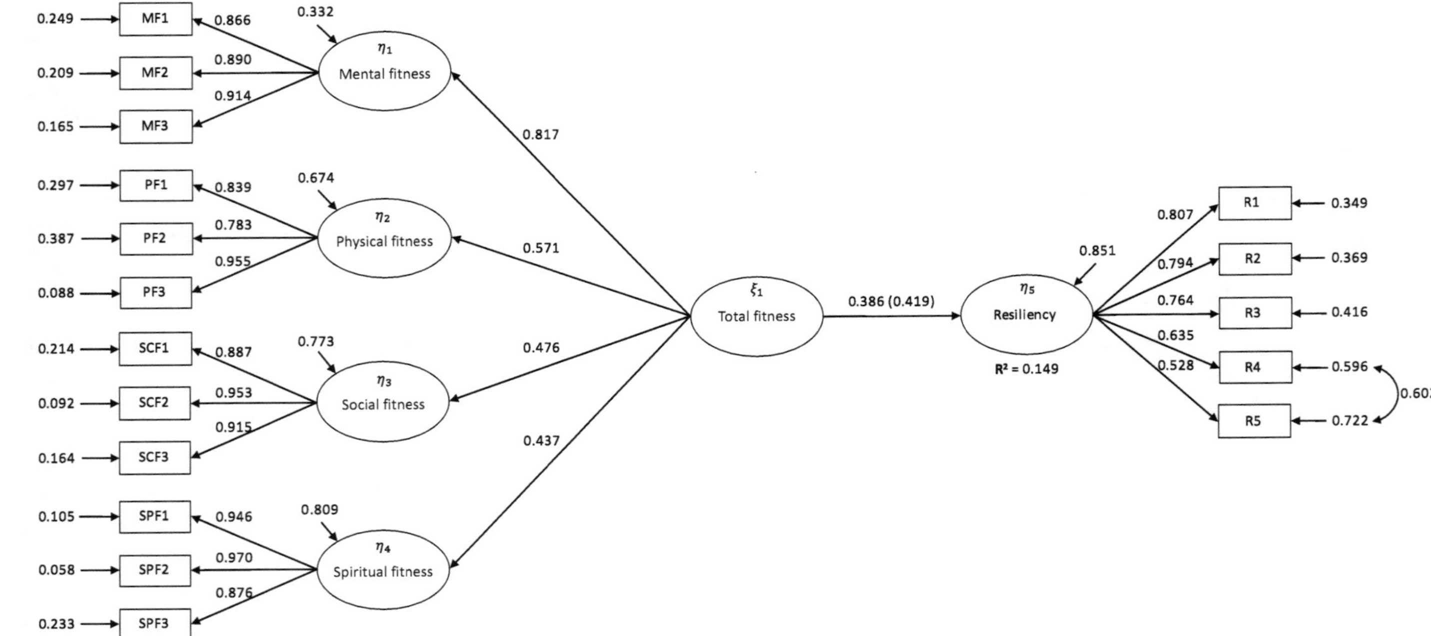

Figure 15.2 Second-order factor model and construct validation with full sample (N = 981)

Final model

Figure 15.2 displays the final second-order structural factor model with the full sample. Model fit indices for this final model were $\chi^2(113) = 431.286, p < 0.001$; RMSEA = 0.054 [upper-bound 90-percent CI: 0.059]; TLI = 0.970; CFI = 0.975. Congruent with the development and validation models, all estimated parameters with the full sample were significant at the $p < 0.001$ level. Standardized factor loadings for resiliency ranged from 0.528 to 0.807. Standardized first-order factor loadings for CAF ranged from 0.783 to 0.970. Standardized second-order factor loadings for CAF ranged from 0.437 to 0.817. Further, total fitness was positively associated with resiliency ($b = 0.386$, $\beta = 0.419$), and 14.9 percent of the variance in resiliency was explained by total fitness. The final model was reanalyzed with MLR as a robustness check; results were identical to those estimated with ML. Refer to Figure 15.2 for more details.

Discussion and implications

Consistent with the USAF-wide CAF program and the inclusive definition of airman, the current study sought to validate a measure of CAF for female civilian spouses of active-duty members. Using data from a sample of USAF *Key Spouses*, our results suggest the CAF measure operates as an appropriate instrument for measuring the domains of mental, physical, social, and spiritual fitness for these spouses. Moreover, our model suggests that a higher-order total fitness construct may drive variation in these subcomponents of fitness. Thus, the items in our analysis can be conceptualized as part of a larger total fitness construct, applicable for further development and use with USAF spouses. Total fitness, as a higher-order factor, is positively and strongly associated with resiliency, providing evidence of construct validity for this instrument among civilian spouses. Overall, these findings align with those in recent analyses of the CAF instrument among active-duty members, Air National Guard/USAF Reserve, and USAF civilian employees (Bowen et al., 2016a, 2016b).

This study set out to examine the use of an easily administered assessment instrument to support the USAF policy requirement for data that will inform the CAF program and provide unit leaders, policymakers, and community human services providers with the information needed for program management to build and sustain its culture of fitness. Like its total force member CAF counterpart (Bowen et al., 2016a, 2016b), our findings suggest the civilian spouse version of the CAF measure also has potential for this capability. Not only can we envision data being collected to support unit and installation leadership fitness programs, this assessment tool offers the potential for the creation of a simple-to-use, valid and reliable, electronic-based self-assessment instrument that can be integrated into toolkits for self-development and the promotion of behaviors that foster and sustain resiliency. For example, the measure could be integrated into the Wingman Toolkit (www.wingmantoolkit.org), which offers information about CAF, resources to support fitness and resilience, and a link to a mobile app that includes tools and features for building resilience within each fitness domain. The results from the present analysis set the stage for such applications of the measure, as well as for incorporating the measure into larger surveys as part of unit-, base-, major command-, and USAF-wide efforts, such as the Community Assessment Survey (Meadows, Miller, and Robson, 2015). In time, data from a representative sample of USAF civilian spouses could be used to develop comparison norms for the CAF, including norms of multiple subgroups.

Limitations and future research

We note some limitations of this study. First, our analysis used data on female *Key Spouses* only. As noted earlier, *Key Spouses* are thought to be among the best-adjusted, most committed civilian spouses; therefore, *Key Spouses* might show low levels of variance in their responses to the CAF items. Thus, the CAF measure might yield greater variance among non-*Key Spouses*—an area worth investigation. As concluded by Dawes (2002), scales that produce greater variance have benefit in examining relationships among variables.

Although our sample was relatively large, participants were not randomly sampled for inclusion. Thus, our parameter estimates might not generalize to all *Key Spouses*; however, our use of development and validation subsamples aids in demonstrating the replicability of our findings, or bolstering our confidence in model selection. We also note that the social fitness items in the CAF used here differ from the items used to measure social fitness in the active-duty member CAF tool (Bowen et al., 2016a, 2016b). Specifically, the three social fitness items were recently revised to shift focus from a person's willingness to seek help from others to a person's feelings of connectedness and being confident help would be available from others, if needed. We believe this shift better reflects the USAF (2014) definition of social fitness (see Table 15.1). Although we cannot be sure of the relative performance of one set of items over the other, our findings show that each set of items performs well within the intended population.

Further research should attempt to include all spouses, including male civilian spouses. Tests of measurement invariance could be conducted to confirm whether the instrument operates similarly for all spouses. Questions also remain regarding measurement invariance across other population subgroups/characteristics with respect to USAF spouses (e.g., number and age of resident children, status as step-parent versus biological parent, pay-grade of member spouse). Measurement invariance across subgroups suggests that an instrument reliably captures the same phenomenon for members of each subgroup—a desirable characteristic of any assessment tool used within a diverse target population such as active-duty USAF members and their families.

Conclusion

As discussed in this chapter, larger efforts to promote a "fit, resilient, and ready force" (USAF, 2014: 3) should include a focus on the fitness and resiliency of the families and partners of active-duty members. The CAF program in the USAF exemplifies this broader focus, whereby both active-duty members and their families are the targets of fitness promotion. Civilian spouses, like their active-duty counterparts, are situated at the nexus of military and family institutions. Thus, civilian spouses are central figures in the meso or organization level triad of military member, family, and work organization. The demands and opportunities associated with this social placement make civilian spouses a valuable focus of the CAF program. We presented and validated a metric for assessing civilian-spouse fitness, which has meaningful implications for USAF leaders, policymakers, and practitioners who aim to promote, support, and measure CAF.

Note

1 The views and opinions contained in this chapter are those of the authors and should not be construed as official Department of the Air Force position, policy, or decision, unless so designated by other authorized documents. Data reported in this chapter were collected through support from the Airman, Family, Wounded Warrior, and Community Operations (HQ AFPC/DPSIA), Air Force Personnel Center, Randolph AFB, TX 78150 (GSA Order ID: 9Q1SFSRAB001). The Office of Human Research Ethics at the University of North Carolina at Chapel Hill determined that the proposed secondary analysis of these data was exempt from human subject review.

Correspondence concerning this article should be addressed to Gary L. Bowen, PhD, School of Social Work, The University of North Carolina at Chapel Hill, 325 Pittsboro Street, Chapel Hill, NC 27599-3550. E-mail: glbowen@email.unc.edu.

References

Air Force Personnel Center (2016). *Air Force Personnel Demographics*. Retrieved from www.afpc.af.mil/library/airforcepersonneldemographics.asp.

Bollen, K. A. (2000). Modeling strategies: in search of the Holy Grail. *Structural Equation Modeling*, 7, 74–81.

Bowen, G. L. (1986). Spouse support and the retention intentions of Air Force members: a basis for program development. *Evaluation and Program Planning*, 9, 209–220.

Bowen, G. L., Jensen, T. M., and Martin, J. A. (2016a). A measure of comprehensive airman fitness: construct validation and invariance across Air Force service components. *Military Behavioral Health*, 4, 149–158.

Bowen, G. L., Jensen, T. M., and Martin, J. A. (2016b). Confirmatory factor analysis of a measure of comprehensive airman fitness. *Military Behavioral Health*, 4, 409–419.

Bowen, G., Jensen, T., and Williams, B. (2017). Prevention of family maltreatment in the U.S. Air Force: a systematic review of research on active duty military personnel. *Journal of Family Social Work*, 20(1), 52–80.

Bowen, G. L. and Martin, J. A. (2011a). *The 2011 Support and Resiliency Inventory: Key Spouses Pilot Test Summary Report*. Charlotte, NC: Flying Bridge Technologies.

Bowen, G. L. and Martin, J. A. (2011b). The resiliency model of role performance of service members, veterans, and their families. *Journal of Human Behavior in the Social Environment*, 21, 162–178.

Bowen, G. L. and Martin, J. A. (2011c). *The Support & Resiliency Inventory: Civilian Spouses* (SRI-CS). Chapel Hill, NC: Bowen & Colleagues.

Bowen, G. L. and Martin, J. A. (2015). Building community capacity in the U.S. Air Force: promoting a community practice strategy. In K. Corcoran and A. R. Roberts (eds.), *Social Workers' Desk Reference*, 3rd edn (pp. 935–940). New York: Oxford University Press.

Bowen, G. L., Martin, J. A., Liston, B. J., and Nelson, J. P. (2009). Building community capacity in the U.S. Air Force: the Community Readiness Consultant Model. In K. Corcoran and A. R. Roberts (eds), *Social Workers' Desk Reference*, 2nd edn (pp. 912–917). New York: Oxford University Press.

Bowen, N. and Guo, S. (2012). *Structural Equation Modeling*. New York: Oxford University Press.

Bowles, S. V., Pollock, L. D., Moore, M., MacDermid Wadsworth, S., Cato, C., Dekle, J. W., . . . Bates, M. J. (2015). Total force fitness: the military family fitness model. *Military Medicine*, 180, 246–258.

Browne, M. W. and Cudeck, R. (1993). Alternative ways of assessing model fit. In K. A. Bollen and J. S. Long (eds), *Testing Structural Equation Models* (pp. 136–162). Newbury Park, CA: Sage.

Casey, G. W., Jr. (2011). Comprehensive Soldier Fitness: a vision for psychological resilience in the U.S. Army. *American Psychologist*, 66, 1–3.

Castaneda, L. W. and Harrell, M. C. (2008). Military spouse employment: a grounded theory approach to experiences and perceptions. *Armed Forces & Society*, 34(3), 389–412.

Chandra, A., Lara-Cinisomo, S., Jaycox, L. H., Tanielian, T., Han, B., Burns, R. M., and Ruder, T. (2011). *Views from the Homefront: The Experiences of Youth and Spouses from Military Families*. Santa Monica, CA: RAND Corporation. Retrieved from http://www.rand.org/content/dam/rand/pubs/technical_reports/2011/RAND_TR913.pdf.

Cheung, G. W. and Rensvold, R. B. (2002). Evaluating goodness-of-fit indexes for testing measurement invariance. *Structural Equation Modeling*, 9, 233–255.

Cooke, T. J. and Speirs, K. (2005). Migration and employment among the civilian spouses of military personnel. *Social Science Quarterly*, 86(2), 343–355.

Crouch, C. L., Adrian, A. L., Adler, A. B., Wood, M. D., and Thomas, J. L. (2017). Military spouses stationed overseas: role of social connectedness on health and well-being. *Military Behavioral Health*, 5, 129–136.

Curran, P. J., West, S. G., and Finch, J. F. (1996). The robustness of test statistics to nonnormality and specification error in confirmatory factor analysis. *Psychological Methods*, 1, 16–29.

Dawes, J. G. (2002). Five point vs eleven point scales: does it make a difference to data characteristics? *Australasian Journal of Market Research*, 10(1), 39–47.

DeVellis, R. (2012). *Scale Development: Theory and Applications*, 3rd edn. Thousand Oaks, CA: Sage.

Donoho, C., Riviere, L., and Adler, A. (2017). The association of deployment-related mental health, community support, and spouse stress in military couples. *Military Behavioral Health*, 5, 109–116.

Eaton, K. M., Hoge, C. W., Messer, S. C., Whitt, A. A., Cabrera, O. A., McGurk, D., . . . Castro, C. A. (2008). Prevalence of mental health problems, treatment need, and barriers to care among primary care-seeking spouses of military service members involved in Iraq and Afghanistan deployments. *Military Medicine*, 173, 1051–1056.

Enders, C. (2010). *Applied Missing Data Analysis*. New York: Guilford.

Fraser, M. W. and Galinsky, M. J. (2010). Steps in intervention research: designing and developing social programs. *Research on Social Work Practice*, 20, 459–466.

Gonzalez, G. C., Singh, R., Schell, T. L., and Weinick, R. M. (2014). *An Evaluation of the Implementation and Perceived Utility of the Airman Resilience Training Program*. Santa Monica, CA: RAND Corporation.

Hengstebeck, N. D., Meadows, S. O., Griffin, B. A., Friedman, E. M., and Beckman, R. (2016). Military integration. In S. Meadows, T. Tanielian, and B. Karney (eds), *The Deployment Life Study: Longitudinal Analysis of Military Families across the Deployment Cycle* (pp. 263–302). Santa Monica, CA: RAND Corporation.

Hosek, J. and MacDermid Wadsworth, S. (2013). Economic conditions of military families. *The Future of Children*, 23, 41–59.

Hu, L. T. and Bentler, P. M. (1999). Cutoff criteria for fit indexes in covariance structure analysis. Conventional criteria versus new alternatives. *Structural Equation Modeling*, 6, 1–55.

Ipsos Public Affairs (2013). *Air Mobility Command 2012 Comprehensive Airman Fitness Survey: Final Methods Report*. Washington, DC: Author.

Jensen, T. and Bowen, G. (2017). The prevention of family maltreatment among airmen: a focus on personal resilience. *Journal of Family Social Work*. Advance online publication. doi: 10.1080/10522158.2017.1410270.

Kline, R. (2011). *Principles and Practice of Structural Equation Modeling*, 3rd edn. New York: Guilford Press.

Lester, P., Peterson, K., Reeves, J., Knauss, L., Glover, D., Mogil, C., . . . Beardslee, W. (2010). The long war and parental combat deployment: effects on military children and at-home spouses. *Journal of the American Academy of Child & Adolescent Psychiatry*, 49(4), 310–320.

MacCallum, R. C., Browne, M. W., and Sugawara, H. M. (1996). Power analysis and determination of sample size for covariance structure modeling. *Psychological Methods*, 1, 130–149.

Meadows, S. O., Miller, L. L., and Robson, S. (2015). *Airman and Family Resilience: Lessons from the Scientific Literature* (RR-106-AF). Santa Monica, CA: RAND Corporation. Retrieved from www.rand.org/pubs/research_reports/RR106.html.

Mullen, E. J. (2004). Outcome measurement: a social work framework for health and mental health policy and practice. *Social Work in Mental Health*, 2, 77–93.

Muthén, L. K. and Muthén, B. O. (2012). *Mplus User's Guide*, 7th edn. Los Angeles, CA: Muthén and Muthén.

Orthner, D., Bowen, G., and Mancini, D. (2003). *The Community Readiness Unit Service Guide for Air Force Space Command Family Support Centers*. Colorado Springs, CO: US Air Force Space Command Family Matters.

Perry-Jenkins, M. and MacDermid Wadsworth, S. (2017). Work and family research and theory: review and analysis from an ecological perspective. *Journal of Family Theory & Review*, 9, 219–237.

Peterson, C., Park, N., and Castro, C. A. (2011). Assessment for the US army comprehensive soldier fitness program: the global assessment tool. *American Psychologist*, 66, 10–18.

Robbins, S. P., Chatterjee, P., and Canda, E. R. (2012). *Contemporary Human Behavior Theory: A Critical Perspective for Social Work*, 3rd edn. Upper Saddle River, NJ: Allyn & Bacon.

Segal, M. W., Lane, M. D., and Fisher, A. G. (2015). Conceptual model of military career and family life course events, intersections, and effects on well-being. *Military Behavioral Health*, 3, 95–107.

StataCorp (2013). Stata statistical software: Release 13. College Station, TX: Author.

Spera, C. (2009). Spouses' ability to cope with deployment and adjust to Air Force family demands. *Armed Forces & Society*, 35, 286–306.

US Department of the Air Force (USAF) (2013, May 7). *Airman and Family Readiness Centers: Air Force instruction 36-3009*. Retrieved from http://static.e-publishing.af.mil/production/1/af_a1/publication/afi36-3009/afi36-3009.pdf.

US Department of the Air Force (USAF) (2014, April 2). *Comprehensive Airman Fitness (CAF): Air Force instruction 90-506*. Washington, DC: Author.

US Department of Defense, Office of the Deputy Assistant Secretary of Defense for Military Community and Family Policy (2015). *Military Family Life Project: Active Duty Spouse Study*. Retrieved from www.militaryonesource.mil/MilFamStudy.

Wright, K. M., Riviere, L. A., Merrill, J. C., and Cabrera, O. A. (2013). Resilience in military families: a review of programs and empirical evidence. In R. R. Sinclair and T. W. Britt (eds), *Building Psychological Resilience in Military Personnel: Theory and Practice* (pp. 167–191). Washington, DC: American Psychological Association.

Part III

Inside the negotiation household

Tensions between the soldier-parent, the partner, and children

16 "In the cross-fire": intimate partner violence in military families

A narrative review and implications for the military organization[1]

Philip Siebler and George Karpetis

Introduction

This chapter will identify and explain the theoretical causes of, and risk factors for, the problem of intimate partner violence (IPV) in the military setting, examine interventions across micro, meso, and macro levels, and discuss the implications of the causes and interventions for policy, practice, and education. Significantly, IPV has been described as a "wicked problem" (Young-Wolff, Kotz, and McCaw, 2016). These researchers contend IPV is difficult to solve, complex to comprehend, stigmatized by society, and a seemingly unmanageable condition. Military organizations internationally are concerned about this social and secretive problem, which can be solved and will be a focus of the final section of this chapter.

This chapter adopts the Australian Department of Defense (DoD) description of IPV (*Intimate Partner Violence*, DCO Website, 2018):

> Intimate partner violence occurs when a current or former partner uses behaviors or threats to make you feel scared, controlled, or intimidated. A relationship in which IPV occurs is an abusive relationship. . .
>
> – **Physical violence**: hitting, pushing, grabbing, biting, choking, shaking, slapping.
>
> – **Sexual violence**: attempted or actual sexual contact without your consent.
>
> – **Threats of physical or sexual abuse**: words, looks or gestures to control or frighten.
>
> – **Psychological or emotional abuse**: humiliating, putting down, isolating, threatening.
>
> – **Stalking**: following, harassing, or unwanted contact that makes you feel afraid.

The chapter will be underpinned by a narrative review of the peer-reviewed literature in relation to IPV in the military setting in the last ten years. A number of terms such as "wife battering," "domestic violence," "partner abuse," "severe emotional abuse," and "family violence," "victims," "survivors," and "perpetrators" are used in the literature depending on the theoretical perspective adopted, to be discussed later in this chapter. This chapter adopts the stance that IPV is interchangeable with terms such as "domestic violence" and "family violence." Whilst IPV can be perpetrated by men or women, overwhelmingly, most victims in military families are current or former female partners. Children and adolescents are also affected (Jones, 2011; State of Victoria, 2014–2016).

Ecological theory (Bronfenbrenner, 1993; Wojda et al., 2017) provides a useful framework for understanding the multiple systems within which families are nested. The ecological approach is one of the most widely used accounts of IPV and offers a comprehensive perspective across all levels and the first author's model (Figure 16.1) of the military family will underpin the narrative review (Siebler, 2009). Figure 16.1 shows how the macrosystem level encompasses all the other system levels. The visual representation is not intended to privilege any level over another. The model supports the notion that responding to IPV requires coordinated approaches at the population, community, institutional, and individual levels.

The scope of the problem

IPV is described as an ingrained global public health and social problem, a human rights issue for girls and women (World Health Organization [WHO], 2010), and as having serious short- and long-term physical and mental health consequences for women and children (Campbell, Brown, and Okwara, 2011; Sparrow, Kwan, Howard, Fear, and MacManus, 2017). According to the WHO (2013: 2):

> . . . overall, 35% of women worldwide have experienced either physical and/or sexual intimate partner violence . . . in some regions 38% of women have experienced intimate partner violence . . . globally, as many as 38% of all murders of women are committed by intimate partners.

Figures show that in Europe 12 women are murdered by intimate partners or other family members per day (United Nations Office on Drugs and Crime, 2011). According to Black et al. (2011), in the US an average of 20 people are physically abused by intimate partners every minute. This equates to more than 10 million abuse victims annually. Globally, WHO estimates that as many as 38 percent of murders of women are committed by an intimate partner. On average, one woman is murdered per week by her current or former partner in Australia (Bryant and Bricknell, 2017). It is a factor involved in 60 percent of Australian homicide cases involving a female victim (Shackelford and Mouzos, 2005), and, imposes a significant financial burden on individuals, families, and society, being estimated to cost the Australian economy $10 billion per annum by 2021 (Commonwealth of Australia, 2009). A Royal Commission into Family Violence, the first of its kind internationally, was established in the Australian State of Victoria in February 2015 in recognition of the harm family violence causes (State of Victoria, 2014–2016).

The military organization is not immune from the effects of IPV in its ranks. Victims in military communities are most likely to be women (66 percent) and the civilian partners of service personnel, who typically have children (Klostermann, Mignone, Kelley, Musson, and Bohall, 2012). Whilst Klostermann et al. do not specify, it is evident that 34 percent of men are also victims. Physical violence is the most frequent form of IPV across studies, accounting for up to 92 percent of all IPV (Rentz, Martin, Gibbs, Clinton-Sherrod, Hardison, and Marshall, 2006). Whilst inconclusive, in some studies, IPV is reported to be more prevalent and more severe than in civilian populations (Stamm, 2009). Prevalence rates of 13–58 percent for veterans and 13–47 percent for active-duty personnel are cited (Jones, 2011). The high variability in rates is considered to be due to methodological limitations (Rodrigues, Funderburk, Keating, and Maisto, 2014). Similar to the general population, risk factors for perpetration among military personnel include previous violence victimization and perpetration, experiencing and witnessing abuse in childhood, and substance misuse and social deprivation (Trevillion et al., 2015). IPV may have a range of consequences for military family victims including death, serious injury, depressive symptoms, PTSD, and substance use disorders (Aronson, Perkins, and Olson, 2014). Between 1995 and 2001 there were 217 domestic homicides in the USA military community (Klostermann, Mignone, Kelley, Musson, and Bohall, 2012). A Canadian study found that IPV affected a minority of military families similar to the general population in Canada (Zamorski and Wiens-Kincaid, 2013).

We found that the bulk of the research emanated from the USA (Jones, 2012). As Zamorski and Wiens-Kincaid (2013) observe, such data may not apply to other countries due to differences in military populations, the stressors faced by families, the services available to them, and prevention strategies in relation to IPV implemented by respective DoD. However, the authors are unaware of any research that examines family violence in general or of the prevalence of IPV in the Australian Defence Force (ADF). Hence, the scope of the problem of IPV is unknown in the ADF setting, although it is reasonable to extrapolate that the prevalence and implications arising for intervention will be similar to other military populations and the general population as a whole.

Whilst prevalence rates are important, addressing and solving the problem in the military is more critical. Accordingly, it is conceivable military organizations could be leaders in transformational change in this area. As a case in point, the Australian Department of Defence has embarked on a *Family and Domestic Violence Strategy 2017–2022* (Commonwealth of Australia, 2017) as a "first step towards creating a more supportive and responsive workplace within the Department of Defence." In addition, the Australian Army produced a video, *Silence is the Accomplice* (Chief of Army speech to National Press Club – Domestic Violence Campaign, 2017), which included first-person accounts of four members of the Army who shared their experiences of family and domestic violence. This demonstrates the Army has taken a leadership role and is serious about addressing the problem.

Causes of, and risk factors for, IPV in the military

Macro level factors include macro-theoretical approaches, culture, and policy (Figure 16.1). A number of theoretical frameworks may, in part, explain domestic violence in the military. Ali and Naylor (2013) examined a broad range of theories and concluded no single theory could explain the phenomenon.

The *cultural spillover theory* (Klostermann, Mignone, Kelley, Musson, and Bohall, 2012) attempts to explain IPV within the military organization and posits

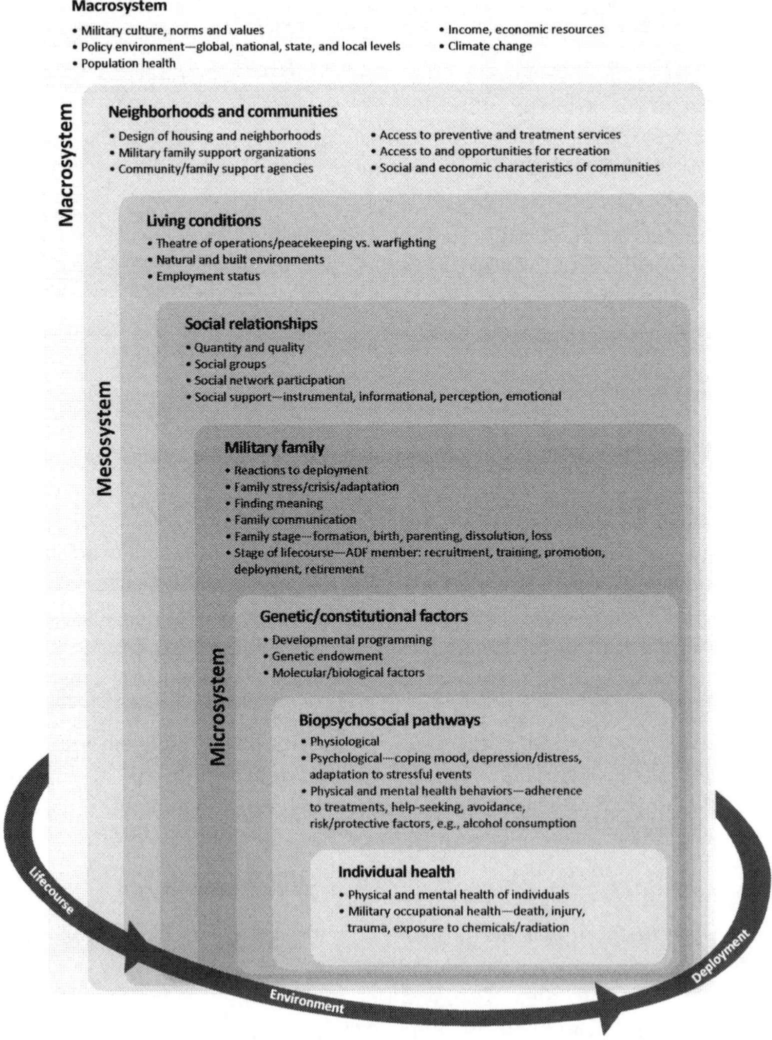

Figure 16.1 An ecological model of the military family for social work

personnel are conditioned when they undergo initial training to learn that violence is acceptable under certain circumstances that may spillover into their intimate lives. Jones (2012) contends the cultural spillover effect is greatest for veterans when they transition to civilian life and must adapt to civilian norms.

The *occupation-related stress model* posits that the inherent risks and danger associated with the hypermasculine military occupation may lead men to bring their work home in the form of violence against women.

According to Ali and Naylor (2013), *feminist theory* argues that IPV is a social problem rather than a private or family matter that has to be addressed by social change. IPV is considered a product of gender power disparity, determined by the patriarchal structures of the society that forces women to remain in a passive state via control tactics by men such as physical, psychological, sexual, and economic abuse (Ali and Naylor, 2013). The military organization crystallizes the notion of a patriarchal structure that legitimates power and authority and violence in the family setting (Jones, 2012).

A range of risk factors or correlates of IPV (Klostermann, Mignone, Kelley, Musson, and Bohall, 2012) are documented, including victim-related characteristics such as pregnancy, new birth, and depression, and perpetrator-related characteristics, such as mental health, alcohol and other drug abuse, childhood trauma, military service, family and relationship conflict, community, and demographic factors.

Military-specific risk factors

Surprisingly little research has been undertaken regarding possible risk factors in military populations such as deployment, traumatic brain injury (TBI), military occupation, and combat exposure (Jones, 2012; Klostermann, Mignone, Kelley, Musson, and Bohall, 2012). Military deployment and reunification creates increased stress levels for couples and contributes to partner aggression (Cesur and Sabia, 2016; Klostermann, Mignone, Kelley, Musson, and Bohall, 2012). Deployment has been shown to be associated with IPV at a risk of four to five times higher when there has been a history of pre-deployment IPV (Jones, 2012). Additional stressors for military couples are work-induced separations from parents, friends, and community. Relocation due to postings may cause isolation for victims, cutting them off from family and other social support systems, leading to a dependency on the perpetrator that prevents the victim from leaving the relationship (Jones, 2012). Relocations may cause partners to face periods of involuntary unemployment while the military member becomes the primary breadwinner (Harrison and Laliberté, 2002). As a consequence, partners are unable to leave violent relationships since they do not have the financial means. IPV has been associated with non-White personnel more than White personnel (Klostermann, Mignone, Kelley, Musson, and Bohall, 2012), age and military rank being more prevalent among younger persons as well as among technicians, administrative staff, and combat troops. IPV has been found to be more prevalent in non-commissioned officers than commissioned officers (Jones, 2012).

IPV is associated with combat exposure, although this relationship is mostly accounted for by a diagnosis of post-traumatic stress disorder (Klostermann, Mignone, Kelley, Musson, and Bohall, 2012). Finally, the male predominance of the military influences perpetration of IPV (Zamorski and Wiens-Kincaid, 2013). Currently, female participation in the ADF is 16.5 percent. The ADF has set targets of 25 percent for female participation in the Air Force and Navy and 15 percent for Army to be achieved by 2023.

Demographic factors

Younger age is associated with IPV in the military for both perpetrators and victims (Campbell, Brown, and Okwara, 2011; Sparrow, Kwan, Howard, Fear, and MacManus, 2017). Female, non-military partners of active-duty personnel, newly married couples, low educational attainment, low socioeconomic status, and lower couple salary are associated with IPV (Campbell, Brown, and Okwara, 2011; Foran, Heyman, and Smith Slep, 2014).

Relationship and family factors

IPV is more common in military couples than their civilian counterparts (Jones, 2012). Cultural spillover theory (above) sought to explain IPV in couples. In their ecological study, relationship dissatisfaction and family coping were associated with IPV (Foran, Heyman, and Smith Slep, 2014). A range of theories have been expounded to describe relationship and perpetrator typologies beyond the scope of this chapter, which are used to inform counselling interventions (Tasso, Whitmarsh, and Ordway, 2016). Indeed, one such theory, attachment theory, posits that a close relationship with an insecurely attached person can generate relational violence (Tasso, Whitmarsh, and Ordway, 2016). Social learning theory contends that violence is learned via observing violence in the family in childhood, described as the intergenerational cycle of violence (Jones, 2012). Children may both experience violence in the home and use violence in their intimate relationship when they become adults (Ali and Naylor, 2013), thus learning to perpetrate violence. This is a circular problem since children exposed to IPV are also significantly more likely to develop depression, use drugs, attempt suicide, and engage in risky sexual behaviors that often lead to the development of sexually transmitted infections (Norman, Byambaa, Butchart, Scott, and Vos, 2012). However, little research has examined how relationship factors in IPV are interconnected with military and other risk factors.

Community factors

The role of the community, a meso level factor, where families develop relationships and interact, is a significant factor that may both contribute to and prevent IPV in military family communities (Foran, Heyman, and Smith Slep, 2014). Community influences include formal supports provided by the military organization, such as installation and unit leaders. This includes base commanders, their subordinate commanders, chaplaincy, and base heath/mental health and family support agencies. In Australia, all larger bases have such formal supports, which will be discussed in the interventions section. In addition, informal supports, such as the social support provided by fellow service members and their families, create a safe, stable, and supporting environment for the military couple (Bowen, Jensen, and Williams, 2017).

Mental health factors for perpetrators

At the individual or micro level, trauma exposure, post-traumatic stress disorder (PTSD), substance use, depression (Rodrigues et al., 2014), anxiety (Sparrow, Kwan, Howard, Fear, and MacManus, 2017), and antisocial personality disorder (Tasso, Whitmarsh, and Ordway, 2016) have been found to be associated with IPV in the military setting. People suffering from mental disorders are reported to have two to three times an increased risk of violence toward others (Trevillion et al., 2015). Studies indicate that 15–20 percent of military personnel report symptoms of PTSD, anxiety, or depression following deployment (Trevillion et al., 2015). However, despite evidence suggesting a causal association between mental disorders and IPV, the extent this applies in the military is not yet known (Trevillion et al., 2015). A recent systematic review (Sparrow, Kwan, Howard, Fear, and MacManus, 2017) found an association between IPV, mental health, and social problems that was more frequently found among veterans than active-duty personnel. There was stronger evidence for an association between IPV and depression/PTSD for veterans than there was for active-duty personnel (Sparrow, Kwan, Howard, Fear, and MacManus, 2017). The authors emphasized the important role of health and welfare workers in the detection and management of IPV and its consequences (Sparrow, Kwan, Howard, Fear, and MacManus, 2017).

Alcohol and substance use among active military personnel or veterans have been associated with an increased risk of perpetrating IPV as 20 percent of IPV incidents were reportedly preceded by alcohol consumption (Jones, 2012). Alcohol abuse has also been associated with PTSD. Alcohol may be used to deal with PTSD symptoms such as intrusive negative thoughts, flashbacks, hyperarousal, or feeling distant from relationships (Klostermann, Mignone, Kelley, Musson, and Bohall, 2012). A number of researchers contend the military has a culture of excess alcohol consumption (Sparrow, Kwan, Howard, Fear, and MacManus, 2017) and that the culture may support military personnel believing that depression/PTSD are weaknesses, less acceptable than an alcohol problem, and thus under-reported.

Discussion

Most research emanates from the USA and Australian research in this field is nonexistent in the military setting. The narrative review found that causal associations between IPV and its predictors are extremely limited (Rodrigues, Funderburk,

Keating, and Maisto, 2014). Whilst the risk factors for IPV among military personnel are similar to those of the general population (Trevillion et al., 2015), the extent to which specific mental disorders are associated with IPV in the military is unclear (Trevillion et al., 2015). There is limited knowledge about the role of alcohol abuse in the occurrence of IPV and limited empirical knowledge regarding the association between military deployment and IPV (Jones, 2012).

A range of theoretical explanations of IPV were found and these influence how programs and services are designed and implemented, as the next section will examine. Although family violence is a significant social problem for the military, there have been few rigorous outcome evaluations undertaken and methodological limitations abound (Rodrigues, Funderburk, Keating, and Maisto, 2014). This includes the lack of obtaining partner reports of IPV in research designs, little use of qualitative research to gain in-depth knowledge of the problem, exclusive use of the Conflict Tactics Scale, and ensuring the confidentiality/anonymity of the research for participants, which was thought to limit participation. As a case in point, IPV research must consider a victim's confidentiality and safety, which is particularly important in the military context to ensure their participation remains confidential from perpetrators (Rodrigues, Funderburk, Keating, and Maisto, 2014). Military personnel and their families practice "extreme secrecy" in relation to private, health, and welfare problems (Harrison, 2006) and as a consequence may fear reprisals such as loss of employment or negative impact on career progression. From a micro level perspective, what is absent from the IPV literature is an understanding of the causes and treatment of power and control behaviors in the intimate relationship of the military couple, which may manifest as aggression and violence. An understanding of the specific psychic mechanisms (Karpetis, 2010; 2012; 2016; 2017a; 2017b) or the social factors involved in IPV may shed light on what types of interventions may be effective.

Theory informs intervention design for perpetrators and victims. The Australian Royal Commission (State of Victoria, 2014–2016) found that conceptualization of IPV as behavior caused by psychological dysfunction or other individual or sociodemographic characteristics, supports a psychotherapeutic approach to intervention. Understanding IPV as the result of gender identities and power relations supports an educational approach to intervention, and points to the need to address social structures that reinforce men's violence against women. The Commission asserted that combining the best aspects of both interventions was desirable—something the military organization needs to consider. The next section examines interventions that were gleaned from the narrative review and discusses their utility in the military setting.

Interventions for IPV

Military organizations recognize that they have a responsibility to address the physical/mental health and behavioral problems that arise from military service for both personnel and their families (Denning, Meisnere, and Warner, 2014). In addition, military organizations are concerned about the consequences of

IPV, including productivity losses, absenteeism, increased health expenditure (Zamorski and Wiens-Kincaid, 2013), having a detrimental impact on operational capability (Commonwealth of Australia, 2017), and "because of the substantial occupational stress that accompanies military service, families of servicemen have been identified by policymakers as a vulnerable population in need of protection" (Cesur and Sabia, 2016). As a consequence, a number of military organizations such as those of the USA and Canada have well-developed policies, programs, and services to address IPV. In 2017 the Australian Department of Defense (DoD) developed its first strategy to address family violence. Whilst the literature reveals a dearth of empirical and clinical interventions addressing IPV (Tasso, Whitmarsh, and Ordway, 2016), there is some promising work emerging, which will be examined next.

Macro level interventions

At the macro-system level, which encompasses institutions, culture, population health, and social and economic policy, good practice is dictated by appropriate policy that enables interventions to occur (Siebler, 2009; Figure 16.1). Whilst the narrative review revealed no military research that provided empirical support for macro level interventions, there is a body of evidence that such interventions are very effective in the wider literature (State of Victoria, 2014–2016). Whilst the narrative review found that programs and practices must be evidence-based, doing nothing was also thought to be ineffective:

> the need for evidence and further research in all these areas in no way precludes taking action now to prevent both intimate partner violence and sexual violence. Those programs that have evidence supporting their effectiveness should be implemented and, where necessary, adapted. Those that have shown promise or appear to have potential can also play an immediate role—provided strenuous efforts are made to incorporate at the outset rigorous outcome evaluations.
>
> (World Health Organization, 2010)

Gender inequality has been identified as the underlying driver of IPV (State of Victoria, 2014–2016), that is, it affects a large proportion of the population or the population as a whole. In addition, perpetrators' attitudes and beliefs must also be considered in responding to family violence.

Macro level approaches addressing gender inequality, culture, and policy are likely to achieve the greatest benefits in reducing violence against women in the long term. These are most likely to be successful in doing so when the impacts of norms and cultures supporting violence against women, gender equality, and rigid gender roles and identities are an integral part of reform (State of Victoria, 2014–2016). Whilst the military is changing with greater target numbers for women in the ADF as cited above, it is predominantly a male culture. A number of writers assert the hyper-masculine culture of the military may contribute to IPV against women (Jones, 2012). In the USA, IPV is a problem of significant concern to military commanders and policymakers have been tasked with the management of risk and resilience and the creation of health, disability, and social policies and programs as a top priority of the United States Armed Forces (Wojda et al., 2017). Moreover, given secretive problems such as IPV have negative consequences for victims and perpetrators, prevention strategies are critical. Wojda et al. (2017) argue that waiting to intervene until the problem comes to the fore is costly and is unlikely to reduce the prevalence of these problems, as the vast proportion of secretive problems go undetected through formal channels such as Command, family support, mental health, and other services. Treatment alone is not a viable strategy for reducing the scope of the problem since it will not stop the problem.

Military culture is, in part, shaped by military commanders. Military leadership has been shown to have a positive impact on ameliorating IPV. As a case in point, Foran, Heyman, and Smith Slep (2014) found that among civilian women, there is evidence that more support from military leaders related to lower clinically significant emotional abuse (CS-EA). CS-EA is a predictor of physical violence. The researchers found that a range of family, community, and workplace factors such as perceived support before and after a deployment from command may inform prevention and treatment efforts.

Whilst there is no research examining any macro level or other intervention in relation to IPV in the Australian military setting, the Australian DoD has implemented a range of initiatives at all ecological levels. Significantly, at the macro level, the then-Australian Chief of Army (CA, now Chief of the Defence Force at time of writing), Lieutenant General Angus Campbell, has highlighted that the senior leadership in Defence was "working to change the attitudes and behaviors that allow such violence to occur, within our workforce and the wider community" (Address to the National Press Club of Australia, 2017: 6). The DoD has created a *Commanders' and Managers' Guide to Responding to Family and Domestic Violence* and the *Defence and Family Violence Domestic Violence Strategy* was released in 2017. In 2016 the CA directed that all Army personnel would watch the videos focused on the topic of IPV, *Hitting Home*, and one created by the Australian Army, *Silence is the Accomplice*, which was also mandatory viewing in 2017 with an associated discussion to increase awareness of the problem. CA reported that the number of domestic violence cases had increased since 2014 from 41 to 125 in 2016 with "people seeking help via support agencies, our medical system and our network of padres" (CA, 2017). No measurable outcome data regarding whether Army personnel and their civilian partners obtained the help they needed was found.

In response to the emergence of Veteran trauma-related problems such as aggression and substance abuse in the criminal justice system, as well as to the difficulties in identifying Veterans in need of intervention in civilian criminal justice contexts, trauma-informed court diversion programs have been developed in the US. Some states have developed innovative policies mandating that court staff inquire about military service and psychiatric history, which are considered in sentencing (Williston, Taft, and Van Haasteren, 2015). This approach connects veterans to specialized treatment services and this is considered within the imposing sentence (Williston, Taft, and Van Haasteren, 2015).

In Australia, in addition to the DoD and the Department of Veterans' Affairs (DVA), the Commonwealth Government delivers support and services through the family law system and the social security section. State and territory governments provide a range of services including justice, policing, domestic violence services, and legal assistance for victims and perpetrators. Recognition of the harm family violence causes led to the establishment of the ground-breaking *Royal Commission into Family Violence* (State of Victoria, 2014–2016). Whilst the report did not focus on the military context, it made a number of recommendations for intervention at all ecological levels that may be applied to the military setting, some of which will be considered in the final section of this chapter.

Meso level interventions

Good practice strategies at this ecological level include an emphasis on military family support organizations, group work, community work, and inter-agency work (Siebler, 2009).

Inclusive of mental health service delivery and the capacity to address IPV, military family support organizations within the DoD and DVA have evolved to a substantial degree internationally and in Australia. For example, all US military installations have a Family Advocacy Program (FAP), which provides an array of services to prevent, identify, and treat IPV of a family member as well as investigate, treat, and recommend punishments for alleged perpetrators (Cesur and Sabia, 2016). In collaboration with the National Resource Centre on Domestic Violence, the FAP has enabled resources for evidence-based interventions (Cesur and Sabia, 2016). The New Parent Support Program, a component of the FAP, enables home visits targeting active-duty parents with children under age 3 identified as being at risk (Denning, Meisnere, and Warner, 2014). The FAP encompasses early childhood development education, parenting education, playgroups, communication-skills training for families and couples, family violence prevention training for leaders, and strengths-based therapy to address family violence. An Australian program available to the ADF, Baby Makes 3, is a universal, evidence-based program that aimed to prevent violence for new parents in the immediate post-birth period. Evaluation found that it promoted equal and respectful relationships for new parents (Flynn, 2011).

Nonetheless, the effectiveness of family violence programs in the military is mixed. Denning, Meisnere, and Warner (2014) were unable to identify any evidence-based programs that addressed the prevention of family violence. A recurring theme in the literature is that programs need to be tailored to the military audience to be effective. The US and Canadian military organizations have a comprehensive array of services embedded within their DoD (Zamorski and Wiens-Kincaid, 2013) whereas the Australian DoD uses the resources of civilian providers who may not understand the nuances of the military organization.

The Canadian Armed Forces (CAF) prevention program includes a CAF-wide Family Violence Awareness Program, Family Crisis Teams, and risk-factor reduction programs for the drivers of IPV that address factors such as mental disorders, high-risk drinking, family conflict, and social isolation. The CAF prevention program mandates annual training for all commanding officers. Further, prevention efforts are coordinated by a Family Violence Advisory Committee (Zamorski and Wiens-Kincaid, 2013).

In addition, newer primary prevention programs, working within a framework of military community support, focus on identifying relationship stressors, improving communication, and reducing other risk factors of IPV—for example, Battlemind Training for Spouses, Air Force Crossroads, and Northstar (Mancini, Nelson, Bowen, and Martin, 2006; Slep and Heyman, 2008). These newer prevention programs provide a mechanism through which at-risk groups may be introduced to services available to help them address relationship problems and develop safety plans to reduce further risk of violence.

Relationship Education (RE) for couples in a group setting has been developed with the aim of teaching the skills required to maintain a healthy, long-term relationship (Bakhurst, Loew, McGuire, Halford, and Markman, 2017). Whilst not an appropriate setting for severe IPV, programs typically address the unique challenges of the military lifestyle, ensuring program delivery is seen as relevant by military couples, and providing relationship education in formats that enhance the accessibility of programs. Whilst findings are mixed, the rationale is that the content of RE on conflict management and positive couple interaction provides useful input to reduce less severe IPV (Bakhurst, Loew, McGuire, Halford, and Markman, 2017).

Using a cognitive-behavioral social information processing model, the *Strength at Home Couples* (SAH-C) program was developed for military couples where relationship difficulties were present and physical and controlling behavior was absent. The need for IPV prevention was an inclusion criterion. The intervention was designed to prevent IPV from occurring. SAH-C is a ten-week group program for couples led by two Doctoral-level facilitators (Taft et al., 2016). The results of this randomized controlled trial provided support for the efficacy of the SAH-C program in preventing physical IPV and reducing psychological IPV in comparison to a Supportive Prevention intervention (Taft et al., 2016). Both service members and their female partners engaged in fewer acts of reported physical and psychological IPV (Taft et al., 2016).

Couple CARE, a US program, has demonstrated some utility in improving couple communication and relationship satisfaction for females up to a 12-month follow-up (Bakhurst, McGuire, and Halford, 2017). One such program, developed for Australian military families, Couple CARE in Uniform, improved relationship satisfaction and communication with no significant difference compared with the control group (Bakhurst, McGuire, and Halford, 2017). The researchers used the Conflict Tactics Scale at pre-intervention and in follow-up to screen for IPV and 9 percent of the small sample reported one incident of physical violence in the last six months whilst a further 9 percent reported two or more occurrences. The researchers decided to retain these couples in the program and "have them closely monitored by their educator" (Bakhurst, McGuire, and Halford, 2017: 178).

Unfortunately, the study made no analysis or discussion of these results and no conclusion can be drawn as to whether RE was an effective intervention. The study demonstrated the difficulties in recruiting and retaining military couples dues to privacy concerns, unwillingness to disclose personal details to a stranger, support from the military for the study, and concerns that the group program may raise problems where none were thought to exist.

Bowen, Jensen, and Williams (2017) identified family protective factors that may decrease the likelihood of family violence in the US Air Force via the Family Advocacy program. These "critical success" variables included formal support services from installation and unit leaders, informal supports, such as the social support of service personnel and their families, and safe, stable, and nurturing family processes. The findings lend credence to the notion that formal and informal supports are effective targets for prevention efforts. Health, welfare, and military leadership therefore have a significant role to play.

Micro level interventions

The microsystem level (Figure 16.1) considers individual/military family risk and protective factors, genetic/constitutional/biological factors, and individual health and well-being (Siebler, 2009). At this level, individual, family, and couple interventions occur and clinicians working with military families must have "the prerequisite knowledgeable and experience in trauma, and military-specific stressors" (Williston, Taft, and Van Haasteren, 2015). As Lewis, Lamson, and White (2016) observe, counsellors and therapists who work with the military implement a range of modalities including long-term therapy to assist military couples. Responding to individual risk factors is an important way of working out how best to target interventions to tackle family violence. It does not excuse violence or allow people to avoid taking responsibility for their behavior. As cited in the previous section, individual risk factors associated with the perpetration of family violence may include alcohol and drug misuse, mental illness, combat exposure, PTSD, and exposure to violence as a child.

The Australian DoD typically has on-base counselling and other services for families and personnel, which are not specifically tailored to address family violence. Social workers refer families to specialized family violence services where appropriate. These may include group programs for perpetrators, trauma-focused counselling for women and children, advocacy, and emergency accommodation. The DoD mental health system encompasses family-sensitive practice and routinely considers IPV in intake assessments, treatment planning, and care monitoring. The DoD website provides information for families in relation to family violence (DCO Website, 2018). Notwithstanding, no published evaluations of any of these services was available and their effectiveness is unknown.

Unless partner safety can be assured, marital/couples' counselling is contraindicated in working with couples where IPV presents due to concerns about placing the victim at further risk of harm. Anecdotally, all helping professional groups employed in health settings such as doctors, nurses, social workers, and psychologists will encompass IPV in their day-to-day practice in working with military families and need to respond appropriately to both victims and perpetrators using best practice.

Returning from a military deployment may present a range of physical and mental health sequelae for personnel and their families. There is no empirical research evidence providing significant support for any mode of therapy for multiple problems, comorbidities, and, in particular, IPV (Aronson, Perkins, and Olson, 2014; Sayers, 2011).

Service members, veterans, and family members who are victims of IPV may choose to seek information and resources available on the internet to maintain their anonymity and privacy, and seek reporting options that maintain confidentiality. Although the literature available on this topic relates to military and veteran IPV victims, information and resources need to be up to date, and relevant. A consistent message regarding the foundation of IPV that is based on current literature needs to be presented so that those seeking information about or help with IPV are not made to feel helpless to influence the situation. An approach that suggests a variety of options should be encouraged, and more explicitly outlined in information and resources pertaining to IPV. Future information and resources published or posted on the internet by military branches, VA, and other IPV service or information sites should include specific information on privacy and limitations to privacy so victims can fully understand what to expect when seeking help for IPV (Brown and Joshi, 2014). As a case in point, the Australian military family support organization, the Defence Community Organisation, places information on its website regarding IPV in the form of a factsheet (DCO Website, 2018). Families are encouraged to contact a range of community services for assistance. No evaluation was available as to whether the website resource was effective for families.

Summary

The narrative review of the military literature in relation to intervention across the ecological levels revealed few programs or services that have a strong evidence base to demonstrate effectiveness. In Australia, the DoD continues to grapple with the problem of family violence and a strategy has been created. It was beyond the scope of this chapter to review the civilian literature although promising approaches are emerging from this wider literature (World Health Organization, 2010; World Health Organization, 2013). No data or research was found for service utilization by ADF families of Australian services and programs such as the National Family Violence Service, 1800 RESPECT (1800 Respect Website, 2018).

The way forward for the military organization

This chapter has examined theoretical approaches to understanding the causes of IPV and interventions. There is no "one size fits all" approach but an international body of research clearly demonstrates that all three ecological levels must be considered to inform the optimal design of policies, programs, and services. The narrative review revealed the research in the military field is very limited and the evidence for the effectiveness of what works for whom and under what circumstances across all levels is mixed. This is not an argument for doing nothing. There is no evidence that incidence of IPV is either higher or lower than in the wider society, but it seems plausible that IPV is correlated with military culture, profession, deployment, and high usage of alcohol. Moreover, there is evidence the DoD is a population group with a higher level and severity of IPV than the community. This further reinforces for all military organizations that IPV is a "wicked problem" and solving it will require a significant investment of resources and a multi-level approach over a long period of time before enduring outcomes will be seen.

Prevention programs at all three ecological levels are needed—macro, meso, and micro. The evidence shows these must not be piecemeal. We recommend the DoD pilots small projects in collaboration with specialist services and creates Memoranda of Understanding that are well designed, evaluable, and reflect best practice.

The military organization wants to act to solve this problem, so what further can the military do? Funding is always a consideration and the military requires the "best bang for its buck," that is, effective outcomes that are sustainable.

First, considering the macro level, internationally and in Australia, the DoD and DVA (or its equivalent) could collaborate with research organizations to support the development and implementation of evidence-based prevention and treatment programs across the above ecological levels for military families that address both risk and protective factors. In Australia this is Australia's National Research Organization for Women's Safety (ANROWS). Accurate prevalence rates of IPV, using concise definitions, are clearly needed as a starting point to help the military understand the scope of the problem.

Further, similar to overseas forces, the ADF has already shown a commitment to addressing the problem via its strategy. Similar to the USA, we recommend the DoD and DVA work collaboratively and utilize the knowledge of specialist peak organizations to operationalize its strategy and convene a Family Violence Task Force to develop whole-of-defense policies and programs. At the military installation or base level, we recommend each base develops a Memorandum of Understanding in Working with Civilian Providers to enhance referral pathways and build community capacity with providers for the ultimate benefit of its base population of military families. Each base is embedded in a formal social system of care with services funded to prevent and intervene in IPV such as police, women's services, perpetrator programs, housing, and mental health. Bowen, Jensen, and Williams' (2017) ecological model to prevent IPV lends strong support to this approach.

In collaboration with research organizations such as universities, the DoD and DVA could research, trial, and evaluate meso and micro level interventions for perpetrators and victims within a two-year timeframe. Current gaps are group and individual programs as the narrative review outlined. This requires the military to open itself up to researchers and strong leadership will be required such as that demonstrated by the Australian Army and its willingness to address the problem.

At the meso level of organizations, we recommend that, at a minimum, all Commanders, managers, health and family support staff such as doctors, nurses, social workers, and psychologists receive tailored, ongoing education in relation to identifying and responding to IPV. Family violence work is a specialized field and staff must be appropriately trained and credentialed. Group programs must be well designed such that they are evaluable and have measurable outcomes for participants, be they victims or perpetrators. Mental health professionals undergo ongoing professional development in family-sensitive practice, risk assessment, and management. In Australia, the DoD already has a system of care via its health contract and this could be leveraged to refer the affected persons to prevention programs and specialist treatment services for victims and perpetrators. Each state in Australia has a well-developed community care system, which the DoD already utilizes. The victims of IPV, namely women and children, require special consideration in ensuring they receive the appropriate level and kind of support. Notwithstanding, these services will themselves need to be evidence-informed and develop an understanding of the military culture to yield effective outcomes. The DoD could be a leader here by funding place-based research to support military-aware practice.

The meso level also needs to build upon the promising programs that are being trialed and evaluated, such as those for perpetrators and victims. Referral pathways for male perpetrators to behavior-change programs need to be developed. Group programs will need to be developed to cater for military-specific factors and for those with serious mental illness or substance abuse. The DoD can collaborate with civilian providers to inform program design. Liaison with police forces will also be important since these services respond to incidents of family violence and may be a pathway to perpetrators and victims receiving the appropriate assistance.

Finally, the micro level has gaps in the knowledge base of which counselling approaches for victims and perpetrators are effective. At an individual level, factors such as exposure to childhood violence, mental illness, and drug and alcohol misuse can fuel or exacerbate family violence. This fact does not in any way minimize or excuse the offending, but does need to inform the intervention for that particular perpetrator. Programs need to reflect the latest knowledge and evidence regarding their capacity to manage risk, achieve attitudinal and behavioral change, address criminogenic factors, reduce re-offending, and meet the needs of victims (State of Victoria, 2014–2016). The military could support research trials with sufficient statistical power to determine which clinical interventions are effective.

The military organization alone cannot solve the problem of IPV but it can address the key drivers of IPV internally and play a key role in preventing IPV in the community. Military organizations are already making significant steps in addressing family violence and they must continue to be a significant agent of transformative change to address this problem, which ultimately benefits its military families and society as a whole.

Note

1 The views expressed in this chapter are those of the authors and should not be taken to represent the policy or standpoint of the Australian Department of Defense.

The authors would like to thank Ms Rachael Mackay, Women's Health Goulburn North East, and Dr John Frederick, Monash University for their constructive feedback in relation to this chapter.

References

1800 Respect Website (2018). *National Sexual Assault, Domestic Family Violence Counselling Service*. www.1800respect.org.au/ (accessed December 3, 2017).

Ali, P. A. and Naylor, P. (2013). Intimate partner violence: a narrative review of the feminist, social and ecological explanations for its causation. *Aggression and Violent Behavior*, 18(6), 611–619.

Aronson, K., Perkins, D., and Olson, J. (2014). Epidemiology of partner abuse within military families. *Journal of Family Social Work*, 17(4), 379–400.

Bakhurst, M., McGuire, A., and Halford, W. (2017). relationship education for military couples: a pilot randomized controlled trial of the effects of couple CARE in uniform. *Journal of Couple & Relationship Therapy*, 16(3), 167–187.

Bakhurst, M., Loew, B., McGuire, A., Halford, W., and Markman, H. (2017). Relationship education for military couples: recommendations for best practice. *Family Process*, 56(2), 302–316.

Black, M., Basile, K., Breiding, M., Smith, S., Walters, M., Merrick, M., Chen, J., and Stevens, M. (2011). *The National Intimate Partner and Sexual Violence Survey: 2010 Summary Report*. Retrieved from www.cdc.gov/violenceprevention/pdf/nisvs_report2010-a.pdf (accessed December 17, 2017).

Bowen, G., Jensen, T., and Williams, B. (2017). Prevention of family maltreatment in the US Air Force: a systematic review of research on active-duty military personnel. *Journal of Family Social Work*, 20(1), 52–80.

Bradley, C. (2007). Veteran status and marital aggression: does military service make a difference? *Journal of Family Violence*, 22(4), 197–209.

Bronfenbrenner, U. (1993). Ecological models of human development. In M. Gauvain and M. Cole (eds), *Readings on the Development of Children*, 2nd edn (pp. 37–43). New York: Freeman.

Brown, A. and Joshi, M. (2014). Intimate partner violence among female service members and veterans: information and resources available through military and non-military websites. *Social Work in Health Care*, 53(8), 714–738.

Bryant W and Bricknell S. (2017). *Homicide in Australia 2012–13 to 2013–14: National Homicide Monitoring Program report*. Statistical Reports No. 2. Canberra: Australian Institute of Criminology. https://aic.gov.au/publications/sr/sr002 (accessed December 3, 2017).

Campbell, C., Brown, E., and Okwara, L. (2011). Addressing sequelae of trauma and interpersonal violence in military children: a review of the literature and case illustration. *Cognitive and Behavioral Practice*, 18(1), 131–143.

Cesur, R. and Sabia, J. (2016). When war comes home: the effect of combat service on domestic violence. *Review of Economics and Statistics*, 98(2), 209–225.

Chief of Army speech to National Press Club (2017). *Domestic Violence Campaign*. Address to the National Press Club of Australia, 16 National Circuit, Barton, Wednesday, August 16, 2017. www.army.gov.au/our-work/speeches-and-transcripts/australian-army-domestic-violence-awareness-silence-is-theaccomplice (accessed November 9, 2017).

Commonwealth of Australia (2017). *Family and Domestic Violence Strategy 2017–2022*. Canberra.

Commonwealth of Australia (2009). *Background Paper to Time for Action: The National Council's Plan for Australia to Reduce Violence against Women and their Children, 2009–2021*. Canberra: ACT.

Defence Community Organisation Website (2018). *Intimate Partner Violence*. www.defence.gov.au/dco/_Master/documents/Handouts/Intimate-partner-violence.pdf (accessed December 3, 2017).

Denning, L., Meisnere, M., and Warner, K. (2014). *Preventing Psychological Disorders in Service Members and Their Families: An Assessment of Programs*. Institute of Medicine. Washington, DC: National Academies Press.

Flynn, D. (2011). *Baby Makes 3: Project Report*. White Horse Community Health Service, Box Hill, Melbourne.

Foran, H., Heyman, R., and Smith Slep, A. (2014). Emotional abuse and its unique ecological correlates among military personnel and spouses. *Psychology of Violence*, 4(2), 128.

Harrison, D. (2006). The role of military culture in military organizations' responses to woman abuse in military families. *The Sociological Review*, 54(3), 546–574.

Harrison, D. and Laliberté, L. (2002). *The First Casualty: Violence against Women in Canadian Military Communities*. Toronto, ON: James Lorimer & Company.

Iverson, K., Vogt, D., Dichter, M., Carpenter, S., Kimerling, R., Street, A., and Gerber, M. (2015). Intimate partner violence and current mental health needs among female veterans. *The Journal of the American Board of Family Medicine*, 28(6), 772–776.

Jones, A. (2012). Intimate partner violence in military couples: a review of the literature. *Aggression and Violent Behavior*, 17(2), 147–157.

Karpetis, G. (2010). Psychodynamic clinical social work practice with parents in child and adolescent mental health services: a case study on the role of the father. *Journal of Social Work Practice*, 24(2), 155–170.

Karpetis, G. (2012). Psychodynamic supportive psychotherapy techniques in clinical social work practice with parents. *Smith College Studies in Social Work*, 82(1), 63–89.

Karpetis, G. (2016). Identifying effective therapeutic mechanisms in psychodynamic parent work. *Smith College Studies in Social Work*, 86(02), 118–135.

Karpetis, G. (2017a). Mental health knowledge gaps in the child protection work with parents: a narrative review of the social work literature. *Journal of Social Work Practice*, 31(3), 353–368.

Karpetis, G. (2017b). Theories on the child protection work with parents: a narrative review of the literature. *Child Welfare*, 95(2), 33–70.

Klostermann, K., Mignone, T., Kelley, M. L., Musson, S., and Bohall, G. (2012). Intimate partner violence in the military: treatment considerations. *Aggression and Violent Behavior*, 17(1), 53–58.

Lewis, M., Lamson, A., and White, M. (2016). The state of dyadic methodology: an analysis of the literature on interventions for military couples. *Journal of Couple and Relationship Therapy*, 15(2), 135–157.

Mancini, J., Nelson J., Bowen, G., and Martin, J. (2006). Preventing intimate partner violence: a community capacity approach. *Journal of Aggression, Maltreatment, and Trauma*, 13, 203–227.

Norman, R., Byambaa, M., Butchart, A., Scott, J., and Vos, T. (2012). The long-term health consequences of child physical abuse, emotional abuse, and neglect: a systematic review and meta-analysis. *PLoS Medicine*, 9, e1001349. doi:10.1371/journal.pmed.1001349.

Rentz, D., Martin, S., Gibbs, D., Clinton-Sherrod, M., Hardison, J., and Marshall, S. (2006). Family violence in the military: a review of the literature. *Trauma, Violence & Abuse*, 7(2), 93–108.

Rodrigues, A., Funderburk, J., Keating, N., and Maisto, S. (2014). A methodological review of intimate partner violence in the military: where do we go from here? *Trauma, Violence, & Abuse*, 16(3), 231–240.

Sayers, S. (2011). Family reintegration diffculties and couples therapy for military veterans and their families. *Cognitive and Behavioral Practice*, 10, 108–119.

Shackelford, T. and Mouzos, J. (2005) Partner killing by men in cohabiting and marital relationships. *Journal of Interpersonal Violence*, 20(10), 1310–1324.

Siebler, P. (2009). *"Military people won't ask for help": Experiences of Deployment of Australian Defense Force Personnel, their Families, and Implications for Social Work.* Unpublished PhD thesis, Monash University [online], available from http://arrow.monash.edu.au/hdl/1959.1/157678 (accessed December 21, 2011).

Slep, A. and Heyman, R. (2008). Public health approaches to family maltreatment prevention: resetting family psychology's sights from the home to the community. *Journal of Family Psychology*, 22, 518–528.

Sparrow, K., Kwan, J., Howard, L., Fear, N., and MacManus, D. (2017). Systematic review of mental health disorders and intimate partner violence victimisation among military populations. *Social Psychiatry and Psychiatric Epidemiology*, 52(9), 1059–1080.

State of Victoria (2014–2016). Royal Commission into Family Violence: summary and recommendations, Parl Paper No 132.

Stamm, S. (2009). Intimate partner violence in the military: securing our country, starting with the home. *Family Court Review*, 47(2), 321–339.

Taft, C., Creech, S., Gallagher, M., Macdonald, A., Murphy, C., and Monson, C. (2016). Stength at home couples program to prevent military partner violence: a randomized controlled trial. *Journal of Consulting and Clinical Psychology*, 84(11), 935–945.

Tasso, A., Whitmarsh, L., and Ordway, A. (2016). Intimate partner violence within military families: intervention guidelines for relational aggressors. *The Family Journal*, 24(2), 114–121.

Trevillion, K., Williamson, E., Thandi, G., Borschmann, R., Oram, S., and Howard, L. M. (2015). A systematic review of mental disorders and perpetration of domestic violence among military populations. *Social Psychiatry and Psychiatric Epidemiology*, 50(9), 1329–1346.

United Nations Office on Drugs and Crime (2011). *2011 Global Study on Homicide*. UNODC; Vienna.

Wojda, A., Heyman, R., Smith Slep, A., Foran, H., Snarr, J., and Oliver, M. (2017). Family violence, suicidality, and substance abuse in active duty military families: an ecological perspective. *Military Behavioural Health*, 5(4), 300–312.

World Health Organization (2010). *Preventing Intimate Partner and Sexual Violence against Women: Taking Action and Generating Evidence*. Geneva: World Health Organization.

World Health Organization (2013). *Responding to Intimate Partner Violence and Sexual Violence against Women: WHO Clinical and Policy Guidelines*. Geneva: World Health Organization.

Williston, S., Taft, C., and Van Haasteren, K. (2015). Military veteran perpetrators of intimate partner violence: challenges and barriers to coordinated intervention. *Aggression and Violent Behavior*, 21, 55–60.

Young-Wolff, K., Kotz, K., and McCaw, B. (2016). Transforming the health care response to intimate partner violence: addressing "wicked problems." *Journal of the American Medical Association*, 315(23), 2517–2518.

Zamorski, M. and Wiens-Kincaid, M. (2013). Cross-sectional prevalence survey of intimate partner violence perpetration and victimization in Canadian military personnel. *BMC Public Health*, 13, 1019.

17 Swedish families' responses to military deployment

Ann-Margreth E. Olsson and Sven-Erik Olsson[1]

Introduction

This study examines Swedish families' responses to their family members being deployed in an international military operation. It aims to contribute to current knowledge by examining the experiences of not only military personnel and their partners, but also their children (including siblings) and parents, through dialogical participatory action research. First, the context of the military and the family in Sweden will be presented. Then, we proceed with describing the design and results of the study. The chapter concludes with a discussion of the findings and implications for research and practice.

The military and the family in Sweden

The concept of family is in a deconstruction process (Gümüscü, Khoo, and Nygren, 2014). Is one parent with children a family? Is a parenting duo with a father and a mother essential? What happens to family when there is a divorce, or when one or both vow to a new person? What about bonus children? How the political administrative system and law respond to challenges posed by this kind of question forms a local context. Surprisingly, for a country that has a reputation as being collectivist/socialist, in Sweden there is a strong focus on individuals being independent and enjoying equal opportunities (Ekström and Hjort, 2010).

In Sweden the levels of fertility are declining and divorce levels are increasing (Ohlsson-Wijk, Turunen, and Andersson, 2017). Sweden is well known as the prototype for Social Democratic welfare states. In public policy, this has resulted in a strong commitment to gender equality, dual-income families and shared family responsibilities, including caring for the children. However, in some areas a gendered pattern has persisted. While labor-market participation seems to be equal (Dreber and Wallace, 2004; OECD, 2018), wages, career patterns, and propensity to stay at home/use child leave benefits are not (Magnusson and Nermo, 2017). Women, especially those having children, engage in part-time work to a much larger extent than men. Ziegert noted that Sweden's supportive legislative programs addressing families and children are focused on establishing a network of support assisting the family system, including making it possible for both parents to work outside the home for large parts of the day (Ziegert, 1987). Ziegert also argued that formal marriage had lost its ideologically and socially special status rendering the difference between marital and extra-marital children largely irrelevant for legal policy (Ziegert, 1987).

The overall principle in Sweden is that everyone, regardless of gender (sex, transgender identity or expression), has the right to have a career *and* family life (Ministry of Integration and Gender Equality, 2009). A survey conducted by the Swedish Union of the Officers revealed that, during a deployment, spouses had lowered their work time in 34 percent of the families with children under 8 years old (Synovate and Officersförbundet, 2008). This also means that 66 percent of the spouses had not reduced their work time. There is still reason to regard the development toward gender equality as a work in progress (Galte Schermer, 2018).

In many countries military families are often given special provisions, such as accommodation, healthcare, social security, schooling, and childcare (see, for example, Moelker, Andres, and Poot, 2006). This is in stark contrast to the generalized welfare policy in Social Democratic welfare states such as Sweden, Denmark, and Norway (Kasearu and Olsson, 2019), and how SAF envisions the relationship between employer and employed. Outside of the brief recruitment phase, three months in duration, it is expected that the individual is responsible for accommodation. Largely the soldier is regarded as a normal citizen that can rely on the Swedish public universal welfare system, though there are some provisions that are made available by the SAF. The universal system gives access to extensive social benefits and services, childcare, and healthcare. In Sweden, family support largely is made available through the same channels that are also open to other citizens.

However, when Sweden started to participate in risky warlike missions, and the Swedish parliament decided to reintroduce a selective form of conscription (Jonsson and Nordlund, 2010; Parliament/Riksdagen, 2010), the need for family support quickly became a political priority. Laws were passed that obliged the SAF to provide support on a scale that makes it possible for the soldier to combine military life with family life as well as participate in community life (Jonsson and Nordlund, 2010). Thus the importance of supporting families of military personnel now is emphasized (Hjortendal-Hellman, 2011).

The SAF recognized that the military and the family mutually influence one another and started to collaborate with (and give financial support to) voluntary organizations that support families and individuals experiencing military deployment. That responses and reactions in families of deployed soldiers influence soldiers' performance, military readiness, and retention in the forces is well established in international military family research (e.g., Chapin, 2009; Hadaway, 1979; Segal and Harris, 1993; Schumm, Bell, and Resnic, 2001).

Study design

This study is part of a comprehensive systemic action study concerning Swedish families of the SAF. It deals with the question of how the families cope with or without the support of the measures made available by the employer and other channels such as healthcare, social services, and voluntary organizations. The study was based on Dialogical Participatory Action Research (DPAR) (Olsson, 2014a, 2014b). This research process involves phased sequences of collaboration, exploring and collecting data/narratives in dialogical meetings, which also could become supportive for the families and/or family members (this being "the action"), the intervention, in conducted action research study.

The study was approved by the Regional Ethics Board in Lund (dnr 2012/459). Methods used are based on dialogical, systemic, and narrative ideas where the participants were asked to narrate about and explore their experiences of emerging social life in the context of deployments. More specifically, dialogical research uses Appreciative Inquiry (AI) (Cooperrider and Whitney, 2003) with a focus on what works, how the families successfully manage whatever arises in context of and in relation to international military deployment in their perspective. The aim was to improve the understanding of the real-world problems by exploring the emerging solutions the family speaks about.

Participants

During family gatherings, organized by SAF or voluntary organizations, families who had a member that was going to be or had been deployed (usually for six months) were invited to participate in the study. Many of the participating families suggested contacting other families in their networks. All families that came forward and were willing to participate were interviewed. This resulted in 135 persons (110 adults and 25 children) participating in dialogical interviews, making their own voices heard (see Tables 17.1 and 17.2). In addition to the 25 children telling about their experiences themselves, narratives about children's responses were collected through their parent(s).

In total, 59 families participated; 33 with their whole family (2–7 family members) and 26 with 1–4 representatives of their family. A diversity of family structures characterized the participating families. There were couples, married or cohabited, with children or not, running a household together or separate from each other, etc. Siblings participated in the study, either living together with one or both of the parents or managing their own households, as well as mothers

Table 17.1 Adults participating in the dialogical interviews[1]

Category	*Women*	*Men*	*Total*
Soldiers/veterans	8	34	42
Home-staying spouses	35	6	41
Parents and other relatives	14	7	21
Siblings	5	5	10
Young adult, 19–25 years old	16	5	21

[1] Note that some participants fall into two categories, for example, those being a veteran and a partner.

Table 17.2 Children participating in interviews

	Boys	*Girls*	*Total*
6 years or younger	2	5	7
7–11	8	4	12
12–15	3	1	4
16–18	2	–	2
Sum	15	10	25

and fathers of the soldiers and other relatives. In total, 110 adults participated: 63 women and 47 men. The study also includes children of soldiers/veterans, of whom 25 participated in dialogical interviews of their own.

Method

Primary data were obtained by means of dialogical semi-structured interviews that were taped after acquiring consent of the participant(s). The researchers recurrently met participating families and/or representatives of extended families, listening to their experiences of the different phases of the deployment cycle (Logan, 1987; Olsson, 2018; Pincus, House, Christenson, and Adler, 2001). The researchers met the participants individually and/or in a group. Themes for the dialogue were prepared by the researchers; however, if the participants wanted to talk about something else important in the context of the deployment, that was given highest priority.

The interviewing researcher did transcription verbatim. Edits were made in consideration of military secrecy and to ensure confidentiality. Participants were all informed of the scope and purpose of the research study and that participation was voluntary. This was done at least once and every time with participating children. As usual in action research the analysis was ongoing during the study and preliminary results were explored with participants and with representatives of the SAF and researchers in different seminars (cf. Reason and Bradbury, 2006a, 2006b). Content analysis was used (Graneheim, Lindgren, and Lundman, 2017) as well as thematic analysis (Braun and Clarke, 2006). The analysis process revealed six ideal types of families' approaches and responses to military deployment.

Ideal types accentuate certain characteristics of a given social phenomenon (Eneroth, 1984). They are abstract simplifications and do not claim to be true in an empirical sense, but if adequately constructed they can be productive in interpreting or reconstructing the logic of social interaction in a certain context (Bengtsson and Nils, 2014). Participants did recognize themselves more or less in all six ideal types (see Table 17.3). Transitions between the ideal types were occurring, which families considered as evolutions.

Table 17.3 Family's responses to military deployment of a family member

	A	*B*	*C*	*D*	*E*	*F*
Ideal type	Partnership	Supporting and mobilizing	Normalization—ordinary life	Adapting and negotiating	Emotional reacting	Suffering
The family's dominating orientation in responses	Joint actions Joint challenges	Mutual support and emerging involvement Mobilizing	Used to and adjusted to military life as the ordinary life	Gender equality Equality Justice Compensation Balancing act	Anger Powerlessness Extroversion, acting out emotional reactions	Sorrow Introversion Closed family system
Communication within the extended primary family	Open communication, dialogical; mutual and spontaneous responsiveness	Open communication; curiousness, many questions for the soldier to answer	Open and continuous communication with intimacy	Open communication, ongoing negotiations and feedback	Competitive and intrusive communication. Mixed feelings of regret, blame, and desire to escape	Reclusivity, closed communication
Managing strategies	If they need something, they ask or arrange support primarily in their network, including services of the community	The family is opening up for emerging possibilities to take part and share experiences Family-members are helpful in supporting others	Familiar with the military, knowing anyhow family members not always so involved Tight family bonds Support from within the extended family	Need and are open for support Use given opportunities in the community, including buying service and support	Support and co-creation of mutual interplay improving family members' safe-feeling and feelings of being secure	In need of that somebody outside the family to pay attention and intervene and take measures of care and support and mobilization

How Swedish families respond to deployment

Partnership

Families who cope with deployment in partnership consider and manage deployment as a joint challenge. Among them were different types of families, including dual-military couples. A married soldier, who was staying at home in Sweden this time while his wife was deployed to Mali, said: "It is part of our job. It's our job. We have chosen this profession and she wants to go, and I want that too. But not at the same time. We have children" (soldier with partner and two small children).

There were also partners with interests and aspirations in different professions, who thought of deployment as an opportunity, a time when the partner at home could devote her/his time completely to her/his own "project" while the soldier was doing her/his:

> So, I thought it was very good for him to go to Kosovo, for then I did my stuff for six months. So, during Kosovo, I worked around the clock for almost half a year . . . Had he been at home then, he would not have seen much of me anyhow.
>
> (Spouse, woman)

Other families considered a deployment a joint project and chose to follow the deployed family member, fulfilling a commission as observer or adviser around the world. This is called a "family deployment," although it did not necessarily imply that the whole family would stay in the same place abroad as the deployed soldier. The family could become divided for long periods of time, sometimes living a few hours away. Family members learned to live and survive in the new country, either on their own or together with others in similar situations. In some families, the children returned to Sweden on their own for boarding school or studies at university. These "family deployments" are talked about as very popular even though the situation is not free of risks. It was not always the soldier who turned out to be at the place that involved the biggest risks and dangers. At times it was the accompanying family members. Families with grown-up children talked about these incidents as positive learning experiences. The children evolved into independent individuals, family ties had been strengthened, and family members developed new skills in transition between new contexts.

Supporting and mobilizing

The interviewed families demonstrated a large amount of support, for the deployed service member, for other families, and for the military operations. Soldiers invite their family members to family meetings during the deployment and the Family Day that takes place just before the departure. The soldier finds it important to establish a feeling of doing it together. He or she invites the spouse or partner to spend a weekend together participating in one of the Prevention and Relationship

Enhancement Programs (PREP-courses; Lübeck and Sarkadi, 2009; Stanley et al., 2014), offered by one of the voluntary organizations and receiving funding from SAF, which are often fully booked (cf. Svenska Soldathemsförbundet, 2018). In this study, there were 18 couples that participated in PREP, which aims to lower risk levels and increase protective factors to further a healthy relationship, among other things by training communication skills, and encouraging participants to remain positive, committed, and connected (Einhorn et al., 2008).

Spouses and other family members also took an active part and interest in the life of other military families, including families of veterans, and found this also satisfying and helpful for themselves. Sometimes they joined one of the voluntary organizations, such as Invidzonen (Adjacent Zone). A spouse with a deployed husband took the initiative to form this organization in order to provide support to other spouses and families. Invidzonen, which currently receives financial support from the SAF, offers different activities and support, such as blogging, chat forums, and phone services.

Families show interest in what is going on in the mission area and inform others in the family network. In the interest of safety, the soldier is subject to restrictions and cannot reveal much of what is going on. Moreover, some things soldiers only expose to fellow soldiers who have had the same or similar experiences. The use of Skype, email, Facebook, and blogs opens up a variation of new opportunities of social interaction, to communicate, be together (or not), and take part in one another's stories.

In these families, most children are happy to bring their parents to school to speak about the deployment, both before and after, showing pictures and making everyone in school aware of the deployment and the country the parent/soldier is visiting. SAF recommends doing so. However, some children preferr that the parents do not inform anyone but the teachers about the deployment (Olsson, 2017).

Normalization—ordinary life

If families have seen it all before and are accustomed to military life and culture, sometimes because they have military ancestry, they have included deployment in the normal activities of family life. Daily life is adjusted to accommodate recurrent periods of deployments and other commissions though negotiations and mutual considerations. However, although they are accustomed to the demands of a military career, they do not identify themselves as a *military* family. They are as any other family.

It is common that adults have grown up with parents or other relatives in the military or at sea. As children, they have become used to taking part in military life. In various ways, soldiers show their family what military life can offer. However, involving the family in the military lifestyle and culture also includes becoming used to a style of orderliness and tidiness as well as a more hierarchical style in decision making that does not always invite the children to democratic participation. There are high expectations and demands on the non-deployed parent's capacity and ability to take care of everything at home when the deployed parent is absent. Soldiers will consult their spouse regarding crucial decisions on career and work performance, but ultimately this is seen as the soldier's call.

The soldier is spoken of as confident with military life, feeling safe and secure in relation to colleagues, in his/her professional role, and in what s/he can disclose to his/her family. Approaching a departure, the soldier invites family members to more intimate family and network meetings just before departure, in addition to the official family meetings organized by the SAF. Relatives are familiar with the context to which the soldier is moving and working in, with whom s/he is associated, and what his/her highest values are at work and at home. They trust the soldier's commanding officer and fellow workers. The soldier and his/her family try to live as normally as possible without making a great deal of an approaching deployment. Couples speak in positive terms of the separation, as an occasion to reawaken their relationship, creating a new opportunity for appreciation and concern for each other. Missing each other and longing for each other also leads to reunification. The children, even if they do not show different behavior, are aware of the difference in being deployed in the homeland and on a mission in war zones. They live with an awareness of the danger even though the youngest children may be more afraid of animals (for example, scorpions) than weapons. In school the children in these families want a school visit of the deployed parent, *but only* if all the other parents also give a talk about their work.

Adapting and negotiating

When one parent is leaving for deployment, there is a need for special arrangements, creating conditions for the stay-at-home partner to continue her/his life without excessive hardship. Family members express expectancy of fairness and compensatory measures that reflect a balance between family members. The stay-at-home parent may say: "It's your turn now, my turn will come later." One partner said: "You have to compromise. He's allowed to go this time, another time it's me. He supports me in so much else, so now it is time for me to support him" (partner, woman).

There are expectations that partners have similar opportunities for personal development and having a career and that they are both responsible for household chores and parenting tasks. When a parent is deployed, children are promised objects to compensate them, like a racing bike, a trip abroad, or what the extra revenue can bring along. It is seen as *imperative* that children's normal recreational activities should be able to continue as usual. The idea is that a child should not suffer from a parent's absence. The aim is to maintain the same routines and same high standards, for instance when it comes to cooked meals, time limits of children's computer and TV time, and bedtime. In order to accomplish this, the family network is mobilized, as well as other help such as house and window cleaners and the delivery of ready-to-use groceries. Relatives help taking care of the children to create "time of their own" (*egentid*) for the stay-at-home parent and to enable her/him to continue study and/or work—caring for her/his own professional career. The stay-at-home partner may even move into the home of her/his parents for some time, or into the home of the soldier's parents. Grandparents enjoy this extra time with their children or grandchildren.

Emotional reaction

Predominantly, it was young couples that spoke about negative energy, emotions, and reactions, accompanied by dissatisfaction and/or problems; but couples with long-lasting relations also experienced this. In many cases, the soldier had declared from the beginning that "I am a soldier" and had revealed plans for participation in a military deployment abroad, which was seen as part of his/her military job and an obligation as a soldier.

> When we met, it was already decided that he should go. I had nothing to say about that. He was very honest and said he had been deployed once before and he will go again. He wanted me to agree, of course, but it was up to me to decide if I could cope with it. He said: "I'll go and I'll be out for a while and for a long time." I did not perceive that I was going to become second in relation to him. I understand that this is his job and something he wants. Should he have it? I do not think I was reflecting on that so much then. I was so in love and I just said: "Yes, yes," then. We'll take that as well. It was, well two months ago, when everything became obvious; it became difficult. When they started commuting to Stockholm. Then I realized, shit, he's really going to go away. In the beginning, I kept it to myself. Then I burst. I was so sorry, I was angry, pissed off. All at once. And he said: "Yes, but you knew this." Yes, but just because I knew, doesn't make it easier.
>
> (Young spouse, woman)

The spouse/partner and other family members appear to have lived with denial or disbelief up to the moment when the time was set for the upcoming deployment. As the reality of the deployment finally sunk in, the soldier and family started preparations. The family appeared upset, worried, or confused about the deployment. The soldier was defied, tried to avoid more bickering about what is going on, and was unsure if the family really wanted to listen to his/her military experiences and unsure about how and what to tell. Some things that could not be shared, he withheld—the unspoken, untold stories. The soldier's family may have cried out for more attention and space in the soldier's life.

When soldiers and family members differ in their views about the importance and meaningfulness of Swedish international military operations, it may result in discord. Questions may be asked as to why the soldier should venture off to a foreign country engaging in dangerous missions when there is so much at home to take care of and protect. Typical questions posed to the soldier are: don't you care about me/us? How can you even think of leaving us? What can be so attractive in participating in a mission? The children may ask themselves: have we been too troublesome here at home? Soldiers are challenged to answer such questions that can be very difficult to answer. They may feel pressed into defending and explaining. It may result in feelings of despair and grief and the soldier being hesitant to leave.

The feelings of the non-deployed spouses/partners alternate between pride and anger directed at the leaving soldier. Mood switches between joy and sorrow, faith and resignation put the family on a rollercoaster. Couples may *go silent* in relation to one another, in particularly in telephone contacts, to protect each other from what might be difficult to sort out at a distance. At the same time, family members at home as well as deployed soldiers develop new activities and relations with others, which means socializing with others instead of their family members. One child asked: "Does dad care more about the children in Afghanistan than about me?"

There seems to be ample material to construct threats. On Campus, men and women intermingle—could it become more than friendship? Stories about love affairs and secret relationships circulate, especially on Facebook—can it be applied to our/my soldier? And inversely, the spouses/partners at home express longing for companionship with both women and men; they go for a walk with a male or female friend, hang out and talk with both men and women. This can be viewed as competition, risking the soldier's place in the relationship. Jealousy and/or envy lies in waiting and may cause difficulties for those involved.

The non-deployed spouse/partner may feel rejected and abandoned. This was not what s/he had imagined as living in a steady-going relationship—caught in a trap of being part of a loving couple, but still feeling alone. Others have each other, come in pairs, hang out in pairs, celebrating Christmas, New Year, birthdays together and can look forward to the approaching weekend with joy. Several options were mentioned in the interviews, but they had to be "secure" and not challenge their relationship with the deployed soldier, such as: a move home to mom and dad to become like a child again, work holidays, celebrations with teammates, and an end to caring about the traditions or moving the dates of their celebrations to the soldier's homecoming. Children chose to not talk with friends about the deployment, but they made exceptions for those who also have/had a parent deployed: "they know what this is about."

Suffering

In some families, a pattern evolves that circles around a theme: *this is the best job for me and it is what it is*. A tension emerges in relation to the soldier's claims considering the nature of the job; going away, exposing oneself to danger are part of the job and the life together. The partner knew it all along. This is what the soldier was trained for, the profession s/he identifies with: "I am a soldier. If you love me—this is who I am."

Children are also expected to accept the demands and conditions of their parents' professional lives. Even if the non-deployed parent tries to avoid showing the children how much s/he is mourning, the children feel their parent's mood and the changed atmosphere at home. In relation to the deployed parent the response of the child varies: they may resort to avoiding and refusing to have any contact or they may find relief in talking with the deployed parent.

In communication, the soldier tends toward silence: if we do not talk about it, problems do not exist. Discussing emotions and dilemmas with outsiders, for example, in a PREP course or family counseling (included in what Social Welfare Service offers in every municipality) would carry the risk of creating and increasing problems. The soldiers speak of feeling apprehensive; they fear that their family's contacts and collaboration with other grieving military families in the network, including voluntary organizations, only aggravate the situation. Some couples choose to reduce communications, the rationale behind this being that the soldier has to be able to concentrate on his/her task and cannot constantly be reminded of the emotional chaos at home. Others apply a different strategy: they focus the discussion on joint projects, for example, the renovation of the kitchen or a new house, training preparation for doing something like "A Swedish Classic" involving skiing, running, swimming, and cycling, or participating in other competitions or events.

Conclusion

The aim of this chapter was to focus on the responses of Swedish families in relation to international military deployment. From a systemic view, the main function of family systems is the proximity and intimacy between family members (Luhmann, 1995). This may be challenged when a soldier is deployed, depending on how the family may see and respond to the deployment. Interestingly, the families participating in this study, even those that had a long ancestry in the military, did not identify themselves as military families—a common term used in international research. In Sweden, just as in Norway and Denmark, the military is not seen as a distinctive and separate entity with special ambitions or aspirations of governance; there is no rift between civil society and the military (Boëne, 2000; Kasearu and Olsson, 2019). There are many institutions (education, healthcare, social insurance, social benefits/welfare) that are universal and financed through taxation. From the interwar period and onwards, Sweden has seen an expansion of programs that support all families in the shape of children's allowances, paid maternal and parental leave, daycare, pre-schools, and so forth. A military family is seen as no different from any other working family. The Swedish approach of equality makes it difficult to position the whole family into the profession of one (or two) of the family members as in the concept of the "military family." This also says something about how these families position themselves in relation to the military system. Instead of being part of the military system, the families position themselves as outsiders, observing the interaction and interplay between their deployed family member and his/her employer. The families wait for recognition. After all, they are aware of their own importance, not only to the soldier, but also to the SAF and Sweden, which are both dependent on soldiers' families for fulfilling the commissions of international deployments. They are doing it together; it is a deployment of the whole family, fulfilled in a joint action.

Note

1 The authors received financial support for the research, authorship, and publication of this article from the Swedish Armed Forces, Kristianstad University and AMOVE AB.

References

Bengtsson, B. and Nils, H. (2014). Generalization by mechanism: thin rationality and ideal-type analysis in case study research. *Philosophy of the Social Sciences*, 44(6), 707–732.

Boëne, B. (2000). *Facing Uncertainty: Report No 2: The Swedish Military in International Perspective*. Stockholm: Försvarshögskolan (Swedish Defence University).

Braun, V. and Clarke, V. (2006). Using thematic analysis in psychology. *Qualitative Research in Psychology*, 3(2), 77–101.

Chapin, M. (2009). Deployment and families: hero stories and horror stories. *Smith College Studies in Social Work*, 79, 263–282.

Cooperrider, D. L. and Whitney, D. (2003). Appreciative inquiry. In M. Gergen and K. J. Gergen (eds), *Social Construction: A Reader* (pp. 173–181). London: SAGE.

Dreber, A. and Wallace, B. (2004). *Villkor för Kvinnor i Karriären. En internationell jämförelse*. Stockholm: SNS Förlag.

Einhorn, L., Williams, T., Stanley, S., Wunderlin, N., Markman, H. J., and Eason, J. (2008). PREP inside and out: mariage eductaion for inmates. *Family Process*, 47(3), 342–356.

Ekström, K. M. and Hjort, T. (2010). Families navigating the landscape of consumption in the Swedish welfare society. *Journal of Macromarketing*, 30(4), 366–374.

Eneroth, B. (1984). *Hur mäter man "vackert"? Grundbok i kvalitativ metod*. Stockholm: Akademilitteratur.

Galte Schermer, I. (2018). Lönegap [Wage Gap]. *Ekonomifakta*. Available at: www.ekonomifakta.se/Fakta/Arbetsmarknad/Jamstalldhet/lonegap/.

Graneheim, U. H., Lindgren, b.-M., and Lundman, B. (2017). Methodological challenges in qualitative content analysis: a discussion paper. *Nurse Education today*, 56, 29–34. doi:http://dx.doi.org/10.1016/j.nedt.2017.06.002.

Gümüscü, A., Khoo, E., and Nygren, L. (2014). Family as raw material—the deconstructed family in the Swedish social services. *Journal of Comparative Social Work*, 2, 1–27.

Hadaway, N. L. (1979). *Preparation for Separation: Preparing the Military Family for Duty-Related Separation. Crisis Intervention Topics*. Washington, DC: US Department of Education.

Hjortendal-Hellman, E. (2011). *Kartläggning av vissa veteransoldatfrågor inom NORDEFCO-samarbetet*. Stockholm: Försvarsdepartementet, Regeringskansliet [Ministry of Defence, The Government Offices].

Jonsson, U. and Nordlund, P. (2010). *Frivilliga soldater istället för plikt – internationella erfarenheter och ekonomiska konsekvenser* (Vol. FOI-R--3053--SE). Stockholm: FQI—Totalförsvarets forskningsinstitut [Swedish Defence Research Agency].

Kasearu, K. and Olsson, A.-M. E. (2019). A systemic perspective on children's well-being in military families in different countries. In A. Skomorovsky (ed.), *Impact of Military Life on Children from Military Families* (pp. 5.1–5.24). STO-TR-HFM-258: STO/NATO – OTAN. North Atlantic Treaty Organization Science and Technology Organization. Neuilly-Sur-Seine: Cedex.

Logan, K. V. (1987). The emotional cycle of deployment. *US Naval Institute Proceedings*, 113, 43–47.

Lübeck, K. and Sarkadi, A. (2009). *Från samverkan till samsyn – en resa genom par, grupper och organisationer. Rapport från ett projekt mer förebyggande parrelationsarbete - PREP-projektet i Mora 2005–2008.* Uppsala: Inst. för kvinnor och barns hälsa, Uppsala universitet, SHS Vårdcentrum och Kommunernas familjerådgivning.

Luhmann, N. (1995). *Social Systems* (J. w. D. B. Bednarz, Trans.). Stanford, CA: Stanford University Press.

Magnusson, C. and Nermo, M. (2017). Gender, parenthood and wage differences: the importance of time-consuming job characteristics. *Social Indicators Research*, 131(2), 797–816.

Ministry of Integration and Gender Equality (2009). New anti-discrimation legislation and a new agency, the Equality Ombudsman. In G. O. o. Sweden (ed.), *Regeringskansliet*. Stockholm.

Moelker, R., Andres, M., and Poot, G. J. A. (2006). Supporting military families: a comparative study in social support. Arrangements for military families (theoretical dimensions and empirical comparison between countries). *Human Dimensions in Military Operations: Military Leaders' Strategies for Addressing Stress and Psychological Support*, 18, 18-11–18-14. www.rto.nato.int/abstracts.asp.

OECD (2018). *Is the Last Mile the Longest? Economic Gains from Gender Equality in Nordic Countries*. Paris: OECD Publishing.

Ohlsson-Wijk, S., Turunen, J., and Andersson, G. (2017). *Family Forerunners? An Overview of Family Demographic Change in Sweden*. Available at: www.suda.su.se/polopoly_fs/1.339366.1499071119!/menu/standard/file/SRRD_2017_13.pdf.

Olsson, A.-M. E. (2014a). Dialogical participatory action research in social work using delta-reflecting teams. In F. Rauch, A. Schuster, T. Stern, M. Pribila, and A. Townsend (eds), *Promoting Change through Action Research* (pp. 163–172). Rotterdam: Sense Publishers.

Olsson, A.-M. E. (2014b). The impact of dialogical participatory action research (DPAR): riding in the peloton of dialogical collaboration. In G. Simon and A. Chard (eds), *Systemic Inquiry Innovations in Reflexive Practice Research* (pp. 230–243). Farnhill: Everything is Connected.

Olsson, A.-M. E. (2017). Barn i svenska "militära familjer"—barns berättelser om hur de reder sig när förälder åker iväg som svensk soldat på utlandsmission [Children in Swedish "military families"—narratives of children about how they manage when a parent is a deployed Swedish soldier and far away in a foreign country]. In B. Nilsson and C. Eva (eds), *Barnsliga sammanhang – Forskning om barns och ungdomars hälsa, välbefinnande och delaktighet* (Vol. 2017: 5, pp. 51–64). Kristianstad: Kristianstad University.

Olsson, A.-M. E. (2018). *Internationell militär insats ur familjeperspektiv –Insatscykler med växlande responser [International Military Deployments in Perspective of Family: Deployment Cycles of Varied Responses]* (Vol. 10). Kristianstad: Kristianstad University Press. URN: urn:nbn:se:hkr:diva-18789.

Parliament/Riksdagen (2010). *Riksdagens Årsbok 2009/10*. Stockholm: Sveriges Riksdag.

Pincus, S. H., House, R., Christenson, J., and Adler, L. E. (2001). The emotional cycle of deployment: a military family perspective. *U.S. Army Medical Department Journal*, April–June, 15–23.

Reason, P. and Bradbury, H. (2006a). Introduction: inquiry and participation in search of world worthy of human aspiration. In P. Reason and H. Bradbury (eds), *Handbook of Action Research* (pp. 1–14). London: SAGE Publications.

Reason, P. and Bradbury, H. (eds) (2006b). *Handbook of Action Research*. London: SAGE Publications.

Schumm, W. R., Bell, D. B., and Resnic, G. (2001). Recent research on family factors and readiness: implications for military leaders. *Psychological Reports*, 89, 153–165.

Segal, M. W. and Harris, J. J. (1993). *What we Know about Army Families*. Alexandria, VA: US Army Research Institute for the Behavioral and Social Sciences.

Singer, A. (2014). Voices heard and unheard: a Scandinavian perspective. *Journal of Social Welfare & Familiy Law*, 36(4), 381–391.

Stanley, S. M., Rhoades, G. K., Loew, B. A., Allen, E. S., Carter, S., Osborne, L. J., and Markman, H. J. (2014). A randomized controlled trial of relationship education in the U.S. Army: 2-year outcomes. *Family Relations*, 63, 482–495.

Svenska Soldathemsförbundet (2018). PREP-kurser. Retrieved from https://soldathem.org/prep-kurser/.

Synovate and Officersförbundet (2008). *Hela familjen gör utlandstjänst. En enkätstudie av de anhörigas upplevelser av utlandtjänsten*. Stockholm. Available at www.officersforbundet.se/globalassets/pdfer/materiel--avtal/foldrar-och-rapporter/hela-familjen-gor-utlandstjanst.pdf.

Ziegert, K. A. (1987). Children's rights and the supportive function of the law: case of Sweden. *Journal Comparative Family Studies*, XVIII (2), 157–178.

18 What happens on-board stays on-board?

The political game of communication between deployed military personnel and their loved ones

Manon Andres and René Moelker

Introduction

Communication is key in family dynamics. It is crucial in maintaining healthy family relationships and also plays a powerful role in political processes within families as "the essence of politics is talk or interaction."[1] Moreover, the dynamics of communication, i.e., the way family members interact, exchange information, and listen to each other, are critical to individual and relationship well-being.

In times of family separation, such as military-induced deployments, communication is mediated by technology. Modern means of communication, such as email, text messaging, internet video and phone, and social networking sites, enable people to stay in touch quite easily, quickly, and frequently. Although depending on the situation, military personnel can communicate with their home front virtually anytime, anyplace, anywhere, often in real time. Communication allows for virtual proximity and upholds connectedness whilst being separated. It provides the opportunity to support each other and helps to manage the stress of separation, which in turn has been shown to have positive effects on family relationships (e.g., Andres, DeAngelis, and McCone, 2015; Baptist et al., 2011; Merolla, 2010; Moelker and Van der Kloet, 2003; Porter, 2014; Rossetto, 2013). However, in addition to being an important resource, the possibility of service members to speak with family members back home in real time has been defined as a mixed blessing as both benefits and drawbacks have been identified, such as high telephone bills, security risks, and maintaining family roles over the telephone (Applewhite and Segal, 1990; Ender, 1995). Furthermore, communication presupposes a dilemma: what to tell and what to withhold. Often with good intentions, such as to avoid distracting the other from work and not giving them cause to worry, people may choose to withhold information instead of being open.

Only few studies have examined communication patterns between deployed military personnel and their families at home using modern communication technologies. Aiming at enhancing our understanding of communication patterns between service personnel and their home front and the tensions associated with it, this study examined: 1) the frequency of communication, communication media, and communication strategies used by Dutch Navy personnel *and* non-deployed partners *while being separated* by deployment; 2) the conditions under which they choose a particular strategy; and 3) how their communication strategies are associated with their well-being and relationship quality. We start with reviewing the literature and a description of the study design.

Communication between service members and the home front

Communication frequency and media

When studying communication between service members and their loved ones, scholars focused on the frequency of communication, the communication media used, and the quality of communication or communication strategies. Recent research shows that, in general, the frequency of communication during deployment is fairly high, often on a daily basis (e.g., Carter et al., 2011; Cigrang et al., 2014; Ponder and Aguirre, 2012). Whereas in former times, telephone communication and "traditional" mail contact were the only or most frequently used communication media (though not used on a daily basis; e.g., Ender, 1995; Schumm, Bell, Ender, and Rice, 2004), in more recent deployments, email and text messaging have become popular means of staying in touch, in addition to phone calls (e.g., Andres and Moelker, 2010; Carter et al., 2011; Carter and Renshaw, 2016b; Cigrang et al., 2014). Studies demonstrate that access to communication technologies varies and can pose difficulties, such as disconnected connections or the stress of missed phone calls (e.g., Hinojosa, Hinojosa, and Hognas, 2012; Lapp et al., 2010; MacDermid et al., 2005; Sahlstein, Maguire, and Timmerman, 2009).

From a family stress and resilience perspective, communication between loved ones is seen as a form of relationship-focused coping, which is distinct from individual coping strategies. It is suggested to affect well-being as it buffers from stress. Moreover, Karney and Crown (2007) conceptualized the way loved ones communicate and interact with each other as part of their adaptive processes, which is assumed to contribute to positive relationship outcomes. However, empirical research findings among military personnel and their home front do not yet provide a clear and consistent understanding of how communication frequency and media are associated with well-being and relationship outcomes.

With respect to communication media, some studies demonstrated the benefits of writing letters, although used less frequently (e.g., Schumm, Bell, Ender, and Rice, 2004). Ponder and Aguirre (2012) found that letters (of all media) and email (of internet-based media) were most predictive of relationship satisfaction. However, Carter and Renshaw (2016a) did not find significant main effects of using either asynchronous (e.g., letters and email) or synchronous (e.g., video and phone calling) communication media during deployment on post-deployment relationship satisfaction.

With respect to communication frequency, some scholars found positive associations between the frequency of communication during deployment and relationship quality afterwards (e.g., Baptist et al., 2011; Ponder and Aguirre,

2012; Schumm, Bell, Ender, and Rice, 2004; Villagran, Canzona, and Ledford, 2013), whereas negative and non-significant correlations were also found (e.g., Carter and Renshaw, 2016a; Joseph and Afifi, 2010). Others emphasized that it is the *quality* rather than the *quantity* that matters (e.g., Andres and Moelker, 2010). For instance, a longitudinal study among Dutch deployed service members and their partners at home showed that, after statistically controlling for pre-deployment levels of relationship quality, active interactions during and after the deployment positively contributed to reconciliation and relationship quality afterwards; at both times, however, service members communicated less openly than partners did (Andres and Moelker, 2010).

Communication strategies

Various communication strategies have been identified in the literature. In their study among heart attack patients and their wives, Coyne and Smith (1991) introduced the constructs of active engagement and protective buffering as forms of relationship-focused coping. Whereas "active engagement is a matter of involving the partner in discussions, inquiring how the partner feels, and other constructive problem solving," they conceptualized protective buffering as "a matter of hiding concerns, denying worries, and yielding to the partner to avoid disagreements" (Coyne and Smith, 1991: 405). Suls, Green, Rose, Lounsbury, and Gordon (1996) extended Coyne and Smith's research, focusing on the protective buffering strategy, and modified the measurement instrument. Although it was introduced as a form of relationship-focused coping, and the concept suggests to buffer (shield the significant other) from stress, both studies found that greater use of protective buffering was associated with greater distress. Joseph and Afifi (2010) applied the construct in their study among military wives, who were also mothers, and whose husbands were deployed. The results showed that the more wives of deployed military personnel perceived their husbands were in dangerous situations, the more likely they were to engage in protective buffering. Moreover, protective buffering was associated with negative health symptoms, and disclosure was related to relationship satisfaction. Other scholars examined related concepts, such as topic avoidance or purposeful avoidance of disclosure. Frisby, Byrnes, Mansson, Booth-Butterfield, and Birmingham (2011) found that topic avoidance and not engaging in everyday talk frequently were associated with higher levels of stress experienced by military couples.

For a variety of reasons, such as to protect the other (from worrying or emotional distress), avoid conflict, preserve the relationship, or to avoid distractions, deployed service members and their partners at home may strategically choose to restrict communication or to avoid discussing certain topics with one's partner (Durham, 2010; Keeling, Woodhead, and Fear, 2015; MacDermid et al., 2005; Rives, 2015). Literature on disclosure and secrecy suggests that sharing information is beneficial for health and well-being; although openness is not without risks (discussed in more detail by Joseph and Afifi, 2010; see also, for instance, Campbell and Renshaw, 2012). It highlights a tension between openness/disclosure/involvement on the one hand and closeness/avoidance/protection on the other hand. This tension is particularly relevant to geographically separated couples, when communication is likely to be different from when they are geographically close (they do not see each other in person and communication is mediated by technology); and even more so during military-induced separations, given the particular tensions these couples face and for whom stress and considerations about safety are prominent.

Method

Procedure and participants

Data used in this chapter are part of a larger study, focusing on deployment experiences of Dutch Navy personnel and their partners. Personnel of all frigates and oceangoing patrol vessels of the Dutch Navy that were deployed between January 2014 and June 2015 were invited to participate in the study. Questionnaires were brought on-board before departure and distributed among the personnel during their four-month deployment. At that same time, questionnaires were sent to the home addresses of non-deployed partners who were registered as contact persons. A letter accompanied the questionnaires, explaining the purpose of the study, emphasizing confidentiality and that participation in the study is voluntary, and stressing the importance of filling out the questionnaire independently. Navy personnel returned their completed surveys anonymously in a (closed) box on-board the ship, which was handed over to the researchers immediately after the ship returned from its mission. Partners used the enclosed envelop to return their completed survey by mail.

In total, 351 questionnaires of Navy personnel and 125 questionnaires of non-deployed partners were returned, resulting in response rates of 46 percent and 57 percent, respectively. Seventy-five percent of the deployed Navy personnel were in a committed relationship (48 percent of them were married, 52 percent were not), 25 percent of the personnel were single; in this study, we used the data of those who were in a committed relationship ($N = 262$). Most deployed service members were male (91 percent) and most non-deployed partners were female (93 percent). The mean age of deployed Navy personnel was 33 years ($SD = 9.00$), varying from 19 to 53 years old. The non-deployed partners were on average 35 years old ($SD = 8.78$), varying from 19 to 54. Little more than half of the respondents (51 percent of the Navy personnel and 58 percent of the non-deployed partners) had children. A large majority of the partners at home (87 percent) had paid employment, of which 26 percent also worked or had worked within the Ministry of Defense.

Measures

In addition to items that assess demographic variables, the questionnaires contained validated scales as well as newly constructed items.

Communication frequency and media. Navy personnel and non-deployed partners were asked how frequently they communicated with their loved one(s) at home or deployed during the deployment via: telephone, text, email, Skype, Facebook, and mail. Response choices were: 1) never, 2) monthly, 3) weekly, or 4) daily. The items were assessed independently and summed to create a variable that indicates the overall frequency of communication, with higher scores indicating higher frequency of communication.

Communication strategies. The questionnaires contained items that assessed the use of two communication strategies: supportive communications and protective reticence.[2] Responses were given on a scale of 1 (strongly disagree) to 5 (strongly agree); higher scores indicate higher use of the particular communication strategy. *Supportive communication* refers to the emotional support people give each other by showing pride and interest in each other when they communicate (five items, e.g., when me and my partner on-board/at home communicate during this deployment: I show interest in his/her experiences, or: I show my partner that I am proud of him/her). Cronbach's alpha coefficients were 0.81 (Navy personnel sample) and 0.83 (non-deployed partners sample). *Protective reticence* is inspired by earlier work on protective buffering (e.g., Coyne and Smith, 1991; Schwarzer and Schulz, 2000; Suls, Green, Rose, Lounsbury, and Gordon, 1997) though we feel that the concept is better framed as protective reticence because nothing is buffered; one purposefully withholds information from the other out of protective considerations. We measured the construct through four items: when me and my partner on-board/at home communicate during this deployment: I avoid everything that could upset him/her; I keep all bad news from him/her; I share all my experiences (reversed); I try to discuss the issue when I feel sore about something (reversed). The Cronbach's alpha coefficient of the scale was 0.71 (both Navy personnel and non-deployed partners sample).

Life events. We assessed respondents' recent experiences with 13 different life stressors, such as the birth of a child, personal injury or illness, having dependent parents, and death of a relative, to examine the conditions under which one may choose a particular communication strategy. Respondents were asked to indicate if they had recently experienced any of the life stressors, using a yes (1) or no (0) response scale and how stressful the event was for them on a 1 (not at all) to 5 (very much) scale. In addition to examining the items independently, we summed scores into two separate variables: a composite of the number of life stressors experienced recently and the mean stress experienced by these events; higher scores indicated more life stressors and more life stress, respectively.

Well-being. The questionnaires included two instruments that measured well-being of the respondents. Respondents were asked to indicate how they felt at the present moment, during the deployment. First, we measured *psychological distress* through the General Health Questionnaire (Dutch edition of the GHQ-12; Goldberg, 1992; Koeter and Ormel, 1991). Responses were given on a scale ranging from 0 (not at all) to 3 (much more than usual). Higher scores indicate higher levels of distress. Cronbach's alpha coefficients were 0.79 (Navy personnel sample) and 0.86 (non-deployed partners sample). Second, we measured *affective well-being*, by six positive and six negative affect items (e.g., sad, uneasy, happy, satisfied; Warr, 1990). Responses were given on a scale ranging from 1 (never) to 6 (always). Negative items were reversed and scores were summed so that higher scores indicate the presence of more positive emotions. Cronbach's alpha coefficients were 0.89 (Navy personnel sample) and 0.93 (non-deployed partners sample).

Relationship quality. Relationship quality was assessed by five items (Norton, 1983), including: "my relationship with my partner is very stable" and "I really feel like part of the team with my partner." Responses were given on a 1 (strongly disagree) to 5 (strongly agree) scale. Higher scores indicate higher levels of relationship quality. Cronbach's alpha coefficients were 0.91 (Navy personnel sample) and 0.93 (non-deployed partners sample).

Results

Communication frequency and media

As shown in Figure 18.1, while being at sea, a large majority of Navy personnel (76 percent) communicated with their loved ones at home on a daily basis via text messages (74 percent of non-deployed partners indicated to communicate by text on a daily basis); another 18 percent of Navy personnel and 17 percent of partners communicated by text on a weekly basis, which made this the most frequently used communication medium. The second-most frequently used medium on a daily basis was Facebook; Navy personnel were more likely to use this medium to stay in contact with their homefront than vice versa. Telephone communication was most often used on a weekly basis: 59 percent of Navy personnel and 51 percent of non-deployed partners phoned once or multiple times a week with their loved one(s) deployed or at home; another 10 percent of Navy personnel and 4 percent of partners communicated by telephone on a daily basis. Roughly a third of the respondents (33 percent of Navy personnel and 31 percent of non-deployed partners) sent emails once or multiple times a week; another 13 percent of Navy personnel and 6 percent of partners communicated by email on a daily basis. Interestingly, Navy personnel were more likely to phone, send emails, and use Facebook on a daily basis than partners. Non-deployed partners were more likely to send mail on a monthly basis (74 percent; 19 percent never) than Navy personnel (56 percent monthly, 40 percent never). Skype was the least often used medium.

One-way between-groups analyses of variance (ANOVAs) revealed that Navy personnel who maintained email contact with their partners at home reported higher levels of relationship quality than those who never emailed (with a significant difference between weekly and never: $M = 4.56$ and $M = 4.25$, respectively). The calculated eta squared was 0.03, which indicated a small effect size.[3] Furthermore, partners who had daily telephone contact with

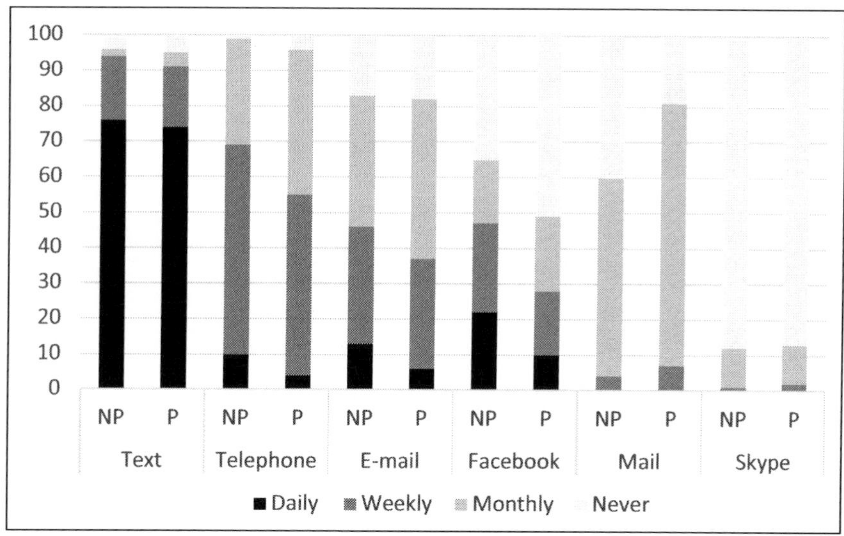

Figure 18.1 Communication frequency by medium for Navy personnel (NP) and non-deployed partners (P)

their deployed Navy partner reported higher levels of distress (measured by the GHQ-12) than those who had less frequent contact by telephone (with a significant difference between daily and weekly telephone contact: $M = 20.67$ and $M = 10.18$, respectively). The calculated eta squared was 0.17, which indicated a large effect size.

Communication strategies

Tables 18.1 and 18.2 present descriptive statistics and correlations of the study variables for Navy personnel and non-deployed partners.[4] The means demonstrate that both Navy personnel and non-deployed partners tend to be fairly supportive in their communication with their loved one at home or deployed ($M_{NP} = 4.10$, $SD = 0.50$; $M_P = 4.38$, $SD = 0.52$). A paired samples t-test of matched data showed that partners were somewhat but significantly more supportive in their communication than Navy personnel ($t\ (85) = -3.11$, $p < 0.01$).[5] The eta squared was 0.10, which indicated a moderate effect size. Protective reticence among both Navy personnel and non-deployed partners was fairly low to moderate ($M_{NP} = 2.64$, $SD = 0.71$; $M_P = 2.27$, $SD = 0.68$); Navy personnel significantly more often put protective reticence into practice than non-deployed partners did ($t\ (85) = 3.17$, $p < 0.01$). Again, the eta squared (0.11) indicated a moderate effect size.

Table 18.1 Descriptive statistics, Navy personnel (N = 262)

	Variable	Mean	SD	*Range*	*1*	*2*	*3*	*4*	*5*	*6*
1	Supportive communication	4.10	0.50	1–5						
2	Protective reticence	2.64	0.71	1–5	−0.21**					
3	Number of life events	2.97	2.42	0–13	−0.04	0.24***				
4	Life stress	0.74	0.66	0–5	−0.01	0.28***	0.94***			
5	Psychological distress	10.35	4.02	0–36	−0.05	0.20**	0.19**	0.27***		
6	Affective well-being	4.48	0.64	1–6	0.10	−0.19**	−0.15*	−0.23***	−0.70***	
7	Relationship quality	4.46	0.59	1–5	0.37***	−0.28***	−0.22**	−0.20**	−0.12	0.08

* $p < 0.05$, ** $p < 0.01$, *** $p < 0.001$.

Table 18.2 Descriptive statistics, non-deployed partners (N = 125)

	Variable	Mean	SD	*Range*	*1*	*2*	*3*	*4*	*5*	*6*
1	Supportive communication	4.38	0.52	1–5						
2	Protective reticence	2.27	0.68	1–5	−0.21*					
3	Number of life events	2.93	2.25	0–13	0.09	0.06				
4	Life stress	0.75	0.69	0–5	−0.02	0.11	0.89***			
5	Psychological distress	11.83	5.21	0–36	−0.25**	0.22*	0.26*	0.29**		
6	Affective well-being	4.37	0.73	1–6	0.27**	−0.22*	−0.19	−0.25**	−0.79***	
7	Relationship quality	4.66	0.51	1–5	0.56***	−0.10	−0.13	−0.17	−0.22*	0.27**

* $p < 0.05$, ** $p < 0.01$, *** $p < 0.001$.

Conditions for choosing communication strategies

Trying to gain more insight into the conditions under which deployed Navy personnel and non-deployed partners choose a particular communication strategy, and in particular when they choose to withhold information from the other, we performed several analyses.

As described earlier, Navy personnel significantly more often engaged in protective reticence than non-deployed partners did. Navy personnel who had a female partner at home (compared with those with a male partner; $t\ (81) = -2.50$, $p < 0.05$, eta squared = 0.07), who had a partner that never worked within the Ministry of Defense (compared with those who had a partner with work experience within the MoD; $t\ (81) = 2.15$, $p < 0.05$, eta squared = 0.05), and those with children (compared with those who did not have children; $t\ (251) = -2.26$, $p < 0.05$, eta squared = 0.02) were more likely to be more protective in their communication with their home front. Furthermore, Navy personnel who recently experienced more life events and who experienced more stress from these events were more likely to engage in protective reticence ($r = 0.24$, $p < 0.001$ and $r = 0.28$, $p < 0.001$, respectively). More specifically, assessing the 13 life stressors individually, Navy personnel who recently experienced injury or illness of a relative ($t\ (248) = -2.79$, $p < 0.01$, eta squared = 0.03), decease of a relative ($t = -2.62\ (250)$, $p < 0.01$, eta squared = 0.03), who experienced problems in the relation with their partner or children ($t\ (243) = -2.32$, $p < 0.05$, eta squared = 0.02 and $t\ (234) = -2.45$, $p < 0.05$, eta squared = 0.02, respectively), who had dependent parents ($t\ (249) = -4.38$, $p < 0.001$, eta squared = 0.07), and/or those who experienced financial difficulties ($t\ (250) = -2.87$, $p < 0.01$, eta squared = 0.03) were more likely to engage in protective reticence when communicating with their home front than those who did not experience these stressors. Interestingly, among non-deployed partners, engaging in protective reticence or being supportive in their communications with deployed Navy personnel to higher or lesser degrees was not associated with the above described conditions.

Communication, well-being, and relationship quality

As shown in Tables 18.1 and 18.2, among both Navy personnel and non-deployed partners, protective reticence was associated with their well-being (i.e., psychological distress and affective well-being). That is, higher levels of protective reticence were associated with higher levels of psychological distress ($r = 0.20$, $p < 0.01$ and $r = 0.22$, $p < 0.05$) and lower levels of affective well-being ($r = -0.19$, $p < 0.01$ and $r = -0.22$, $p < 0.05$). Moreover, only among Navy personnel, higher levels of protective reticence were associated with lower levels of relationship quality ($r = -0.28$, $p < 0.001$).

Among both Navy personnel and non-deployed partners, higher levels of supportive communication were associated with higher levels of relationship quality ($r = 0.37$, $p < 0.001$ and $r = 0.56$, $p < 0.001$). Only among non-deployed partners, engaging in supportive communication was associated with their well-being.

That is, higher levels of supportive communication were associated with lower levels of psychological distress ($r = -0.25, p < 0.01$) and higher levels of affective well-being ($r = 0.27, p < 0.01$).

Hierarchical regression analyses revealed that, when taking the life events Navy personnel and non-deployed partners recently experienced into account, protective reticence negatively impacted their well-being. Moreover, it negatively affects the relationship quality reported by Navy personnel (Table 18.3). The variance explained is fairly low though (ranging between 5 and 11 percent). Among Navy personnel, Sobel tests provided support for statistical significant mediation effects, which suggests that deployed Navy personnel who recently experienced more life stressors are more likely to engage in protective reticence, which in turn negatively impacts their well-being and relationship quality.

Similar analyses were performed with supportive communication. Among Navy personnel, while taking life stressors into account, higher levels of supportive communication positively predicted relationship quality ($\beta = 0.36$, $p < 0.001$, $R^2 = 0.18$); it did not affect their well-being. Among non-deployed partners, supportive communication also affects their relationship quality, even more strongly ($\beta = 0.58, p < 0.001, R^2 = 0.35$); it also positively affects their

Table 18.3 Impact protective reticence on well-being and relationship quality

Navy Personnel	Affective well-being			Psychological distress			Relationship quality		
Step predictor	B	SE B	*β*	B	SE B	*β*	B	SE B	*β*
1 Constant	4.60	0.07		9.42	0.42		4.62	0.06	
Life stressors	–0.04	0.02	–0.15*	0.31	0.11	0.19**	–0.05	0.02	–0.22**
2 Constant	4.95	0.16		7.19	1.03		5.09	0.15	
Life stressors	–0.03	0.02	–0.11	0.25	0.11	0.15*	–0.04	0.02	–0.16*
Protective reticence	–0.15	0.06	–0.16*	0.92	0.39	0.16*	–0.20	0.06	–0.24***
df			222			215			221
Total R^2			0.05			0.06			0.10
Partners	Affective well-being			Psychological distress			Relationship quality		
Step predictor	B	SE B	*β*	B	SE B	*β*	B	SE B	*β*
1 Constant	4.55	0.12		10.10	0.87				
Life stressors	–0.06	0.03	–0.19	0.59	0.24	0.26*			n/s
2 Constant	5.04	0.27		6.61	1.90				
Life stressors	–0.06	0.03	–0.18	0.56	0.23	0.24*			n/s
Protective reticence	–0.22	0.11	–0.21*	1.58	0.77	0.21*			n/s
df			91			88			
Total R^2			0.08			0.11			

* $p < 0.05$, ** $p < 0.01$, *** $p < 0.001$.

well-being (affective well-being: $\beta = 0.29$, $p < 0.01$, $R^2 = 0.12$; psychological distress: $\beta = -0.27$, $p < 0.01$, $R^2 = 0.14$).

Given the cross-sectional nature of the data, however, we cannot draw causal conclusions; therefore, we also examined the alternatives. Supportive communication could be more prevalent among those in higher functioning relationships and those experiencing less distress, while engaging in protective reticence could be more prevalent among those experiencing lower well-being and those in lower functioning relationships; thus, well-being and relationship quality could be conditions under which one engages in a particular communication strategy. To examine this, we performed additional regression analyses, with the communication strategies as dependent variables and life stressors, well-being, and relationship quality as predictors. While taking life stressors (and well-being) into account, higher levels of relationship quality were associated with higher levels of supportive communication, both among deployed Navy personnel ($\beta = 0.38$, $p < 0.001$, $R^2 = 0.15$) and non-deployed partners ($\beta = 0.54$, $p < 0.001$, $R^2 = 0.37$). Furthermore, while taking life stressors (and well-being) into account, lower levels of relationship quality reported by Navy personnel were associated with higher levels of protective reticence ($\beta = -0.22$, $p < 0.01$, $R^2 = 0.13$); no significant effects were shown among non-deployed partners.

Conclusion and discussion

This study examined communication patterns between Navy personnel *and* non-deployed partners *while being separated by deployment*, and the tensions associated with it. The results showed that Navy personnel on-board a ship stayed in touch with their home front on a regular basis, by using both asynchronous and synchronous communication media (Carter and Renshaw, 2016a). Text messages were the most frequently used communication medium. Furthermore, on a daily basis, Navy personnel were more likely to phone, send emails, and use Facebook than partners; whereas on a monthly basis, non-deployed partners were more likely to send traditional mail. Among Navy personnel, email contact was associated with higher levels of relationship quality; a finding that supports previous research that demonstrates the benefits of writing (e.g., Ponder and Aguirre, 2012; Schumm, Bell, Ender, and Rice, 2004). Among non-deployed partners, more frequent telephone contact (i.e., on a daily basis) was associated with higher levels of distress.

Both Navy personnel and non-deployed partners tend to be fairly supportive in their communication with their loved one at home or deployed; partners were somewhat but statistically significantly more supportive in their communication than Navy personnel. Navy personnel significantly more often put protective reticence into practice than non-deployed partners did. Those who had a female partner at home, with no work experience within the MoD, and those with children, were more likely to withhold information out of protective considerations. The gender (being male or female) and professional perspective (being service member or not, with service members not always being able or allowed to share everything) was also demonstrated in earlier research (e.g., Andres and Moelker, 2010).

Furthermore, Navy personnel who recently experienced more life events and more stress from these events were more likely to apply the strategy of protective reticence. In particular, those who recently experienced injury or illness of a relative, death of a relative, who experienced problems in the relation with their partner or children, who had dependent parents, and/or those who experienced financial difficulties were more likely to withhold information from their loved ones at home. The degree of protective reticence may depend on what (one perceives) the other can manage. Vulnerability may be something personal, but may also depend on the pile-up of stressors. Our findings regarding the experience of life events suggest that service members make strategic considerations as to what to tell and withhold from their loved ones at home, plausibly with good intentions, such as not to burden their home front (even more). Among non-deployed partners, engaging in protective reticence (or being supportive in their communications with deployed Navy personnel to higher or lesser degrees) was not associated with the above described conditions.

The findings of this study suggest that supportive communication is a healthy communication strategy (in particular for non-deployed partners), whereas protective reticence is not. That is, supportive communication is positively associated with well-being (among non-deployed partners) and relationship quality (among both Navy personnel and non-deployed partners), whereas protective reticence is negatively associated with well-being (among both) and relationship quality (among Navy personnel). These findings confirm earlier research findings in different contexts (e.g., Coyne and Smith, 1991; Joseph and Afifi, 2010; Suls, Green, Rose, Lounsbury, and Gordon, 1997). Researchers agree on the importance and benefits of supportive communications among romantic partners in maintaining well-being and relationship quality, especially in times of stress and separation. The findings of our study suggest that supportive communication is particularly beneficial for the perceived well-being and relationship quality of partners at the home front, whereas protective reticence seems to have more disastrous implications for deployed service members. Having said that, this does not suggest that one should relieve their feelings and share difficulties with their beloved unlimitedly. Certain issues are hard to solve at a distance, other things may be hard to understand, and burdening others with these matters may adversely affect their well-being. Previous research suggests that openness and sharing information is not without risks (discussed by Joseph and Afifi, 2010; see also Campbell and Renshaw, 2012). It highlights the tension between openness/disclosure/involvement on the one hand and closeness/avoidance/protection on the other hand. It points to the dilemma and struggle every couple faces and it forms an additional challenge to families or couples experiencing (military-induced) separation: what to tell and what to withhold?

Given the cross-sectional nature of our data, we also examined whether well-being and relationship quality could serve as a condition under which one engages in a particular communication strategy. The findings demonstrate that supportive communication was more prevalent among those in higher functioning relationships, while engaging in protective reticence was more prevalent among those in lower functioning relationships.

We examined communication patterns *during* deployment, but what is the role of technology in enhancing or restricting the quality of interactions? Previous research showed that partners of service members who returned home from deployment were disappointed that the intense communication they had during the separation, by writing emails and letters, immediately ended when their military partner returned home. Physical closeness diminishes the desire and necessity to write elaborate and personal letters to each other. Moreover, after reunion, different factors may hinder both service members and their loved ones from sharing their experiences (Andres and Rietveld, 2012). More longitudinal, but also more in-depth research is needed to gain more insight in these political processes of communication within (military) families.

Notes

1 www.aalep.eu/what-political-communication.
2 Factor analysis confirmed the existence of two separate constructs.
3 According to Cohen's (1988) guidelines, 0.01 is considered a small effect, 0.06 a medium effect, and 0.14 a large effect.
4 We assessed scatterplots in order to detect possible curvilinear relationships between the variables, which we did not find.
5 Data of 86 couples could be matched.

References

Andres, M. D., DeAngelis, K., and McCone, D. (2015). Reintegration, reconciliation and relationship quality. In R. Moelker, M. Andres, G. Bowen, and P. Manigart (eds), *Military Families and War in the 21st Century. Comparative Perspectives* (pp. 145–160). New York: Routledge.

Andres, M. D. and Moelker, R. (2010) Sweethearts or strangers? Couples' reconciliation following military deployment. In M. Andres, *Behind Family Lines. Family Members' Adaptations to Military-Induced Separations* (Doctoral dissertation, pp. 147–176). Breda, the Netherlands: Broese & Peereboom.

Andres, M. and Rietveld, N. (2012). It's not over till it's over: sharing memories at the home front. In J. van der Meulen, A. Vogelaar, R. Beeres, and J. Soeters (eds), *Mission Uruzgan: Collaborating in Multiple Coalitions for Afghanistan* (pp. 295–307). Amsterdam: Pallas.

Baptist, J. A., Amanor-Boadu, Y., Garrett, K., Nelson Goff, B. S., Collum, J., Gamble, P., Gurss, H., Sanders-Hahs, E., Strader, L., and Wick, S. (2011). Military marriages: the aftermath of Operation Iraqi Freedom (OIF) and Operation Enduring Freedom (OEF) deployments. *Contemporary Family Therapy*, 33(3), 199–214.

Bodenmann, G., Pihet, S., and Kayser, K. (2006). The relationship between dyadic coping and marital quality: a 2-year longitudinal study. *Journal of Family Psychology*, 20(3), 485–493.

Broadbent, D. E., Cooper P. F., FitzGerald P., and Parkes K. R. (1982). The cognitive failures questionnaire (CFQ) and its correlates. *British Journal of Clinical Psychology*, 21, 1–16.

Campbell, S. B. and Renshaw, K. D. (2012). Distress in spouses of Vietnam veterans: associations with communication about deployment experiences. *Journal of Family Psychology*, 26, 18–25.

Carter, S. P., Loew, B., Allen, A., Stanley, S. Rhoades, G., and Markman, H. (2011). Relationships between soldiers' PTSD symptoms and spousal communication during deployment. *Journal of Traumatic Stress*, 24, 352–355.

Carter, S. P. and Renshaw, K. D. (2016a). Communication via different media during military deployments and postdeployment relationship satisfaction. *Military Behavioral Health*, 4(3), 260–268.

Carter, S. P. and Renshaw, K. D. (2016b). Spousal communication during military deployments: a review. *Journal of Family Issues*, 37(16), 2309–2332.

Cigrang, J. A., Wayne Talcott, G., Tatum, J., Baker, M., Cassidy, D., Sonnek, S., Snyder, D. K., Balderrama-Durbin, C., Heyman, R., and Slep, A. (2014). Intimate partner communication from the war zone: a prospective study of relationship functioning, communication frequency, and combat effectiveness. *Journal of Marital and Family Therapy*, 40(3), 332–343.

Coyne, J. C. and Smith, D. A. (1991). Couples coping with a myocardinal infarction: a contextual perspective on wives' distress. *Journal of Personality and Social Psychology*, 61, 404–412.

Durham, S. W. (2010). In their own words: staying connected in a combat environment. *Military Medicine*, 175, 554–559.

Ender, M. G. (1995). G.I. phone home: the use of telecommunications by the soldiers of Operation Just Cause. *Armed Forces & Society*, 21, 435–454.

Frisby, B. N., Byrnes, K., Mansson, D. H., Booth-Butterfield, M., and Birmingham, M. K. (2011). Topic avoidance, everyday talk, and stress in romantic military and non-military couples. *Communication Studies*, 62(3), 241–257.

Goldberg, D. (1992). *General Health Questionnaire (GHQ-12)*. Windsor: NFER-Nelson

Hinojosa, R., Hinojosa, M. S., and Hognas, R. S. (2012). Problems with veteran-family communication during Operation Enduring Freedom/Operation Iraqi Freedom military deployment. *Military Medicine*, 177, 191–197.

Houston, J. B., Pfefferbaum, B., Sherman, M. D., Melson, A. G., and Brand, M. W. (2013). Family communication across the military deployment experience: child and spouse report of communication frequency and quality and associated emotions, behaviors, and reactions. *Journal of Loss and Trauma*, 18, 103–119.

Joseph, A. L. and Afifi, T. D. (2010). Military wives' stressful disclosure to their deployed husbands: the role of protective buffering. *Journal of Applied Communication Research*, 38, 412–434.

Karney, B. R. and Crown, J. S. (2007). *Families Under Stress: An Assessment of Data, Theory, and Research on Marriage and Divorce in the Military*. Santa Monica, CA: Rand Corporation, National Defense Research Institute.

Keeling, M., Woodhead, C., and Fear, N. (2015). Interpretative phenomenological analysis of soldier's experiences of being married and serving in the British Army. *Marriage & Family Review*, 52(6), 511–534.

Kim, I., Kawamura, A., Jerney-Davis, M. Kim, R., Raphael, D., and Lau, J. (2005). *Relational Maintenance during Deployment: Communication between Spouses*. Paper presented at the International Communication Association Conference, New York.

Koeter, M. and Ormel, J. (1991). *General Health Questionnaire. Nederlandse bewerking – Handleiding*. Lisse, the Netherlands: Swets & Zeitlinger.

Lapp, C. A., Taft, L. B., Tollefson, T., Hoepner, A., Moore, K., and Divyak, K. (2010). Stress and coping on the home front: guard and reserve spouses searching for a new normal. *Journal of Family Nursing*, 16, 45–67.

MacDermid, S., Schwarz, R., Faber, A., Adkins, J., Mishkind, M., and Weiss, H. (2005). Military fathers on the front lines. In W. Marsiglio, K. Roy, and G. L. Fox (eds), *Situated Fathering: A Focus on Physical and Social Spaces* (pp. 209–239). Lanham, MD: Rowman & Littlefield.

Maguire, K. C., Heinemann-LaFave, D., and Sahlstein, E. (2013). "To be so connected, yet not at all": relational presence, absence, and maintenance in the context of a wartime deployment. *Western Journal of Communication*, 77, 249–271.

Merolla, A. J. (2010). Relational maintenance during military deployment: perspectives of wives of deployed US soldiers. *Journal of Applied Communication Research*, 38(1), 4–26.

Moelker, R. and Van der Kloet, I. E. (2003). Military families and the armed forces: a two-sided affair? In G. Caforio (ed.), *Handbook of the Sociology of the Military* (pp. 201–223). New York: Kluwer

Norton, R. (1983). Measuring marital quality: a critical look at the dependent variable. *Journal of Marriage and the Family*, 45, 141–151.

Ponder, W. N. and Aguirre, R. T. (2012). Internet-based spousal communication during deployment: does it increase post-deployment marital satisfaction? *Advances in Social Work*, 13, 216–228.

Porter, T. (2014). *Relational Maintenance: Experiences of Left Behind Civilian Male Spouses during the Deployment of their Military Wives* (doctoral dissertation). Retrieved from http://search.proquest.com/docview/1549542644.

Rives, A. P. (2015). *To Tell or not To Tell: A Study of Naval Aviator Wives' Disclosure Practices during Deployment and Perceived Influence on Officer Retention* (doctoral dissertation). Retrieved from http://search.proquest.com/docview/1675962319.

Rossetto, K. R. (2013). Relational coping during deployment: managing communication and connection in relationships. *Personal Relationships*, 20, 568–586.

Sahlstein, E., Maguire, K. C., and Timmerman, L. (2009). Contradictions and praxis contextualized by wartime deployment: wives' perspectives revealed through relational dialectics. *Communincation Monographs*, 76, 421–442.

Schumm, W. R., Bell, D. B., Ender, M. G., and Rice, R. E. (2004). Expectations, use, and evaluation of communication media among deployed peacekeepers. *Armed Forces & Society*, 30, 649–662.

Schwarzer, R. and Schulz, U. (2000). *Berlin Social Support Scales (BSSS)*. Retrieved from: www.coping.de.

Suls, J., Green, P., Rose, G., Lounsbury, P., and Gordon, E. (1997). Hiding worries from one's spouse: associations between coping via protective buffering and distress in male post-myocardial infarction patients and their wives. *Journal of Behavioral Medicine*, 20(4), 333–349.

Villagran, M., Canzona, M. R., and Ledford, C. J. (2013). The milspouse battle rhythm: communicating resilience throughout the deployment cycle. *Health Communication*, 28, 778–788.

Warr, P. (1990). The measurement of well-being and other aspects of mental health. *Journal of Occupational Psychology*, 63, 193–210.

Wilson, S. R., Chernichky, S. M., Wilkum, K., and Owlett, J. S. (2014). Do family communication patterns buffer children from difficulties associated with a parent's military deployment? Examining deployed and at-home parents' perspectives. *Journal of Family Communication*, 14(1), 32–52.

Wong, L. and Gerras, S. (2010). *The Effects of Multiple Deployments on Army Adolescents*. Carlisle, PA: Strategic Studies Institute, United States Army War College.

19 Single parents in the Canadian Armed Forces

The impact of military life on psychological distress

Alla Skomorovsky, Amanda Bullock, and Cynthia Wan

Introduction

Little is known about the impact of work and family stressors on the psychological functioning of single-parent Canadian Armed Forces (CAF) families. It is unclear which stressors play a unique role in single parents' psychological distress and whether the impact of these stressors is directly or indirectly related to work–family conflict. Given that the prevalence of single-parent CAF families continues to rise in tandem with the rate in the Canadian population (Statistics Canada, 2012; Tanner et al., 2008), it is necessary to understand the path between stressors and well-being among single-parent CAF members. Accordingly, this study examined the impact of military life stressors and parental strain on psychological distress among single CAF parents and the mediating role of work–family conflict in this path.

The challenges of single-parenthood may be exacerbated in the military because military personnel are more prone to occupational stress resulting from temporary (e.g., deployment) and chronic (e.g., long and unusual hours) hardships (Skomorovsky and Bullock, 2015; Skomorovsky and Hujaleh, 2016; Skomorovsky, Norris, Bullock, and Smith Evans, 2016). These military stressors are consistently linked to members' elevated rates of mental health impairment, risk of injury, and poor physical health (Bedno et al., 2014; Hourant, Williams, and Kress, 2006). The effects of occupational stress can also adversely affect the military's effectiveness as occupational stress contributes to increased absenteeism, low productivity, lack of organizational commitment, and interpersonal problems (see Hourant, Williams, and Kress, 2006).

Recent research on single CAF parents found high levels of financial strain, work overload, and concern for their children and high rates of work–family conflict (Skomorovsky and Bullock, 2015; Skomorovsky and Hujaleh, 2016). Compared with their civilian counterparts, single military parents may be more susceptible to experience role conflict because they face the combined stressors of single-parenthood and the military lifestyle (Booth and Lederer, 2012). This compounding of stressors may make single military parents more vulnerable to psychological health problems (e.g., Blanchard, 2012). Indeed, evidence indicates the strong impact of work–family conflict on health, including greater psychological strain and somatic complaints, poorer well-being, and reduced life satisfaction (e.g., Amstad, Meier, Fasel, Elfering, and Semmer, 2011). Recent focus group research with single CAF parents has revealed they experience a high degree of psychological distress, work–family conflict, and parental strain (see Skomorovsky and Bullock, 2016).

In addition to examining work–family conflict as an outcome variable or a unique predictor of an outcome variable, mainly the health and well-being of the employee (e.g., Amstad, Meier, Fasel, Elfering, and Semmer, 2011; Frone, Russell, and Cooper, 1997), there has been growing interest in examining work–family conflict as a mediator in the relation between work-related stressors and various health outcomes. Although various pathways and relations have been examined, studies have consistently demonstrated that work–family conflict partially mediated the relation between occupational stressors and work-, family-, and health-related outcomes—specifically, satisfaction with work and family and perceived levels of stress (e.g., Holliday, Wayne, Casper, Matthews, and Allen, 2013). Notwithstanding this research, comparatively few studies have examined the mediating effects of work–family conflict in a military context, including single-parent military families. Given the importance of work–family conflict in these pathways and the relatively higher influence of work-related stressors among military personnel, we suspected that work–family conflict would play a crucial role in single CAF parents' reported levels of psychological distress and parental strain.

Method

Procedure and participants

Regular Force male and female CAF members who had children 19 years of age and younger and were single, divorced, separated, or widowed were selected to participate in this study. Single CAF parents were sent emails containing a URL link for English and French versions of the survey. Of the 3211 single CAF parents who received a link to the survey, 1260 responded. The final sample consisted of 552 single parents who completed at least 65 percent of the survey, yielding an adjusted response rate of 17.2 percent. Out of those who reported their demographic characteristics, the distribution of the sample was relatively even between men (56.7 percent; $n = 289$) and women (43.3 percent; $n = 221$), with an average age of 40.14 years ($SD = 6.85$). By rank, 401 were non-commissioned members (80.9 percent) and 49 were officers (19.1 percent). Single CAF parents were mainly in the Canadian Army (51.8 percent; $n = 266$) or the Royal Canadian Air Force (34.4 percent; $n = 177$). Out of those who reported the nature of their single status, the majority of the sample were divorced ($n = 231$; 45.7 percent), followed by 29.2 percent who were separated ($n = 148$), 21.9 percent who were single and never married ($n = 111$), and 3.2 percent who were widowed ($n = 16$). The majority of single CAF parents self-identified as being the primary caregiver

(75.3 percent; $n = 382$) and mainly had one (48.8 percent; $n = 251$) or two (40.3 percent; $n = 207$) dependent children. Finally, 100 single CAF parents (19.5 percent) reported having children with special needs.

Measures

Occupational stressors. Military-related stressors were measured with three subscales from the Canadian Forces Occupational Stress Questionnaire (CF-OSQ; Kelloway and Barling, 1994) and an additional subscale created for the survey. Each of the subscales from the CF-OSQ contained four items and demonstrated excellent internal consistency (Kelloway and Barling, 1994). The subscales were quantitative load, which assessed the number of tasks to be carried out in a given timeframe ($\alpha = 0.87$); work schedule, which assessed lack of notice for overtime and the amount of overtime and irregular hours ($\alpha = 0.87$); and posting stress, which assessed the amount of stress related to postings ($\alpha = 0.79$). One item on the postings subscale was rephrased to tailor it to the single-parent sample. The original item "Every time I am posted my spouse has to find a new job" was replaced with "Postings are a major stressor to me." In addition, the terms *spouse* and *wife* were replaced with *my family* throughout the subscale. The deployment stress subscale, which measures the amount of stress related to deployment, was created for the present survey. It was constructed to parallel the four items on the postings subscale (e.g., "Deployments are a major stress to me"; $\alpha = 0.75$). Two additional items were added to deployment subscale, "I have sufficient support from the CAF while I am deployed" and "It would be difficult for my child(ren) to cope if I were deployed." Participants rated their agreement with items on the five subscales on a five-point Likert-type scale, ranging from 0 (*strongly disagree*) to 4 (*strongly agree*).

Parental challenges. The Parental Strain Scale (Baruch and Barnett, 1986) was used to measure the extent to which stressors, such as financial strain, heavy demands and responsibilities, and children's academic performance were challenging for single parents (e.g., "Is financial strain a concern for you?" and "Are heavy demands and responsibilities a concern for you?" The scale contained 14 items rated on a five-point scale ranging from 1 (*not at all*) to 5 (*extremely*; $\alpha = 0.85$).

Work–family conflict. Twelve items were adapted from the Work–Parent Inter-Role Conflict Scale (Day and Chamberlain, 2006) to assess work–family conflict. Participants were asked to rate the extent to which their responsibilities as service members and as parents conflicted (e.g., "It is hard to balance my roles as a service member and as a parent" and "My work and parental responsibilities often conflict") on a five-point scale ranging from 1 (*strongly disagree*) to 5 (*strongly agree*). Items were averaged to compute the total score for the scale ($\alpha = 0.92$).

Psychological distress. Psychological distress was measured using the Kessler Psychological Distress scale (Kessler et al., 2002). This ten-item scale measures the frequency respondents experienced anxiety and depressive symptoms—ranging from 1 (*none of the time*) to 5 (*all of the time*)—in the four weeks prior to completing the survey (e.g., "Did you feel tired-out for no good reason?", "Did you feel nervous?", "Did you feel so sad that nothing could cheer you up?"). Responses were averaged to calculate the total score for the scale. This scale was found to have high internal consistency ($\alpha = 0.93$).

Results

Descriptive results

Descriptive information presented in Table 19.1 indicates that, overall, single CAF parents had relatively low levels of psychological distress. The levels of work–family conflict were not found to be high, with the mean slightly higher than the average. Of the parental and occupational stressors, the rates of posting and deployment stress were highest.

Family group comparisons

To examine whether the effects of the variables of interest (occupational stressors, parental strain, work–family conflict, and psychological distress) differed between various family structures and related factors, a series of one-way Multivariate Analyses of Variance (MANOVAs) were conducted. In the first step, separate one-way MANOVAs were conducted for each of the following family factors: parental sex, relationship status, number of children, primary caregiver status (i.e., whether the study participant is the primary caregiver), and the presence of a child with special needs. The preliminary one-way MANOVAs indicated that the variables of interest only differed as a function of parental sex, $F\,(7{,}479) = 8.84$, Wilks's $\Lambda = 0.89$, $p < 0.001$; primary caregiver status, $F\,(7{,}477) = 9.32$, Wilks's

Table 19.1 Descriptive information and correlation matrix (*N*s range from 512 to 518)

	M (SD)	*Range*	*1*	*2*	*3*	*4*	*5*	*6*
Psychological distress	2.13 (0.84)	1–5	–					
Work–family conflict	3.23 (0.76)	1–5	0.44***	–				
Parental strain	2.80 (0.84)	1–5	0.33***	0.40***	–			
Deployment stress	3.44 (0.82)	1–5	0.23***	0.32**	0.21***	–		
Posting stress	3.82 (1.14)	1–5	0.18***	0.20**	0.16***	0.33***	–	
Work scheduling	2.80 (1.05)	1–5	0.19***	0.44**	0.22***	0.03	0.12**	–
Quantitative load	3.20 (0.97)	1–5	0.19***	0.44**	0.25***	0.18**	0.17***	0.58***

Notes. $*p < 0.05$, $**p < 0.01$, $***p < 0.001$. M = mean; SD = standard deviation.

$\Lambda = 0.88$, $p < 0.001$; and presence of a child with special needs, $F(7{,}481) = 4.20$, Wilks's $\Lambda = 0.94$, $p < 0.001$. On average, male single parents reported experiencing significantly lower deployment stress than female single parents ($M = 3.34$ vs. 3.58; $F(1{,}485) = 10.28$, $p = 0.001$), but male single parents reported significantly higher work schedule stress ($M = 2.99$ vs. 2.56; $F(1{,}485) = 20.84$, $p < 0.001$) and posting stress ($M = 3.98$ vs. 3.63; $F(1{,}485) = 11.48$, $p = 0.001$) than female single parents. Furthermore, primary caregivers also experienced significantly higher deployment stress ($M = 3.59$ vs. 3.00, $F(1{,}483) = 51.32$, $p < 0.001$) and work–family conflict ($M = 3.28$ vs. 3.10, $F(1{,}483) = 5.13$, $p = 0.024$) than non-primary caregivers (no group differences were found among the other variables of interest (*ps* = 0.080 to 0.897)). Finally, the one-way MANOVA results revealed that single parents with a child with special needs typically reported experiencing higher deployment stress ($M = 3.60$ vs. 3.40, $F(1{,}487) = 4.28$, $p = 0.039$) and parental strain ($M = 42.72$ vs. 38.20, $F(1{,}487) = 12.55$, $p < 0.001$), but lower quantitative load ($M = 2.99$ vs. 3.25, $F(1{,}487) = 5.52$, $p = 0.019$) than single parents without a child with special needs (no significant group differences were detected for the other occupational stressors (*ps* = 0.179 to 0.613).

In the second step, a 2 × 2 × 2 MANOVA was computed to examine whether there was an interaction between parental sex, primary caregiver status, and the presence of a child with special needs, and whether the effects of the variable of interest differed after taking the three factors into account (Table 19.2). When taking all this into account, we did not find significant main effects of parental sex ($p = 0.192$) or the presence of a child with special needs ($p = 0.144$). However,

Table 19.2 Summary of 2 × 2 × 2 MANOVA omnibus results: effects of occupational stressors, parental strain, work–family conflict, and psychological distress as a function of parental sex, primary caregiver status, and presence of a child with special needs

	F	p	*Wilks's Λ*
Main effects			
A) Parental sex	1.43	0.192	0.98
B) Primary caregiver status	2.77	**0.008**	0.96
C) Presence of a child with special needs	1.56	0.144	0.98
Interactions			
A × B	1.17	0.103	0.97
A × C	0.39	0.909	0.99
B × C	0.51	0.829	0.99
A × B × C	0.99	0.714	0.65
Between subject effects: primary caregiver status			
Psychological distress	0.004	0.948	
Work–family conflict	2.64	0.105	
Deployment stress	7.98	**0.005**	
Posting	2.37	0.124	
Work-scheduling	0.15	0.702	
Quantitative load	2.91	0.089	

Note. *Univariate ANOVA results reported when applicable*

we did find a significant main effect of primary caregiver status, F (7,459) = 2.77, Wilks's Λ = 0.96, p = 0.008. Participants identified as primary caregivers experienced significantly higher deployment stress than participants who were not primary caregivers, F (1,465) = 7.98, p = 0.005 (M = 3.59, SD = 0.77 vs. M = 2.98, SD = 0.82, respectively). No significant two- or three-way interactions between the factors were found.

The role of stressors and work–family conflict in psychological distress among single CAF parents

A multiple regression analysis examined the roles of occupational stressors, parental strain, and work–family conflict in psychological distress of single CAF parents. The stressors experienced by single parents significantly predicted 23 percent of the variance of psychological distress, $R^2 = 0.227$, F (6, 502) = 24.547, $p < 0.001$. Although all types of these stressors were related to greater psychological distress, only parental strain and work–family conflict were each uniquely predictive of psychological distress, over and above the other stressors (Table 19.3).

Mediation analyses

We tested the mediating role of work–family conflict in the path between stressors (i.e., occupational stressors and parental strain) and psychological distress using Hayes' (2013) PROCESS macro for mediational analyses in SPSS version 23. This macro estimates path coefficients for mediator models and generates bootstrap confidence intervals for the total, indirect, and direct effects of an independent variable (X) on a dependent variable (Y) through a proposed mediator variable (M), adjusting for covariates (C), if necessary. Using this approach, we conducted five separate analyses to assess the indirect effect of the deployment stress (X), posting stress (X), work scheduling (X), quantitative load (X), and parental strain (X) on psychological distress (Y_1) through work–family conflict (M), each time controlling for the other four variables (C); see Table 19.4 for a summary of the results.

Table 19.3 Multiple regression analyses of the role of stressors on distress among single CAF parents

	R²	*Pearson* r	*β*
Stressors Occupational stress	0.227***		
Deployment stress		0.225***	0.059
Posting stress		0.179***	0.068
Work scheduling		0.190***	0.003
Work load		0.194***	−0.022
Parental strain		0.332***	0.173***
Work–family conflict		0.436***	0.336***

Notes. *$p < 0.05$, ***$p < 0.001$. Pearson r correlations are slightly different from the ones reported in Table 18.1 due to the differences in the sample sizes in these statistical analyses.

Table 19.4 Mediating role of work–family conflict in the path between parental strain and work stressors and psychological distress: results of bootstrap analysis

	Coefficient	SE	t	p
Parental strain				
IV to work–family conflict	0.01	0.00	6.80	< 0.001
Direct effect of work–family conflict on DV	0.35	0.05	6.61	< 0.001
Total effect of parental strain on DV	0.02	0.00	5.89	< 0.001
Direct effect of parental strain on DV	0.01	0.00	3.91	< 0.001
Partial effect of control variables				
Workload	–0.01	0.04	–0.34	ns
Work schedule	0.00	0.04	0.07	ns
Posting stress	0.05	0.03	1.57	ns
Deployment stress	0.05	0.05	1.16	ns
	Bootstrapping 95-percent CI			
	Lower	**Upper**		
Work–family conflict	0.00	0.01		
Workload				
IV to work–family conflict	0.14	0.04	3.94	< 0.001
Direct effect of work–family conflict on DV	0.35	0.05	6.62	< 0.001
Total effect of work load on DV	0.04	0.05	0.80	ns
Direct effect of work load on DV	–0.01	0.04	–0.34	ns
Partial effect of control variables				
Parental strain	0.01	0.00	3.91	< 0.001
Work schedule	0.00	0.04	0.07	ns
Posting stress	0.05	0.03	1.59	ns
Deployment stress	0.05	0.05	1.16	ns
	Bootstrapping 95-percent CI			
	Lower	**Upper**		
Work–family conflict	0.02	0.09		
Work schedule				
IV to work–family conflict	0.20	0.03	6.19	< 0.001
Direct effect of work–family conflict on DV	0.35	0.05	6.62	< 0.001
Total effect of work schedule on DV	0.08	0.04	1.85	ns
Direct effect of work schedule on DV	0.00	0.04	0.07	ns
Partial effect of control variables				
Parental strain	0.01	0.00	3.91	< 0.001
Workload	–0.01	0.04	–0.34	ns
Posting stress				
Deployment stress				
	Bootstrapping 95-percent CI			
	Lower	**Upper**		
Work–family conflict	0.04	0.11		

(continued)

Table 19.4 (continued)

	Coefficient	SE	t	p
Posting stress				
IV to work–family conflict effects	0.01	0.03	0.50	ns
Direct effect of work–family conflict on DV	0.35	0.05	6.62	< 0.001
Total effect of posting stress on DV	0.05	0.03	1.66	ns
Direct effect of posting stress on DV	0.05	0.03	1.59	ns
Partial effect of control variables				
Parental strain	0.01	0.00	3.91	< 0.001
Workload	–0.01	0.04	–0.34	ns
Work schedule	0.00	0.04	0.07	ns
Deployment stress	0.05	0.05	1.16	ns
	Bootstrapping 95-percent CI			
	Lower	**Upper**		
Work–family conflict	–0.02	0.03		
Deployment stress				
IV to work–family conflict effects	0.22	0.04	5.92	< 0.001
Direct effect of work–family conflict on DV	0.35	0.05	6.62	< 0.001
Total effect of deployment stress on DV	0.13	0.05	2.85	< 0.01
Direct effect of deployment stress on DV	0.05	0.05	1.16	ns
Partial effect of control variables				
Parental strain	0.01	0.00	3.91	< 0.001
Workload	–0.01	0.04	–0.34	ns
Work schedule	0.00	0.04	0.07	ns
Posting stress	0.05	0.03	1.59	ns
	Bootstrapping 95-percent CI			
	Lower	**Upper**		
Work–family conflict	0.05	0.12		

Model summary: $R^2 = 0.223$, $F(6, 488) = 23.30$, $p < 0.001$; level of confidence for confidence intervals: 95; Number of bootstrap resamples: 5000

In the first analysis, the independent variable, parental strain, significantly predicted work–family conflict and psychological distress. The confidence intervals corresponding to the indirect effect did not contain 0, indicating a significant indirect effect of parental strain on psychological distress through work–family conflict. Specifically, single parents with greater parental strain reported greater work–family conflict, which in turn was associated with greater psychological distress. As both the direct and indirect effects of parental strain were significant, it seems that work–family conflict partially mediated the path.

We found a similar trend of results in the second and third analyses, so the results are reported together: the independent variables, workload and work schedule, predicted work–family conflict, but did not predict psychological distress when other stress-related variables were statistically controlled for. The effects of workload and work schedule on psychological distress became non-significant when taking into account parental strain. Moreover, there was no evidence for the mediation effect given that both the direct and indirect effects of workload and work schedule (through work–family conflict) were not significant.

In the fourth analysis, the independent variable, posting stress, did not predict work–family conflict and psychological distress when other stress-related variables were controlled for. The effects of posting stress became non-significant when taking into account other stressors, especially parental strain. The confidence intervals corresponding to the indirect effect contained 0, indicating a lack of indirect effects of posting stress on psychological distress.

Finally, in the fifth analysis, the independent variable, deployment stress, significantly predicted work–family conflict and psychological distress. The confidence intervals indicated a significant indirect effect of deployment stress on psychological distress through work–family conflict: single parents with greater deployment stress reported greater work–family conflict, which in turn was associated with greater psychological distress. As the direct effect of deployment stress became non-significant (when statistically controlling for work–family conflict), work–family conflict appeared to fully mediate the path between deployment stress and psychological distress.

Discussion

Our study examined the influence of occupational stressors and parental strain on psychological distress among single CAF parents and the mediating role of work–family conflict in the path between these stressors and psychological distress.

Influence of family factors on stressors, work–family conflict, and psychological distress

Our findings indicated that the combined effects of occupational stressors and work–family conflict differed based on three key family factors: parental sex, primary caregiver status, and whether the child had special needs. These family characteristics played an important role in the levels of occupational stressors and work–family conflict among single CAF parents. However, when considering these family factors together, the effects of occupational stress and work–family conflict only differed as a function of primary caregiver status. Being a primary caregiver appears to greatly determine the extent of occupational stress and work–family conflict. It is also worth noting that, of the four occupational stressors examined, only deployment stress significantly differed as a function of the primary caregiver status—that is, primary caregivers reported notably higher deployment stress than non-primary caregivers. It is not surprising that single CAF primary caregivers would experience more deployment stress than other CAF families. Indeed, deployed CAF parents had been found to report reduced psychological well-being and higher family tension (Gewirtz and McMorris, 2015; Lara-Cinisomo et al., 2012).

Influence of occupational and parental stressors on psychological distress

Overall, the roles of occupational and parental stressors and work–family conflict in greater psychological distress are consistent with previous research (e.g., Blanchard, 2012; Dobreva-Martinova, Villeneuve, Strickland, and Matheson, 2002). However, once the other stressors were statistically controlled for, parental strain and work–family conflict became the key predictors of psychological distress. It is possible that parental strain plays a more important role in the well-being of single parents as they feel solely responsible for the child, especially if the other parent plays a minimal or no parenting role. Experiencing parental strain and feeling unable to meet one's parental obligations may cause a high level of stress and contribute to greater psychological distress than other stressors. In addition, it is possible that parental responsibilities are more related to psychological distress because there are no specific resources or organizational training to help them prepare for single-parenthood.

The mediating role of work–family conflict

Our finding that work–family conflict was one of the key risks of psychological distress is consistent with previous research (e.g., Cheeseman, Ferguson, and Cohen, 2011). Indeed, since single parents have fewer resources than two-parent families, it is understandable that they may experience more work–family conflict and higher levels of distress (Crosier, Butterworth, and Rodgers, 2007). Consistent with this, work–family conflict partially mediated the path between parental strain and psychological distress, and fully mediated the path between deployment stress and psychological distress among single CAF members. Interestingly, work–family conflict did not mediate the path between posting stress and psychological distress; nor was the lack of mediation explained by strong direct effects of posting stress on psychological distress. Parental strain may play a more important role in psychological distress than other stressors, including posting stress. Alternatively, posting stress may temporarily reduce one's life satisfaction instead of causing psychological distress. Therefore, it is recommended to explore the impact of posting stress on the psychological distress of single CAF parents.

Finally, our findings only revealed significant indirect effects of work load and work schedule on psychological distress through work–family conflict. It is possible that the roles of these variables were diminished after accounting for other variables. Our results indicate that parental strain may be more influential than the other predictors. But this might also indicate an important interaction between these stressors and parental strain—that is, single parents with occupational stressors only experience considerable psychological distress if their parental strain is high. Therefore, it is important to further examine the relations between these variables in explaining psychological distress among single parents while conducting moderated mediation accounting for interactions between these occupational stressors and parental strain.

Limitations

The present study contributes to the literature on the influence of different types of stressors on psychological distress among single CAF parents and the mediating role of work–family conflict. However, various methodological constraints may have negatively affected the generalizability of the results, including the low response rate. First, the survey was voluntary, so it is possible that individuals who experienced greater work–family conflict or higher levels of occupational stressors chose not to participate. Second, CAF members who have easier access to computers, CAF members who are not deployed, CAF parents who may have more resources available (a greater social support network), and female CAF members may be overrepresented in the sample; therefore, the results may not be generalizable to the CAF population. Third, the cross-sectional nature of the study precludes drawing inferences about the direction of the relations between occupational stressors, work–family conflict, and psychological distress. For example, psychological distress may contribute to the perceptions of occupational stressors and work–family conflict. Alternatively, increased work–family conflict may contribute to increased perceptions of occupational or parental stressors. Furthermore, other factors might affect the well-being of single parents, such as parental and child age, and accessibility of and satisfaction with social support (DeVoe and Ross, 2012) that were not examined in the present study.

Practical implications

Despite the limitations, the findings reveal the importance of mitigating parental strain among single CAF parents and assisting them in establishing a better work–family balance via formal and informal social support. Military organizations have employed various family-centered preventive interventions to reduce psychological distress and to promote and foster resilience among military families. Such programs and interventions appear to help single-parent families (Tucker and Kelley, 2009), and they may be particularly important during deployments.

One such program is resilience training called Families Overcoming Under Stress (FOCUS; Lester et al., 2012; Mogil et al., 2015) that is widely used in the US and is available in some of the Canadian Military Family Resource Centers. It provides education and skills training to military parents and children so they are able to cope with deployment-related stressors, and facilitates understanding and communication between family members to improve family resiliency. However, neither FOCUS nor other preventive intervention program offers programming tailored to the needs of single-parent military members. Thus, we encourage researchers to adapt FOCUS or develop a similar program to address the unique needs of single-parent CAF members. Although formal support programs may be a useful resource, receiving informal support (e.g., from friends or relatives) helps reducing psychological distress related to childcare arrangements and responsibilities (Bowling and Sherman, 2008). Given the importance of both formal and informal social support in improving psychological distress (Smith et al., 2013), we recommend future researchers explore the role of social support in mitigating distress while accounting for work–family balance, parental strain, and psychological distress.

To conclude, this study has demonstrated the roles of various stressors and some underlying mechanisms in psychological well-being of single CAF parents. The results could be used to improve treatment and prevention programs and, ultimately, enhance the well-being of military families. Programs oriented toward helping single parents establish a better work–family balance could be highly valuable for these families under stress. Future research could consider examining the types of organizational programs currently available for single military parents and identifying the gaps in the existing programs and improvements that could be made to them.

References

Amstad, F. T., Meier, L. L., Fasel, U., Elfering, A., and Semmer, N. K. (2011). A meta-analysis of work–family conflict and various outcomes with a special emphasis on cross-domain versus matching-domain relations. *Journal of Occupational Health Psychology*, 16, 151–169.

Baruch, G. K. and Barnett, R. C. (1986). Consequences of fathers' participation in family work: parent's role strain and well-being. *Journal of Personality and Social Psychology*, 51, 983–992.

Bedno, S., Hauret, K., Loringer, K., Kao, T., Mallon, T., and Jones, B. (2014). Effects of personal and occupational stress on injuries in a young, physically active population: a survey of military personnel. *Military Medicine*, 179, 1313–1318.

Blanchard, S. (2012). Are the needs of single parents serving in the Air Force being met? *Advances in Social Work*, 13, 83–97.

Booth, B. and Lederer, S. (2012). Military families in an era of persistent conflict. In J. H. Laurence and M. D. Matthews (eds), *Oxford Handbook of Military Psychology* (pp. 365–380), Oxford; New York: Oxford University.

Bowling, U. B. and Sherman, M. D. (2008). Welcoming them home: supporting service members and their families in navigating the tasks of reintegration. *Professional Psychology: Research and Practice*, 39, 451–458.

Cheeseman, S., Ferguson, C., and Cohen, L. (2011). The experience of single mothers: community and other external influences relating to resilience. *Australian Community Psychologist*, 23, 32–49.

Crosier, T., Butterworth, P., and Rodgers, B. (2007). Mental health problems among single and partnered mothers: the role of financial hardship and social support. *Social Psychiatry and Psychiatric Epidemiology*, 42, 6–13.

Day, A. L. and Chamberlain, T. C. (2006). Committing to your work, spouse, and children: implications for work–family conflict. *Journal of Vocational Behavior*, 68(1), 116–130.

DeVoe, E. and Ross, A. (2012). The parenting cycle of deployment. *Military Medicine*, 177(2), 184–190.

Dobreva-Martinova, T., Villeneuve, M., Strickland, L., and Matheson, K. (2002). Occupational role stress in the Canadian forces: its association with individual and organizational well-being. *Canadian Journal of Behavioural Science/Revue canadienne des sciences du comportement*, 34(2), 111.

Families Overcoming Under Stress (FOCUS) (2017). FOCUS: resilience training for military families. Retrieved from https://focusproject.org/.

Frone, M. R., Russell, M., and Cooper, M. L. (1997). Relation of work–family conflict to health outcomes: a four-year longitudinal study of employed parents. *Journal of Occupational and Organizational Psychology*, 70, 325–335.

Gewirtz, A. H. and McMorris, B. J. (2015). Family adjustment of deployed and non-deployed mothers in families with a parent deployed to Iraq or Afghanistan. *Professional Psychology, Research, and Practice*, 45, 465–477.

Holliday Wayne, J., Casper, W. J., Matthews, R. A., and Allen, T. D. (2013). Family-supportive organization perceptions and organizational commitment: the mediating role of work–family conflict and enrichment and partner attitudes. *Journal of Applied Psychology*, 98, 606–622.

Hourant, L., Williams, T., and Kress, A. (2006). Stress, mental health, and job performance among active duty military personnel: findings from the 2002 Department of Defense Health-Related Behaviors Survey. *Military Medicine*, 171, 849–856.

Kelloway, E. K. and Barling, J. (1994). *Development of the Canadian Forces Occupational Stress Questionnaire*. Willowdale, ON: Canadian Forces Applied Research Unit.

Kessler, R., Andrews, G., Colpe, L., Hiripi, E., Mroczek, D., Norman, S., Walters, E., and Zaslavsky, A. (2002). Short screening scales to monitor population prevalence and trends in non-specific psychological distress. *Psychological Medicine*, 32, 959–956.

Lara-Cinisomo, S., Chandra, A., Burns, R. M., Jaycox, L. H., Tanielian, T., Ruder, T., and Han, B. (2012). A mixed-method approach to understanding the experiences of non-deployed military caregivers. *Maternal and Child Health*, 16, 374–384.

Lester, P., Saltzman, W. R., Woodward, K., Glover, D., Leskin, G. A., Bursch, B., ..., and Beardslee, W. (2012). Evaluation of a family-centered prevention intervention for military children and families facing wartime deployments. *American Journal of Public Health*, 102, S48–54.

Mogil, C., Hajal, Nastassia, Garcia, E., Paley, B., Milburn, N., and Lester, P. (2015). FOCUS for early childhood: a virtual home visiting program for military families with young children. *Contemporary Family Therapy*, 37, 199–208.

Skomorovsky, A. and Bullock, A. (2015). *The Impact of Military Life on Single-Parent Military Families: Well-Being and Resilience* (Director General Military Personnel Research and Analysis Scientific Report DRDC-2015-R099). Ottawa, ON: Defence Research and Development Canada.

Skomorovsky, A. and Hujaleh, F. (2016). *Impact of Military Life on Single-Parent Military Families* (Director General Military Personnel Research and Analysis Scientific Report DRDC-RDDC-2016-R9999). Ottawa, ON: Defence Research and Development Canada.

Skomorovsky, A., Norris, D., Bullock, A., and Smith Evans, K. (2016). The impact of military life on children's well-being and child-parent relationships from single-parent military families. *Journal of Military, Veteran and Family Health*, 2, 29–36.

Smith, B. N., Vaughn, R. A., Vogt, D., King, D. W., King, L. A., and Shipherd, J. C. (2013). Main and interactive effects of social support in predicting mental health symptoms in men and women following military stressor exposure. *Anxiety, Stress, & Coping*, 26, 52–69.

Statistics Canada (2012). *Fifty Years of Families in Canada: 1951–2011* (No: 98-312-X2011003). Retrieved from: www.statcan.gc.ca.

Tanner, L., Coulthard, J., Fraser, K., Otis, N., Sudom, K., and Wang, Z. (2008). *Family Support in the Canadian Forces: An Overview of Research Conducted since 1990* (Director General Military Personnel Research and Analysis Technical Note 2008–24). Ottawa, ON: Centre for Operational Research and Analysis and Director General Military Personnel Research and Analysis.

Tucker, M. and Kelley, M. (2009). Social support and life stress as related to the psychological distress of single enlisted Navy mothers. *Military Psychology*, 2, S82–S97.

20 The life situation of military fathers

Perspectives of family planning and fatherhood of officers in the Austrian Armed Forces

Gottfried Reiter

Introduction

The military requires frequent relocations and deployments, which may be detrimental to family structure or have a negative impact on the organization of everyday private life and the practice of fatherhood (e.g., Adams, Hall, and Thomson, 2009; Pickering, 2006; Tomforde, 2015). In recent decades, the mobility of soldiers has increased considerably through international military cooperation. The commitment of the Austrian Armed Forces (AAF) to missions abroad has intensified since 1989. Deployments abroad may delay decisions to start a family and may also impact fatherhood and parenting. In this context a strong traditional role allocation, which occurs especially among officers with frequent absences, is remarkable (see Balbo and Mills, 2011; Applewhite and Mays, 1996; Booth, Segal, and Bell, 2007; Huffman, Culbertson, and Castro, 2008; Karney and Crown, 2007a, 2007b).

Just as demands in the military domain have changed in recent decades, so have demands in the family domain, including demands on fathers (Marsiglio, Amato, Day, and Lamb, 2000; Marsiglio and Cohan, 2000). Fathers may be confronted with controversial role expectations: they should be breadwinner, educator, and sensitive partner in one person (Halrynjo, 2009; Lamp, 2000). Fulfilling these expectations is challenging for men in jobs that require high mobility and flexibility. For these men the compatibility of family and work becomes difficult. In this context it is not surprising that after the birth of the first child a re-traditional effect is visible. For example, due to the many absences and the low presence in everyday family life, the mother performs mainly the child education (Guillaume and Pochic, 2009; Kelty, Kleykamp, and Segal, 2010).

The Austrian Armed Forces (AAF) has about 30,000 soldiers. It consists of professional soldiers and conscripts as well as about 25,000 reserve soldiers. By constitution the military system in Austria ordains that every eligible male Austrian citizen has to be conscripted. Women can serve as a volunteer in the Army (BMLV, 2018). About 2800 professional officers serve in the AAF. They have to complete a three-year training at the FH bachelor's degree program at the Theresian Military Academy. After completion of the training, they have the rank of lieutenant and the academic degree "Bachelor of Military Arts." In order for the officers to become professional soldiers for life, they must have served abroad. This is often a requirement for promotion to higher posts.

In Austria, professional soldiers are legally entitled to parental leave. It can be used until the child's second birthday and must last at least two months. In addition, there is the possibility to consume a "father's early leave" for the joint care of the child with the mother in the first weeks of life. A take-up is provided for a maximum of four unpaid weeks. In addition, all professional soldiers have the opportunity to use block time. This should increase the compatibility of work and private life. If there are no military interests against it, regulars must be present from 0900 to 1400 hours. The remaining time from 0730 to 0900 hours and from 1400 to 1545 hours is the individual's responsibility. One can take over 20 plus or minus hours in the next month, which increases the flexible use of time (HELP, 2018).

This chapter focuses on what professional challenges arise for officers of the AAF in the realization of family planning or the practice of fatherhood. In particular, the following questions will be answered.

1 What are important considerations for officers in starting a family?
2 What challenges do they experience in the practice of fatherhood?

Method

For the study a qualitative approach was chosen with a focus on the work–life balance of officers of the AAF (Reiter, 2016). Data were collected through semi-structured interviews. The invitation to the interview was made personally or by phone. Finally, 13 interviews were conducted between April and December 2014.

Officers that met the following criteria were invited to participate.[1]

(1) They should have been separated from their families due to job requirements for at least three months in the past year.
(2) They should live in a stable partnership and have children under 15 years of age.
(3) They should represent a very broad spectrum of different types of work (special forces, stand-by units, etc.).

The interviews were transcribed. All data that would allow conclusions to the person were deleted. In addition, the names were coded: the first interviewee was named Alex, the second Bernd, the third Conrad, and so on. An overview of respondents is represented in Table 20.1.

Topic analysis was used for interpretation of the data. In topic analysis the interpretation is reduced in favor of the manifest content. The idea is to identify the characteristic elements of the thematic presentation to make the differences in the representation of a theme and its context of argumentation visible (Froschauer and Lueger, 2003). Topic analysis essentially consists of five constructive components, each step increases the complexity of the summary and thereby the thematic structure of one or more texts. The interesting text sections are summarized and structured by using topics. The five constructing components of text reduction are based on the following questions: what is an important topic and in which passages in the text is this expressed? What are the most important characteristics of

Table 20.1 Sample overview

No.	*Name*	*Age*	*Marital status*	*Number of children*	*Branch*
1	Alex	37	Married	3	Combat unit
2	Bernd	30	Married	2	Combat unit
3	Conrad	42	Married	2	Combat unit
4	Daniel	32	Married	2	Combat unit
5	Erich	35	Married	1	Combat-support unit
6	Fritz	38	Married	2	Combat-support unit
7	Gerald	33	Cohabitation	2	Combat unit
8	Harald	32	Married	2	Combat-support unit
9	Ingo	33	Married	2	Combat-support unit
10	Jörg	38	Cohabitation	1	Combat unit
11	Karl	41	Married	1	Combat-support unit
12	Ludwig	37	Married	2	Combat-support unit
13	Michael	33	Married	2	Combat-support unit

a topic and in what context do they appear? In what sequence are topics raised? Where are the differences between the narratives? How can the characteristics of a topic be integrated into the research question? (Froschauer and Lueger, 2003; Figure 20.1). For the interviewed officers the main issues in context of family planning and family life were the impact of military service, foreign deployment, and the value of children.

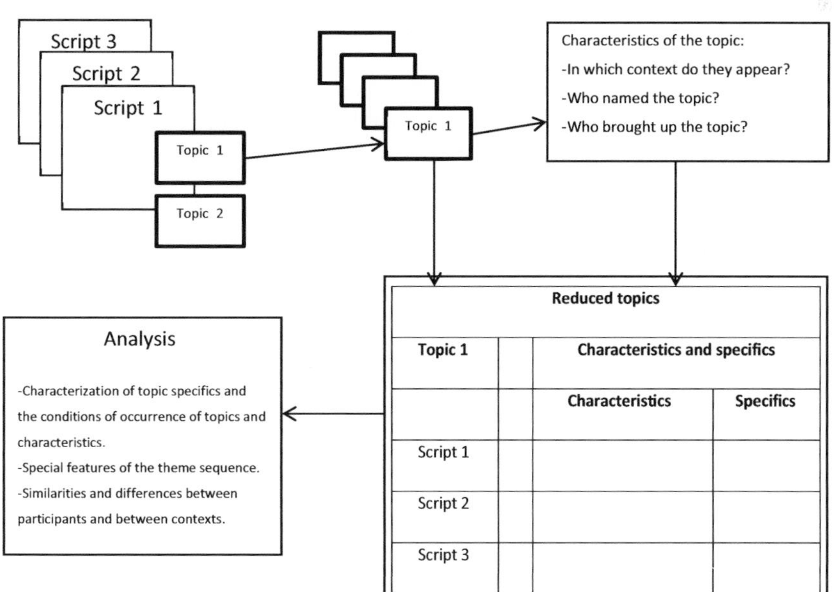

Figure 20.1 Topic analysis

Source: Froschauer and Lueger (2003: 162).

Results

Family planning and realization

The interviews revealed that the high demands on mobility and flexibility influence officers' family planning. Some officers were rational in their decisions to start a family.

Daniel: In the last year of the Military Academy, we said: children yes, but when is the optimal time? Well, you never find the optimal time, because you're always on the road somewhere. And then we decided, ok, I have never had such a regulated service like at the academy. So we made a decision. The first child comes in the last year of the training. The birth is to take place on this day, recalculated nine months ago, one month as a reserve, done, and exactly one week as planned was the birthday.

Daniel shows how rational the negotiation process for family planning was. Daniel and his wife used the predictability of the training at the Military Academy. Especially in the first years after training, officers are confronted with high mobility and flexibility requirements.

The completion of a foreign assignment is an integral part an officer's career. However, missions abroad cause ambivalence. On the one hand, they delay starting a family, while on the other hand, they create the necessary financial resources for a family. For Harald the higher income during missions is the "starting capital for the further future plan." In addition, the foreign assignment is also a duty that has to be fulfilled.

Bernd: The child planning was definitely dependent on the foreign assignment. We would really like to have another child, but the service is no longer a restriction, because I have fulfilled the assignment abroad as a duty that has to be fulfilled. And if I go abroad again, it will be synchronized with the kids.

It seems that in Bernd's case the fulfillment of service has priority over family planning. Nevertheless, after the birth of the first child, a reappraisal of the life orientation takes place.

The timing of family realization depends not only on foreign assignments or the willingness to be mobile and flexible. Officers' identification with their role as military leader also seems to play a role. Karl: "Until I realized that my military company works, I wanted to start a family. Because I had the confidence, I am now an officer, I can lead the company . . . so I had confidence in my military role." The consolidation of the officer's role and confidence in one's abilities and profession are the basic prerequisites for Karl for starting a family. In this context, the military service has priority over family planning. In the first years after training, life plans seem to be dominated by professional expectations, the military environment, the search for challenges, and personal development. Also for Conrad, the first few years after his training are characterized by a high willingness to be mobile and flexible; he feels that committed relationships hinder the fulfillment of military expectations. Conrad: "Basically, in my personal life plan it was never planned to have a committed relationship before the thirtieth year. Because of the requirements of the military profession and the associated freedoms in terms of capabilities and availability."

This reflects the difficulties of compatibility of family and work. It seems that with the increasing desire for active fatherhood, the compatibility problem becomes a concern and officers are likely to postpone their plans to start a family because they want to be available for the military. This is also shown by Gerald, whose partner wanted to start a family earlier:

> She really wanted to have children very early on, actually at 20 . . . I said, I do not want to, I want to finish my training. I was also not sure if she was the right woman for life. After my second assignment abroad, since I was already over 30, it occurred to me, yes, now I would like to start with children.

An additional characteristic of the family formation of officers is the availability of a private residential building. It is noticeable that the majority of respondents prefer a home in a rural area with a local kindergarten or elementary school. Fritz: "We said we start a family when the house is finished, when the nursery is ready." Erich also links the realization of the wish to have a child with the existence of a private residential building. Here, too, the military requirements caused a delay to the family planning. Erich and his wife changed their place of work and residence four times until the year 2010. Only when a professional transfer could be avoided, the couple talked about starting a family. Erich: "Children were never really an issue for us until 2010 . . . and when we bought a house, of course we talked about having children."

The realization of family planning seems to depend on the planning of professional relocation and mobility. Likewise, a high predictability of the professional requirements would benefit an earlier desire for having a family and children. Something similar can be observed with Ingo: "We waited for the right time . . . until we knew that we wanted to stay here [place of work and residence], then we said that we now start planning to have children." Only because of the certainty to stay longer at the current posting they were able to buy a home and start realizing their family planning.

Practice of fatherhood

The following section presents the different challenges and behaviors of fatherhood. First of all, a majority of the respondents experienced a reorientation of priorities after the birth of a child.

Bernd: Since then everything is different. That with the military, which used to be a matter of course, with sleeping in barracks, it does not matter now. . . because that's just not possible anymore. There has been a clear shift of focus in the private sphere . . . I do not want to be so much away from the children.

At this stage of the family cycle, there seems to be a discrepancy between military expectations and officers' ideas of fatherhood. At least temporarily, Bernd identifies more with the family and wants to be more present in everyday life at home. This can be interpreted as a breakup of traditional role models. For the military, this course of action can be a potential obstacle to future tasks, especially when long separations are expected from the family.

Another challenge is described by Alex. His foreign assignment, shortly after the birth of his child, conflicts with his family obligations. His wife had to play the role of a single mother during the deployment, which affected them both. Alex: "The second assignment abroad, my son was half a year old . . . He went through difficult phases, sleeping, etc., my wife was very stressed. And that has had a negative effect on my professional life."

Another perspective is shown by Fritz and Ludwig: a foreign assignment would benefit their career, but they felt "letting-down" their family was egoistic. These officers deliberately refrained from frequent absences in order to relieve their partner and to prevent potential problems for the children (for example, a possible decline in learning success). Fritz: "As long as the two children are not really firm somewhere in school, for me a foreign assignment is not really in question . . . I just want to make the learning conditions as stable as possible." Ludwig: "I have not had a foreign assignment because I say I do not want that while the children are still young." Here a high responsibility in the family area can be observed. The focus is mainly on the needs of the children, although shorter absences are accepted. The paternal identity seems to be determined by job and family affiliation. Likewise, this can be seen as a breaking-up of traditional gender roles.

Erich especially addresses the problem of available time. To solve his, he forgoes his own leisure activities. The subordination of one's own interests in favor of time with the child(ren) points to a desired emotional relationship, which increasingly becomes more difficult with the duration of absences.

Erich: I was a weekender [only being home on weekends] and after five weeks my little daughter did not let me take care of her . . . it's not easy with the bulk of absences . . . I'm currently doing nothing but family when I'm at home. You cannot buy children, because you can earn the affection only with time and dedication. . . then I was four weeks at home and it was great again, but now [Note: again, a weekender for 11 weeks] I notice again every week how it gets a bit worse again.

Erich points to the negative consequences of frequent absences for cementing the father-child relationship. Due to his low presence in everyday family life, the child has become alienated from him. As a consequence, Erich tries to reduce his official engagement. Career disadvantages are deliberately accepted. The supposition seems plausible that high official burdens, combined with unfulfilled beliefs of fatherhood, have a negative impact on service motivation. Compensating the loss of time by the fathers can be problematic, especially if it suffers the own regeneration and results in a permanent shortage of time.

Conrad: You come home in the evening and the kids then see you as the playmate. Of course, at the weekend, you also get the kids, although you have little time to regenerate again. Not that you do not want to have anything to do with the children, but at some point you also want to have time for yourself . . . but sometimes the children need a strong hand . . . and I'm no different to my children than to my soldiers, just family-friendly and with a different tone.

Activities with the children are limited to the evening, the weekends, and the holidays. In the available time Conrad acts primarily as a playmate. In doing so, he resorts to practiced military patterns of behavior when the children need a "strong hand." The comparison of his children with subordinate soldiers suggests that educational activity has authoritarian features.

Mother–child centering

Due to the many absences, the wives carry out the main part of parenting. The officers arrange themselves often without much discrepancy or they act on equal terms with the partner.

Ingo: The boss is always the woman, that's pretty clear. There are enough situations in childcare that are extremely demanding. . . we just talk about it. Well, we do not have any major discrepancies, but there has been always lively discussion.

Ingo's organization of everyday family life and parenting takes place together with his wife. The action pattern refers to a concept of co-parenting. The organization of family life as well as the practice of paternity is favored at Ingo by a satisfactory job position with low and plannable absences. Ambitious career thinking "in a hundred thousand directions" as well as personal self-realization are reduced to the minimum in favor of the family. Something similar can be observed with Harald. Also in his life the wife is the highest decision-making authority in child education. Harald: "I would say we are equal partners. Of course she has . . . the main educational part and I always ask if that's okay if I decide that one way or the other."

A completely different way of acting is described by Gerald. This couple practice a clear separation of duties.

Gerald: I'm responsible, so it's arranged, for the money-making. And she is responsible, so that everything fits intern the family. Starts from the household to the child's education. This has been classically conservative, shared, and we can both live well with this separation.

For Gerald, his job has a high priority. His function as a father is primarily perceived through the provision of economic resources. For the practice of fatherhood, this behavior can indicate that everyday life is characterized by the securing of what has been worked out (e.g., payments and obligations).

Jürgen presents another interesting approach to fatherhood. He also lives with his wife by the traditional role allocation. Interestingly, Jürgen was the only one who took a three-month parental leave.

Jürgen: Terrible . . . it's nice to play with my child, but I'm not born to be the playmate for babies, including infants. This is not my world, I do not care. I love my baby for ten minutes, and after that it's going to end in work. . . I'm not a nurse. I've become a soldier. And I'm looking forward to the time when the youngest can walk. That's more fun, I like it. Carrying children around is not my business.

Interesting in this observation is that Jürgen's life is defined by the soldier's profession, while he has an aversion for emotional "work." This may indicate a low level of motivation in participating in parenting in the early years of life. He also describes time accounts in context of military service as "one of the biggest idiocies I've ever seen in the Army." As a commander, Jürgen is used to having his soldiers available from 0730–1545 hours. With the implementation of time accounting this structure is missing for him.[2] Jürgen uses the time account to stay longer in the working world. In this context, arranging time for yourself can increase your own quality of life and satisfaction.

Another challenge is presented by Conrad. For him, responsibilities as a commander are an obstacle for him to take parental leave.

Conrad: Parental leave was never an issue for us. First, because my wife used it two years for the first child and maybe with the second child, I could still have done half-a-year. Problem was that I was always in commander functions at this time . . . then I took over the responsibility for the period when I was commander, and never gave it up.

This suggests that for Conrad leadership responsibilities prevent an egalitarian role allocation within the family and restrict the practice of paternity. This happens especially when leadership tasks combined with permanent availability at the workplace exists.

In contrast to the interviewees mentioned above, Karl vehemently strives for active fatherhood. He deliberately plans time together with his child and tries to balance his own needs. As a consequence, Karl has been transferred to a job that favors reconciliation between the profession and the desired practice of fatherhood.

Karl: I have never resisted [the change to another post], as long as it is a function where I can play a key role in the family. In my opinion, this is one of the most important things, not just talking about education or giving advice to the woman on how education is, education you have to be able to see . . . It may come back differently when he's out of school. Of course, then I can devote myself more flexibly to the military again, without letting the family too much out of the center.

Especially in the first years of parenting Karl seeks very close contact with his son. This action is supported by Karl's high self-management of the job and the intensive use of the time account. But that does not mean that the profession plays a subordinate role in the long term. Karl wants to return to greater flexibility in favor of the military when his child gets older.

Grandparents

In order to manage the family and professional challenges, the officers often are supported by the children's grandparents. They contribute significantly to childcare.

Daniel: The children are happy that they can sleep with their grandparents. We make a casual evening, go to the movies, eat something, and have time just for us. Because it is not supposed to be that we are just a machine, raise children and live 08/15.

Fritz: The big advantage is that we have our parents-in-law as neighbors. The mother-in-law is freshly retired and can take on volunteer work on behalf of our children.

The integration of the grandparents in family processes is important for these couples, to give themselves time to break up routines in everyday life and invest time in their relationship. Likewise, the assumption seems plausible that the support of the grandparents increases the quality of the officers' partnership. Grandparents can serve as a kind of "social safety net" for the partner, if the officer is confronted with high absences. This is especially true when difficult family situations have to be overcome.

Bernd: When she had to go to the hospital and I was not there, that was already difficult. I've assessed if the problem could be solved by her family or if I had to go home immediately. And we said that it's possible in her family unit.

At the time, Bernd was entrusted with a leadership task that required him to be responsible and fully committed to his soldiers. The grandparents act here as cooperative actors, which facilitate the military task fulfillment for Bernd.

In contrast to the support the grandparents provide, there may also be conflicts with them. For instance, when the grandfather seems to become more important as a male caregiver than the father.

Erich: Then suddenly the grandfather, who comes by once a week, is more important with persistence of the absence. There should be no jealousy. It asks less for me and more for the grandparents any envy or jealousy of the grandparents or the mother is simply misplaced. You just have to accept that and see that you win the heart of the little girl again.

Here, above all, the emotional aspects of frequent absences become recognizable. The low availability in everyday life can lead to emotional stress and reduce the commitment to the military of the officer. In contrast, Michael tries to avoid frequent absences in favor of the social structure of his children. He deliberately refrains from lucrative job offers and career opportunities. Nevertheless, he also is dependent on the support of his grandparents.

Michael: I had a civilian foreign offer that I declined because of the family. Now my children, especially the boy, are at an age where there is already a circle of friends. So he already has friendships. On the one hand I do not want to tear it out. On the other hand, we depend on the structure of our home, because my wife also works. And we just need grandma and grandpa.

Quality time and fixed rituals

Many of the interviewed officers try to spend as much time as possible with their children on the weekends, which indicates that officers want to be actively available for their children. Alex is trying to make up for lost time with the family and children on the weekends by deliberately avoiding intensive maintenance of other social contacts.

Alex: It's all about the kids. When I get home, the kids are on top of me and just before driving on Sunday or Monday in the morning I shake them off again. We have our rituals, like Sunday mornings—this is our walking day. We walk without mom and have our adventures. We do something almost every weekend. Either skiing, swimming, hiking, or just trying to make the most of the time, not just hanging out at home and letting the day go by.

Joint activities with children have high priority for Alex. It is based on fixed rituals, which should structure the family's everyday activities on the weekends.

Remarkable is the high proportion of physically stimulating and demanding activities in which the mother may not be included.

In contrast to Alex, Daniel does not limit his free time, but includes his children in all activities. Gender-specific differentiations are given little consideration here. The daughter and the son are involved in the, especially male connoted, actions: "Yes, if you ask the girl, for example, cylinder head gasket change, then she does it." The rational, optimal use of the available time is a common course of action in this family. Daniel: "I always say, it depends on how you use the time. When I come home, I let myself intensively tell everything that they have done, then play, then read aloud at night, and just spend time together." Similar to Alex, established rituals should also simplify the return to paternal life after absences. The assumption seems to be that high mobility demands increase the ritualization of everyday life in the family.

Daniel: The process is always the same. Whether I am here or not, it does not really matter, because it always runs the same way [the routines in everyday life of the family] . . . When I join in, I'll just get in the right phase of where they are.

A completely different situation can be observed with Michael. He has comparatively low absences. As a result, a compensation of the time on the weekend is not necessary. Paternity is characterized by presence, responsibility, and commitment in everyday life. This allows him to arrange career and leisure interests (e.g., football training). Gender-specific divisions of housework or functional assignments to father and mother are largely avoided.

Michael: It is common that when I come home, we still do something together with the children. Eating together . . . My wife cleans up afterwards, I wash the children. Then we divide up again, where I mostly read the story with the boy and she with the girl.

The time together with the children happens in the hours after work until bedtime. Here common inner-family rituals and structures are also established. Michael is a comprehensive participant in child-related care and nursing activities. The assumption seems plausible that a frequent availability of officers in the family favors an egalitarian role distribution.

Fritz has a completely different way of dealing with paternity. During the interview, he never spoke of a common father-child time. Rather, he tries to provide services to the children by delegating activities to other people.

Fritz: You want to offer something to the children. I mean, if I do not allow my daughter to go to the music school and dance, then she's coming home from school, doing homework, then that's it? I want to offer her opportunities and the same to the boy too.

Fritz wants to provide resources that are used to promote children's development. In this context, the practice of fatherhood has a high relevance to the future. The high number of developmental events the children participate in (dance school, music school, etc.) indicate a style of education that aims to discipline the children to autonomous personalities with achievement orientation.

Conclusion

Officers' decisions to start a family are influenced by the demands for mobility and flexibility, self-fulfillment, the assumption of leadership responsibility, and the completion of training. For the majority of respondents, a deployment abroad delays starting a family. Foreign assignments are mainly used to provide financial resources for starting a family. With the birth of a child a declining willingness to mobility, at least temporarily, can be seen. In the private sphere, a solid partnership and proximity to the grandparents is intended. This can be the reason why problems with compatibility between work and family are not mentioned by the respondents.

The most important challenge for the practice of fatherhood is the available time. The lack of time affects especially those officers who are in commander positions and who are confronted with frequent absences. In general, with the birth of the first child, a reorientation of life to the benefit of the family as well as a decreasing willingness to mobility is identified.

Remarkable is the consistently strong traditional role allocation, which occurs especially in officers with frequent absences. If the duty is determined by a few absences, then even egalitarian tendencies are visible. In general, there is a high degree of aversion to parental leave.

All officers see themselves as responsible for their children and spend quality time with their children in the available time. Basically, three ways of acting can be identified. The first is used by frequently absent fathers. Here, the majority of child education is delegated to the wife, while the paternal involvement in the family is rather low. Time together is restricted to the evenings, weekends, and on vacation. It may happen that the officer completely gives up his own hobbies or involves the children in his interests of leisure activities. It is not uncommon to use fixed rituals, which should make it easier for the officer to "get in" the family. The second course of action is found in fathers who are rarely absent. A compensation of time at the weekend is not necessary. Paternity is characterized by presence, responsibility, and commitment in everyday life. One's own leisure activities can be largely pursued. Likewise, parts of an egalitarian division of housework can be observed here. The third mode of action presents fathers who have a low involvement in everyday life, although the family is addressed as a top priority in life. The role of fathers in these cases is to provide opportunities to promote development by supporting children through external facilities.

In this chapter we see that the available time with the children, from the point of view of the officers, is of high quality. Future research could focus on the perspective of the wife. Moreover, future research could focus on questions like: How do children experience the often-absent father? How does a foreign assignment affect the school success of the children? And what are the differences in the practice of paternity between military and civilian leaders?

Notes

1 The same sample was used in the PhD thesis (see Reiter, 2016).
2 See introduction.

References

Adams, B. D., Hall, C. D. T., and Thomson, M. T. (2009). *Military Individual Readiness, État de préparation militaire de l'individu*. North York, ON: Defence Research and Development Canada Toronto.

Applewhite, L. and Mays, R. (1996). Parent-child separation: a comparison of maternally and paternally separated children in military families. *Child and Adolescent Social Work Journal*, 13(1), 23–39.

BMLV (2018). *Aufgaben der Streitkräfte*. Available at www.bundesheer.at/sk/index.shtml (accessed March 6, 2018).

Balbo, N. and Mills, M. (2011). The influence of the family network on the realization of fertility intentions. *Vienna Yearbook of Population Research*, 9, 179–206.

Booth, B., Segal, M. W., and Bell. D. B. (2007). *What We Know about Army Families: 2007 Update*. Department of the Army, Family and Morale, Welfare and Recreation Command. Available at: www.army.mil/fmwrc/documents/research/whatweknow 2007.pdf (accessed October 4, 2012).

Froschauer, U. and Lueger, M. (2003). *Das qualitative Interview*. Wien: Facultas.

Guillaume, C. and Pochic, S. (2009). What would you sacrifice? Access to top management and the work–life balance. *Gender, Work & Organization*, 16(1), 14–36.

Halrynjo, S. (2009). Men's work–life conflict: career, care and self-realization. Patterns of privileges and dilemmas. *Gender, Work & Organization*, 16(1), 98–125.

HELP (2018). *Väterkarenz und Väterfrühkarenz* ("Papamonat"). Available at: www.help.gv.at/Portal.Node/hlpd/public/content/359/Seite.3590009.html (accessed March 6, 2018).

Huffman, A. H., Culbertson, S. S., and Castro, C. A. (2008). Family-friendly environments and U.S. Army soldiers' performance and work outcomes. *Military Psychology*, 20, 253–270.

Kelty, R., Kleykamp, M., and Segal, D. R. (2010). The military and the transition to adulthood. *The Future of Children*, 20, 181–207.

Karney, B. R. and Crown, J. S. (2007a). *Does Deployment Keep Military Marriages Together or Break them Apart? Evidence from Afghanistan and Iraq*. Available at: www.netbooks-services.de/MediaFiles/Texts/3/9781441970633_Exzerpt_001.pdf (accessed October 4, 2012).

Karney, B. R. and Crown, J. S. (2007b). *Families under Stress: An Assessment of Data, Theory and Research on Marriage and Divorce in the Military*. Available at www.dtic.mil/cgi-bin/GetTRDoc?AD=ADA465553 (accessed October 4, 2012).

Lamb, M. E. (2000). The history of research on father involvement: an overview. *Marriage & Family Review*, 29, 23–42.

Marsiglio, W., Amato, P., Day, R. D., and Lamb, M. E. (2000). Scholarship on fatherhood in the 1990s and beyond. *Journal of Marriage and Family*, 62(4), 1173–1191.

Marsiglio, W. and Cohan, M. (2000). Contextualizing father involvement and paternal influence: sociological and qualitative themes. *Marriage & Family Review*, 29, 75–95.

Pickering, D. (2006) *The Relationship between Work-Life Conflict/Work-Life Balance and Operational Effectiveness in the Canadian Forces*. Toronto, ON: Defence R&D Canada. Technical Report. Available at: www.dtic.mil/dtic/fulltext/u2/a473654.pdf (accessed June 6, 2013).

Reiter, G. (2016). *Die work-life-balance von offizieren des Österreichischen Bundesheeres*. Balti: Südwestdeutscher Verlag für Hochschulschriften.

Tomforde, M. (2015). The emotional cycle of deployment. In R. Moelker, M. Andres, G. Bowen, and P. Manigart (eds), *Military Families and War in the 21st Century* (pp. 87–106). London and New York: Routledge.

21 Boots and bottles

Navigating the triumphs and challenges of early childhood in military families

Catherine Mogil and Blair Paley

Introduction

Military families face numerous challenges to communication, roles, routines, and relationships. Aspects of military life can impact child and family development throughout childhood, but may have unique consequences during early childhood, both in terms of child development but also in how the family formulates and adapts during this critical period. Understanding how these challenges are undertaken by military families with young children has broad public health implications as approximately 38 percent of the 1.7 million children living in military families are between the ages of birth and 5 years old in the US military alone (DoD, 2016). During early childhood, parents play a central role in helping their children navigate important physical, cognitive, social, and emotional milestones. For the military family, this phase can be complicated when paired with revolving parental absences (often involving risk) and the attendant disruptions of daily family life, the need to co-parent at a distance during such absences, and possibly parental post-traumatic stress or other injury. Focusing on the first five years of life for children and their families, this chapter will discuss the most significant challenges of early childhood and how military families adapt to navigate this major transition during military service.

The complexity of military life

Although research indicates that many military children and families adapt very well to the circumstances that military employment represent, there are features of military life that may present particular challenges to families. Namely, there is tiered risk associated with length of parental separations, particularly those related to deployment, and parental injury (Cozza, 2016), and these risks appear to be somewhat greater for young children (Barker and Berry, 2009; Chartrand, Frank, White, and Shope, 2008; Gewirtz, Pinna, Hanson, and Brockberg, 2014). Absences due to trainings, trips, or missions can tax a family as the military parent rotates in and out of family routine and interactions in daily life (Moeller, Culler, Hamilton, Aronson, and Perkins, 2015). In some countries, a parent may work at a military site or on a ship during the week and return home on the weekend, and in others the parent may be away training for months at a time. Even in countries where the military member may be home every night, the critical aspects of military duty may require long hours causing the parent to leave the house before a child awakes and return home long after bedtime. For young children who are almost entirely dependent upon their parents and rely on them to create a world that is safe and predictable, ongoing parental absences may threaten their sense of security (Osofsky and Chartrand, 2013).

Over the last 15 years, a hallmark of military life in many countries has been wartime deployment, which brings a unique set of challenges to military families and has been associated with increased utilization rates in pediatric healthcare settings (Gorman, Eide, and Hisle-Gorman, 2010) and behavioral problems in early childhood (Barker and Berry, 2009; Chartrand, Frank, White, and Shope, 2008; Gewirtz, Pinna, Hanson, and Brockberg, 2014). Absences related to deployments may be especially difficult for young children who likely do not have the cognitive capacity to understand the reason for the parent's absences or the coping strategies to help them tolerate the separation, nor are the options for bridging the distance as readily accessible for young children (e.g., an infant cannot communicate with the absent parent via an email exchange or a phone conversation as could an older child). For young children, parents occupy almost the totality of their interpersonal world, and thus when one of them (or the only one in the case of single parents) is deployed, their absence may create a much greater void than it might for older children. Furthermore, for the parent who remains at home, they are likely simultaneously attempting to manage their child's distress and or confusion about the other parent's absence, as well as managing their own anxiety about the safety of their spouse or partner. The at-home parent may be unsure about how to provide developmentally appropriate information about deployment (Strong and Lee, 2017) and the additional stress may impair their ability to model appropriate affective regulation and provide the emotional support that is needed by the young child.

Moreover, during early childhood the loss of time together may be especially salient given the dramatically accelerated pace of development during the child's first years (Trautmann, Alhusen, and Gross, 2015). A parent who is deployed for a year during a child's infancy and returns when their child is walking and talking may feel as if they are meeting their child for the first time. Parental absence due to military deployment also brings with it the need to prepare for the possibility of parental injury or even death. There are logistical considerations for parents as they navigate wills, custody decisions, and financial plans, but with this also comes emotional uncertainty, both for parents and for children.

Regardless of the reason for the separation (deployment or other military-related duties), separations and reunions require logistical shifts in the daily routines and rituals of family life, the burden of which rests on the remaining parent. Military families may adapt by reorganizing schedules and roles, but military families also face the duties, responsibilities, milestones, and hardships that other families face. In the context of change, a military family may also be navigating pregnancy, childhood illness, or accidents that can be taxing without the added challenges of the absence of a co-parent in the face of danger (Strong and Lee, 2017). The adjustments made to adapt to military separations can also be difficult for young children who tend to thrive on consistency and knowing what to expect each day. For example, if a parent who consistently manages bedtime routines is suddenly unable to do so, the routine may change from an expectable course that cues the child's body to begin the sleep process. A child who regularly gets a bath and a bedtime story will begin to get tired when the bath and story are read to them. If this process is disrupted, they may have trouble falling asleep until they are able to adjust to a new routine and new sleep cues.

Once the family is reunited, it can be difficult for a parent who has accommodated new responsibilities and adapted to single care-giving to hand back over parenting tasks to fully reintegrate the family (Strong and Lee, 2017). The recently returned parent may also have difficulty resuming previous roles (Dayton, Walsh, Muzik, Erwin, and Rosenblum, 2014; Lee et al., 2013; Louie and Cromer, 2014; Walsh et al., 2014; Willerton, Schwarz, Wadsworth, and Oglesby, 2011). Service members may feel disconnected from their child and their role as parent and be reluctant to ask for advice from the co-parent. Reflecting on their absence, military parents often express a sense of guilt about missing key developmental and family milestones and may not feel empowered to make discipline decisions.

All of these key parenting tasks of early childhood are rendered with even greater complexity by virtue of the fact that they do not occur in a vacuum. The parent–child relationship unfolds within a larger system that often (but not always) includes a spouse/partner and potentially more than one child. Thus, a parent is often negotiating these tasks in concert (or not) with a co-parent, which may create either a sense of collaboration and mutual support or lead to increased conflict that impacts both the marital and parent–child relationships. More broadly, when one family member is affected by certain stressors, it is likely that this impact will reverberate throughout the family (Paley, Lester, and Mogil, 2013). Some studies suggest that spouses and partners of military service members experience increased rates of depression (Kendler, Kawkowski, and Prescott, 1999; Kessler, 1997), which may be even higher for parents raising young children (Barker and Berry, 2009). This is compounded by the exhaustion and social isolation, which is often associated with the increased responsibility for a suddenly single caregiver during the deployment of a coparent (Strong and Lee, 2017). In the US, military families relocate frequently, which can further limit available social support that might otherwise offer instrumental support and limit isolation. In addition, there is some evidence that risk for child maltreatment, particularly neglect, increases with the number of months a parent is deployed (Gibbs, Martin, Kupper, and Johnson, 2007; McCarroll et al., 2010; Rentz et al., 2007). The spouse/partners ability to successfully navigate the deployment process is paramount for young children, as infants, toddlers, and preschoolers rely on the at-home parent to adapt to the role shift and adjust routines and rituals accordingly (Osofsky and Chartrand, 2013). Combat-related mental health symptoms represent an additional risk, not just for the service member, but also for the young child (Hisle-Gorman et al., 2015). In fact, the impact of combat-related injury affects the entire family. For example, if one parent is dealing with a physical or psychological injury, the other parent and the children will likely be impacted by the aftermath of these injuries as well. With younger children who have limited verbal capacities to ask questions or express confusion or concern about their parent whose altered behavior or appearance they do not understand, this impact may be expressed in the form of regressive, fearful, or oppositional behavior, which can add further to an already heighted stress level in the family. Although necessary, the treatment process can create more physical distance between the young child and their injured caregiver as parents might undergo additional hospitalizations, rehabilitation, and mental health treatment (Culler and Saathoff-Wells, 2018).

Infancy

The transition to parenthood and/or the addition of a new baby into the family represent important alterations in the family system. The microsystem must adjust to incorporate the complex developmental needs of a newborn infant into the family. Parents reorganize around basic functions such as a baby's sleep/wake cycle and feeding needs. Roles of family members are negotiated with the addition of each new child and are renegotiated as the child develops and his physical and emotional needs change over time.

One of the key developmental tasks of infancy is the child's establishment of close emotional bonds with their parents or other primary caregivers. These early attachment relationships take central focus as they set the stage for the child's ability to navigate the world and serve as a template for future relationships. Decades of research on parent–child attachment relationships highlight the importance of a strong emotional bond between child and caregivers in providing the child with a sense of security. When parents respond sensitively and consistently to the child's needs, the child develops a mental model of others as a reliable source of comfort, and of themselves as worthy of that predictable and nurturing response. Conversely, when parents respond insensitively (and perhaps even harshly) and/or inconsistently, the child develops a view of others as unreliable and even potentially threatening. The quality of infant-caregiver attachment has been shown to predict how a child explores their environment and regulates their physical and emotional states. Conversely, poor-quality attachment relationships in infancy have been associated with lower problem-solving ability, later peer aggression, greater frustration during play, and heightened response to stress.

An attachment perspective can be useful in understanding children's responses to separations from a parent during deployment. When a primary attachment figure leaves, some of a child's usual resources for dealing with stressful circumstances or emotionally distressing events are no longer available. Children may naturally rely on the non-deployed parent for more comfort, soothing, and reassurance than normal during the deployed parent's absence. However, the non-deployed parent's own coping abilities and resources may be taxed during deployment, as he/she manages extra household responsibilities or assumes the responsibilities of both parents, all while dealing with concerns about the deployed parent. There has been limited examination of parent–child attachment relationships in military families but there is some evidence that the separations they experience may impact those relationships. In a study of military families with young children, Barker and Berry (2009) found that child behavior problems and intense attachment behaviors at reunion increased with the number of deployments.

Importantly, attachment relationships are built through repeated interactions between parent and child over time, and when there are sudden and/or prolonged disruptions to those interactions due to parental absence, the quality of the attachment relationship may be compromised. Researchers have highlighted the importance of synchrony in early parent–child relationships and as a predictor of the quality of parent–child attachment (Isabella and Belsky, 1991). Feldman (2012) has described that "over time and daily experience, parent and child adjust to the specific cues of the attachment partner and this biobehavioral synchrony provides the foundation for the parent–infant bond" (p. 42). Children whose parents are suddenly deployed, perhaps without the opportunity to say goodbye or provide reassurance of their return, may have greater difficulty viewing this parent as a dependable source of comfort. Furthermore, parents who experience frequent and/or prolonged separations from their young child have less of an opportunity to develop synchrony through a foundation of daily interactions. Moreover, these parents may also have fewer opportunities to make repairs when they become "out of sync" with their child. Frequent deployments may be highly disruptive to the daily rhythms of a parent's interaction with their young child, as each impending departure may create stress for not only the service member but for the other parent as well, and disrupt normal routines of caregiving (e.g., feeding, playing, bedtime rituals) that are a key part of developing synchrony. Similarly, each return from deployment may require a period of the parent and child "getting to know each other" all over again. This is not to suggest that military parents and children cannot establish secure attachment relationships, but rather that they made be more challenging by the parent's repeated comings and goings.

Another and related major development task of infancy is building the earliest foundations of the child's capacity for self-regulation, largely by relying on their primary caregivers as a source of external regulation. When a child is born, they are completely reliant on their parents to help them regulate their physiological states, as they are the source of feeding, changing diapers, putting the infant to sleep, and ensuring the infant is neither too cold nor too hot. Similarly, as the infant begins experiencing basic emotions of pleasure and anger, the parent plays a key role in helping the child modulate those experiences. During bouts of play, the child may experience periods of contentment or even intense joy and excitement (e.g., giggling or happily screaming in response to a game of "peek-a-boo" with their parent) that the parent may reinforce by mirroring the infant's affective states. At other times, the child may experience frustration, fear, or sadness, expressing their distress through crying, fussiness, or clinging, to which the parent ideally responds with some kind of soothing. Parents also provide external regulation by shaping their child's environment through the establishment of daily routines (e.g., a regular feeding schedule) and rituals (e.g., reading or singing at bedtime), and the creation of nurturing physical spaces (e.g., a quiet bedroom to promote healthy sleep; age-appropriate toys and books in a safe play area to promote physical, cognitive, and language development). Infants can be sensitive to changes in their schedules, routines, or physical environment, or to the presence or availability of caregivers, and some features of military life, such as family relocations or deployments, may make it challenging for parents to create and maintain a caregiving environment that supports infant regulation.

Toddlerhood

The second year of life is marked by mastery of walking and talking. Toddlerhood begins with clumsy toddling in the start of the second year of life and ends with improved coordination, running, and the ability to walk backwards. There is also an explosion of connections in the language areas of the brain between the first and second year of life. Toddlers begin to pair the symbolism of words with their experiences, resulting in quadrupling of vocabulary in year two. As children's verbal abilities expand, so does their capacity to relate their internal experiences to others. Children's increased capacity to express themselves may help parents better understand their children's needs, motivations, and feelings, and thus allow them to respond more sensitively and effectively to their child.

Enhanced motor skills bring an ability to move about the world more easily and to wander farther and farther away from the primary caregiver. When parents support a child's autonomy, exploration emerges and toddlers learn through trial and error. With each new success, neural connections continue to be formed and a bit more independence from the parent is gained. Through exploration, children also learn that there are consequences for their actions—both positive and negative. Through repetition, toddlers master many physical tasks and begin to learn what works and what doesn't work, until they stumble upon a new strategy that works better.

The limbic system of the brain, responsible for emotional regulation, also matures rapidly during toddlerhood. Emotions of pride and shame emerge as they experience success and failure. Because children in the toddler phase are highly attuned to parent cues, parents continue to play a critical role during this period—that of limiting the autonomy of the toddler. The emotional reaction of a parent provides signals to the child about whether an experience is positive or negative. For example, as a child produces new words parents often provide open displays of joy and approval. Similarly, as a child takes his first steps, parents may applaud and provide encouragement. Conversely, as a child becomes curious about something that is dangerous or toddles too far outside of the parent's comfort zone, the child may be met with disproval, anxiety or fear—parent cues that indicate disproval and can result in shame experiences for the child. The normal stress that parents experience when trying to gauge how much latitude they allow a toddler who is taking developmentally normative risks may be exacerbated by having a deployed spouse/partner who may be in harm's way. Issues of danger and risk may take on heightened meaning in military families that impact how a parent reacts to a toddler who is attempting to figure out what is safe and what is not, and may lead the parent to precipitously cut off the toddler's efforts at exploration. The trial-and-error approach to exploration, along with the sensitivity to parents' negative cues, can result in many frustrating experiences for the toddler. As such, the toddler finds ways to express their disappointment. The "terrible twos," as the period is often referred to, may introduce tantrums into the everyday life of the family. Toddlers experience "big" emotions like sadness but do not yet have the coping skills to manage their disappointments. They may seem irritable but lack the vocabulary to describe their emotional experiences.

As external emotional regulators, the parents' role during this period continues to focus on soothing the toddler. Through modeling of appropriate strategies for self-soothing, the child watches and learns what helps their parent to calm down. Over time, the child will internalize these models of coping and begin to use them on their own.

As toddlers struggle with their desire for greater independence coupled with the reality of both their own developmental constraints as well as limits imposed by parents and other caregivers, the absence (or inconsistent presence) of one primary caregiver may heighten family stress around that struggle. For example, if one parent typically assumes the role of authority figure in the family and that parent is either physically absent (e.g., due to a deployment) or psychologically unavailable (e.g., due to injury), the toddler may test limits and boundaries to an even greater degree.

Preschool years

Year three and four of life are commonly referred to as the preschool years. Many of the milestones that began during the second year begin to mature during the preschool years. For example, there is a significant increase in verbal skills and verbal reasoning and what is often described as a vocabulary "explosion." At the beginning of the third year, a child may be able to produce around 200 words, which doubles or triples during the following year. Preschoolers also begin stringing words together into short sentences.

The preschool-aged child also develops more words to express feelings, although the emotional vocabulary may still not be enough to capture the complex feelings of this stage. Preschoolers begin to distinguish negative emotions; for example, they start to understand the difference in how sadness feels different from anger. In this stage, they also start to better recognize the nonverbal emotional cues of others. In other words, they can read nonverbal cues of happiness, sadness, or disappointment. As a result of understanding how others are feeling, they begin to show the first signs of empathy. Empathy is initially only possible for family members or caregivers who are close to the child. As such, the way in which empathy is expressed is largely dependent on the unique context of the family. If preschoolers see their parents express empathy by giving a hug or saying sorry, then the child will be more likely to express it in a similar way.

As preschoolers begin to go out into the world and interact with others, and even begin playing with other children, the parents' job is to help the child navigate social interactions. In preschool, the child will encounter other helpful adults such as teachers and classroom aids. The child will take their cues from their parent about how to develop relationships with other helpful adults. As the child's relationships with adults outside the home are strengthened, this can pose an additional challenge for the parent. Although still the primary attachment figure, a parent can experience a sense of loss as their child starts to rely on other trusted care providers for support and guidance. Preschoolers may react differently to a parents' military deployment than in previous years. Preschoolers are likely to have a clearer awareness of the absence of a parent than do younger children. They may emotionally respond to this awareness by regressing from previously attained developmental milestones (regression in toilet training, thumb sucking, sleep disturbance, clinginess, and separation anxiety). They may also demonstrate signs of irritability, depression, aggression, or somatic complaints. Due to their active imaginations, preschoolers may develop idiosyncratic or personalized explanations regarding the deployment of a parent, e.g., "Daddy/Mommy left because I was angry at him/her." These inaccuracies can best be addressed through brief, accurate, and concrete information related to the deployment. Preschoolers' growing awareness of their parent's absence and of the potential danger their parent faces (Paris, Acker, Ross, and DeVoe, 2011) may make them more prone to behavioral difficulties. Compared to younger children of deployed parents, 3-to-5-year-olds were found to exhibit higher rates of behavior problems (Flake, Davis, Johnson, and Middleton, 2009).

Transition to kindergarten

As children emerge from the preschool years and begin to enter their years of formal schooling, a number of developmental tasks become more salient. Children's awareness of and capacity to communicate about and regulate their feelings continue to grow, as do adults' (e.g., parents, teachers) expectations for more regulated behavior (e.g., following directions, staying in one's seat in class or at the dinner table). Children also must navigate an increasingly complex social environment as they begin to develop more stable friendships. Their ability to navigate these relationships partly rests on their maturing cognitive skills, including theory of mind and executive function skills. Their capacity for theory of mind allows them to begin recognizing that individuals' perceptions may not always match the objective world. Executive function skills include working memory (i.e., the ability to hold multiple pieces of information in one's mind and act on that information), inhibitory control (i.e., being able to control one's impulses), cognitive flexibility, and planning, sequencing, and organizing, and contribute to children's ability to have reciprocal social conversations, problem-solve when encountering an obstacle, and engage in complex imaginative play with other children.

The transition into formal schooling is one of the biggest developmental changes in a young child's life, wherein school becomes one of the primary agents of socialization through the child's relationships with both teachers and peers. For military families, this transition may be complicated by interacting with a school system that may not be aware of the particular challenges faced by military families. For example, the typical difficulties that some children can experience around separations may become potentiated in children of service members. For example, the child may become anxious about being dropped off at school if they are worried that the parent might be gone when they get home from school. Normal school day separations may also become much more meaningful for a child who is worried about the well-being of the remaining parent, as they view them as potentially their only caregiver if something happens to the other parent. Children in military families may also be vulnerable to teasing either about their parent's deployment or involvement in combat (Barker and Berry, 2009).

How military families adapt successfully

The impact that deployment has on young children appears to be mediated through a pathway of parental trauma, combat-related mental health challenges, and the wear-and-tear stress associated with military life. Resilience-enhancing programs, like Familes OverComing Under Stress for Early Childhood (FOCUS-EC), also make use of the parental pathway to enhance child resilience and bolster family coping by supporting coordinated leadership and strengthening relationships across the family. Given parental-mediated risk and protective factors for child well-being, it is important to enhance parental functioning of the most at-risk military families (i.e., recently deployed parents, multiply deployed parents, and parents with psychological and physical injuries).

It is no secret that young children can tax a parents' patience and leave them feeling ineffective during tantrums, emotional outbursts, and behavioral dysregulation. Teaching parents positive behavioral support skills can help enhance the parents' sense of self-efficacy. This may include sharing information about staging the child's environment so that is physically safe, not overstimulating, and responsive to the needs of the young child (e.g., placing appropriate items where the child can reach them).

Given that a young child's ability to better regulate emotions develops as they grow, information about how parents can support and shape these skills is key. Emotion coaching is a set of skills that help parents support their child's emotional regulation. For example, a young child may experience two primary emotional states, pleasure and anger. When a parent is able to expand the child's emotional experiences to include in-between states, such as annoyance or frustration, they have more opportunity to intervene to help the child cope before they are in an anger state. In other words, the parent can help expand the range of the child's emotional experiences and coping responses over time. This may start with modeling appropriate expression of emotion, even for distressed states. For example, a parent may narrate their own experience of being frustrated when cut off in traffic. If a parent adds how they cope with their frustration (e.g., "mommy is frustrated but I am going to take a deep breath to calm down), they begin to show their child that managing difficult feelings is possible. Parents can also narrate their child's emotional world by labeling what feelings the parent thinks the child may be experiencing (e.g., "it looks like you're mad") and adding how the child can start to feel better (e.g., "it looks like you might want a hug to help you calm down"). When emotion coaching is integrated into the home experience, it teaches the child that their feelings are important, seen, and that they are able to manage those "big" emotions.

Parents who balance their child's need for autonomy with the parent's need for protection help their child better develop a positive sense of self. This can be particularly challenging during the evolving context of deployment when risk and safety may be on the mind of both the young child and the parent. If parents are too limiting (parenting out of fear) or too permissive, the world can seem unsafe to a young child.

Maintaining parenting at a distance can reduce the ambiguous loss that is experienced during deployments. There are numerous strategies that military families often use to help the child maintain connection to the absent parent. For young children, this can mean keeping a picture of the deployed parent close by and accessible (at the child's level) and incorporating it into daily rituals (kissing daddy goodnight or sending mommy a morning wish) or playing a recording of the deployed parenting reading a book to the child (with the other parent listening and reading too). It can also be done through verbal statements from the at-home parent that incorporate the absent parent into the parenting role. For example, the parent may say, "your mother and I agree that it is important to eat vegetables" or "Daddy told me that he loves you a lot!" Maintaining parenting at a distance also has benefit for the deployed parent. When developmental milestones are shared regularly through email reports, pictures, videos, telephone reports, or Skype calls, the returning parent may feel more connected to their young child, more effective as a parent, and more engaged in supporting their young child's development. Of course, it is also important to strengthen the entire family system. This may include the marital relationship—paying special attention to reducing marital discord and enhancing emotional and physical intimacy, the co-parenting relationship, so that roles are balanced, synchronous, and coordinated—and the entire family-level interactions.

Planning and preparation are trademarks of military operations. The solider trains up and becomes mission-ready prior to leaving for tactical undertakings. Unfortunately, the same is not always true for the military family. Although readiness programs and workshops may be available to military parents, they don't often take full advantage of the services or do not feel that the programs meet the unique needs of their own family. Readiness has logistical considerations as well as social/emotional aspects. When families are able to preventively enhance family relationships, increase connection among family members, and bolster social support before a transition, they may better be able to weather changes. Further, anticipating challenges can help parents plan for how they might communicate during distressing times. Some couples find it helpful to agree upon a set of guidelines for communication during a deployment. For example, a parent may learn that it is difficult for the military member to share about the difficult experiences during military operations so the couple may agree that they will focus on what is going on at home and what happened in the barracks and avoid discussion of what happened during a specific mission, or the parent at home may share that they need to be asked about their day at the start of the conversation. Parents may also want to agree upon a set of household rules that they want to uphold during deployment and which ones may require flexibility and judgment from the at-home parent. For example, they may agree that they still want their children to attend daycare during the deployment, but that the parent at home can make decisions about bedtime routines.

It is important that support is practical and enhances a parents' ability to manage not only their own needs, but also the needs of their young children. For many military parents, access to trusted childcare is a concern (Strong and Lee, 2017) that may prevent them from accessing other social networks and support services. This is particularly true in the US where universal access to high-quality childcare is not routinely available for families living distally from military installations where child development centers are available during the day.

Particularly for mental health services, stigma is a barrier to seeking treatment for many military members and their families. Concerns about whether seeking help will affect their career or make them appear weak or unable to cope exist for many service members. Embedding trauma-informed care into less-stigmatized service structures may help. For example, offering parenting support in school locations or behavioral health screening and resources during routine medical care can help improve access to care in a destigmatized manner. When referrals for mental health treatment are necessary, making sure that providers are aware of the unique challenges of military life and sensitivities around confidentiality (both for operational security but also for career impact) can help military families feel more comfortable and open to care for depression, anxiety, and PTSD.

When intervention is warranted, it is important that interventions incorporate the needs of young children in their lens. Many families with young children may not access services if they feel that they do not have practical application to the developmental needs of young children and the unique aspects of parenting infants, toddlers, and preschoolers. Further, most mental health treatments utilize intervention strategies that require insight-oriented or talk therapy into the treatment protocol but are inappropriate for very young children (Paris, Acker, Ross, and DeVoe, 2011). Given that many military families have children aged 0–5 years, it is important that interventions for military families not only incorporate trauma-informed strategies and convey an understanding of the military context, but also meet the needs of young children. FOCUS-EC (Mogil, Hajal, and Garcia, 2015) and Strong Families, Strong Forces (DeVoe, Paris, Emmert-Aronson, Ross, and Acker, 2017) are such interventions.

References

Barker, L. H. and Berry, K. D. (2009). Developmental issues impacting military families with young children during single and multiple deployments. *Military Medicine*, 174 (10), 1033–1040.

Chartrand, M. M., Frank, D. A., White, L. F., and Shope, T. R. (2008). Effect of parents' wartime deployment on the behavior of young children in military families. *Archives of Pediatrics and Adolescent Medicine*, 162(11), 1009–1014.

Cozza S. J. (2016). Parenting in military families faced with combat-related injury, illness, or death in parenting and children's resilience in military families. In A. H. Gewirtz and A. M. Youssef (eds), *Parenting and Children's Resilience in Military Families*, pp. 151–174. New York: Springer.

Culler E., Saathoff-Wells T. (2018). Young children in military families. In J. Szente (ed.), *Assisting Young Children Caught in Disasters: Educating the Young Child* (Advances in Theory and Research, Implications for Practice), vol. 13. Cham: Springer.

Dayton, C. J., Walsh, T. B., Muzik, M., Erwin, M., and Rosenblum, K. L. (2014). Strong, safe, and secure: negotiating early fathering and military service across the deployment cycle. *Infant Mental Health Journal*, 35(5), 509–520.

Department of Defense (DoD), Office of the Deputy Assistant Secretary of Defense for Military Community and Family Policy (ODASD (MC&FP) (2016). *Demographics Profile of the Military Community*. Washington, DC: Office of the Deputy Assistant Secretary of Defense. Available at: http://download.militaryonesource.mil/12038/MOS/Reports/2016-Demographics-Report.pdf.

DeVoe, E. R., Paris, R., Emmert-Aronson, B., Ross, A., and Acker, M. (2017). A randomized clinical trial of a postdeployment parenting intervention for service members and their families with very young children. *Psychological Trauma: Theory, Research, Practice, and Policy*, 9(Suppl 1), 25–34.

Feldman, R. (2012). Parent-infant synchrony: a biobehavioral model of mutual influences in the formation of affiliative bonds. *Monographs of the Society for Research in Child Development*. Wiley Online Library, 77, 42–51.

Flake, E. M., Davis, B. E., Johnson, P. L., Middleton, L. S. (2009). The psychosocial effects of deployment on military children. *Journal of Developmental and Behavioral Pediatrics*, 30(4), 271–278.

Gewirtz, A. H., Pinna, K. L., Hanson, S. K., and Brockberg, D. (2014). Promoting parenting to support reintegrating military families: after deployment, adaptive parenting tools. *Psychological Services*, 11(1), 31.

Gibbs, D. A., Martin, S. L., Kupper, L., and Johnson, R. (2007). Child maltreatment in enlisted soldiers' families during combat-related deployments. *JAMA*, 298, 528–535.

Gorman, G. H., Eide, M., and Hisle-Gorman, E. (2010). Wartime military deployment and increased pediatric mental and behavioral health complaints. *Pediatrics*, 126(6), 1058–1066.

Hisle-Gorman, E., Harrington, D., Nylund, C. M., Tercyak, K. P., Anthony, B. J., and Gorman, G. H. (2015). Impact of parents' wartime military deployment and injury on young children's safety and mental health. *Journal of the American Academy of Child and Adolescent Psychiatry*, 54(4), 294–301.

Isabella, R. A. and Belsky, J. (1991). Interactional synchrony and the origins of infant-mother attachment: a replication study. *Child Development*, 62, 373–384.

Kendler, K. S., Kawkowski, L. M., and Prescott, C. A. (1999). Causal relationship between stressful life events and the onset of major depression. *American Journal of Psychiatry*, 156, 837–841.

Kessler, R. C. (1997). The effects of stressful life events on depression. *Annual Review of Psychology*, 48, 191–214.

Lee, S. J., Neugut, T. B., Rosenblum, K. L., Tolman, R. M., Travis, W. J., and Walker, M. H. (2013). Sources of parenting support in early fatherhood: perspectives of United States Air Force members. *Children and Youth Services Review*, 35(5), 908–915.

Louie, A. D. and Cromer, L. D. (2014). Parent-child attachment during the deployment cycle: impact on reintegration parenting stress. *Professional Psychology: Research and Practice*, 45(6), 496–503.

McCarroll, J. E., Ursano, R. J., Liu, X., Thayer, L. E., Newby, J. H., Norwood, A. E., and Fullerton, C. S. (2010). Deployment and the probability of spousal aggression by US Army soldiers. *Military Medicine*, 175(5), 352–356.

Moeller, J. D., Culler, E. D., Hamilton, M. D., Aronson, K. R., and Perkins, D. F. (2015). The effects of military-connected parental absence on the behavioral and academic functioning of children: a literature review. *Journal of Children's Services*, 10(3), 291–306.

Mogil, C., Hajal, N., Garcia, E., Kiff, C., Paley, B., Milburn, N. and Lester, P. (2015). FOCUS for early childhood: a virtual home visiting program for military families with young children. *Contemporary Family Therapy*, 37(3), 199–208.

Osofsky, J. D. and Chartrand, L. C. M. M. (2013). Military children from birth to five years. the future of children. *US Air Force*, 23(2), 61–77.

Paley, B., Lester, P., and Mogil, C. (2013). Family systems and ecological perspectives on the impact of deployment on military families. *Clinical Child and Family Psychology Review*, 16(3), 245–265.

Paris, R., Acker, M. L., Ross, A. M., and DeVoe, E. R. (2011). When military parents come home: building "strong families strong forces," a home-based intervention for military families with very young children. *Zero to Three*, 32(2), 36–42.

Rentz, E. D., Marshall, S. W., Loomis, D., Casteel, C., Martin, S. L., and Gibbs, D. (2007). Effect of deployment on the occurrence of child maltreatment in military and nonmilitary families. *American Journal of Epidemiology*, 165, 1199–1206.

Strong, J. and Lee, J. J. (2017). Exploring the deployment and reintegration experiences of active duty military families with young children. *Journal of Human Behavior in the Social Environment*, 27(8), 817–834.

Trautmann, J., Alhusen, T., and Gross, D. (2015). Impact of deployment on military families with young children: a systematic review. *Nursing Outlook*, 63, 656–679.

Walsh, T. B., Dayton, C. J., Erwin, M. S., Muzik, M., Busuito, A., and Rosenblum, K. L. (2014). Fathering after military deployment: parenting challenges and goals of fathers of young children. *Health and Social Work*, 39(1), 35–44.

Willerton, E., Schwarz, R.L., Wadsworth, S. M., and Oglesby, M. S. (2011). Military fathers' perspectives on involvement. *Journal of Family Psychology*, 25(4), 521–530.

22 Epilogue: dating from a distance

Love and separation in a networked society

René Moelker and Manon Andres

For those who are at times far away and yet so close

Introduction: love under stress of deployment-induced separation

In this study (this book) we explored the politics of relations that are under stress, negotiating military and family life. When love is under stress, tensions can be resolved by trying to keep the relationship as good as it can be. A practical resolve at the micro individual level comes from "dating from a distance," meaning that couples can balance the power relations between them by relatively simple techniques of communication. Although simple, they are grounded in complex insights into the changes that define modern love.

International research has shown that relations do deteriorate when they shift into being long-distance relationships, caused by deployment-induced separation. The statistics indicate that 40 percent of all long-distance relationships break up; four-and-a-half months is the average time it takes for a long-distance relationship to break up if it is not going to work.[1] From this data we may tentatively extrapolate that the period from halfway to three-quarters of the way through a military deployment is the most difficult. Later on in the deployment, there might be "channel fever," the anticipatory stress one experiences in the anticipation of homecoming. In the British and Dutch Navies, passing the channel meant that one was almost home, hence the name "channel fever." At this stage, people (including spouses back home) are nervous, but they do not break up. On the contrary, they will soon enter the phase of marital reconciliation. Sometimes, a deployment makes a relationship stronger, but more often relationships deteriorate. Longitudinal research among deployed military personnel and their spouses shows that relationship satisfaction after the deployment is significantly lower than before the deployment; 18 percent of the relationships deteriorate considerably, whereas 11 percent improve significantly (Andres, 2010). In all stages, couples negotiate and renegotiate their relationship because it is always in flux, ever-changing, and not always for the best. So how to make the best of it? How to make each other's lives a little bit happier?

The answer also depends on negotiations at the level of the state and the organization for it is a political process at three intertwined levels with always three or more actors involved (see the framework presented in Chapter 1 of this volume). The bargain is sometimes formal or informal, explicit or implicit, and more or less trades of care provisions and remuneration against loyalty, support, and labor. At the state level, modernizing processes result in a shift from institutional to occupational types of covenant. At the organizational level, one can observe a variety of arrangements that sometimes strongly rely on self-help on the one hand, while they may depend on traditional family support systems on the other. At the individual level, we observe a development from command households to negotiation households (Swaan, 1982).

First, we will discuss what modern love looks like and especially how long-distance relationships can be managed within the framework of the negotiation household. Second, we will discuss the implications of changes in political negotiation regarding the state and organization level in an effort to get beyond the concept of the greedy institution.

Keeping up the romance during deployment in a networked society

Love

Falling in love is the easiest thing. For example, *The New York Times* published a 36-question interview schedule that future partners can use during dating (Jones, 2015). The questions rise in difficulty level. Examples are

> What would constitute a "perfect" day for you? . . . What do you value most in a friendship? . . . What is your most treasured memory? . . . Share with your partner an embarrassing moment in your life . . . Tell your partner something that you like about him/her.

After 36 questions, either it works or it is perfectly clear it is never going to work! The session ends with staring into each other's eyes for four full minutes—extremely difficult to do, but it enhances the empathic moment. Falling in love is thus only a projection of empathy onto the other and basically these are our own desires and emotions that we project. Falling in love is only a narcistic projection of one's own desires onto the other, onto the wished-for relationship in hope for reciprocity and empathic mutual identification. But the narcistic projection is a precondition for many things, among others for direct gratification, for getting to know each other, and for developing enduring relationships. Without self-love, love is impossible. Thus, love follows its own cycle (Hofstede, 1991), which can also be applied to the love affair between two countries having to work together in a military headquarters (Moelker, Soeters, and Hagen, 2007) because it is all about two parties negotiating a working relationship. The cycle describes the politics of collaboration between two partners and how it is not much different from a love affair. During the first stage high expectations result in feelings of mutual sympathy, butterflies, and even some kind of excitement and euphoria. In the next stage, however, mutual sympathy will decrease, because both parties increasingly see each other's weaknesses and problems. This may even result in what is commonly known as a "culture shock" or "reality check," realizing the other is different. During the following acculturation phase, routinization and normalization will occur. Partners negotiate positive and negative experiences, they are being balanced, and finally (in phase four) they come to a new equilibrium. This new equilibrium, however, is seldom higher than during the first phase of euphoria but this is what we normally describe as the stage where there is "love" between the two parties. There are many definitions of love, popular and scientific, but one that is both classic and still valid is given by Erich Fromm (1956):

> Love means to commit oneself without guarantee, to give oneself completely in the hope that our love will produce love in the loved person. Love is an act of faith, and whoever is of little faith is also of little love.

For being in love Fromm deems care, responsibility, respect, and knowledge to be required essentials. Without care a relationship dwindles. Partners take responsibility for each other. Partners have to know and respect one another's boundaries. Respect is not the same as adoration. Adoration often is temporal, while respect can persist in the long run.

Modern love in a networked society

Most servicemen during separation fear that their partner will find another lover. We cannot count on relationships being cast in concrete, tied together with golden bands, for "Your partner never belongs to you. At best he/she is on loan with an option to renew" (Perel, 2017). Thus, soldiers and partners fear infidelity and soldiers sometimes erect a "Wall of Shame" on which the pictures of the infidel partner are posted. They dread the day they receive a "Dear John" or "Dear Mary" email. Most people in a long-distance relationship discover that they are always worried they are being cheated on but it also happens that soldiers start affairs among themselves, with translators or with someone from the indigenous population. They sometimes cheat on their partner back home. Since you don't want to lose that person because you feel comfortable, you will start to lose touch with reality and the people who are right there for you.

The greedy family concept is still valid (DeAngelis and Segal, 2015) but it is in need of elaboration or else we need to go beyond it. From the side of the family, three revolutions about reproduction (Perel, 2017) have impacted the politics regarding relationships. In the first revolution, sex is separated from production. The nineteenth-century division of labor caused a separation from homework and factory work and also caused children to be recognized as children instead of miniature adults who could also be productive workers. This reduced the importance of the patriarchate as a system, because the family no longer was the primary production unit. The second revolution in the sixties and seventies separated sex from reproduction. Contraceptives (the pill) gave back to women the control over their bodies. They could have children if and when they wanted. The third revolution in the twenty-first century relates to gender being dissociated from biology. Gender now becomes a matter of choice. This revolution coincides with the advent of the network society.

Women have gained power because of all these revolutions. The power is multiplied because in a network society all someone has to do to coerce power in a relationship is to block the other from communication. Power balances are shifting tremendously. Boyd and Ellison (2008: 211), define social networks as:

> web-based services that allow individuals to (1) construct a public or semi-public profile within a bounded system, (2) articulate a list of other users with whom they share a connection, and (3) view and traverse their list of connections and those made by others within the system.

In all countries, social networks play a central role in communication. Whereas in former times, telephone communication and traditional mail contact were the only or most frequently used communication media during deployments (though not used on a daily basis; e.g., Ender, 1995; Schumm, Bell, Ender, and Rice, 2004), in more recent deployments, email and text messaging have become popular means of staying in touch, in addition to phone calls (e.g., Andres and Moelker, 2010; Carter et al., 2011; see also Chapter 18 in this book). Facebook is also frequently used.

Networked relationships promote and enable communication and make dating during separation feasible. But there are risks to dating from a distance. One can too easily defriend a disappointing or deceitful partner from Facebook, Instagram, or other social media. Internet communication empowers both partners in the relationship, but power must be utilized with velvet gloves or preferably not at all because there are more effective ways of dialogue. The internet equalizes power in the relationship, but although the spouses have much power one should be careful in using it. Blocking the other out from communication is the last resort, for it is the lifeline of the relationship. Use communication not to punish your loved one but to discuss matters and to promote further understanding in cases of unclarity.

Staying in love: politics of communication

Modern demands set high standards on our partners. The ideal partner, also during deployment-induced separation, is empathic, caring, sexy, attentive, a good dad and/or mum, and a good conversationalist. . . most importantly, not possessive. But how to achieve all those objectives if one only has long-distance communication tools available? For example, what should one tell and what should one not tell?

Coyne and Smith (1991) introduced the constructs of active engagement (supportive communication) and protective buffering as forms of relationship management. Whereas "active engagement is a matter of involving the partner in discussions, inquiring how the partner feels, and other constructive problem solving," they conceptualized protective buffering as "a matter of hiding concerns, denying worries, and yielding to the partner to avoid disagreements" (Coyne and Smith, 1991: 405). Protective buffering is applied if the other is perceived to be under stress and in need of protection because it is feared that the information might do more damage than good.

However, findings from our Dutch Navy study (Chapter 18) reveal that supportive communication is a healthy strategy, in particular for non-deployed partners, as it is positively associated with well-being and relationship quality, whereas protective reticence is not, which confirms earlier research findings in different contexts (e.g., Coyne and Smith, 1991; Joseph and Afifi, 2010; Suls, Green, Rose, Lounsbury, and Gordon, 1997). Researchers agree on the importance and benefits of supportive communications among romantic partners in maintaining well-being and relationship quality, especially in times of stress and separation. The findings of our study suggest that supportive communication is particularly beneficial for the perceived well-being and relationship quality of partners at the home front, whereas protective reticence seems to have more disastrous implications for deployed service members.

Tips and tools for dating from a distance

Nowhere in academic literature of scholarly teaching is it discussed how to improve communication and keep up the romance. Strangely, in pre-deployment courses neither relationship skills nor sex are discussed. However, providing tips and tools could very much contribute to relationship quality and one only has to use one's imagination. Here we provide some examples that serve as illustration only, but the list should be tailor-made and fitted to the relationship.

- Compile a "Missing You Emergency Box." When you are really missing him/her, you can choose something from the box.
- Record and send him/her a tape of songs that remind you of him/her.
- Make a screensaver with pictures of the two of you and send a copy to him/her.
- Learn to say "I Love You" in several foreign languages, and write those to each other.
- Pretend you are stranded on a desert island and write him/her a love letter. Place the message in a bottle and send it to him/her.
- Write a book or a chapter in a book together.
- Make a batch of his/her favorite cookies and send them to him/her.
- Share some of your goals for the next five years.
- Do not cut yourself off from others: go to social meetings and have fun.
- Do not avoid problems: discuss with others and your loved one.
- Keep sexual intimacy alive: have flirty video chats.
- Prepare the homecoming together.
- Plan a holiday/time together.

Getting beyond the "greedy institution"

The concept of the greedy institution is still valid (DeAngelis and Segal, 2015), but regarding the politics of military families the concept does need elaboration. Basically, the greedy institution concept is a double-dyadic concept. There are tensions between the Armed Forces organization and the soldier and there are tensions between the soldier and the family. The soldier is caught between these institutions and has to find ways to resolve the tensions. It is a functionalist construct since the tensions need to be resolved in order to further the well-functioning of the Armed Forces, the soldier, and the family but the construct does not well enough explain changes in the system since it is focused on regaining equilibrium. The double-dyadic concept is too dichotomous to catch the complexities of present-day military families. The construct wants to better the system, but it does not challenge the system and that is why we need to go beyond the dyadic concept and move on to triadic modeling of military families.

In this book we discussed triads at societal, organization, and family level. At societal level, state, the Armed Forces, and the home front are bound together by tensions that make one big balancing act. At the organization level, the stakeholders are the soldier, the work organization, and the military family. At the family level, the military parent, the parent, and the child are the rivaling (or collaborating) parties. Politics and agency (who gets what, when, and how) lend the triads their dynamic potential for change.

Three different axes of tensions

Moreover, the levels are interconnected and the interconnectedness is revealed by comparative analyses of military families worldwide, an analysis that is provided for in the chapters of this volume. Three axes connect and/or intersect the levels of analysis. These are:

- institution versus occupation
- self-help versus familiar arrangements
- command versus negotiation households

The actors negotiate formal and informal contracts with each other that are pictures of temporary equilibrium. The formal contract regulates mutual obligations, work for remuneration, formal rights and duties, fringe benefits, and so on. The informal contract is not spelled out, and contains amongst others moral obligations, allegiance and loyalty, informal care arrangements, and social support. In the United Kingdom, the semi-informal macro contract is archaically denoted "the covenant." At the family level and the organizational level, we often refer to the informal unwritten contract as the "psychological contract." When the contract is broken, or feels broken, the fault lines are revealed to the public eye. Strife and political agency will then give a certain dynamic to the systems until the actors have obtained their objectives (some will be ascending, winning, others will lose) and again a kind of agreement evolves.

The first axis is derived from Moskos' (1977) opposition of institution versus occupation. The Armed Forces have always been an instrument of state formation and in this respect contributed to national identity. Often but not always conscription was part of state building. In this respect it makes sense that the Armed Forces and military families were institutionalized. In a comparative endeavor, such as presented in this book, one can clearly demonstrate the evident differences between countries. Brazil, for example, is more institutional compared to Portugal and many other Western countries that have a more occupational makeup. Differences in geography, in risk perception, and tasking of the military define the contours of this institution-occupation divide. Finland and the Baltic states also show institutional tendencies because of the imminent threat of a neighboring country, albeit, just as in South America, in modern forms. Therefore, relocation of servicemen is, as discussed in Chapter 12 on Finland, a source of tensions. Sweden on the contrary has highly occupational characteristics and the implication for military families goes so far that "military families" do not exist. In Sweden there are families of soldiers, but no military families. Swedes don't identify with the "military family" concept. Care provisions are within the normal arrangements the welfare state already provides so the Armed Forces do not have to and are not allowed to act like the old-fashioned patriarch. The axis institution versus occupation thus works out differently on the family triads in all these different countries. The interplay between the three levels—society, organization, family—is thus also constituted differently. The resulting micro, macro, and meso contracts are thus also different.

The axis self-help versus family arrangements does not necessarily correlate with the axis institutional versus occupational. In some countries the state and/or the organization provides support as part of the tripartite contract between families, the Armed Forces, and the state. In some countries people resort to their families. In others it is up to individual initiative to take care of themself. Culture, tradition, geography, and infrastructure do play a role in the differences between countries, but also the fact that in some countries the Armed Forces are peripheral or core institutions. Negotiations along this axis determine the outcomes. Some countries have, despite appearances, mixed models. The US and Canada are both individualist countries where individual responsibility is the credo, but they do acknowledge and value community service and local leadership stepping into care arrangements that often also are private community initiatives. Along this axis we also elaborated on the concept of work–family conflict and support arrangements. One of the findings is that the tensions between military and family not only result from time, strain, or behavior, but also, as Masson explains, from deeply rooted beliefs on gender roles. This is exemplified in the chapters on fatherhood and child-rearing.

The third axis, command versus negotiation households, refers to a general development whereby families cannot automatically be coerced, nor can family members be bossed around at will. Violence in the family, as described in the Australian case, is legally banned in all nations in our sample. Like the French-Russian comparison pointed out, the work that is being done by Army wives is still "free labor" and the logic of exploitation still applies, but things gradually are changing. The experience South American soldiers had with peacekeeping in Haiti still proves that the burden of emotion work lies on families who are supporting the deployed soldiers. But all this is taken for granted less and less frequently. Negotiation with the family is outside the chain of command, so there is always the question of how families are co-opted into the system, or not. The United Kingdom and the US still provide military housing and thus still have a strong impact on family life, but even though this is the case, more subtle ways of political work are required. Command households and coercion no longer enjoy legitimacy and states and organizational authorities will have to succumb to seduction.

Seductive capital

Bourdieu coined the concept of symbolic violence and Connell that of the gender regime. Concepts like these, and especially the manner in which Elias defined habitus as second-nature, help us understand why the greedy institutions concept, although still valid in essence, is no longer sufficient as a tool in understanding military families. This volume analyzes the political processes of negotiation and contract-forging that results in a figuration where the occupational, the self-help arrangement, and the negotiation household seem to point in the direction of the emergent structuring of modern military families. Spruce (in this book) rightly remarks that: “The power relationships could change once partners become aware and use their unrecognized power, and rather than just being a victim of symbolic violence they could become a reciprocal source” of symbolic capital. Modern love is accommodated within these structures and all agents within the triad are seduced to play their part with or without knowing what that part exactly is, what the larger structure is, and how they are exploited to serve the objectives of state and military organizations. Since coercion has lost legitimacy, cooperation, consciously or unconsciously, is brought about by cooption and seduction. Those who hold more seductive capital (benefits, kindliness, support) are able to bestow existing systems, i.e., the military family as auxiliary to the Armed Forces organization, its sustainability. The nice and friendly organization is helping out military families, but the help is not altruistically motivated. It serves the organization’s interests.

Note

1 https://deesdatingdiary.files.wordpress.com/2016/10/making-a-long-distance-relationship-work-infographic.jpg (accessed November 28, 2018).

References

Andres, M. D. and Moelker, R. (2010). Sweethearts or strangers? Couples’ reconciliation following military deployment. In M. Andres, *Behind Family Lines: Family Members’ Adaptations to Military-Induced Separations* (doctoral dissertation, pp. 147–176). Breda, the Netherlands: Broese & Peereboom.

DeAngelis, K. and Segal, M. (2015). Transitions in the military and the family as greedy institutions: original concept and current applicability. In R. Moelker, M. Andres,

G. Bowen, and P. Manigart (eds), *Military Families and War in the 21st Century. Comparative Perspectives* (pp. 22–42). London: Routledge.

Boyd, D. and Ellison, N. (2008). Social network sites: definition, history, and scholarship. *Journal of Computer-Mediated Communication*, 13, 210–230.

Carter, S. P., Loew, B., Allen, A., Stanley, S. Rhoades, G., and Markman, H. (2011). Relationships between soldiers' PTSD symptoms and spousal communication during deployment. *Journal of Traumatic Stress*, 24, 352–355.

Carter, S. P. and Renshaw, K. D. (2016). Communication via different media during military deployments and post deployment relationship satisfaction. *Military Behavioral Health*, 4(3), 260–268.

Coyne, J. C. and Smith, D. A. (1991). Couples coping with a myocardinal infarction: a contextual perspective on wives' distress. *Journal of Personality and Social Psychology*, 61, 404–412.

Ender, M. G. (1995). G.I. phone home: the use of telecommunications by the soldiers of Operation Just Cause. *Armed Forces & Society*, 21, 435–454.

Fromm, E. (1956). *The Art of Loving*. New York: Harper and Row.

Hofstede, G. H. (1991) *Cultures and Organizations: Software of the Mind*. London: McGraw-Hill.

Joseph, A. L. and Afifi, T. D. (2010). Military wives' stressful disclosure to their deployed husbands: the role of protective buffering. *Journal of Applied Communication Research*, 38, 412–434.

Jones, D. (2015, January 9). The 36 questions that lead to love. *The New York Times*. Retrieved from www.nytimes.com/2015/01/11/fashion/no-37-big-wedding-or-small.html.

Moelker, R., Soeters, J., and Hagen, U. vom (2007). Sympathy, the cement of interoperability: findings on ten years of German-Netherlands military cooperation. *Armed Forces & Society*, 33, 496–517.

Moskos, C. (1977). From institution to occupation: trends in military organization. *Armed Forces & Society*, 31(1), 388–401.

Perel, E. (2017). *The State of Affairs: Rethinking Infidelity*. London: Hodder and Stoughton General Division.

Suls, J., Green, P., Rose, G., Lounsbury, P., and Gordon, E. (1997). Hiding worries from one's spouse: associations between coping via protective buffering and distress in male post-myocardial infarction patients and their wives. *Journal of Behavioral Medicine*, 20(4), 333–349.

Schumm, W. R., Bell, D. B., Ender, M. G., and Rice, R. E. (2004). Expectations, use, and evaluation of communication media among deployed peacekeepers. *Armed Forces & Society*, 30, 649–662.

Swaan, A. de (1982). Uitgaansbeperking en uitgaansangst. Over de verschuiving van bevelshuishouding naar onderhandelingshuishouding. [A ban on going out may lead to fear of the streets. The shift from command household to negotiation household], in A. de Swaan (ed.), *De mens is de mens een zorg* (pp. 81–115). Amsterdam: Meulenhoff.

Index